Intro

Well, I'll admit I'm not a walking thesaurus. Writing this book has been one of the greatest challenges I've ever undertaken. I have so much I want to say and opinions I want to share but it's been difficult articulating them all into words. I found an editor online close to where I live to hopefully help and he requested a few hundred words of my manuscript to evaluate. He sent me an email back saying this isn't a book "per se" but a lament on life. I thought to myself, "Can't I lament about life in a book?" It definitely made me question myself and the whole process but I've pressed forward regardless. What does he know anyways? He sure wasn't blessed with the gift of encouragement, nor being a salesman for that matter.

I'm not a writer by trade, I'm a carpenter so it's been a true test of patience and focus for me, to say the least. When something doesn't fit or go right at work I just grab a sledgehammer or cut it down with a skilsaw. Unfortunately, writing a book takes a little more intellectual dexterity than that. It's been a challenge but has also given me a purpose and outlet through the pandemic and a severe car accident I was involved in. Words are a powerful way of communicating and I've had to work diligently at trying to be clear and transparent in sharing my opinions and in conveying how I feel, especially with the goal of influencing people to God.

The title "Blind in Affliction" can mean many things to many people and that's why I chose it. For some reason those words together draw you in and make you think. When it comes to the cover, I remember years ago I was walking my dog on the beach and seeing this eagle up ahead on the shoreline, surrounded by crows. They were cawing at him relentlessly and there was even some dive bombing him from the air. For some reason that imprint stuck in my mind, and to me, it's an analogy of how relentless this world can be and how blind we can be in it's affliction, no matter who we are. An eagle has the strongest eyesight in the animal kingdom and is America's symbol of freedom but even they get pestered all day long. The eagle finally broke free and flew away but these crows were nasty and unrelenting. I always saw eagle's as this majestic creature full of grace and beauty, which they are, but that day I saw being an eagle as an exhausting burden to live up to, especially with a murder of crows constantly tormenting you.

I also picture another eagle soaring over the New York city harbor by the Statue of Liberty and what that symbolizes now amidst this pandemic and the aftermath of 9/11. To me it's a fascinating contradiction in how we perceive and represent freedom to be without God and how far that liberty has taken us.

The world's in serious trouble and many can't see through themselves to understand why. My book is centered around the cause of that from a biblical perspective and how relevant the Christian faith is in regards to our world's calamity.

Blind In Affliction

Chapter 1

"My Lament On Life"

The Accident

I'm writing this book with a heavy heart. Life at times can throw us some unexpected curveballs and I've definitely received one recently. My life these past few years has been extremely difficult to endure and has been filled with severe frustration and physical pain. I am still blessed relatively speaking to a large percentage of the world, which I am thankful for, and trying not to take for granted, but my afflictions are still real and are affecting my overall health, peace of mind and enjoyment of life. There's that old saying, "It's all relative I guess" but that can be a hard pill to swallow in the present moment, as reality persists alongside our dreams and ambitions. Finding joy and giving thanks can be challenging at times amidst frustrating and restricting circumstances. I was smoked by a drunk driver in my truck about three years ago and I'm still battling through the aftermath of it all. I'm lucky to be alive considering the impact, but still suffer from severe neck and back pain due to the whiplash. I pulled over to use the phone and some guy smashed into me from behind, drunk on his cell phone. He was probably going between 80-100 km an hour and if it weren't for me driving a suburban and being a bigger frame, I'd either be paralyzed or dead. I was also wearing a seatbelt which would have launched me through the windshield otherwise. It felt like a 300 lb sledgehammer hit me right between the shoulder blades. It was a serious jolt to my whole body and has caused many other issues including extensive nerve damage, more inclusively to my left side. I also suffered a severe concussion which has brought on constant headaches, insomnia and memory loss, (which doesn't help in writing a book.) I always saw concussions as the result of the actual abrasion but they're also attributed to the rattling of the brain in its shell which can take years to resettle, if ever. It's all been a difficult and lonely road in recovery to say the least. In situations like these a person truly finds out who they are and who their support system is, and for me, I wish my support system was a little stronger to be honest. I have two divorced adopted parents that are still alive but have shown no concern or empathy for me whatsoever. Our family was broken apart years ago and I never made a family of my own, so it's left me to deal with my circumstances on my own in faith. I am slowly getting better but it's been an extreme test of perseverance for me physically, emotionally, financially and spiritually. Before I got hit I was a big strong guy with my life ahead of me, who for the most part was productively contributing to society, with my troubles in the past, but now I've definitely been limited in my capabilities. It's amazing how one man's ignorance and sinful disregard for the law can have such a negative and rippling effect on so many lives. He's obviously affected mine and the path I was on, but he apparently has three little kids at home himself, so I'm sure it's caused a severe effect in his own situation and household. With this being said my faith has been tested and come into question on all levels. I got hit as a born-again believer in Jesus Christ and with the gospel now ingrained in my loins, I find myself bearing the christian stripes of circumstance, surrender and the most difficult and admirable task of living a blameless life. Blameless is an interesting word the Bible uses in defining those in faith because it's believing regardless of our circumstances, as though you may have an inclination or find reason to blame God, but choose otherwise. I can look at the incident from several perspectives. Was it a premotivated or predestined fate? Was it some sort of chastisement or lesson from God or was it merely another sinful act of injustice on a collision course to an unfortunate victim? Either way, it happened to me in faith and the questions and answers don't reverse the repercussions of the offense. I'll admit, it's hard to process it all and reason with sometimes. There's a popular new country song out that's lyrics are along the same lines regarding God and faith. The singer must have lost a friend in a car accident and these questions came to light herself. The song goes,

> If I ever get to heaven
> You know I got a long list of questions
> Like how do you make a snowflake?
> Are you angry when the earth quakes?
> How does the sky change in a minute?
> How do you keep this big rock spinnin?
> And why can't you stop a car from crashing?
> Forgive me, I'm just askin,
> I bet somewhere, there's a yearbook
> In a box under a bed
> With a senior picture missing
> In loving memory instead
> And somewhere there's a mother
> Who stopped going to church
> 'Cause your plan quit making sense down here on earth.

It's a riveting song for sure but regardless, like her, I'm forced to deal with it either way as many others are in their circumstances.

I can't play reality in reverse and change the outcome. This isn't a fictional movie where we can suspend time in mid-air and manipulate the story or procession, this is real life and sometimes life is as real as a heart attack. I can ask "why me?" as much as I want and chase sympathy around like a dog after its tale, but consequences to ourselves and others are a persisting result of our choices and the influence we generate. If there were no consequences to our choices and God were protecting us from every sin or mistake, we'd see time being suspended all around us like the Matrix, but it's not. There's been millions of deaths and people injured or paralyzed from accidents with no answers to why inclusively to any individual whether they're believers in faith or not. There was a pastor who would cross the US/Canada border with a bunch of jerry cans close to where I live to save money. One day he filled them up and was waiting in the border line to come home when a Porsche flew down one lane, lost control and careened into his van igniting the gasoline and killing him. Sometimes it can only be explained as being in the wrong place at the wrong time. Much like him, I could have driven a different way home or even left a split-second earlier or later, but the past is gone and I can't go back to my previous position in life. It's a humbling reality I find myself in. Emotionally and psychologically it can be obsessively difficult to persevere through. It's not just the physical pain, it's the emotional struggle and isolation that's just as hard to deal with, especially as an active person and someone with faith in the forefront of my mind. I compare it to the analogy of a blind person and if it's more painful for them to lose their sight after knowing what it's like to see or if they're born that way from birth and not knowing what they're missing. Either way, it's definitely been a struggle but with more time on my hands I've had the opportunity to read and research things I didn't have time for previously. I've been able to study religions, history and all sorts of cults and secret societies, but more importantly I've got to study the Bible and the history that surrounds it. It's been a fascinating journey and I've come to a far deeper understanding and clarity of the Christian faith and its roots morally, historically and spiritually which has more solidified my standing to it's undeniable relevance, but then my own personal dilemma has hindered my capacity to embrace and proclaim what I've learned and believe to others with joy and assurance. My head is full of knowledge but my lips seem silenced and hesitant in articulation due to my circumstances and how people would perceive my faith in light of my situation. There's been a fierce battle within my mind through all of this that goes beyond what I can express in words and I know many in faith feel the same way. I wouldn't be honest if I said doubts haven't periodically entered my mind. It's only natural considering my circumstances. Not necessarily doubts in what I believe about Jesus and the bible, but what I believe in and how it concerns myself. I've felt so bound up with emotion and torn at times throughout the day because of this guy's drunken stupidity and act of negligence. I've been forced to ask the ultimate question, whether I only perceive faith as a means for gain and for God to bless me in this life, or do I actually truly love God and revere him for his forgiveness and salvation and seek the life to come? Do I see what God has accomplished through Jesus Christ on the cross as my defining stance and posture on life and faith, despite my circumstances? I'm a perfect case study for these questions to be asked, because if my faith is the cause of my circumstance and every situation that confronts me, then I'd have my faith to blame for my circumstances whether they be good or bad wouldn't I? But again, God calls us to be blameless.

Defining Faith

Faith can be difficult to substantiate and define because faith in its purest form exemplified in the Bible would definitely be defined through and no matter what our circumstances are, especially considering the accessibility to prosperity in their generations and from their perspective. I feel we've certainly come off course defining faith ourselves in this day and age. They were far more oppressed and afflicted than I can even comprehend. These kinds of questions are legitimate and they bind our world in its perception of true faith. To be honest, they should generate an opinion especially with so many beliefs and circumstances out there, and again, it makes the actual word faith a complex and elusive word to solidify and define. I guess if we were to solidify the word faith and be able to hold on to it, dictate it and control it, we wouldn't need faith at all, our faith would be in and of ourselves. There's always been relentless circulating opinions and contention on the subject throughout history and there always will be because opinions differentiate in accordance to positionary circumstances. There's also residual implications to our own free will and moral conscience that present questions between consequence, coincidence and providence that are stumbling blocks to truly ascertain. Google defines spiritual faith as a strong belief in God or in the doctrines of a religion, based on spiritual apprehension rather than proof. I agree with Google's definition to some degree because I don't see the Christian faith as a faith that defines itself solely by the result of your own individual circumstances or experiences for that matter. If that were the case our faith would be comparative, conditional and circumstantial. There's just more to it than that and I feel it proves itself more in our disregard for it and in the consequences that proceed in the aftermath. The result and proof of faith and it's relevance should be seen in the conduct that precedes the believer which to me is far more important and relevant to the reality we live in. People seem all ears to faith-filled, inspiring words that bring health and prosperity their way and are easily drawn to those in favorable positions but the true gospel takes the journey of faith to a whole other level of understanding and enlightenment. There's a relationship and confirmation that's formed in the light of scripture that goes far deeper than what we can feel, touch or experience. There's so many avenues and perceptions faith can take the carnal unregenerate man in its own imagination and perspectives, especially in a world driven by self belief and narcissism. We can be in any position and say faith got us there but if we're finding truth and peace of mind in our perceived faith no matter what it is and we are compelled to share it with those in disfavorable positions, then our circumstances may get worse and probably should at times, especially attempting to confront the consequential issues and emotions and walk admits them. A true missionary gives up his or her own circumstances to give aid and help teach and resolve the circumstances of others. They are willfully and selflessly dying to their own needs in faith to serve the needs of others. This to me is faith working proactively. I guess the question then could or should be, what is the objective of faith?

Again, I'm a perfect case study for all these questions because I never had faith or believed in anything spiritual my whole life, but now becoming a Christian, all of these questions have risen within me intently amidst my own circumstances as a believer. I definitely see undeniable truth in my faith but how I confront that interactively can be a challenging objective and it's also been difficult how I confront it all within myself. Do I actually revere God as the Lord over my life, trust him and seek a personal relationship with him regardless of my circumstances or again, is my supposed faith some sort of contrived impersonal expectation?

The Internal Struggle

This current state of mind I'm in has brought me to such a submissive level and true sense of humility that I've never been before. My situation has unearthed a vulnerability within me that I feel a lot of people, including myself, are scared to admit. As men, we hate feeling vulnerable and not being in control. Something in our pride and masculinity says it's all a weakness. This kind of personal contemplation is emotionally intrusive and can trigger a lot of fear and painful trauma that many people are simply not willing to be transparent about within themselves or to others. I feel we shouldn't fear this kind of personal analysis as much as we do, we should embrace it, because we can't conquer our fears unless we confront them and learn the basis for them, which the Christian faith certainly compels the world to do. I think we all have voids and moments of supposed weakness and anxiety throughout the duration of our lives but we're afraid to reveal them to others for fear of being ridiculed, humiliated or rejected. We know they're there but have just enough control over our lives and our identity to where we feel they don't need to be unearthed or brought to the surface. The problem is who we are in our identity when we lose that control. Either way it seems people are unempathetic these days and won't listen long enough to even hear your voice outside of their own objectives and affirmations, let alone sympathize with your problems. We've come to believe we are all alone in our problems and suffer in the fear of confronting them. The general mindset I see around me is a medicated state of emotional unrest and fear.

A few years ago there were three NHL hockey players who took their own lives due to depression and severe anxiety, or what has now been diagnosed as mental health or mental illness. These were three healthy, wealthy guys in the prime of their careers and living their supposed dream, who physically feared no one as hockey fighters, but something inside their mind wasn't right and overcame them to such a degree that they couldn't resolve it within themselves and decided to bow out of life all together. It's such a drastic, sad and avoidable conclusion but it happens to people in all different situations in life around the world, whether they're poor or rich or male or female. No matter our social standing, financial position or in what culture we live in, the perception we have of ourselves can be incessantly debilitating and sometimes too consuming to overcome. I see diagnosing depression and anxiety as a mental health issue justifiable, but calling it an actual illness is probably doing more harm than they realize. In my opinion it's further ostracizing people from something that's extremely common within us all. Some people definitely have chemical imbalances genetically that need to be properly medicated but depression to me shouldn't be ostracized or considered abnormal at all, in fact, I would say if you're not depressed and feeling anxious at times, especially considering the state of the world right now, you're actually abnormal and probably an uncompassionate narcissist yourself. The truth is it's natural to feel these emotions in life but it's important we know their origin and how to process them productively especially from a spiritual perspective. We've come to vainly define it all as mental illness, then we push forward with our dependence on the compassion and empathy of others as its savior as we look in the rear-view mirror. I see mental health as the ability and courage to confront these issues together with faith, truth, support and rationality but the world has come to define it as a secluded illness because it doesn't coincide with the promotion of health and prosperity and they are what make profit and drive the economic machine forward. Whatever our opinions are on the subject, the problems persist and escalate. The suicide rate has climbed over 30% since 1999 with over 40,000 deaths in America last year alone. That's a startling figure especially in its progressive consistency and in a country that lives to its own praise and is the center of influence around the world.

Our tendency is to suppress all these emotions and feelings inside or else medicate and escape from them entirely. People feel all alone in their struggles and have fallen victim to the voices in their head and to the fears, pressures and anxieties of life. The fears have grown and persisted to where they've interfered with the enjoyment and fulfilment of life. I know some people with so much social anxiety they confine themselves inside to where no one has a chance to make eye contact or judge them. They live in crippling fear and anxiety of social interaction with seclusion as their only refuge. At times I've felt that way myself, to be honest. The mind can be a hurricane with nothing to hold on to, especially when we don't know how to handle the storms and valleys of life and the cause of them. It can be a persisting debilitation for many trapped in their own head and identity. Little do we realize what lies under the surface and in the hearts of men and women all over the world and how similar we all are in our hearts' genuine desire. What seems to divide us interactively and spiritually would actually unite us if only we had more courage and transparency to share, and people would have more compassion to listen and not to judge. If you look at the soldiers of two opposing armies, both have their mind set on the same dreams and aspirations when they get back home from battle, but it's been a recurring theme throughout history. How much different can we truly be? It's like we're the same people fighting against ourselves. Unfortunately, we've become so divided in trying to find a residing and foundational focus to draw from and guide us. We war and kill each other with no productive resolution but also do it with our claim of forming a resolution. Unfortunately this was the state of mind the world was in leading up to the cross and the whole purpose of its objective and all we're doing by disregarding it now is following suit and reverting back to the state we were in then.

Another hockey player around the same time came out in public confessing his own personal struggles with depression, fear and anxiety. He stated that the fears and anxiety almost killed him and would drive him into debilitating panic attacks. He said he more feared the scrutiny and ridicule from his teammates than anything. What's interesting is that when he finally came out and spoke about his internal struggles, very few people scrutinized him at all, in fact they embraced him for his courage and transparency and has now become a forerunner, endorsing mental health awareness around the league and beyond. It just shows that yes the world can be judgmental but a lot of that is a disillusion and what we build up in our minds in the perception we have of ourselves. So much of our anxiety is based on what the world is telling us we should be and our own self analysis compares itself to that supposed requirement. From a spiritual perspective I would say this is satan's greatest achievement. He's defined self worth for us and we've become consumed in our own self deprecation.

Self Deprecation

I was at a friend's house a while ago sitting by the pool in the sun. Him and his girlfriend were swimming while I was laying on the fold-out chair on the deck. The sun was in my eyes so I merely threw my towel over my head to cover my eyes from the sun because I had no hat. A couple of days later his girlfriend texted me in a rage expressing how horrible and judgmental I was for covering my head because of her apparent weight issue. She went on a rant about how I was a woman-hater and disrespectful to her and him and to never come around their house again. For two days all these insecurities built up in her mind of how one person supposedly perceived her and she attacked that supposed perception. Her fears took control over her mind and all these preconceived notions and insinuations took precedence over truth and rationality. Her fears also took precedence over our relationship and the trust we'd grown accustomed to beforehand. None of what she presumed even entered into my mind. All I did was throw a towel over my head because of the sun. She literally ended a friendship wholeheartedly from the basis of her own fears. It's just another observation I've noticed in myself and in other people with an obscured view of themselves and without a secure identity and purpose in life. It all stems from the fear of rejection, unacceptance and the pressure the world puts on us to aspire to be someone we're not. It's become a world of deception and a crossfire of these false insinuations everywhere we look and is where much of the spiritual world is at war. I've come to realize through this accident that my whole life before Christ was a struggle with these issues in acceptance, rejection and complex trauma and I had nowhere to turn for help or support. I reacted and made poor decisions that merely compounded the problem and escalated the fears in my mind. I can now see that so much of my aggression was based on the fears I had from the opinion I had of myself. I wasn't even aware of this depth of insecurity within me especially as an adult, because I never cared enough about myself or had the courage to confess them to myself. Again, I felt I had just enough control over my life to keep these emotions from the surface.

Confronting Fear and Trauma

Since becoming a Christian, God has revealed a lot of my carnal blindness and exposed my sin, but this accident has forced me to look even deeper into my actual character. It's natural to be complacent when you're healthy and satisfied, but life isn't that way for many people and most certainly isn't for me right now. My situation has triggered a lot of deep emotional pain and childhood trauma that I thought I'd buried long ago, but now realize they deeply affected me and I've always hid from them or suppressed them. I was always so lonely and angry growing up with no resolution. The anger wasn't necessarily at anyone in particular, it was because there was no father figure or support system for me to confide in. There was also no loving, nurturing mother to encourage or console me, and I finally grew emotionally cold and callous. I built up walls so big I myself couldn't penetrate them. It's like I formed a protective shell or false identity for myself when my true identity was hiding away in a battered mess of emotional despondence. I would have done anything to not feel alone no matter how damaging it was to me or to the world around me. Despondency is defined as the state of being extremely low in spirits, dejected, discouraged or feeling hopeless, and that's how I felt my whole life before coming to the Lord. It's a fragile life when we are hiding from who we are and when our confidence is based on how we presume others are perceiving us, much like my friend's girlfriend. I think that's how a lot of people live their lives these days. We sometimes see ourselves through other people's eyes and we don't like what we see, because we haven't accepted ourselves for who we are. We also haven't learned of the Lord's acceptance which leaves us extremely sensitive, empty and vulnerable. We actually judge ourselves in other people's eyes even before they've made an assumption and then we blame or judge them for their response in our presumed insinuation. It's like their initial response is so frightening that we're always walking around in fear of the response, depending upon it for our security. For many of us, it's come to a point that we won't even make eye contact with people anymore. This is a paralyzing deception many have succumbed to in our world. Much of our anger and divisiveness is based on our own inferiority complexes and much of our superiority complexes are based on our own insecurities. It's actually an identity crisis this world is facing and at war with more than anything and is why when I interact with people and our eyes meet, no matter what mood I'm in, I try to smile and say hi because you just don't know what kind of insecurities people have built up towards themselves these days in their mind.

I remember being in a grocery store line up awhile ago and dropping half my groceries all over the floor. There were onions rolling down the isles and stuff flying everywhere. I was embarrassed but handled it well and joked about it with all the people in the line up. I finally got to the cashier and she commended me on how I handled it. I simply said, "It's healthy to be embarrassed," and she nearly broke down in tears. She was kind of tall, shy and awkward looking and it's like she lived in fear of that insecurity her whole life. I'm not always that secure within myself but that day I was and it brought a sense of levity and peace to the situation.

How This Relates To Faith

The natural pride and ignorance of man would deem this all as irrelevant or a weakness but I'm going to embrace these feelings and emotions that I think we all share as a strength and dig deeper into the true basis for them in my own self analysis and confession to hopefully help others find my life's challenges relatable and give a reason for faith, hope and eventual change. I also want people to see the Bible for its intended purpose psychologically and spiritually and represent Christ in a way that's relative to the circumstances we're facing and living in. It makes me think of the incessant toil of perfectionism in our everyday affairs, whether it be the social pressures we put on ourselves or some sort of religious pressure. Sometimes we're so meticulous and obsessive to perform every immediate and minut task to affirm ourselves religiously or uphold our reputation but who are we really trying to please? Why do we care so much about how we present ourselves to be to others? It becomes an exhausting persona to live up to and we're only fooling ourselves because we're all imperfect people deep down inside. It's actually an obsessive compulsive social disorder that many of us are deceived by and feel trapped in. It's like we're enslaving ourselves by our own false persona. Ultimately, we all make mistakes and under the surface we are all broken to some degree, but if we'd admit that, then our strength and peace of mind would actually be found in our admittance because we can't be someone we're not. We also can't relate to people in an elevated perception of ourselves and ultimately God sees through to our heart either way. Until we see God this way, we walk in contradiction of ourselves and who we truly are. This kind of sincerity is the sanctifying mystery behind acceptance that God embraces and where religion utterly fails.

I see so many people hiding behind a false sense of security or mask, disguising themselves in fear of revealing their true identity. It's like millions of intertwining masks in a collision course of insinuation and false perception that's just too difficult for many to endure. I know for myself that whatever tough and rough exterior I've presented to those I've interacted with on my journey, it was always just the mask I used to hide from the broken, insecure child within me. I was so sensitive to criticism growing up that I felt if I could physically or verbally intimidate people they'd be too scared to cast any judgment upon me. It actually worked to some degree but then I was always in conflict within myself and my true identity because deep down that's not who I was or who I was created to be. I had to live up to the pressure and expectation I put on myself and I feel that's where many of us live in contradiction with ourselves. It's not only the pressure I put on myself but the identity I felt I had to live up to. I also now see through Christ, that that is more of an inferiority rather than a superiority complex and only God could bring me to that understanding and clarity. I was too hurt by people and resentful of the world to adhere to any philosophy, psychology or opinions from man about myself and I was far too stubborn, cynical and abrasive to listen. I like the definition of cynical, it says; believing that people are motivated by self-interest and distrustful of human sincerity and integrity. These are the repercussions when our faith is in man and not in God. I'll admit I was a pretty scary and volatile guy at times before Christ, but God sees under the skin and into the hearts of us all and pursues us regardless of our trauma or ignorance. I feel for people imprisoned, that aren't necessarily evil or horrible people but have merely reacted emotionally to their trauma and circumstances, and that one decision has cost them years of their life, if not all of them. I'm not justifying the sin but definitely sympathizing with the reaction. Sometimes our emotions show that we care but we're just too scared to reveal them for fear of getting hurt. I'm lucky I'm not behind bars myself but God in all his sovereignty is an internal diplomat and truly wants to heal each one of us however bad or lost we think we are, whatever trauma we've endured or whatever mistakes we've made. It can be tough love in its most rigorous form at times because it's about exposing our pride and relinquishing our control but it's what a lot of us need to begin healing and rejuvenation. Ultimately, it's only in a broken state that we can relate and communicate productively. It's a strong quality and development in our character when we can break ourselves down and laugh at ourselves and our past. It's also in knowing and accepting we're forgiven that we can learn to forgive, even ourselves. The first word in relationship is to relate and that's what God desires in his relationship with us and with others. He says in 2 Corinthians that "his strength is made perfect in weakness," and that becomes so relevant in our interaction with others. We are all yearning so deeply to be released from the anxieties of life and the pressures we put on ourselves and I see now how God has provided a far more intriguing and sustainable way than people realize for us to heal and find refuge, direction and purpose. He becomes the anchor in the hurricanes of life and the foundation to build upon. Faith isn't merely a formula or methodology we use to gain prosperity as many people are teaching, it's a journey into our hearts and into our character, where prosperity can never take us, in fact prosperity only takes us further behind our own masks of pride and inferiority. God came to show us the meaning of life and defined love to the world by the giving of himself.

He didn't just leave us here to our own devices and say, "To hell with you all" which I wouldn't necessarily blame him, considering our sinful ignorance. Like myself, many of us don't even understand what true love is therefore God selflessly exemplified it for us in Christ. 1 John 3:16 says, "Hereby we perceive the love of God, because he laid down his life for us."

I feel people are reacting prematurely in their unsecured emotions, self-destructing and eventually harming themselves and those closest to them in the process. There's evidence of that in every statistic these days. Unfortunately, they're also hurting God and interfering with his providence, callings and mercy upon their lives. Instead of turning to him we're turning inwardly and destroying ourselves in the process. Without God we just don't have the capacity to fully understand what's taking place within us spirituality or psychologically. I just watched an interview with Michael Phelps about anxiety and depression. He was promoting mental health to the world which is courageous and noble, don't get me wrong, but his only solution was to reach out to somebody, that's it, there was no mention of faith whatsoever. The problem is, that leaves us dependent upon man to save us, but faith goes far deeper into the root of anxiety and depression than the world perceives. It's so much easier to see when you're released from it, but so hard to see when you're trapped within it. We're actually fighting for what's destroying us and we just can't see it. Hence, the title of the book, "Blind in Affliction."

Matthew 11:28 says, "Come to me, all you who labour and are heavy laden, and I will give you rest. Take my yoke upon you and learn from me, for I am gentle and lowly in heart, and you will find rest for your souls. For my yoke is easy and my burden is light." Our emotions blind us and cloud our judgment but he's come to help us identify with our emotional and spiritual discourse and reverse the psychological and physical implications through grace. I say physical as well because stress and anxiety are the leading cause of many of the ailments and diseases in our bodies. These are irrefutable facts that even science attests to. God came to give his life to atone for our sin and bring us to heaven but he also came to live and walk with us this side of heaven and save us from so much of our impulsive decisions and problematic discourse. It's all a spiritual veil that's unknown to the unwilling, unbelieving world. The carnal man and woman without Christ pushes forward undeterred by its surroundings and the ramifications of sin, living unto its own cause, but so much of what we're pushing towards is an illusion set before our eyes. Unfortunately, I see a world imploding as time is of the essence and in need of a savior and I want to help any way I can, before it's too late. I don't have much for resources right now but I can certainly reveal what's being revealed to me and in me. I have nothing in me that claims any wisdom of my own or any sort of religious entitlement. My gifts are giving and discernment for the most part and I struggle with pretty much everything else. In all honesty, without God, I'm a complete disaster. There's just something about that book that transforms our entire perception of reality when we open its pages in a sincere way. Again, I'm not a religious person whatsoever or claim any specific denomination or position in any church. Sometimes outside of the four walls I feel can give you a wider and more conclusive observational perspective than within. We put so much emphasis on what's going on inside the four walls of the church that we forget to bring it outside. I feel with that overemphasis we've actually brought the problem within at times with unnecessary contention, over analyzing our service religiously apart from grace. I'm on a journey in faith myself and am learning every day like the rest of us, but it takes a leap of faith to begin this journey. I was lost and blind in my own afflictions but God intervened and reached in when he knew I needed him the most. It was like I was on the raging river of a life not knowing of the massive waterfall up ahead. I was maxed out in my own capacity and God's mercy saved me and defined itself to me in all its omnipotence.

Back To The Accident

I've spent my life in the construction industry building houses for the last 25 years, which has brought me relative security and financial stability along the way. I never really got ahead but I also never got too far behind. Unfortunately now I'm at a crossroads. I'm completely at the mercy of faith. My body is broken and I'm financially strapped, barely getting by. I don't even have the money to professionally edit this book, to be honest. It's a position I've never found myself in to this degree. It's hard on my pride not to be in control physically and what goes in and out of my wallet. I've had plenty of emotional and financial struggles along the way and plenty of bumps and bruises physically, but this accident is different. I've felt trapped, hopeless and inadequate throughout the day dealing with the insurance company and legal firms over something I didn't do. I'm hoping one day justice will prevail but until then I'm left in parel and justice itself is a wavering institution of corruption and manipulation in of itself. It's become a socialistic monopoly and I see them all as professional extortionists more than anything. I have to present the truth of my case to a nearly bankrupt and repeatedly fraudulent organization who assumes and aims to prove I'm a liar, knowing full well they're lying to me and to themselves. They also bribe their own employees with bonuses to lie under oath to the legal system, their own system, to me and to the judge. They have such a massive undisclosed overhead to work with through the court system that they simply starve you out until you cave-in or die. People in my position are forced to settle because they run out of resources, so they merely prolong the inevitable. The insurance company is greedy and has manipulated it all for their own benefit, the lawyers are simply waiting for victims' phone calls to fill their own pockets and the public has abused the entire system as well. It's become a revolving contradictory hypocrisy that has unfortunately defeated its own purpose and the honest man who pays his or her insurance for coverage, loses out in incidents like mine. It's all been so corrupted, just like so much of our system and society. People behind the scenes just take advantage and fill their pockets with the excess overhead and hide it all in the paperwork.

I was summoned to undergo a full ICBC appointed physical a while ago. I stood across the office from this pugnant and smug man, who was supposedly there to give a professional medical analysis of my injuries and their progression. It just so happens I was completely seized up and I could hardly move my neck. My hands were purple due to the lack of circulation and nerve damage. I showed him but he shrugged his shoulders as if it were irrelevant and unimportant. He merely bumped my knees and elbows to test for nerve response and the meeting was over in 15 minutes. The guy was literally paid off to fly across the country from Toronto the day before because of his credentials to lie and fraudulently sign off papers concerning my case. I have to hire a lawyer to defend against a hired liar. What a despicable and corrupt world we live in. I guarantee he didn't even see the pictures of my truck in the accident or even know what happened. Again, I look at it as a form of entrapment or extortion in a way. If I work they'll say I'm fine and if I don't they'll say I'm milking it, so they starve you out until you're broke and have to go back to work and then they follow you around with cameras to prove their case. They've even rejected my doctor and occupational therapists request for retraining to further entrap me. Again, to me it's all a monopoly bordering on socialism that I actually pay to protect me. It's been a crazy battle and I feel for people going through these situations with legitimate injuries like mine. It's left me in a state of uncertainty moving forward into the future with my career, my health and my social life.

New Perspective

This all being said, my faith and spiritual life have dramatically grown. I would never have considered writing a book like this or compelled to do so unless I realized the deep need for God within myself and for others. I've been forced to take a step back out of the rat race and release my previous ambitions and grip on life, however that looked previously. I'm not in the relentless daily grind, stuck in rush-hour traffic like I was for so many years, living cheque to cheque, trying to stay afloat. It's humbled me and given me a chance to see life from a different perspective. It's become such an enslaved 9 to 5 system that seems to control the lives and minds of the modern world and it was also controlling me, but I've inadvertently been released from it all together. It's been a strange transition in anxiety and stress. My whole life I fiercely laboured to get a break and now I've been given a justifiable and unescapable excuse to be in one. My body is broken but I now see my mind was broken in the daily grind of life trying to get ahead and that state of mind was I feel more unhealthy and destructive than what I'm going through now. I see things differently than I ever could or would have otherwise. Life has become a relentless and exhausting race for validation that never seems to reach its promoted goal. It's like I'm two completely different people in the same body. Whether this was God's intention, he only knows but my receptors have been opened to a whole new world around me that I'd never even acknowledged before.

I go to the pool everyday for my rehab and see all sorts of people hobbling around with restrictions, ailments and injuries like me. I've gained a far deeper respect and sympathy for not only those struggling through injuries like mine, but those who are less fortunate around the world. Those marginalized, living in severe poverty and affliction, blind to a deeper eternal hope and merely reacting emotionally to their trauma and unfortunate circumstances.

I've definitely been convicted of how selfish and narcissistic I was living previously. Psalms 119 says, "Before I was afflicted I went astray, but now I keep your word…it is good for me that I have been afflicted that I may learn your statutes." Not easy words to hear but definitely true in so many respects to humility in my life. Health and prosperity become unrealistic and unrelatable illusions when we're faced with mental or physical limitations ourselves. It's not only our limitations, it's our geographic accessibility that's a hard pill to swallow as well. I can also see now that so much of our world's anxiety and psychological trauma is attributed to the illusion and generic promotion of health and prosperity being advertised due to the comparison and envy it generates. It's become a form of bondage that the majority of us just can't identify with. Proverbs 27:4 says, "Wrath is cruel, and anger is outrageous; but who is able to stand before envy?" It's like watching the news and seeing all the daily devastation happening around the world but never being a victim of it yourself. You almost judge and scrutinize it all but when you actually become the victim, it changes your perspective entirely. You come to appreciate life in a whole new way. I've been brought to tears and deeply affected by it all. I seem to complacently gloss over all the small blessings in everyday life before my accident, but now everything seems far more precious and vital. My heart was cold in my health but now it's been warmed and tenderized in it's pain. It's all brought me to my knees in desperation which has it's intriguing way of building character development and actually coming to know God personally.

My friend's daughter had a similar accident with a bus where she ended up needing reconstructive surgery on her face. She was in a severe battle with her injuries for years and admits that that's when she truly came to know God personally and intimately. I guess the question then is, who is this God of the Bible if bad things happen to good people, especially to those in faith? That's the question people ask as an excuse to disregard God completely. They just expect life to work out perfectly in their favour with no interruptions, but that's just not true reality. The answer is that we live in a fallen world and sin affects us all. It's the grey area in defining faith that can be so convoluted and misrepresented in our own carnal narcissism and greed because biblical faith doesn't conclude in this world, it persists and perseveres through this sinful world for the promise of the world to come. My friend's daughter comes from a missionary family who are all Christians and look what happened to her. I know another couple that had a ministry washing the feet of street people and were killed in a head-on collision, leaving three children behind. I see people all through my congregation suffering through all sorts of financial problems and physical ailments, it's just a part of life. In Paul's second letter to the Thessalonians he says, "I boast of you in all the churches of God for your patience and faith in all your persecutions and tribulations that you endure." Honestly, I don't see Christians being any less susceptible to some of life's afflictions but I definitely see them inviting less their way. God does punish people as does the law in a carnal sense but sin on its own has its repercussions that hurt and affect whoever they come in contact with. That's the reality of my accident that I just have to accept and live with. Common sense tells us that our good decisions change our circumstances which is true to a degree, but the world is an interactive world and if we think or expect everyone to be living perfect lives around us and God manipulating each one for our benefit, we're only deceiving ourselves and narcissistically using faith as a word to do so. I just don't see the God of the Bible existing to enshrine us all who believe in perfect blissful harmony and us living as invincible rubberized vessels. It's an unrealistic expectation especially in this day and age. Life is full of compromising interaction, contention and interruptions along the way for us all. I see him as the God of truth, guidance and healing through our circumstances and as the world's sin becomes more prevalent and escalates, the circumstances in it will get worse and worse and our expectations of him will become more unrealistic if health and wealth are our expectations. God would never push us further into complacency, it's just not in his character to do so. The truth is there is a void in this world without a relationship with God and without prayer. We're doing whatever we can to fill this void, but the valley keeps widening and getting deeper and deeper. The eyes of this world have become too enamoured and impulsive with life's attaining diversions to find true humility, appreciation, focus and understanding when they're open. We find who we truly are when our eyes are closed in self-observation and reverence to God. We think we understand it all when we're in control but we realize very quickly when that control gets taken away how inferior and fragile we all truly are and this coronavirus pandemic is proof of that. This is why there's such an incessant battle for the control over our lives because people hate the feeling of inferiority. Interesting how the beginning of the word inferiority is "In fear" and the basis for inferiority is in seeking acceptance and affirmation and that's what God releases us from in faith. The problem with the battle for control is control opposes the idea of faith and without faith there is no God and without God we're left to our own incentives and priorities. I just see the brokenness in all of this and in the heart of man, and how we are in need of clarity and healing. There's a war going on in the minds of men and women over control, affirmation, acceptance and approval that is dividing us all and driving us into a mad frenzy. It's a psychological and spiritual code red no matter how coerced we are to generally view the world and believe otherwise. The world is driven by this fixated illusion and promotion of health and prosperity because that's what makes profit and drives our incentives but it's not the true state of the world and reality we're living in. It's just an illusion the lens has deceived us all into believing. It's almost as though advertising and the media have become our greatest adversaries. I just couldn't see it all as clearly before my faith in God and especially after this accident. I seem to be trapped in some sort of narcissistic, narrow-minded race for self attainment and validation myself, disregarding the needs of others and the concerns for the world. My own self-preservation was two steps ahead of my compassion, humility and empathy. There was no intellect outside of my own self-entitled progression but now I've been humbled and a part of me wants to reach out and help, when before I would have just cast a blind eye.

Chapter 2

Time And Need For Change

The carnal spirit is growing dangerously narcissistic and sociopathic and those of us with hearts for change need to dig our heels in deeper through this inevitable storm and use our gifts to bring the hope of salvation to this lost and broken world while there's still time. We are not only facing a pandemic physically, we're facing a social pandemic of epic proportions that triggers so much of our reactive state of mind. We can't change the world's course but we can change the destiny of the souls residing in it. I Googled sociopath and it's defined as a person with a personality disorder manifesting itself in extreme antisocial attitudes and behaviour and a lack of conscience. I feel this is how we're becoming in society but I also find it fascinating that it defines it as a disorder and a lack of conscience as though order and conscience have apparently been previously defined and established by our minds. Social media as it is so-called, is not producing socially interactive qualities as we presume, in fact I see it actually forming these sociopathic disorders. It's called the information superhighway, but all the information seems to be leading us on is a highway to an abyss of emotionally interactive despondency and fear. It's amazing to have all of this information at our fingertips now but if we're not using it in a productive way then I don't see the point in the innovation and accessibility. If we can't interact with each other cohesively then what value is all this knowledge and technology either way? My birth mother was considered a genius but couldn't get out the front door without falling on her face because her mind was overcome with the torment of over-analysis. It consumed her into a state of fear and paranoia. My point is that if all the information creates is an awareness or consciousness then all we are by not acting upon it, is over informed hypocrites and contradictions of ourselves. I'd rather be wise to it all than consider myself wise in the knowledge I attain from it. Ultimately, we have no excuse excusing ourselves and have grown generally unempathetic as a whole in society especially with it all staring us in the face. We live to serve ourselves and unless our actions benefit ourselves, the majority of us don't get involved because everything advertised to us is for the benefit of ourselves. Unfortunately we don't realize that the advertiser lives for the benefit of himself and his priorities.

There's just so many people suffering from cancer and various other diseases that need empathy, help, support and hope. People in wheelchairs, paralyzed or with dementia and mental illness. People abused sexually, living in fear and regrets. Children neglected without support or guidance. There's war veterans with PTSD and amputees, people blind, handicapped or deaf and the list goes on and on, but on top of the list, what I see is a world that feels so alone. There is no unity or community in narcissism and if all we are concerned for is our own well-being and self-preservation then all these concerns merely remain concerns and those afflicted are left unto themselves. Again, these concerns merely resolve themselves in the compassion of others but without community support each problem is seen as an isolated burden to our selfish objectives. I see our loneliness and isolation as the primary root of our problems and the greatest internal pain of all because of how we react emotionally to it. It's become a devastating world with our faith and hope solely in itself. It's a world fuelled by extraction and those of us without anything to extract from, are left in vulnerable and disparaging positions. The enclosed and isolated mind can become desperate, impersonal and unpredictable. We're just too emotionally and interactively designed beings to be productive in isolation and without community interaction. We were created for relationship and without it we suffer and there's undeniable proof of that everywhere we look. This is the mundane spiritual void we're all feeling interactively in our day-to-day lives and we wouldn't react so emotionally if it weren't true. There's an emptiness and spiritual void from soul to soul without faith and common ground that affects us all internally and proactively. When we serve and support each other we feel like we're a part of something bigger than ourselves. Unfortunately when we live to serve ourselves, all we're left with is ourselves even if we gain the whole world. When we live to serve ourselves, no matter how big an island we build, we're still alone on that island. I know from personal experience before Christ, and now going through this accident how difficult, lonely and debilitating life can be on your own. I've been bound up and isolated at home so much since the accident that without faith I'd have gone completely crazy. Those of us who are emotionally, spiritually or financially secure need to unite together in a driven amalgamation of philanthropy and give up our time and resources for the greater cause or it will all just continue to escalate. These truths are undeniable but it's such a hard world to convince and compel to change. We just don't seem to bear these initiatives or convictions anymore. It's so much easier to divert that focus and revert it to ourselves into our own needs and desires. So much of life has a hold of our attention and priorities these days. It's so easy to just change the channel whether it be on TV, on the Internet or in your mind into the impulses of life, ignoring the needs of others. I know for myself that I'm always one button away from a desire to be temporarily satisfied and we are all guilty of that to some degree, but the world is called to a deeper purpose and initiative in Christ, a purpose and mission to step out of our complacent comfort zone and our own needs, to serve one another in empathy, compassion, self-sacrifice and love. The love of God is not defined in how we draw a benefit from him to ourselves, it's defined in how Jesus exemplified love as an example for us to follow. Without God and his commands and convictions, the mindset of the world simply becomes more and more selfish and narcissistic.

The Narcissistic World

I was driving on the main highway where I live a few years ago and the traffic started backing up really bad. We were bumper to bumper for about twenty minutes until we finally reached the problem. There was a lady broken down in one lane holding up the traffic with a broken front steering arm. Me and my friend pulled to the side, hopped out and got her over to the side of the road. I held the tire straight while he pushed from the back. I look back now and realize for twenty minutes at least a hundred cars would have driven by her and no one helped. Not one person thought to lend a hand and it was a fairly attractive middle-aged woman to boot. Whether they thought about it or not, they still didn't do it. I see a lot of it as blatant selfishness but I also see how socially programmed and system dependent we've become complying and conforming to the system. It's like we've become instinctual rather than distinctual. There's no independence in our character and we've become so divided psychologically from car to car and from house to house. We'd rather roll up our windows, complain and pass these problems by, but of course if we were the ones broken down, we'd love for someone to stop and help us in our distress or misfortunes and we'd complain if they didn't. I think a lot of it too is that we don't like putting ourselves out there for the fear of being embarrassed or scrutinized. Whatever it is, it's becoming a compounding problem in our world and again, we can't love our neighbour as ourselves if all we do is live for ourselves, but this is the ever increasing social pandemic and evolving contradiction we live in. We're just not bearing these initiatives in life anymore. It's almost as if these acts of kindness are so rare, they'll make headlines on the news when people find out about them. We're expecting life to rejuvenate and regulate itself outside of ourselves and we point fingers in judgment and complain when things fall apart around us, but we are all contributing to the problem however small our choices seem and however insignificant they presume to be. Interestingly, the word ignorance starts with ignore, the word responsibility is the ability to respond and the word accountability is the ability to give an account. Again we have no excuse, excusing ourselves especially when we use these words regularly. We've even come to blame the government as scapegoats for the justification to not govern ourselves. It's easy to sit back while the news is on and form opinions as the world crumbles around us but what are each of us doing to make a difference? We assume there's a moral obligation by people other than ourselves to resolve our world's problems and make a pathway for us to not have to. Most people do nothing but live inside their own opinionated bubble and I think there's something about watching others suffer that gives us pleasure and a sense of pride and entitlement. It's just so much easier to tear people down than to build them up or lend a hand. We've become flapping jaws of bitterness, disservice, gossip, gluttony and entitlement more than anything. Entitlement is defined as the belief that one is inherently deserving of privileges or special treatment and that's how much of this world has become, especially here in the western world. While soldiers and police officers are out sacrificing their lives for our peace of mind and freedom, the majority of us have become thankless, complacent and unappreciative grumblers. Even if the government is reckless with our money, what are we really doing with the freedom we pay for and what these services pay for with their lives? Some say we're a product of our environment which is true to a certain degree but we're also generating this environment by not investing in it ourselves. God sees it all unfolding and will judge according to our contribution and resources and our accessibility to them. We just seem to live and die too and for ourselves while our communities become more and more divided. It reminds me of Alexander Ovechkin and how nearly his whole career he couldn't win in the playoffs. He seemingly played his own individual game to elevate his ego, fame and statistics. Over the years the scrutiny wore on him until he finally changed his attitude and mindset to start playing for the team and the benefit of everyone around him. He then, of course, won the Stanley Cup. The point is what he learned was that it wasn't all about him. He was only on the ice for a third of the game and when he was taking penalties his team had to fight shorthanded for his mistakes and that is what a community does in support of each other. We are designed to serve each other and when we do we feel a sense of purpose and belonging. We also get far more accomplished together. It's just an analogy I see in comparison to the spirit of the world. This is where the carnal spirit of man has overwhelmingly failed and where the spirit and revelation of Christ reigns and transforms us in our purpose, initiative and thinking process through his Word. It's like he turns on a supernatural operating valve in our soul and rewires some sort of predisposed intuition within us through his spirit and in our faith. The more we draw to him and his character through his Word, the more the truth of our own general depravity gets exposed especially in regards to narcissism. The initial transition can be a difficult journey to embark upon but it's still the truth and it's where I'm finding my own personal struggle between actual true faith from an obedient, blameless and submissive heart defined in the scriptures, and a faith seemingly dictated and manipulated to fulfill my own desire for self-preservation, conforming the definition of the word faith for my own benefit. I guess if this were the case my faith would merely follow suit with the spirit of the world and nothing in me would change, nothing in the world would change, and there would be no need for the Bible or the revelation of Jesus Christ. It's hard letting go of the carnal aspirations we have or have set for ourselves in this life and allow the bigger picture to reveal itself into our hearts, but it's the only way to see God's eternal hope in salvation as justifiable cause to do so. For us to hold on to our security in the world as our profession of faith, is almost to deny our faith entirely and live in contradiction to its objective. It's a deep and powerful subject to unearth because if the overriding objective of faith is salvation and for the greater good then again, I have to release the reins and control I have in this life and trust in the vision and calling another entity has upon my life. This is the binding struggle within man's will and pride and where true faith gets defined. Trust in itself can be an extremely difficult word to confide in these days. People seem ruthless in pursuit of their objectives and priorities as though the world is standing in their way. I've struggled vigorously with it in my own mind but ultimately that's what faith is. It's to surrender to an objective that's not of your own.

More of Defining Faith

The difficulty I'm seeing is the presumed directive we're entrusting in, not only in the world but concerning faith, from the voices and conformity of man. Unfortunately faith has become like a chameleon in this western society and throughout the world, shaping itself to our appeasement, preferences and interpretations and blinding us as true reality and relativity persist alongside. Sure the word faith flows easy from the lips when we're healthy, money is in our pockets and our senses are being gratified by the pleasures of the world, but what is faith when our hands and pockets are empty and ungratified? What is faith in relation to history and in restriction and disability? What is faith in oppression and disfavor? What is faith when we realize the state of the world and we are the ones called and compelled to initiate the change and to call out its sin? What is faith in abstinence and obedience? These questions are all too real right now in this world wide epidemic and in how people have perceived the result and outcome of faith to be. The carnal mind lives to accommodate not to regenerate. It reminds me of Martin Luther King and the severe burden that went on in his heart. He literally walked in the exemplification of the objective of true faith. He had a whole life to live outside of his ministry and vision for desegregation. He had a wife and family to care, nurture and provide for separate from his ministry. I'm sure he had dreams and desires for his own success and personal tranquillity like all of us do and it's only natural to feel that way. He had every justifiable right to step back out of the limelight and scrutiny he was under to live for his own cause and the cause of his family but he saw the need and greater cause as a means to die to his own. His faith wasn't in or for himself, his faith was in God and the vision God called upon his life. Whether he made mistakes or was off on his theology, God persisted alongside and honoured his faith regardless of his own personal failures. He was a martyr to a cause that was far bigger than that of his own and he knew it and pursued it regardless. I remember watching one of his last speeches and you could see how torn he was between the two persuasions. All he was doing was calling out the world in it's hypocrisy and blindness to the truth but many people hated him for it because they didn't want their lies and control being altered or exposed. I can't even imagine the feeling of being the designated target in a sniper's rifle and consciously knowing it wherever you went. Much like Jesus he was like a lamb being led to slaughter. You could see him in peril and anxiety as he spoke in his last days but he was bound and determined to persevere for the cause of injustice and equality. 1 Peter 4:1-5 says, "Therefore since Christ suffered for us in the flesh, arm yourselves also with the same mind, for he who has suffered in the flesh has ceased from sin, that he no longer should live the rest of his time in the flesh for the lusts of men, but for the will of God." You could see the spirit of God driving Martin Luther King through his fears in faith. The truth of death's inevitability did not derail him, in fact, it was his overriding ambition as he belted out those famous words in his speech, "I have seen the promised land!" This to me is the truest depiction of unrelenting faith defined in the scriptures. It's standing behind what you believe in regardless of the consequences and not compromising your morals. Again, faith is an unwavering belief regardless of circumstances, regardless of opinions or scrutiny, and not losing sight of the objective in fear. It's one thing to have an opinion and hide behind a computer screen or telephone, but it's another to verbally express that opinion and draw millions of opinions and scrutiny to yourself. To me that's the greatest form of courage, love and faith and no one can deny that, especially if it's based on moral convictions. Martin Luther King's life has become such a profound and courageous proclamation of truth and sincere faith that has changed and revolutionized the world. His life and legacy live on and has become one of the historical pillars and most revolutionary embodiments for transformation and influence the world has ever seen, and his faith ultimately rested upon Jesus Christ. Without Jesus setting the precedence and compelling him, who would Martin Luther King aspire to be or have to confide in to drive his will through his own limitations and fears?

I think the world needs to reconsider its insinuations upon the true Christian faith and come to realize the undeniable impact Jesus has had on shaping our moral consciousness and not simply disregard it all due to false interpretation. Anyone who has found strength or freedom from desegregation by Martin Luther King's impact, actually has his faith to thank and the vision and sovereignty God had set upon his life. They also have the faith of Christ to thank, who exemplified and initiated faith's objective for the world to follow. Galatians 2:20 says, "I am crucified with Christ, it is no longer I who live, but Christ lives in me, and the life which I now live in the flesh I live by the faith of the Son of God, who loved me and gave himself for me." Much of truth is in sacrifice and in the willingness to sacrifice ourselves for the cause of the truth.

The modern world doesn't realize that many of its privileges and much of its productivity and piece of mind have been implemented by historical pillars of faith and perseverance. What much of the world now considers as irrelevant has actually formed our moral consciousness and structure fundamentally, and if looked at through a historical lens would be seen as our only relevance and structure. Ultimately there is no secured promise in living for yourself in this world but there is a substantial promise dying to yourself in faith and this is what people like Martin Luther King and so many millions of others have based their foundation, hope and dependence upon. It's in our willingness to bear the sufferings of this life that express what our faith means to us. Romans 5:3-4 says, "We glory in tribulations, knowing that tribulations produce perseverance, and perseverance character and character hope." Romans 8 says, "For I consider that the sufferings of this present time are not worthy to be compared with the glory which shall be revealed in us..... we ourselves groan within ourselves, eagerly waiting for the adoption, the redemption of our body. For we were saved in this hope, but hope that is seen is not hope, for why does one still hope for what he sees? But if we hope for what we do not see, we eagerly wait for it with perseverance."

2 Corinthians 4:17 says, "For our light affliction, which is but for a moment, is working for us a far more exceeding and eternal weight of glory, while we do not look at the things which are seen, but at the things which are not seen. For the things which are seen are temporary, but the things which are not seen are eternal." I'm not saying we all have to bear that significant of a burden nor are we all called to do so but we will all give account and have our cross to bear in the end.

False Teachers

I've been studying different teachers these past few years and even more so now lying idle at home through this accident. It's fascinating hearing all the contrasting interpretations and opinions circulating the internet these days and as time has progressed in the past few decades. Some of it can be extremely deceptive in trying to find truth that aligns with scripture. Unfortunately, what I see is many are defining faith as some sort of circumstantial formula, antidote or method to draw people in to a false hope by means of gain, prosperity or experience, alluring the desires of the flesh but disregarding the needs of the heart and subsequently dishonoring and blatantly disregarding the gospel entirely. They'll use partial truth forming their own contrived interpretation of God, using scripture out of context to lure people into an apparent benefit, reverting it all back to themselves to justify their own benefit, then stand affirmed as though faith got them there and as though that's the only desired result of faith. They've turned faith into a methodology for their own desired outcome and security and they're selling that anticipation. I've studied the Bible quite extensively and haven't found one justifying reference to a Biblical teacher or prophet becoming rich at the expense of others, in fact it's the complete opposite especially considering the life of Jesus and his apostles. They're literally being paid to tell people what they want to hear, not what they need to hear for salvation. It's all in complete opposition to self sacrifice because I'm sure if they weren't getting rich doing it, they wouldn't do it at all and they'd have nothing to speak about. There is no call to use the Bible to propagate wealth, in fact the call of God and the job of the Holy Spirit within us who believe, is to draw us continually into sincerity, charity and humility, not compel us to prosperity. It's ludicrous and appalling how far this has gotten and the influence it's generated. Philippians 4:8-9 says, "Whatever things are true, whatever things are noble, whatever things are just, whatever things are pure, whatever things are lovely, whatever things are of good report, if there is any virtue and if there is anything praiseworthy, meditate on these things. The things which you learned and received and heard and saw in me, these do, and the God of peace will be with you." This kind of narcissism and greed they're teaching is the entire problem with our world's philosophy and divisiveness whether it be in religion, politics, spiritual premonitions, carma or the apparent universal law of attraction. It's always a self-motivated carnal desire for benefit. These teachers profess Christianity but don't put their feet in anyone else's shoes nor do they put them in the shoes of Jesus or those in the Bible. Again, they simply promote health and prosperity to bank on the anticipation of it. 1 Timothy 6:3-12 says, "If anyone teaches otherwise and does not consent to wholesome words, even the words of our Lord Jesus Christ, and to the doctrine which accords with Godliness, he is proud, knowing nothing, but is obsessed with disputes and arguments over words, from which come envy, strife, reviling, evil suspicions, useless wranglings of men of corrupt minds and destitute of the truth, who suppose that godliness is a means of gain. From such withdraw yourself. Now godliness with contentment is great gain. For we brought nothing into this world, and it is certain we can carry nothing out. And having food and clothing, with these we shall be content. But those who desire to be rich fall into temptation and a snare, and into many foolish and harmful lusts which drown men into destruction and perdition. For the love of money is a root of all kinds of evil, for which some have strayed from the faith in their greediness, and pierced themselves through with many sorrows. But you, O man of God, flee these things and pursue righteousness, godliness, faith, love, patience, gentleness. Fight the good fight of faith, lay hold on eternal life, to which you were also called." It's like 99% of these scriptures pass right through these teachers' minds in their faithless self-dependence. They'll take scripture out of context as though each page is a personal credit card and run people right out the door to their bank machine to justify and contribute to their cause. They're not acknowledging the heart behind the giver or living in reference to his Word, mercy or vision, they're merely using him and his name as a ploy for their own. They are actually only prosperous themselves due to the biblical negligence and scriptural illiteracy of their supporters. A friend sent me a quote from a televangelist named Kenneth Copeland who's accumulated hundreds of millions of dollars from supposed Christian teaching, it said, "No matter your position or profession, God has designed a system to prosper you." These words definitely sound inspiring and optimistic but unfortunately for his disciples that system wasn't in place and they were the pillars of faith, nor is that system in place for millions today or in history dying of cancer or with terminal illness. Ultimately it wasn't in place for our crucified savior who they're professing to follow and is a ludicrous statement historically, geographically and economically. This system wasn't in place for tens of millions of Christians around the world throughout history and now going through this pandemic, not to mention oppressed and regulated societies of communism and socialism. I watched a documentary on the Mexican drug cartels where a system of financial prosperity certainly didn't exist for civilians. It's crazy how many notes I've written down concerning this issue and how irritated I am by these imposters. They've determined faith for everyone as some sort of generic or general term unto health and prosperity so people buy into the promotion. They're actually defining false prophecy in how they're foretelling and giving foreknowledge of the future into everyone's individual lives. Unfortunately now through this global pandemic you can see how unprophetic their words have been all along as accessibility to health and wealth don't look so promising or optimistic on the horizon as they've presumed them to be, even here in our western democracy. I Googled the word presumptuous and it was interesting the definitions that came to light. It says going beyond what is right or proper. Taking things for granted, being overconfident, being too bold or forward, showing overconfidence, or going beyond what is right or proper because of an excess of self-confidence or arrogance. Finally it says failing to observe the limits of what is permitted or appropriate. This describes these teachers to a tee and is in such opposition to the truth of scripture and those in the Bible who God uses as examples of true faith. In fact, the bible specifically states we will suffer and even be persecuted in faith because we are not being conformed by the lust, deception and allure of the world. Romans 12:2 specifically says, "Do not be conformed to this world but be transformed by the renewing of your mind, that you might prove what is that good and acceptable and perfect will of God." Again, I'm not sure what book they're reading because literally every author warns us of these types of heretical teachers and for us as Christians to turn from the lust and covetousness of the world. I've written down some more scriptures for reference concerning the topic. 1 Thessalonians 1:3-5 says, "We are bound to thank God always for you, brethren, as it is fitting, because your faith grows exceedingly, and the love of every one of you all abounds towards each other, so that we ourselves boast of you among the Churches of God for your patience and faith in all your persecutions and tribulations that you endure, which is manifest evidence of the righteous Judgment of God, that you may be counted worthy of the kingdom of God, for which you also suffer." 2 Peter 2:1-3,18 say, "There were also false prophets among the people, even as there will be false teachers among you, who will secretly bring in destructive heresies, even denying the Lord who bought them.....and many will follow their destructive ways, because of whom the way of truth will be blasphemed. By covetousness they will exploit you with deceptive words....when they speak great swelling words of vanity they allure the lust of the flesh, through wantonness, the ones who have actually escaped from those who live in error. While they promised them liberty, they themselves are the servants of corruption, for of whom a man is overcome, the same is brought into bondage." Philippians 3:18-19 says, "For many walk, of whom I have told you often, and now tell you even weeping, that they are the enemies of the Cross of Christ. Whose end is destruction, whose God is their belly, and whose glory is in their shame, who mind earthly things." Colossians 3:2 simply says, "Set your affection on things above, not on things on the earth." Galatians 1:8-10 says, "But if we, or an angel from heaven, preach any other gospel to you than what we have preached to you, let him be accursed. As we have said before, so now I say again, if anyone preaches any other gospel to you then what you have received, let him be accursed. For do I now persuade men, or God? Or do I seek to please men? For if I still pleased men, I would not be a servant of Christ." 1 John 2:15-17 says, "Do not love the world or the things in the world. If anyone loves the world, the love of the Father is not in him. For all that is in the world, the lust of the flesh, the lust of the eyes, and the pride of life is not of the Father but is of the world. And the world is passing away and the lust of it but he who does the will of God abides forever." 1 Peter 2:11 says, "Beloved, I beg you as strangers and pilgrims, abstain from fleshly lusts which war against the soul." Hebrews 13:5-9 says, "Let your conduct be without covetousness, be content with such things as you have. For he himself has said, "I will never leave you nor forsake you".......do not be carried about with divers and strange doctrines. For it is good that the heart be established by grace." Philippians 3:7-8 says, "What things were gain to me, these I have counted loss for Christ. Yet indeed I also count all things loss for the excellence of the knowledge of Christ Jesus my Lord, for whom I have suffered the loss of all things, and count them as rubbish, that I may gain Christ and be found in him, not having my own righteousness, which is from the law but that which is through the faith of Christ, the righteousness which is from God by faith; that I may know him and the power of his resurrection and the fellowship of his sufferings." There are endless scriptures concerning false teachers but one more is Colossians 3:5 which says, "Therefore put to death your members which are on the earth; fornication, uncleanness, evil desire, and covetousness, which is idolatry. Because of these things the wrath of God is coming upon the sons of disobedience, in which you yourself once walked when you lived in them." It's incredible that the book these false teachers claim to know and follow actually convicts them more than any other book in the world. The end of Colossians specifically says that covetousness is idolatry and that is exactly what they are endorsing through the prosperity gospel. God would never call us to exclusively serve ourselves and use faith as our defining incentive to do so, but their entire depiction of God is to use faith in him as a means to serve ourselves and use their promotion as an endorsement to that outcome. Jude 1:16 says, "These are murmurs and complainers, walking after their own lusts, and their mouth speaks great swelling words of vanity, having people admire them because of advantage." Again, this is a horrible misrepresentation in it's disassociation, and I see it actually forming a deeper narcissism than that of the world because they're willfully justifying their conscience in relation to God. They're prophetically projecting the favour of God to the world before even introducing them to how to come to know God through repentance and his sacrifice on the cross. It's so backwards and it angers me even writing this stuff down because as we come to know God through his Word, our faith is substantiated by abstaining from the very desires that they are emphatically and prophetically promoting. All that's happening in the ears of their supporters is their unsaved unregenerate mind attaches itself to whatever form of teaching inspires and justifies their desires and pursuit of the world. It's like a firefighter bringing gasoline to an inferno. To me it's along the lines of a multi-level marketing or ponzi scheme but it's unfortunately deceiving millions in the process as they stand affirmed and exalted in their blatant compromise. All they are doing is promoting positionary and situational control from their own accessibility to finance which ultimately has been paid for by the lie of faith and their lack of it. They've conveniently incorporated wealth into their own faith to form their own security blanket, meanwhile having all their possessions insured for fire and theft. I can't believe they can stand behind a pulpit without conviction like they do but it just goes to show how far people will go for money. It's become a seductive platform for demons and merely been conjoined with the narcissistic spirit satan has enhanced through our impulsive worldly desires and what God restrains and redeems us from in faith and the spirits he exposes. They are literally teaching the unbelieving world to be selfish and are forming a godless, self-centered philosophy as a means to do so to become your own god. They are defining the act of love as or from the benefit received and as our materialistic needs continually being met as though God is some impersonal dispenser or hand to sign checks without an identity of his own. Again, their supporters are simply searching for words to justify their own greed and ignorance. It's as though God has become a bank machine that only they know the code to and they extort people to reveal it to them. They're searing the wilful sacrifice of love on the cross as though it's insufficient for them. 1 John 3:16-18 says, "By this we know the love of God, because he laid down his life for us and we also ought to lay down our lives for the brethren, but whoever has this world's goods, and sees his brother in need, and shuts up his heart from him, how does the love of God abide in him? My little children let us not love in word or in tongue, but in deed and in truth." I know I'm on a bit of a rant but this stuff infuriates me to no end. I read a few pages online of Joel Olsteen's book "Your best life now" and it startled me. Not only is it a best-seller, if you Google his name it says Joel Olsteen is an American pastor, televangelist, and author, who has been called the most popular preacher on the planet and is often listed as one of the most influential religious leaders in the world. Influential is the adjective that bothers me most. People love his inspiring words and prophetic proclamations over their lives, but I want us all to compare these next words in light of the worldwide pandemic and see how they relate to reality. Joel Osteen says, "To experience this immeasurable favor, you must rid yourself of that small-minded thinking and start expecting God's blessings, start anticipating promotion and supernatural increase. You must conceive it in your heart and mind before you can receive it. In other words you must make room for increase in your own thinking, then God will bring those things to pass." These kinds of preachers look like heretical monsters amidst this modern-day crisis but they continue on during this pandemic preaching prosperity. It's literally psychotic. They should all shut up, go home and start emptying their bank accounts for salvations cause as far as I'm concerned. With every word they've spoken over the years they've driven the nails deeper into Christ's hands and feet on the cross, voicing their displeasure of its insufficiency and inadequacy. They don't address God's mercy, nor have they defined mercy in their own hearts and minds. Mercy is a love that responds to human need in an unexpected or unmerited way. Google defines mercy as compassion or forbearance shown especially to an offender or to one subject to one's power and we are all that way in the eyes of God. Faith has become an entitlement to them for them to control and in their lack of surrender. They just don't address the love in the sacrifice of Jesus Christ and how it initiates our accountability which leads us into the gospel of repentance and salvation. They won't do it because it's too confrontational and offensive and it opposes their primary objective, which is money. They merely attribute the result of faith as a measuring stick and an automatic transition into favour as though they "should" receive something, but it has a reverse effect on how someone would measure faith conditionally. I've come to despise the word "should" as a Christian because "should" is a word that to me dictates an expectation and is in complete contrast to mercy. You can't control God's hand of mercy because it contradicts itself in its meaning. It's like two muskox colliding from 50 yards apart and seeing the ripple effect through their loins. This is an extremely destructive heresy. These teachers are damaging people around the world far deeper than they realize in how they attribute faith in God to be especially in relation to opportunity and accessibility. It's equivalent to the influence America's idolatry has had on the world.

True Faith in Contrast

The difference between true faith is there's actually a lot of disfavor that can arise from the world, from satan and from God himself becoming a Christian in a true conversion. The more of an impact you make for the gospel, the more pushback you'll get from the devil especially behind a pulpit, but these teachers aren't compelled to warn us of that or prepare us because the transformation, sanctification and spiritual battle hasn't happened within them. They should read the screwtape letters by CS Lewis and see how intelligent demons are in allowing us to follow our carnal aspirations and teach and inspire others to do so as well. There is also a fear and reverence of the Lord in knowing what you've been forgiven from that should proceed from the lips of those in faith that I just don't hear from them at all. Psalm 130 says, "If you, Lord, should mark iniquities, O Lord, who could stand? But there is forgiveness with you, that you may be feared." They just seem to have no fear of God whatsoever when Proverbs 9:10 specifically says, "The fear of the Lord is the beginning of wisdom, and the knowledge of the Holy One is understanding." Hebrews 12:3-5 says, "Do not despise the chastening of the Lord, nor be discouraged when you are rebuked by him, for whom the Lord loves he chastens, and scourges every son whom he receives. If you endure chastening, God deals with you as with sons; for what son is there whom a father does not chasten. But if you are without chastening, of which "all" have become partakers, then you are illegitimate and not sons. Furthermore, we have had human fathers who correct us, and we paid them respect. Shall we not more readily be in subjection to the Father of spirits and live? For they indeed for a few days chastened us as seemed best to them, but He for our profit, that we may be partakers of his Holiness. Now no chastening seems to be joyful for the present, but painful, nevertheless, afterward it yields the peaceable fruit of righteousness to those who have been trained by it." 1 Peter 4:12-13 says, "Beloved, do not think it strange concerning the fiery trial which is to try you, as though some strange thing happened to you, but rejoice to the extent that you partake of Christ's sufferings, that when his glory is revealed, you may also be glad with exceeding Joy. If you are reproached for the name of Christ, blessed are you, for the Spirit of glory and of God rest upon you."

You see the contrast in this new age teaching in light of actual scripture? To me it's all a sadistic seduction of lies and deception they use to liquidate our resources and they import it around the world receiving tithes and offerings to do so. All they attribute spiritual warfare to, is a speed bump in their way to their desired goal but they don't realize their desired goal in this life is satan's desired goal for them. The problem is the hope in the heart of man is left broken, empty and deceived and the world looks down at Christianity in a hypocritical and convoluted misrepresentation. It ultimately does more damage than good because of the influence and perception it generates, and the intentions unbelievers attribute to God. They only see God's love in what they receive from their own measure of faith and it destroys people all over the world who are marginalized and without access to health and resources, especially with the american dream and ideology as their promotion. These teachers again aren't putting their feet in anyone's shoes or acknowledging the diversities in cultures in regards to accessibility and prosperity geographically. It's just so bad on so many levels. I have come to hate it with every fabric of my being. Think of those with health conditions and mental illness or those in poverty stricken, diseased infested countries. Countries war torn or overrun by ruthless drug cartels like I said before. It gives them no hope and no future and further instills into their heart their own inadequacy and worthlessness. It's actually telling them God hates them due to their circumstances with every word from their mouth because all their gospel is, is a promotion of financial accessibility. They've defined faith circumstantially and that is extremely destructive, irresponsible and naive. It's one thing to say you believe in God, but it's another to represent an established one who's defined his identity in a book and use him and that book for your own benefit. One scripture concerning those who are wealthy is in 1 Timothy 6:17:18, it says, "Command those who are rich in this world not to be high-minded, nor to trust in uncertain riches but in the Living God, who gives us richly all things to enjoy. Let them do good, that they be rich in good works ready to give, willing to share, storing up for themselves a good foundation for the time to come, that they may hold on to eternal life."

The truth of prosperity is many around the world do have access to it. The blessings and gifts of God's creation that he has provided the world, are just merciful characteristics of his personality that millions have had and still have access to. The problem unfortunately is billions don't. It's unfortunate that some don't, but faith isn't defined by that measure. The evilest men in the world have access to more wealth and prosperity than any of us and it doesn't mean God's favour is upon them, in fact it's much the contrary. Some believers would even say, the only way they truly came to faith and to know God is when they were at their wits end either with their health or with their inaccessibility to finances, but these new age charlatans have come to blame our lack of faith to our lack of benefit as though the more we believe the more we will receive. The truth is anyone can walk through the automatic door of a grocery store and buy whatever they want whether they're good or evil or if they're full of faith or completely ignorant of it. In fact, the more evil and faithless I am, the more selfish and gluttonous I probably am, so the more indulgence undoubtedly would consume me. The point is that the true needs of men and women aren't met in what we continuously consume or possess. These are temporal stimulations and satisfactions that get forgotten and unappreciated the more the outcomes are reached and faith only becomes the purpose in the evidence of what you receive. If my basis for faith solely resides in my senses then my senses need to be continuously gratified to substantiate my faith. Again, it's dangerous teaching this stuff because if our emotions are established by our senses and impulses, we're actually simultaneously being conformed and controlled by them. We are temporarily elevated in our senses and stimulation, but unsustained in our emotions, because these impulses only last so long and it's just impossible to maintain that continual level of gratification and remain in humility and in line with God's word and directive.

It reminds me of a show years ago that was about multi million-dollar lottery winners, and how their lives proceeded after they cashed in their ticket. At first it was fun of course, buying a bunch of stuff, as it would be for any of us, but their lives fell apart shortly after in the vanity of it all. All their relationships became contrived and presumptuous because everyone just saw them as a bank machine. They eventually loathed ever winning anything. The money unfortunately became their identity and no one loved them for who they truly were anymore. It became a lonely place to be with more access to money than they could spend in a lifetime. It not only showed the emptiness of affluence and prosperity, it showed the relational perspective from the hand of the giver and how they are always used to attain a benefit, much like how some have come to perceive God. Deep down it hurts to be used, and we all have felt that in the course of our lives, especially when we invest time and energy into someone, but none of us see God in this perspective anymore. We don't even consider the time he invests in us personally and unconditionally. The truth is when we come to know the source we have much more appreciation for the resource. Also, the more we come to know God's spirit through his Word the less we'd be inclined to become selfish, ostentatious or pretentious. The desire for prosperity becomes a non-inclusive proclamation of contrived faith that is unrelative to each individual and their personal circumstances.

It's an extremely vain, non relational and shallow perception of God that people are unfortunately falling for, and it allows the demonic world to flourish in the false perception and anticipation. Again, they quite simply sell the anticipation of what they promote.

Truth of Scripture

Much of scripture is inclusive to the situation, at the specific time and for a specific person or purpose and not necessarily inclusive to our own circumstances now as a general consensus. Also, much of Jesus's miracles were merely fulfilment of Old Testament prophecies to prove who he was and his power, but even with all the proof before their eyes they denied him as many do now. Jesus even says, "Only a wicked and adulterous generation demands a sign," and I feel much of what he did was to prove they would deny him regardless of the miracles they witnessed to ingrain a deeper understanding of faith relationally for future generations. What's inclusive to God is a relationship with him through the revelation of Jesus Christ. Anything else is a vein depiction and needs to be properly analyzed in context maturely and sincerely or else it can be used for heretical coercion. The truth is that we need sanity to be established by forgiveness and grace and that is what God has provided in Jesus Christ. Hebrews 13:9 says, "Do not be carried about with various and strange doctrines, for it is good that the heart is established by grace."

All this has truly brought the scriptures alive for me in a powerful and sobering reality. It's ignited my pen to paper as relatable grievances many face and wrestle with throughout the world as believers and non-believers. I can see God's truths revealing themselves all around me and I yearn to clarify and substantiate biblical relevance and help solidify and define the Christian faith and all its unfortunate misconceptions for the outside world looking in and the inside looking out. I guess I could say the inside looking in as well. If we only look at faith in what we can see, it continuously pushes against the truth of the Gospel because Hebrews 11:1 specifically says that faith is the substance of things hoped for, and the evidence of things not seen. If we start defining faith by our own determination and imagination we're rejecting God's own definition of it. The bible is prophetic in its progression as it inevitably counts down in procession, but faith doesn't progressively evolve alongside or change its course. These new age teachers are substituting true faith with unresearched and unrealistic expectations and are not being relevant to the dissipation of resources in relation to time now, nor are they being relevant to the historical growth in accessibility to resources and amenities. They haven't researched the history of false teachers or false prophets, because they'd only be exposing and condemning themselves. They are leading people on an emotional rollercoaster of contrived opportunism. Our hopes and dreams may never come to fruition in this world, especially if they're based on carnal worldly desires because the carnal mind is in opposition to God.

Romans 8:6-8 says, "To be carnally minded is death, but to be spiritually minded is life and peace. Because the carnal mind is enmity against God, for it is not subject to the law of God, nor indeed can be. So then, those who are in the flesh cannot please God." Outside of true biblical faith, we are resting our hope upon the carnal mind and putting our faith in a world that's deeply sinful and rapidly fading away. These teachers are speaking into our lives and generating aspirations which seem optimistic but again tomorrow isn't as promised as they claim it to be. It's a selfish, naive and uneducated thing to speak of infinite prosperity as the world closes in to its apocalyptic end. It's also naive and ignorant not to recognize that the spirit was manifest and faith in Christ was established, recognized and accepted in a time when there wasn't an awareness or accessibility to prosperity and affluence as there is now. There wasn't worldwide communication and technology. There wasn't transportation like we see today nor the accessibility to comfort, convenience and resources.

They wouldn't have known our benefits and the amenities of today therefore they certainly wouldn't proclaim faith in attaining them. They are simply selling Jesus as a product and unfortunately not preparing people for the valleys in life and the valleys that lie ahead. Again, their faith looks like an empty void amidst this pandemic and all the prophetic words they've spoken over the years are merely suspended in midair. All the promises and foretold promotions, all the words of inspiration and overflow of finances are again, hanging in mid-air as time elapses. It's like skating over a lake in the winter while it's frozen but the truth is it's only seasonal and you can't be on top all year round. The ice will melt and if you're not careful and wise while the seasons change, you'll fall through the cracks and drown. It's not only the cracks, it's the weight of what you're carrying. I also see it as comparable to the lottery corporation in how they advertise wealth and prosperity to lure millions into buying a ticket, but only one wins and then they keep the undisclosed extra for themselves. It's like embezzlement much like our government and how they use the taxpayers money to finance it. Ultimately, the fulfilment emphasized and promoted never keeps pace with the desire and the lack of attainment leaves people empty and unsatisfied, yearning for more and more of an unrealistic bar that's been set so high. People actually start becoming critical and even blame the god they think they know because they've been taught and have built their faith up as an expectation to stimulate their desires and impulses. These false teachers are actually what satan uses to deepen people's faith and dependency in the world and turn them from salvation. To me it actually shows a lack of faith because they continuously need proof for its assurance. Again, the impulse may never meet the requirement and anticipation of our imagination especially with our imaginations being so manipulated. The faith that God instills in our hearts is for salvation in the world to come and for us to let go of our impulsive yearnings and cravings in this world. Martin Luther King is a perfect example because he had absolutely no money yet the impact of his faith has become timeless. I see biblical faith as a means to see through the global deception and diversion and to discern truth from error. It helps us persevere through the contention of the world and in the contemplation of our minds. A hope unseen especially from an eternal source and perspective gives us who believe a far deeper sense of gratitude, relief, and awareness. It brings independence and hope to those marginalized and limited in their capabilities and accessibilities. It gives empowerment amidst inadequacy, comparison and mediocracy. It provides sustenance and clarity through all the opinions, scrutiny and contention that surround us. It offers comfort and rest to those whose health is dwindling and are nearing the end of their lives and it also brings conviction when conviction is needed. Faith is a lifeline in all aspects of our life and a powerful word when seen through its intended scriptural lens. Hebrews 12 says that Jesus was the author and finisher of our faith, therefore if he is the example for us to follow in defining faith then we as Christians need to deeper analyze Jesus's faith and stop creating a faith of our own.

The Battle For Truth

All this being said, it's still not easy. Life is a spiritual battlezone between truth and deception and between pride and surrender. As the screwtape letters insist, demons are aware of all our habitual nuances and tendencies outside of sincere faith. It's hard releasing our impulses and trusting in a love and promise outside of ourselves and what we can see or touch. That's why it's called faith, but again it isn't easy dying to yourself and being patient for something that at times seems so far away. Few pulpits talk about heaven and the life to come these days, let alone hell. It's too confrontational so they mostly gravitate their focus on this immediate world and our individual needs and assurances, but again, this world is on unsecured grounds and with biblical compromise comes unsecured and unestablished faith. I realize it's a hard balance especially with young families who are working hard with hopes and dreams for the future. No one wants to see children suffer anymore than they have to. It's also hard for people in general, who just appreciate God and his creation but we also need the severity of truth as a reminder of our eternal hope. I guarantee this pandemic has made many in the faith question their biblical literacy in relation to eschatology. If I were to be prophetic right now, I would say it's not a good idea to start making babies with what looms ahead. We need to be careful where the word optimism can lead us. Again, they sound like inspirational words I hear from these pastors in megachurches saying God has a plan for your life, but God's actual plan for our lives was to reconcile us back to himself by his sacrifice on the cross through Jesus Christ and until this is established in our hearts, the rest is irrelevant.

The plan for us now is to use our gifts individually and together as a Church community to draw people to the hope of salvation, not for their hope in this world and this includes our own children. They'll fill massive stadiums and auditoriums seemingly to live vicariously through the carnal voice of an inspirational speaker but we're not questioning their intentions or our own aspirations in relation to the Word of God. We're allowing someone else to dictate them for us in our own passive-aggressive, unsecured, complacent inferiority and lack of hermeneutics. We're hearing what we want to hear to justify our own ignorance. I'm not even sure who they're speaking to, to be honest. They're definitely not speaking to born again christians because christians should see right through them and they aren't speaking to non-believers other than to justify them in the self-serving narcissistic course they were already on. They are actually severely detrimental to anyone who listens to them. The truth is that we are all independent people with independent minds and wills that need to take this seriously and properly evaluate our own faith in our own independent study with God and his Word. When we start following the wrong voice, we get so easily derailed in our own carnal ambitions and unsecured understanding. Unfortunately, the opposite of security is insecurity and that's where many are finding themselves in regards to faith these days. People shouldn't have to be told what to believe, they should believe, because they've made their own personal decision and declaration to do so. 1 John 2:26-27 says, "These things I have written to you concerning those who try to deceive you. The anointing which you have received from him abides in you, and you do not need that anyone teach you, but as the same anointing teaches you concerning all things, and is true, and is not a lie, and just as it has taught you, you will abide in him." I don't think Gods saying we can't learn from those who are experienced and mature in the faith, but the spirit is the discerning mediator that aligns with scripture and has the overall authority to us as individuals regardless of man's interpretation. When we're being told what we should believe from a position of entitlement and self intention, all sorts of vain proclamations and control arise, much like Catholicism. I'm going to bite my tongue through this pen for a few pages concerning their ridiculous religion, but many of these so-called Christian denominations are literally defining heresy and apostasy with every word that leaves their mouth and they have since their inception whether it be Catholicism, prosperity preaching, Jehovah Witnesses, Mormons and many others. Google defines apostasy as an act of refusing to continue to follow, obey, or recognize a particular faith and that's exactly what many have done and are still doing. Heresy is defined much the same and says it's any belief or theory that is strongly at variance with established beliefs or customs, in particular the accepted beliefs of a church or religious organization. They are blatantly professing and exemplifying the very hypocrisy and sin God convicts them of in his Word and through his spirit. I'll be honest in saying that I have no idea what they're talking about in relation to the bible, especially Catholicism. It's amazing the downfall and rippling effect that arises when men feel as though they've arrived and gain a position in a seat of authority.

Even if 95% of their words sound inspired by God and are seemingly in line with God's word, their intentions are ultimately for their own control and agenda and those influenced use their profession as a means to justify their own. It's not just in prosperity, it's in the religious conformity of guilt through the law that they claim the entitlement over. Sometimes that 5% is like a drop of rat poison in a glass of Kool-Aid and unfortunately it's poisoned the world in its perception of the true Christian faith. The reason why I'm so strong in emphasizing all this is because this is the general perception of the Christian faith around the world whether it be in televangelism or in Christian literature on the bookshelves. It's become like an industry and this is a large percentage of imported theology the world has grown accustomed to hearing, whether it be in prosperity, prophecy or in Catholicism. Again, it all becomes like a chameleon in the theories of our selfish carnal imagination and entitlement. 1 Thessalonians 2:3-6 says, "Our exhortation did not come from error or uncleanness, nor was it in deceit. But as we have been approved by God to be entrusted with the gospel, even so we speak, not as pleasing men, but God who tests our hearts. For neither at any time did we use flattering words, as you know, nor a cloak of covetousness, God is witness, nor did we seek glory from men."

So much of supposed faith seems contrived to me these days, kind of like two baseball players on opposing teams playing in a game. They'll hit a base hit or a home run and do a sign of a cross on their chest, then point to the sky as if that were God's individual intention for their lives. It may be a partial giving of thanks, so I'll try to be careful judging their intentions, but what are they giving thanks for, is the question? It seems to me there's supposed faith is again, a vain, contrived and conceited belief for their own personal benefit and accolades, because in the end one team will eventually lose and both players were supposedly pointing to the same God. The point is God is not vain at all in his own personal declaration and has established and defined faith through Jesus Christ. The Word of God is deep and hits the core intentions of our being. It goes far deeper than just being all about you, all the time. Hebrews 4:12 says, "The Word of God is living and powerful, and sharper than any two-edged sword, piercing even the division of soul and spirit, and of joints and marrow, and is a discerner of the thoughts and intents of the heart. And there is no creature hidden from his sight, but all things are naked and open to the eyes of him to whom we must give account." There's no harm in having faith for realistic things of this world and God does show favour to those who are obedient and mature, but we certainly can't dictate God and manipulate his steering wheel. In doing so we leapfrog over forgiveness and mercy and over repentance and humility. We also leapfrog over the salvation of the world into which we are called. If you look again at it from a baseball perspective, there are hundreds of players on different teams rounding bases all year long pointing to the sky in supposed faith, but at the end of the season only one team wins with players on the team with no faith at all. We now see through this Coronavirus and with all these professional sports being suspended how trivial it all is in light of scripture. This is why our conclusive declaration of faith isn't solely in the individual treasures, accolades or recognition of this world. It doesn't mean God won't help us in and through our individual needs or even use us as an inspiration to others, it just means we need to be more realistic and relative in our understanding of God in our ambitions influentially, because validation and equity are both vanity to God. When we bear the selfless initiatives and influence of God we can see our ambition and God's will in a more mature, humble, sober and productive directive and consensus than that of our own. If faith never brings us affluent prosperity, we need to hold to the faith and promise that this world isn't our conclusive destination. Faith in the real Jesus would never produce this kind of spirit within the heart of man because prosperity and the desire for it generate envy and comparison and with comparison comes pride and division. 1 James 4:1 says, "Where do wars and fights come from among you? Do they not come from your desires for pleasure that war in your members? You lust and do not have. You murder and covet and cannot obtain. You fight and war. Yet you do not have because you do not ask. You ask and do not receive, because you ask amiss, that you may spend it on your pleasures." As soon as the spirit of comparison triggers our emotions and forms an opinion in our minds, we either become entitled in our ego and judgment or we become inferior in our frustration and inadequacy. Either way we refrain ourselves from supporting each other in unity and that's what incites the division. It isn't a coincidence or ironic that in a comparative and envious world people suffer for lack of support. This is what the American dream produces and the outcome of it. It's what generates the spirit of suicide and murder in the heart of man and where so much abuse and hostility happens within our homes and communities. Comparison is in continual conflict and opposition to love and support if you analyze it in a psychological way. We don't bear each other's burdens and again, we can't love our neighbours as ourselves if all we are is living for ourselves in comparison. The carnal spirit of man attributes wisdom in how we've devised the reception of personal gain to ourselves and stands affirmed in that entitlement, but true wisdom sees through all that self-serving narcissism and is wise to it for the benefit of us all unto salvation. This is the wisdom of the spirit of God and in the revelation of Jesus Christ. Anything else is devised by the carnal intent and intellect of man.

My Own Struggle

With my own afflictions set before me with this accident, I'll admit I've struggled intensely in my head with all the above. It's as though my mind is torn between self-promotion, devotion and demotion and this accident hasn't helped me resolve the three. It's not only the accident, it's me and the perception I have of myself that I've always struggled with even before the accident. It's been a spiritual war to say the least. The devil can be an idol beast and incessant in his accusations towards us who believe and are called for a higher purpose. He also knows those who are called but just don't know it yet and tries to destroy them before finding God and making an impact. I say that as a warning because I've been there. Regardless, I've always struggled with self-confidence and initiating conversations with people with spiritual resistance or not. I'm not really one for small talk or intellectual dialect so it's been difficult engaging people through the process of life and faith. It can be awkward and uncomfortable to confront these kinds of issues interactively with people, especially family and friends. I have a hard time communicating all the head knowledge into compatible, productive interaction with grace at times. The majority of my extroverted personality growing up involved drugs and alcohol and a diluted version of my true self, so this transition has been challenging to say the least. Even without blanketed nerves with substance abuse, I still struggle with confidence around people especially when life is grinding me through its gears like it is now. It's much easier conversing when life brings some contentment and relative fulfilment, especially from a financial perspective, so it's easy to see why people buy into voices that justify those means. This being said, my identity in the world has come into question on all levels. A part of me is still hanging on to it when I know deep down God just wants me to let go, but it's hard. I feel I don't have a voice in conversation because, again, people these days attribute faith to our individual status, financial position or reputation in life and resolve their perception of it in relation to mine. They don't see a reason for faith in an undesirable position and they'll merely say, "Look at where faith has got you" or, "If there's a God then why this or why that?" and to them that justifies their unbelief. It takes a lot of courage to hold on to your beliefs and convictions in faith when you're dealing with conflict or difficult circumstances yourself. People naturally hate dying to themselves in compromise. I see people around me in more favorable positions and get jealous and envious myself. It's only natural but can be even more so without a greater perspective, appreciation and hope. Psalm 73 says, "Truly God is good to Israel, such as are pure in heart. But as for me, my feet had almost stumbled; My steps had nearly slipped. For I was envious of the boastful, when I saw the prosperity of the wicked. ..their strength is firm. They are not in trouble as other men."

Even if it's not all from jealousy and envy, the majority of us naturally yearn for the good things of the world and when we see other people in positions that we desire ourselves, it can be deflating and demoralizing. The problem from a spiritual perspective, is the devil knows our level of perspective and is there waiting to pounce on any emotional weakness and enhance our reactive propensity and division. He is relentless and persistent at times like a sadistic little fly in the eardrum, coercing me to sin and turning me against my faith but I can't fall victim to his lies. I can stare right at them through the light of scripture in faith and in the forefront of my mind because I'm wise to his identity and I'm wise to his objectives. Scripture says, "The spirit is willing but the flesh is weak," and, "Greater is he that is in you than he who is in the world," and it's so true when battling through the spiritual war in your mind.

It's definitely challenging being disciplined and consistent in faith and surrender but when I am, I find rest for my soul because I'm surrendering to a faith that's previously been established by Christ and not subjecting myself to a faith or strength of my own. I also find when I surrender to God in humility and remain disciplined, I stay in line with his directive for my life and the devil has no avenue to accuse or entice me. God's convictions and promises for the afterlife keep me disciplined in faith and I don't react to my circumstances and offenses that are irrelevant to the bigger picture and eternal perspective. I still have the thoughts, emotions and desires at times, which are natural and satan can affect them, but my faith overcomes them and compels me to carry on morally in God's objective and forgiveness, even if I make mistakes along the way. Sometimes it's not only satan to blame, it's our fallen nature that supersedes our will which can be hard to overcome. The enticement of the world and the shame at times can seem relentless but it's all part of the maturing and sanctification process in faith. Romans 8:1 says, "There is therefore now no condemnation to those who are in Christ Jesus, who do not walk according to the flesh, but according to the spirit." 1 James 12-16 says, "Blessed is the man who endures temptation, for when he has been approved, he will receive the crown of the life which the Lord has promised to those who love him. Let no one say when he is tempted, I am tempted by God, for God cannot be tempted by evil, nor does he himself tempt anyone. But each one is tempted when he is drawn away by his own desires and enticed. Then, when desire has conceived, it gives birth to sin, and sin, when it is full-grown, brings forth death. Do not be deceived, my beloved brethren."

Truthfully, there's a supernatural contentment that is in Christ that exceeds the world's impulsive contentment that I'm compelled and fascinated by, and I'm not ashamed to yield to and admit. It's not necessarily in experiencing life but appreciating and experiencing the grace of life. Philippians 4:6-7 says, "Be anxious for nothing, but in everything by prayer and supplication, with thanksgiving, let your requests be known to God; and the peace of God, which surpasses all understanding, will guard your hearts and minds through Christ Jesus."

The War With The Devil

The devil has been demoted and given up his place in service to God and all he has is our downfall and sadistic glory to live for. That's why life and even faith at times can seem unrelenting in our own strength because he and his minions are literally that pathetically cruel in persistence and are far more evil than we are good, especially without God's righteous fortitude as our sustaining strength. It's a jealous rage within our conscious will that satan persists to be god over, but true faith holds him captive and powerless because Jesus overcame the impulses and emotions that the devil holds us captive in and his Spirit now lives in us that believe and intercedes on our behalf. Romans 8:34-39 says, "Who is he who condemns? It is Christ who died, and furthermore is also risen, who is even at the right hand of God, who also makes intercession for us. Who shall separate us from the love of Christ? Shall tribulation, or distress, or persecution, or famine, or nakedness, or peril, or sword? Yet in all these things we are more than conquerors through him who loved us. For I am persuaded that neither death nor life, nor angels, nor principalities, nor powers, nor things present, nor things to come, nor height, nor depth, nor any other created thing shall be able to separate us from the love of God which is in Christ Jesus our lord." When we hear satan's persisting voice of guilt or condemnation, we know it's a lie because his identity has been exposed and he's already been judged by God long ago, and God calls us forgiven in Christ.

Collosians 2:13-17 says, "And you, being dead in your trespasses, he has made alive together with him, having forgiven all your trespasses, having wiped out the handwriting of requirements that were against us, which was contrary to us. And he has taken it out of the way, having nailed it to his cross. Having disarmed principalities and powers, he made a public spectacle of them, triumphing over them in it. So let no one judge you in food or in drink, or in regarding a festival or a new moon or sabbath, which are a shadow of things to come, but the substance is of Christ." If you look at it from an earthly perspective, we have these supreme court judges that are held to the highest regard and ethical standard, but if we were to find out they had a hidden life full of sin and debauchery, we'd turn the judgment back on them in their hypocrisy. It's similar to the devil and how he gave up his position to serve his own selfish desires and now lives to become a false god in our minds. He's that hypocritical judge that has committed far worse offenses than what he condemns us for. John 8:44 says, "He was a murderer from the beginning, and does not stand in the truth, because there is no truth in him. When he speaks a lie, he speaks of his own, for he is a liar and the father of it."

He's been disarmed in our faith when we truly understand it from a spiritual perspective because the devil gave up his opportunity with God that we still have and that enrages him. Unfortunately, when the world defines faith from a carnal capacity without Jesus, the devil is smart enough to allow and comply with our natural propensity because his ultimate objective is the salvation of our souls. What fascinates me is that I feel much of the world outside of biblical faith actually believes that satan exists, but unless we identify with him from the biblical perspective he merely uses it all for his objective in our disassociation. You can see how people with misguided faith or no faith at all fall victim and succumb to the lies and fears going on in their head especially when they're unaware of the enemy they're fighting. The devil is sophisticated and it can be a debilitating and tormenting persistence without a solution in our own wisdom and strength. I know where they're coming from and my message in this book is that there is hope. I can see now far deeper into the mind of God and the deliverance he provides through the Word of God that equips us in the warfare of our minds. Ephesians 6:13-17 says, "Therefore take up the whole armour of God, that you may be able to withstand in the evil day…. having girded your waist with truth, having put on the breastplate of righteousness, and having shod your feet with the preparation of the gospel of peace, above all, taking the shield of faith with which you will be able to quench all the fiery darts of the wicked one. And take the helmet of salvation, and the sword of the spirit, which is the Word of God."

Dissolving Misconceptions

God has given the world a free gift, I repeat a free gift, to release us from this internal struggle and bondage that many of us feel confused and trapped in. My reason for writing this book is a lot to do with dissolving people's misconceptions of the spirit within the Bible and its relevance. It wasn't generated within the heart of man therefore we cannot hold the entitlement or claim over its significance or directive, nor can we dictate it. Man likes to build cathedrals and create overbearing systems of conformity to appear religious and to be in control but God is uncontrollable and uncontainable. John 3:7-8 simply says, "You must be born again. The wind blows where it wishes, and you hear the sound of it, but cannot tell where it comes from and where it goes. So is everyone who is born of the Spirit." This one scripture literally destroys religious entitlement altogether. It declares God's independence from it and defines faith with only a few words. When we do it our way, we religiously obscure God's identity and objective and abuse his grace and sovereignty in our misinterpretation and misrepresentation. 1 Kings 8:27 says, "Will God indeed dwell on the earth? Behold, Heaven and the heaven of Heavens cannot contain you. How much less this temple which I have built." Acts 7:48-49 says, "The Most High does not dwell in temples made with hands, as the prophet says; Heaven is my throne and earth is my footstool. What house will you build for me? Says the Lord, or what is the place of my rest? Has my hand not made all these things?" God does not need four walls to prove or dictate his providence, he is an omnipresent being who intercedes in the hearts and minds of men and women all over the world and he'll draw whomever he wishes to himself in his time and for his purpose. He is not more present in a large congregation as he is in a small one either. Mathew 18:20 says, "Where two or three are gathered together in my name, there I am in the midst of them."

We couldn't contain him before the world began so I don't see how or why we think we can now. God will walk with us independently regardless of man's systems or control methods. He's beyond the law, in fact, he fulfilled the law in Christ, therefore we're free from its burden in faith and those who are holding onto it haven't understood the full revelation of Jesus Christ. I didn't have to perform a religious act or pay a tithe, nor did I walk through some ritualistic cathedral or make confessions to an ordained priest, I simply believed from my heart and in that sincerity, God entered in voluntarily. Hebrews 7:15-16 says, "There arises another priest who has come, not according to the law of a fleshly commandment, but according to the power of an endless life." There is now a spirit stronger within me that continues to contend over my will, awareness and peace of mind that just wasn't there before. God interceded within my consciousness and actually lives to condemn that religiosity. Hebrews 7:25 says, "Therefore He is also able to save to the uttermost those who come to God through Him, since He always lives to intercede for them." Again, this is the selfless sanctifying love of God the world is ultimately denying and disregarding. He negates so much of the chatter, anxiety and fear in my mind, interceding through the confirmation of his Word. It's supernatural and is the spiritual transformation and regeneration that transcends logic or reason within our Christian faith. Where science, physics, philosophy, the theory of evolution or whatever else humanity has conjured up to justify itself, can produce no answers. One day I lived for sin to justify myself in it, and upon believing realized the uncompromising need for the justice of it in the world and in myself. Romans 5:1 says, "Therefore, having been justified by faith, we have peace with God through our Lord Jesus Christ." It's a supernatural deliverance in our belief where the word faith is truly defined in and by Jesus Christ. It can't be a system of religious conformity or regulations because we're actually professing to God that our religious ordinances are collectively more productive and revolutionary than him. Honestly, I just hate the misconceptions people have of Christianity and desperately want to clarify it all. It's so frustrating once you study the bible for yourself. People will never be justified in unbelief but they're certainly justified in their skepticism through the apostasy and heresy of man over the centuries.

The Person of Jesus Christ

This battle is real and pressing in all around us but true faith can overcome it all because it was overcome by Jesus Christ. I put my feet in his shoes and mine become a far lighter burden to bear no matter what my circumstances are. He came to overcome faith's objective and to become the dimensional bridge for us to evaluate and conceptualize. It was the faith of him that becomes our saving grace and delivers us into our eternal hope and redemption that we abide in. I only have my own burden to bear but he trapped himself in a human vessel and bore humanities burden that holds us captive by the power of the law. It's beyond revolutionary, it is the revolution and basis for our internal resolution between mind, body, soul and spirit. It's a challenging mystery to unravel and grasp at times, don't get me wrong, but if we can't figure out how our own soul and spirit operate, how do we expect to understand God's? People will say, "If he's God why would he need to have faith in himself? But there's a will between spirit and flesh that are in conflict with each other as we all well know, and God took on that same conflict in Christ. The difference is he didn't compromise his will in it's procession to the intention of its cause. There was an outcome to his destiny that he was fully conscious of in his spirit that took faith to carry out while in procession in his flesh, all the way to the cross.

The more I come to realize this persisting battle in the human mind, human heart and my own carnal weaknesses, the more it all gives prevalence and points to the grace, truth and power exemplified through the person of Jesus Christ and how the word holy is truly defined. I guess the question is, who was the word holy defined by if it wasn't defined by him? Google defines holy as exalted or worthy of complete devotion as one perfect in goodness and righteousness, but again, how does this define itself outside of Jesus Christ? Man defines strength by masculinity through its pride, physical fortitude or toughness, but God initiates and substantiates strength metaphysically which is an impartation outside of our capabilities to this magnitude. Metaphysics is defined as the branch of philosophy that examines the fundamental nature of reality, including the relationship between mind and matter, between substance and attribute, and between potentiality and actuality. Jesus Christ literally defines the word in one person and is an incredibly profound and prolific embodiment of truth that for me has become undeniable. His strength is in and for the influence that proceeds and is generated. We praise and idolize men and women for their fame, fortune, achievements and in the legacies they leave behind but God has upheld the world through Christ and sustained it in far more influential and fundamental ways than we realize. He had everything being God, but he became nothing and acquired nothing to become everything to those with nothing, who in the end, will acquire it all. It's a selfless sacrificial martyrdom to the highest degree from the one with the highest pedigree. When I've stood alone amidst my own turmoil and anxieties in life, I've fallen apart into a confused, frail and agitated mess. I was held captive by my fears and emotions, but he wasn't overcome by the anxiety and emotions that compounded upon him. He didn't fall inferior to them, he actually drew the world and all its contention to himself voluntarily and used the burden as an opportunity to teach us to re-evaluate our own self consciousness and convict the world of the harm it's causing itself, disregarding his own life in the process. It takes an extremely courageous and determined individual to uphold that level of independence, willpower and moral fortitude. I'm part of a club called Toastmasters close to where I live that teaches you how to public speak and it's a weekly reminder of how inferior and insecure we all are in the eyes of judgment, scrutiny and opinions when their focus is upon us. In fact, public speaking has been voted the number one fear of man in surveys in America and around the world for years. People are actually more fearful of dying than they are of speaking in front of people. There's something about a captive audience that debilitates us when their eyes are drawn towards us, however small the audience is. I'm getting a bit better but for the most part I'm like a leaf in a windstorm up there. People in the club do it for areas of business or social anxiety where they can't beat the fears that build up inside them. The position of leadership and influence definitely takes a lot of bravery. I started it because I was involved in a soup kitchen years ago that required a short speech before the food was served and I realized when I was up there that I had no idea what I was doing. I froze up and crumbled under the pressure of it all. It was like a muscle that had never been trained or exercised, like the entire perception you have of yourself and all the opinions you've generated for the world are an open book to be examined and evaluated. It freaked me out to be honest, but that's the amazement of Jesus, is how he was not shaken or deterred. He was a rebel with a cause, and in a sense, a full-blown introverted extrovert. Again, it's one thing to have an opinion but it's another to change the course of time and history with that opinion and with every word out of your mouth. My point is that God put himself in this position in Jesus Christ and rendered the fears powerless over his own love-desired obligation to initiate a transformation for the world to openly scrutinize. The difference with him is there's nothing to scrutinize.

I'm learning that within my own personal struggles and fears and within the contention of my mind lies the purpose that implored his directive and lies the truth, deliverance and revelation behind the spirit of God within the Bible. This same spirit was in Christ reconciling the world to God on the cross and is now the sanctifying and redeeming power within me and those who believe. He also defined love with every step he took and every word out of his mouth.

The world doesn't see it because it doesn't believe but all it takes to see it is to believe and the truth begins to unravel before your very eyes and within your heart.

Dissolving More Misconceptions

I had all the same naive, immature and pompous insinuations that I hear from people now when being confronted with the idea of God and the Bible. I'd make unresearched comments and unmerited accusations or assumptions disregarding the Bible as illegitimate nonsense all the while it's truth was unfolding in me, around me and throughout the world. I had never even opened it or read a sentence and most of the people I've interacted with concerning the issue are the same. They might even have one on their bookshelf or somewhere in their attic but it's merely laying dormant, collecting dust. They won't open it because they've already made an assumption of its purpose and integrity or they just feel justified in their own life. Whether there's a little dust on it on the bookshelf or it's an inch thick laying in the attic, the words are in their prophetic procession either way and even more so in the midst of this pandemic. People will say it was written by man so how can it be trusted or they'll say it's been rewritten so many times that it must be flawed. They'll even say religion has caused all the wars in history and the list goes on and on in how people disregard God's Word and its relevance. I was much the same and would just go on my way in my own vindicated ignorance with literally no literary research invested whatsoever. We don't realize the first half of the word ignorance is to ignore and we don't quite realize the gravity of what we're ignoring. The bible says people perish for lack of understanding and it's become more and more evident in our world. Sin is an encroaching disease that eats away at the world like a parasite and is worse than any virus or pandemic the world has ever seen. As the consequence of sin has accumulated, again, the truth of the Bible gets exposed and that little book on the shelf collecting dust becomes more and more relevant. The whole book is a warning for us to stop but we continue to ignore it's warning as though our way is better. It holds so many keys to the doors we've locked in our carnality. Simple research expels so many of our naive assumptions and misconceptions but we just don't care to do it anymore. When it comes to religion causing all the wars in history as I've heard many use as an excuse to disregard christianity, that's just blatant ignorance. Mayo Zedong killed 60 million people under his regime as an atheist. Joseph Stalin killed 40 million and Hitler 30 million. King Leopold ll of Belgium murdered 8 million and Hidek Tojo of Japan 5 million. The list goes on and on in cultures all over the world throughout history and to this very day of regimes mass-murdering and warring over control and power as godless atheists with no fear of the eternal judgment of God. America has had approximately 15000 murders a year for decades and very few are religiously motivated. We just don't properly evaluate whether the fear of God is there to save us from ourselves or does our irreverence to it actually propel us to be consciously liberated otherwise. For me personally, I needed that fear to change the intentions of my heart and evaluate the perception I had of God and of myself.

At the end of the day it doesn't matter how the world perceives the bible if its words are prophetically unravelling around us as we speak, and the life-altering significance within a man or women's confession and testimony bares the undeniable claim to the bible's truth and the spirits prevalence at work in someone's life and heart. I'm living proof of this myself as millions of others have been around the world throughout history. The greatest miracle I see in the world and most relevant and crucial, is when someone turns from their sin and doesn't claim that transition or conversion to be generated from within themselves. All these other miracles or spiritual premonitions are a diversion to the truth of God's eternal objective unto repentance, regeneration and salvation. The transformation happens within you of course, but you're not claiming it as coming from you. If it did you wouldn't need to believe in something other than yourself for it to happen. It's amazing to see all the misconceptions reveal and unravel themselves in a new believer and the truth getting exposed and established in their minds. A genuine conversion to Christ is completely life altering. It's like God opens your eyes to a whole new cognizance like an old muscle car being stripped down to bare metal and being rebuilt from the ground up with new parts. It's God's supernatural vaccination that just can't be compared to anything the world generates. Again, it's just not derived from man's intellect, wisdom or imagination. It can only be of God because we don't produce the inclinations to prophetically proceed themselves. Our foreknowledge is just too limited and narrow minded. When it comes to the bible's literary procession, we did not historically amalgamate together from generation to generation to produce this eclectic of a perogative or storyline, therefore the only alternative is that it is from a higher power and to us as Christians, that power is of God. It's incomprehensible to the human imagination. We're too selfish, self-centered and unattentive in our carnal capacity and depravity. It's impossible for it not to be true on these simple facts alone. Even with all our technology and information nowadays, we can't produce a progressively compounding prophecy like the bible because sin has become the overriding power that blinds our world and only God can see through the power of sin and it's end result.

A Lost And Evil World

We're completely lost without him and in a world so evil now where our own governments and banking systems are extorting the world on every level and to ignorantly call the bible irrelevant actually makes you irrelevant. The whole world has become enslaved to the lender and deceived by sin. I'm going to talk more about this stuff later in the book but the powers of evil are extremely prevalent and extremely relevant right now into which the majority are oblivious. They have the whole world under duress and have insidiously infiltrated almost every aspect of our lives right under our noses. Duress is defined as making someone do something against their will, or making someone perform an illegal act, by using threats, coercion or other illicit means. This is where the powers of impunity can influence our lives. The goal is globalization through centralization and very few understand to what level that extends and impacts our lives. I don't care what people's opinions are concerning covid 19 but this is the "real deal" that the Bible warns us about in Revelation. Our government here in Canada is actually giving 1000$ fines out now if you're unvaccinated but I've researched the biochemistry behind it extensively and it is severely detrimental to our health and future. If you think otherwise you have been deceived into believing a false narrative. They're manipulating our genetics synthetically which is extremely dangerous and using chemicals like polyethylene glycol which is extremely allergenic and derived from petroleum. Bill Gates' own words he admits to wanting to depopulate the world and common sense tells you that the only way to do that is by murder and infertility. Every mandate has a lucrative incentive or commission attached to it and every variant earns these pharmaceutical companies billions of dollars. Unfortunately these psychopaths and our government are all shareholders and proponents to the cause. There's so many variables to science and they're abusing every avenue of it in our naivety to justify legislation and push their sadistic agenda forward. There's far bigger narratives and invested interests at the end of that needle than people realize, don't kid yourself. There's not only invested interests, there's conflict of interest behind every door you open. It's about greed, power, money and control and that's the bottom line. I watched a video someone put together of dozens of news feeds across America simultaneously narrating the exact same words from their teleprompters. It was one of the creepiest things I've ever seen. What's even creepier is these media outlets are sponsored by Pfizer themselves! The whole pandemic is a global sham but if we don't comply and get vaccinated they'll soon ostracize us and not allow us to buy, sell or travel just as the bible indicates. That's the world we'll see in the very near future. Much of it will start happening before this book gets published. I'm trapped between a rock and a hard place, access to regular amenities or a deadly man-made vaccine from the most dangerous, litigated pharmaceutical companies in the world. Unfortunately the adverse effects, I feel, will be far more severe than covid itself, not only biologically but economically as well. It's pretty scary when you have to sign a waiver of consent to the nonliability of adverse effects. That shows a corporation with no credibility and no confidence in the product they've manufactured. It's even scarier when the adverse effects aren't allowed to be released to the media by our government. I've known of several cases of severe adverse effects just within my small group of friends. If you dig deeper you can find the truth but the main sources for data and information are all fraudulent and biased. I watched an interview on sportsnet where one of the teams had several cases of covid throughout the locker room. What's interesting is the coach came on an interview saying that the testing is unreliable because of all the false positives. Here you have a professional sports team with access to the best technology not trusting the testing system two years into the pandemic. What does that say for the population? It's all a scam and this is how they've manipulated so much of what we presume to be our reality. As of June 25, 2021, Eudravigilance (the European database of suspected adverse drug reactions) reported 13,867 deaths in addition to 1,354,336 injuries from these vaccines but no mainstream media outlets reported this information. There's several highly qualified virologists and immunologists including Nobel prize winners and former employees of Pfizer and Gavi, as well as medical professionals who are warning against the dangers of the vaccines, the distribution process, as well as the corruption, censorship, and immorality tied to the handling of the covid pandemic. The problem is not only are we being withheld information and lied to, many information platforms and social media apps like YouTube, Instagram and Facebook have been deleting videos that go against the CDC and World Health Organization recommendations. They're even deleting social media accounts despite how well-qualified, and well supported the information being shared is by data and science. It's called social engineering much like how the Rockefeller Foundation donated over 13 million dollars to combat misinformation and censor dissenting voices. How's that not a conflict of interest? They have an agenda and they have the money and resources to push it forward. That's how the power of technocracy can work and we're witnessing the implications of it. Only 330 kids in America have died of covid19 and they were all immune compromised or diabetic. This is a far less number than the flu itself yet they're mandating children to get vaccinated as well? Why? It just makes no rational sense. To me this is pure evil and goes against our human rights and ethical principles as a democracy. When we can't make our own conscientious objective decisions on our own, especially in regards to our body, that's when tyranny has begun its assault on our human rights and privileges. These are the rights we've fought wars over and established our constitutions upon. We're being forced to put something into our bodies that hasn't even been approved by the FDA when there's legitimately safe and provingly effective treatments like Ivermectin already on the market. It's literally insane how morbid this has become. The FDA itself admits that the covid-19 vaccines have not undergone the same type of review as regular FDA approved products and that their vaccine clinical trials usually take upwards of 7 years. It hasn't been tested on children, pregnant women, immunocompromised or people suffering from chronic health conditions whatsoever. People argue that it's just like any other vaccine we've taken in the past but it's not, it's a new technology being forced into us by fear, propaganda and intimidation. My old boss just got Bell's Palsy after the second shot and another friend had to quit his job as a police officer with severe chest pains from Myocarditis. A nurse in Toronto was recorded in a rally saying over 800 still born babies have occurred in pregnancy since the vaccine mandates were set. The year prior was less than ten. The landscape on my jobsite's wife was concerned about getting vaccinated as she was in her final trimester. He told her he'd lose her as a client if she did because of all the miscarriages and stillborns happening. I could go on forever with this stuff but ultimately it's impossible to say these vaccines are safe when no legitimate testing has been done. We're basically an experiment but the pending question is, are the adverse effects irreversible and detrimental to our health? This is a justifiable and legitimate question to ask especially in regards to children. To me it just shows the true power of propaganda and the influence the media can generate in polarizing a set narrative. It's like we're living in the pages of their global enquirer. Polarize means to divide into sharply opposing factions or political groups. It's also defined by causing something, especially something that contains different people or opinions, to divide into two completely opposing groups. People just can't see how manipulated we've become and how everything we see is a scripted illusion set before our eyes. We had one 14 year old child supposedly die of covid here in Canada. It was all over the news as apparent proof of how deadly the virus can be but the parents then came out shortly after saying their kid had stage 4 brain cancer and his death wasn't a result of covid at all. The child may have had the virus but like thousands of other cases, he didn't die of the virus and that is where these numbers are being enhanced and over exaggerated. The news eventually had to make a public apology but the point is that the numbers and reports just aren't lining up with true facts. Thousands of doctors and nurses are walking off their jobs due to all the coercion going on but their stories are just not being heard. They're definitely skewing and enhancing the numbers but the question you have to ask yourself is why? Our Provincial Health Officer here in British Columbia wrote a book recently that stated she just does what she's told and isn't in a place to share an opinion of her own. Again, there's collusion, bribery and corruption behind every door you open. People are slowly waking up to it all but their agenda seems viciously unrelenting. Unfortunately, without critical independent research there is no way for the actual truth to get through to the public and that's what's so sinister and frustrating. These elite globalist lunatics are masters of gratuity and almost every avenue has been paid off or censored. The public is always two steps behind the actual narrative that's being orchestrated. Covid's actual letters are an abbreviation for Certification Of Vaccination ID. We're all diverted by a supposed virus while the actual narrative is staring us all in the face behind the letters in the word. They've even called the Coronavirus, the luciferian tracking system in America and its 6 letters actually add up to 66. It's all an interrogative monitoring system that's being implemented that again, the naive, unbelieving world is oblivious to. Again, they just believe the mainstream news and media outlets with no independent research of their own. Unfortunately, it's about to set much of Biblical prophecy in motion that the majority will be unprepared for. The stage is being set but what's even crazier is the majority are in support of it all and think people like me are the problem. I'm not a conspiracy theorist, I'm a critical thinker and am simply concerned about our health and what people in places of power and hierarchy are conspiring to do. The actual problem is both arguments in regards to the vaccines are ethically justifiable, but that's the sophistication behind the narrative within the vaccine that people don't realize. I'd be all for the vaccine myself if saving the world was the narrative behind it, but it's not, it's the global elite's premeditated plan to depopulate and further enslave the world. It's like we're trapped between two legitimate principles and we're all feeling compromised and divided between the two. Presidents in countries like Haiti, Tanzania, and Burundi who have denied the vaccines were mysteriously assassinated. Coincidence? I don't think so. If you don't comply, you die, it's that simple. You just don't argue against the narrative. They do not want independent research or critical thinkers in this world, they want compliance. They've even begun the technology of installing chips under our skin to eventually control and monitor our every move and how they can regulate us even more. It's all a trap and sounds morbidly psychotic, but again, the bible indicates these exact words throughout the epistles and in Revelation. It specifically states that anyone who doesn't receive the mark in their right hand or their forehead will be denied the ability to buy or sell. Whether this is a precursor to that, only time will tell, but regardless, I feel the stage is being set and anyone who argues otherwise is naive and has been lulled into complacency. An even better word is preconditioned. There's biblical scholars and theologians far more into this stuff than myself but sin and evil are deathly real and again, this pandemic is simply a precursor for justifying the eradication of the currency and forcing the implementation of global interrogation and mandatory vaccinations. Covid is merely their subplot to justify each one of these steps moving forward to eventually control the world through the database. A subplot is defined as a narrative thread that is woven through a book to support the elements of the main plot. It says a subplot can build out the conflict in the main plot or it can be a vehicle for a secondary character's storyline. Welcome to our New World Order. It's all part of an underground world that's undermining much of what we presume to be our security. It's like we're living in their alternative reality or smoke screen. It's the topic of controversy and contention right now with everybody but very few can pinpoint what's truly taking place. People just want to move on with their lives, hopeful of the future but they're clueless to what future that will become, especially with technology as advanced as it is. Apart from depopulation, there's many other variables behind the virus but ultimately it's how these global elite psychopaths inflate and crash the system economically, further bankrupting each country from the interest generated and through insider trading. It's all a premotivated agenda as we all become more and more dependent and enslaved to the lender from the bottom to the top like a game of dominoes, and then it all comes crashing down. Everyone chases the mirage, living beyond their means and dependent upon the system, then they crash the system and impound and repossess the resources. Economically, it's actually quite simple. The banks are ironically lending money out right now with historically low interest rates but people don't realize that with inflation so high, all they're doing is making more money on their investments and sucking the world dry like a sponge. These people hold a lot of power and are extremely sophisticated in the systems and economics of our world. Unfortunately, people are expendable in reaching their desired goal whether it be economically or biologically through these vaccine mandates. This entire world is a conspiring monopoly that the majority are oblivious to and 9/11 and this pandemic are all a part of the narrative. I just wish people would take the bible more seriously especially in regards to the powers of evil in our world.

Back To The Bible And Dissolving Misconceptions

I could go on and on in reference to the bible because there's just too many layers of epiphany that follow the belief and research for it to be generated by man, especially with the prerogative to draw sin out of man in repentance and warn us of all this stuff that will transpire in the future. In regards to sin, we're just not that good in our priorities and in our ethical transparency. Plus, if the words were written for financial gain or control as many presume them to be, why would they convict the very people who are in the faith, especially its leaders? It would make no sense to do that if that were its intention and inspiration. There's layers upon layers that the deepest philosophers, theologians and scholars around the world take years to study and identify with. It transcends all human logic and reason. I guess if it were derived from man we could simply write a sequel to the Bible and continue its supposed fictional and mythical fairytale. It would make a fortune!

The truth is we can't, this isn't Star Wars and those who have inclined to do so or even manipulated the words have imploded in their futile efforts, immaturity and greed, leading themselves and millions astray in the process.

Back in the late eighteen hundreds a man named Charles Taze Russell did that very thing. He was involved in the occult and Freemasonry which don't hold much virtue or integrity in themselves. He started the Jehovah Witnesses by professing the imminent return of Jesus and even distributing newspapers predicting the day. Thousands bought into it through his fear tactics and supposed biblical knowledge, then he used the finances he received to continue his alternative freemasonry agenda deceiving millions even to this day with false prophecies and propaganda. He manipulated the words and deity of Christ in the bible to conform people to his deception, praying on their insecurities. At his grave site in Pennsylvania is a massive Illuminati pyramid that stands about 6 feet high with an open bible inscribed in stone. I could go on about this stuff for hundreds of pages but it's just so interesting how true evil consciously infiltrates the truth and how in our disregard of the truth we victimize ourselves and get led astray. It's fascinating the foreknowledge of the Bible and how it exposes and warns us of these very people and factions much like the Jehovah Witnesses and how it reveals to us the cause of their means. Revelation 20:10 says, "And the devil that deceived them was cast into the lake of fire and brimstone, where the beast and the false prophet are, and shall be tormented day and night forever and ever."

So much of the Bible exposes false teachers and religious deception but without us studying and acknowledging it, we are held in our own preconceived notions, which is such a shame. It's all there in the Word, and is incredibly relevant and insightful in all spiritual exposition. There's just too much historical proof for it all to be a fictional fabrication. We could buy a ticket to Israel, land in the airport, and take a tour guide over to Jerusalem and even Bethlehem, spending the day visiting the surrounding archives. Millions of people do it year-round and have for decades. Does the unbelieving world need to grind the dirt of Israel in its teeth to believe? The unbelieving world has a problem in it's insinuations because a supposed mythical book doesn't generate soil. It's all been unearthed to expose the supposed mythical insinuations and contradictions. It's incredible what archaeologists have discovered throughout Israel that align with the biblical records and how precise the artifacts and archives are to the dispensation of time, even hundreds of years before Christ. The world is so incessant in disregarding the Bible in any supposed contradiction to prove it's irrelevance but all it does is contradict itself in its own justification to sin. For centuries the pool of bethsaida was an apparent myth to unbelievers and used as a contradiction to discredit the Bible's accuracy and authenticity but was then found by archaeologists in perfect form in 2005 as the Bible insisted, as many others have over the years. The word "tel" which originated in Israel is defined as an artificial mound formed from the accumulated remains of mud bricks and other refuse of generations of people living on the same site for hundreds or thousands of years. Tel Aviv is one of these cities where so much history has been proven to have taken place. The list is endless of archaeological discoveries like Solomon's Temple, the Philistines Cemetery and literally entire cities carved out of rock. There's the underground cisterns from the Ottoman empire, Roman basilicas and artwork and inscriptions everywhere. They're unearthing it all still to this day. City officials were widening highway 38 recently near Tel Beit Shemesh when workers discovered a first century synagogue. This is just one of several found that align with the Biblical records. One of the craziest archeological discoveries was Sodom and Gomorrah in Saudi Arabia where they've found entire cities burned by raining sulphur. All scientists can say is that it's a natural phenomenon but it's exactly where the bible describes it to be and exactly how.

Ultimately, no tourist returns home from travelling to Israel and the surrounding countries and says this stuff isn't real and doesn't exist. I guess the question then if all this stuff is real is, what are we denying? Ultimately, we're denying the historic record and deity of Jesus Christ, which bears severe consequences to the world and to us as individuals. Something in us wants undeniable proof but there's more proof then people realize, even from a scientific standpoint. Judaism denies the deity of Christ but believes he existed, as does Islam. It's even written of Jesus in the Quran. We just dont want to admit to his deity because of the significance his declaration bears. If we were to unbiasedly rewind the course of history and document which historical figure has made more of an impact, and has turned more people from their sin, Jesus would be the forerunner around the world. Why is this relevant, because sin is the world's problem. It's the inescapable and undeniable truth. It's so much bigger than physical proof of insurance to me anyways and a myth doesn't produce a continual generational revolution in who it influences ethically. There's a spirit that's alive and has relentlessly pursued humanity through its discourse no matter our opinion to its prevalence or in our defining stance on sin. The Word of God has transformed countries fundamentally and is the foundation of constitutions. If it weren't true and relevant it would have all died in its early stages and infancy, but it's grown and sustained itself throughout history to be the only prophetic relevance of our modern world. Anything that brings the pride of a man or woman to their knees in repentance is spiritually alive and present, living and active and needs to be reconsidered and re-evaluated for its relevance and significance.

The world has generated thousands of spiritual gurus like the Dalai Lama and Deepak Chopra with their supposed premonitions and prophetic enlightenment's but doesn't specifically target or confront the outlining problem of sin and the repercussions of it as the Bible does. Again, the Bible even convicts the very people that claim its belief. 1 Peter 4:17 says, "For the time has come for the judgment to begin at the house of God, and if it first begins with us, what will be the end of those who do not obey the gospel of God? 1 Corinthians 5:11-12 says, "Now I have written to you not to keep company with anyone named a brother, who is sexually immoral, or covetous, or an adulterer, or a reviler, or a drunkard, or an extortioner, not even to eat with such a person. For what have I to do with judging those who are outside? Do you not judge those who are inside?"

My point is that it's unbiased in it's conviction of sin and even more so to those who believe. It's just too bold, offensive and abrasive for men's standard of morality. The world's philosophy is usually based on feelings and is molded to appease these feelings, emotions and needs. Unfortunately a train doesn't stop for a feather on the tracks and true love confronts the issues that are destroying us head-on without compromise. Whether we like it or not it doesn't detract from the core issues it exposes or who it affects. Years ago someone died near to where I live walking on the railroad tracks with their headphones on. It's obviously a horrible tragedy and could have been so easily avoided, but it happened. This person had tuned out the world around them and complacently strided ahead not aware of the danger that was coming and they'd put themselves in. That for me is what the world is doing disregarding the Bible and the inevitable judgment of our souls. It's the defining mirror of observation for the soul's restraint and cognizance. It compels the world to initiate a rational, non-religious self-analysis and to question its own purpose, consciousness and ethical standards in every country and culture around the world. Common sense alone would tell us that's what the world needs right now and has needed throughout history. God sees our oral register as insufficient to the accountability of our conscious and memory bank, so he generated a written word to be accountable to and to study for reference, direction and dialect. It's brilliant and the wisdom of it is beyond the realm of our inclination. The life of Jesus and the sacrifice he made is the purest form of love we could ever ask for from our creator and the Word of God is the greatest gift we could ask for. It's one thing to understand how we operate and form an opinion but it's another to reform it into a tangible form of literature.

The Bible crushes my stubborn and cynical heart so easily with only a few paragraphs or words. My mind can hardly ascertain its multifaceted complexity from cover to cover. I want you to read the next scriptures from 1 Corinthians 4 and ask yourselves if this is derived from man? And just as a side note, if it isn't inspired by God, then there's only one other alternative and that to me is impossible for a competent person to believe. It says, "Therefore since we have this ministry, as we have received mercy, we do not lose heart, but we have renounced the hidden things of shame, not walking in craftiness, nor handling the Word of God deceitfully, but by manifestation of the truth commending ourselves to every man's conscience in the sight of God. But even if our gospel is veiled it is veiled to those who are perishing, whose minds the God of this age has blinded, who do not believe, lest the light of the gospel of the glory of Christ, who is the image of God, should shine on them. For we do not preach ourselves, but Christ Jesus the Lord, and ourselves your servants for Christ sake. For it is God who commanded the light to shine out of the darkness, who has shined in our hearts to give the light of the knowledge of the glory of God in the face of Jesus Christ." I don't see how a carnal man could even perceive or articulate this in his mind to write it without supernatural inspiration. 2 Timothy 3:16 says, "All scripture is given by inspiration of God, and is profitable for doctrine, for reproof, for correction, and for instruction in righteousness. 2 Peter 1:20-21 says, "Knowing this first, that no prophecy of the scripture is of any private interpretation. For the prophecy came not in old time by the will of man, but holy men of God spoke as they were moved by the

Holy Spirit." I'm writing this to those that are skeptical to help you see through the cloud of misconception because man lives to glorify itself and these words do the complete opposite. Galatians 1:10 says, "Do I now persuade men, or God? Or do I seek to please men? For if I still pleased men, I would not be a servant of Christ."

It's a stumbling block to the pride and complacency of men and provides so many justifiable answers to why there's so much conflict around us and within ourselves. The Word doesn't lie, it envelops me and so many in such an intriguing, transformational and thought-provoking way. It's pages are few in comparison to the world's, yet hold so much power and insight into the intelligence of God and his moral construct and infallibility. The words of the world and all the literature it's composed are bound to itself and will die unto themselves but the words of God are from the world above and beyond where the carnal mind hasn't infected its impression. The only impression that gets infected is when we heretically change and infect it much like the Jehovah Witnesses or Catholicism. There's a holy veil and dominion that encompasses the world just outside our imagination and dimension that God enthrones by the power of His Word. He's invited us into that spectrum and given us a glimpse into a realm of thought that we can't fathom in our limitations. Psalms 138:2 says, "I will worship toward your Holy Temple, and praise your name for your loving kindness and for your truth, for you have magnified your Word above all your name."

Justifiable Compliance

Sin has separated us from God and the world needs to ask itself whether it's sin is worth holding onto for the promise of a paradise beyond our imagination. I feel it's justifiable compliance and through that compliance and surrender he supernaturally infuses a regeneration and hope within you that is unexplainable to the carnal man. Merely fulfilling the law does not release the bondage, it just proves that you're conscious of it. It's the impartation of his spirit that opens your eyes. 2 Corinthians 3:14-17 says, "But their minds were blinded. For until this day the same veil remains unlifted in the reading of the Old Testament, because the veil is taken away in Christ. But even to this day, when Moses is read, a veil lies on their heart. Nevertheless when one turns to the Lord, the veil is taken away. Now the Lord is the spirit, and where the spirit of the Lord is, there is Liberty." Faith in Christ is inclusively liberating and I feel can literally change the chemical imbalance within our brains. Where the law has failed to compel our will and conscience to change into compatible grace, God has accomplished this for us in himself through the revelation of Jesus Christ. I'll meet a true, mature, born again Christian and within only a few words we're at ease and united in an eternal brotherhood and bond of love and understanding regardless of our colour, ethnicity, culture or status in life. Anyone being incompatible or contentious is still trying to be validated in their own mind and hasn't been released from their carnal bondage and slavery. It's a spirit of sincerity and humility that I just don't see in the world outside of true faith in Jesus Christ. Don't get me wrong, there are still millions of friendly and loving people circling the globe with good morals, but true Christians have confronted and wrestled with their own personal sin and inferiority and they know where God takes the heart to, what he extracts from it and what he inserts into it. My little church I go to is full of people with every ethnicity in the world, there's Chinese, German, Korean, English, Italian and many others that are all united in the same bond of peace without prejudice, serving each other as a community. There's churches in cultures all over the world with the centerpiece being Jesus Christ and his teaching of love and communion as the focal point of their faith, whether you're in Brooklyn New York, Iceland, Uganda or the jungles of Brazil. There's a clarity, contentment and humility that God produces within our broken human condition that is endearing to witness and be a part of. His Word instills a hope that roots itself so deep within the soul that is irrefutable to those that believe. I'm still relatively new to the faith and of course with my situation I wrestle with many things in my mind, but I've met some mature Christians over the years who carry themselves with such grace, humility and dignity that have endured far more than myself. Again, there's a joy and contentment in Christ that far exceeds that of the world's joy, where the acceptance of the world is irrelevant to your motives and desires. It's not an experiential joy, it's a joy of servitude, gratitude, compliance and hope within a body of believers. I don't know how else to put it into words to draw people to the pages of the Bible in an alluring and intellectual way. I'm trying with my words to endear you to his words but it's an interesting challenge. It's hard articulating something that only he has the wisdom to articulate. To be honest, I've had to fast while writing this at times to humble my mind and redirect my own objectives to allow God to carry out his objective in me. I literally have to starve myself and shut out the attractions and distractions of the world for my sincerity to express God's exclusive distinction. Deep down I want people to go to heaven and to be released from the pain and trauma they feel here in this fallen world. I always used to think those words were strange when people would say "born again Christian" as many others do, but it's merely a rebirth of the human heart and spirit that was blind to the truth of God and the revelation of Jesus Christ. It's not some obscure religious practice or ritual you've got to go through, it's merely being washed clean and forgiven of your sin by the blood of Jesus Christ. Titus 3:5 says, "Not by works of righteousness which we have done, but according to his mercy he saved us, by the washing of regeneration, and renewing of the Holy Spirit." 1 Peter 1:22-23 says, "Seeing you have purified your souls in obeying the truth through the spirit unto unfeigned love of the brethren, see that you love one another with a pure heart fervently: Being born again, not of corruptible seed, but of incorruptible, by the Word of God, which lives and abides forever."

More Misconceptions and Contention

I understand the indifference and confusion in coming to faith. I can also relate to the pain in people and where their fears and misconceptions come from. I've struggled with the whole idea of church and sitting in the pews like many of us do. I wasn't a church person growing up nor was any of my family. I loathed the thought of religion or any system of conformity and control, but again, so much of my misconception was unmerited ignorance that got released through God's Word and seeing a devoted church family first hand. I'm part of a street church on the downtown eastside where we serve the homeless and addicted. It's incredible to see everyone united together and dying to themselves to provide a service for the community. It's a powerful thing to be a part of. I realize there's contention within the body of Christ at times that can be frustrating and concerning but there's contention in any family. There's been contention ever since Jesus was on the cross and when christianity began, but there's also unconditional love and understanding in God's Word that reconciles itself in forgiveness that's far stronger than that of the world. 1 Corinthians 11:18-19 Paul says, "I hear that there are divisions among you; and I partly believe it. For there must also be heresies among you, that they which are approved may be manifest among you." To be honest, there's severe and concerning matters facing this world that need addressing and ultimately, it's far more endearing to see people fall on the right path than be on no path at all. Even when there are disagreements or personality clashes, there's an overriding general objective that dissolves the contention into remission. The teaching of Christ is extremely unifying and powerful in its admonition and it also compels us to face the core issues of life, which can be difficult. It's part of life and the reality we live in. My point is, I don't see a reason or excuse to turn from God for these issues. I'd suggest if the contention or compromise is to a point where it's interfering with your relationship with God and church community then simply find a different church or take some time on your own with God.

My church has really helped me through my trials and tribulations from this accident. I don't feel judged and always get a handful of hugs and support that I don't get from my family or old friends and for those that are scared of church or even get anxiety in groups of people, Christ is welcoming to that insecurity and no one can take that away from us who have faith and believe. I was at a big church before where I didn't feel connected and I simply found another one that was more of what I was looking for. I'll admit, I've felt insecure about going to church even as a Christian but there's a community and a support system there that is foreign to me elsewhere. God's created this refuge for millions around the world every day whose hearts yearn for supportive interaction and fellowship to help them through their struggles and to give them encouragement in this life and hope for the life to come. This is the purpose and directive of God's Church and through the teaching of his Word, to love one another unconditionally and influence the world in our communion, compatibility and service to one another and to the world. We're to all use our gifts in an amalgamation and united front of service to the world that is in need of a saviour. We're called by God to be obedient, selfless and blameless and to live beyond reproach to draw the world in, so it gives no reason to find fault or accusation. We're to be wise in our words and in our ethical conduct and to be forgiving and patient in suffering. We're to live by example without compromising our own convictions but also not imposing our convictions upon the world, especially in a physical sense. James 1:19 says, "Be swift to hear, slow to speak, and slow to anger." We're compelled to convey our opinions however unwavering that might seem, but not to ignorantly criticize or scrutinize the opinions and perceptions of the world. Again, for me this is all justifiable compliance to adhere to and is a united and sustainable productivity that I see the world missing out on in it's misconceptions and noncompliance. The majority of the world's brokenness stems from the trauma of a severed family and from divided opinions and control, so God provided a solution for all who are seeking refuge by the sacrifice of himself. His sacrifice is like a unifying global martyrdom. I just don't see how God could more clearly demonstrate his love for us. He laid himself bare and emptied himself for an internal and eternal resolution. God literally allowed the world to berate and murder him on that cross for it to see its own religious hypocrisy and to exemplify his contribution to the cause. 2 Corinthians 5:18-21 says, "Now all things are of God, who has reconciled us to himself through Jesus Christ, and has given us the ministry of reconciliation, that is, that God was in Christ reconciling the world to himself, not imputing their trespasses to them, and has committed to us the word of reconciliation. Now then, we are ambassadors for Christ, as though God were pleading through us, we implore you on Christ's behalf, be reconciled to God. For he made him who knew no sin to be sin for us, that we might become the righteousness of God in him." Those of us who have understood the severity and gravity of this sacrifice should be compelled to adhere to the bigger picture and objective no matter our own circumstances. Ultimately it's about putting aside our own agenda, swallowing our pride and working together. It's so important for us to understand the sacrificial system put in place leading up to the cross and how it exemplifies the severity of sin, between life and death. Israel was so stubborn that they needed to actually witness with their eyes the life and blood exiting the sacrificial offerings for God to convey to them the severity of their sin. 1 Samuel 15:22-23 says, "To obey is better than sacrifice, and to heed than the fat of rams. For rebellion is as the sin of witchcraft, and stubbornness is as iniquity and idolatry. Because you have rejected the Word of the Lord, he has also rejected you." He implored them to understand and acknowledge his merciful hand but again, they became stubborn and complacent grumblers, bound by their own justified determination, much like we are today, but unfortunately the final sacrifice has been made by God himself.

However you see it as unfortunate or fortunate, there is no offering sufficient enough, nor will we be justified by any other means in his eyes. Acts 4:17 says, "Nor is there salvation in any other, for there is no other name under Heaven given among men by which we must be saved."

Hypocrisy

I see many in the faith getting it right, full of grace and maturity, following God's word in reverence and baring the objective, but I unfortunately see many getting it wrong and compromising like these prosperity preachers, which gives more reason for the world to turn away. The number one excuse I hear from people to not believe is them stating that "Christians are all hypocrites." They look at the church as the supposed moral and ethical standard for our society in our profession of faith and when they see any bit of hypocrisy or contradiction they'll use it to justify their unbelief. It's such a tragic misconception that literally crushes us as true Christians and makes evangelism and faith extremely difficult to endure at times. Again, I was there and made the same insinuations, but the problem is the world is trying to find Jesus in people and when we aren't his perfect representation they somehow attribute the failings to him and don't realize it's us that fail to live up to his standards and follow his Word and convictions. It doesn't mean the teachings are wrong, it means we're just not following them. It's definitely man that is flawed, not him or his Word. All that does is point more to the infallibility of him and his Word because if we didn't agree with it then again, where is the contradiction and what are we admonishing as unbelievers?

When I actually started studying the word for myself, these contradictions pulled me even closer to its truth rather than turn me away. The word hypocrisy can't define itself unless there's a set moral precedence or there wouldn't be anything to be hypocritical about and unfortunately that precedence is what the world is ignoring even though it innately lives by the moral consciousness itself. The contradiction gives Jesus' ethical standard more prevalence in the world if it's conscientious of the hypocrisy and in that it further condemns itself. The angrier we get as unbelievers at hypocrisy the more we're admitting to our awareness of the standard that's been set. For instance, if I find a Christian leader caught in some sort of infidelity and I'm angry about it, I'm agreeing with monogamy as the standard in marriage. We're actually contradicting ourselves by admonishing the contradiction in our own confession.

I can see now the righteous fury of God though, especially to those who supposedly bear his name and don't see past their own selfish needs to bear his influence on the world. It's not just hypocrisy, we can be so immature and contentious in overemphasizing irrelevance, and carry on about issues merely to prove or affirm our point, but it just takes away from the sacrifice of God. Even worse are those who willfully sin that are in leadership. Ravi Zacharias being a perfect example of this in the ripple effect it causes the church and influence on the world.

Either way people in majority don't believe regardless of the actions and perceptions of the church. I've heard the number is below 10% here in western Canada of actual born-again believers and it's rapidly declining. People believe in various supposed gods, but not the God of the bible and Christianity anymore. Avoiding the truth is always easier than facing it, but we sure don't like facing the consequences of truth as they unravel and this pandemic is a perfect example of that. We as true believers can see the scriptures unfolding around us in plain sight but it's so challenging to penetrate a world so deceived, self-determined and complacently unaware.

Chapter 3

The World's Ignorance

It's become a repugnant and vain coexistence full of opinionated and unappreciative people everywhere you look these days. I live in one of the most desirable places to live in the world. Our resources are beyond plentiful. The water doesn't stop when you turn on the tap. We actually import over 20 percent of the world's drinking water. The grocery stores have been fully stocked for decades up until covid-19 and even through this crisis there was just a temporary shortage of toilet paper for a week or so. We seem to have access to infinite supply and abundance so naturally the carnal mind doesn't see a need for the gospel and doesn't want to hear it. We claim life, its resources and the accessibility to them for our own, with no apologies. Our posture is evidence of that everywhere you look, but where that has brought temporal satisfaction, it's also generated envy, greed, desperation and depression. In a capitalist system the greedy capitalize, further inflating the infrastructure which in turn magnifies it all economically and psychologically. We don't seem to function well together without the conviction for compassion or community interaction. The lack of thankfulness and appreciation in the human spirit generates selfishness and pride and unfortunately with that comes isolation, division and fear. The majority of us have become overstimulated, narcissistic and complacent gluttons. Gratification is great when it's appreciated as a gift but our society as a whole does not see it that way. It's about me and it's about now and there's no excuse or room for interruptions anymore. The rear-view mirror is a hiccup to what's through our windshield and we've come to expect everything and give thanks for nothing. There's no fear of God whatsoever in the majority of people you meet. I wonder why and how God allows us to live with absolutely no reverence or acknowledgement of him whatsoever. We've just come to smuggly believe that if there is a God, he "should" be at our every individual beck and call, all day everyday in all circumstances and if he isn't, we disregard him as non-existent or even blame or curse him for the cause of life's afflictions. It's that word "should" that's so ignorant to me as though he should be there as an expectation, even in our blatant disregard and unbelief. People will say if there's a God then "why this?" or "why that?" and again, will simply justify their own procession, but how can we blame a God we don't follow or believe in and how can we curse a God we don't feel exists? For me, mercy continues to define itself through all of this ignorance. Even though we're ultimately denying God's relevance we're completely at the mercy of his merciful hand and we just don't see it. There's two wills that have to be willing to form a relationship and we don't see God as always being willing unto our grave. The truth behind denial is that there is a willfully conscious decision to do so, much as there is with being defiant. I feel most people would attest to there being some moral truth to Jesus and the Bible and even to the accountability of their own conscience to some degree, but aren't compelling themselves to analyze or adhere to either of them for fear of being confronted or confronting their own sin and being held accountable. We've been blinded by the pursuit of the world and that has taken over our priorities. This is the bridge where so many people struggle to cross concerning faith but the further we've separated ourselves from accountability and correction, especially God's correction, the more our subconscious has transformed itself into self vindication. The problem with self vindication no matter how small it may seem, is that it gradually builds into sinful liberation especially with satan alongside in our unbelief. If we're the only ones to be accountable to, then we live by the standard that we set for ourselves. This is why the greatest gift given to man is a standard to live by and a standard outside of ourselves to be accountable to. The convictions are actually there to save us, not to enslave us. Imagine a world where we didn't age like we do and our conscience would constantly be vindicated without the fear of eternal judgment and accountability. If we were all 100% certain there was no punishment for our sin when we die, imagine the debauchery that would take place around us. It's bad enough as it is but that's what science and so much of what we see on television and in the movies is projecting and insinuating to all of us. They're insisting that we are all mortals and for us to live for today and against our better judgment. This is an extremely dangerous philosophy on life and has severe implications and collateral damage. 1 Corinthians 15:32-34 Paul says, "What advantage is it to me? If the dead do not rise, let us eat and drink for tomorrow we die!. Do not be deceived," he says, "Evil company corrupts good habits. Awake to righteousness, and do not sin, for some do not have the knowledge of God." Again, these murderous regimes throughout history were possessed by irreverent atheist monsters that relished in their vindicated impunity. One of Hitler's famous quotes says, "I want to raise a generation of young people devoid of a conscience, imperialistic, relentless and cruel. My task is to free man from the dirty and degrading ideas of a conscience and morality." They concluded in their minds the non-existence of God and their insatiable yearning for power and control overcame them, fueling their pride and dictatorship into a murderous rage. My point again is the fear of God, however slight that is in our conscious mind, is actually there to save us from what we do otherwise.

Defining Freedom and Judgment

It's a spiritual war over the mind that is inclusively targeting our will's decisiveness and the truth of its implications. God is after it because of the damage it causes, but satan is after it for the damage it causes. Unfortunately we're just not living in spiritual or general terms, we're just living for and unto ourselves so we don't recognize the general influence and spiritual implications as a whole.

Freedom can be defined in several ways especially in a democracy like America. We can allow our individual feelings and senses to define liberation for us and not adhere to any kind of moral structure or compliance. We can exercise our human rights and appease the desires of our flesh in all the impulses being advertised. We can practice any religion or form whatever identity we want without apology and without a concern for the world or the community that surrounds us. It's become the power of pride and indifference that we've come to embrace. That's what our carnal definition of freedom has become without God. It's the philosophy and ideology we've generated for ourselves that lives to justify itself, however it feels entitled. Open the floodgates in tolerance, it's sex, drugs and rock and roll all day long if you want. Put your party hat on, tip the night fantastic and enjoy the one night stand and 24/7 free for all. That's the dream being advertised and the freedom they're fighting for and have established in America, or, you can be free from it from the forgiveness of it and that's what God offers in Jesus Christ. Only then are we truly liberated because we're not deceived in it and not condemned by it anymore.

Interestingly Las Vegas is the pinnacle of that American freedom but everyone knows it as "Sin City." Ultimately, each individual has their own impulsive vessel to live in and their own mind and conscience to evaluate and we are not compelled as Christians to look down upon or judge that comparatively as though we hold some sort of self-righteous entitlement or position, but we are compelled by God not to compromise our own convictions and use rational judgment amidst all of the chaos and offer our own opinion and an identity to those lost in their own.

Much like freedom, the word judgment I feel has been miss evaluated in so many aspects because in a moral sense we all use rational judgment for every conscious decision we make. As parents we use rational discernment and judgment to parent our kids and we do it instinctively out of love to protect them from themselves and what they don't know or haven't experienced yet. We also protect them from the mistakes we've already made, which is us judging ourselves. We have to use judgement to help our friends or those in need especially if we see something destroying their lives. We have to use rational judgment when we drive or when we walk across the street or we'll die. Every time you're in a left turn lane waiting to go through the light, the judgment is in your hands. Not only that, we're trusting in the judgment of the vehicles coming towards us. Everytime we're on the sidewalk we naturally look both ways before crossing the street. We use judgement in what we eat and drink and the list goes on and on. It's common sense, but I feel Christians are misunderstood in regards to judgement and to our fault have at times misunderstood it ourselves and become entitled and hypocritical. It's definitely a fine line differentiating between the two in how we impose it upon people because for me if I'm critically judging someone comparatively, all I'm doing is condemning myself and living against God's Word. Romans 2:1-3 says, "Therefore you are inexcusable, oh man, whoever you are who judge, for in whatever you judge another you condemn yourself, for you who judge practice the same things. But we know that the judgment of God is according to the truth against those who practice such things. And do you think this, oh man, you who judge those practicing such things, and doing the same, that you will escape the judgement of God?" Again, no one likes to be judged or scrutinized comparatively, that's what builds such an insecurity within us all, therefore we all need to define the word judgement maturely and rationally or we just stay lost in it's misinterpretation. This is why it's become so challenging to evangelize in light of the words judgement and tolerance. I guess the question is, where or who does the moral standard of discernment fall on in regards to governing life and tolerance? It's become such a misunderstanding concerning christianity because we all feel the same emotions in life whether we're believers or unbelievers. I have lust and anger throughout the day like the rest of the world. I get bitter, envious and unforgiving at times, it's just natural, but I won't justify the action or reaction to appease or satisfy the emotions because I see the effects of the actions and I'm baring an ethical influence and discipline as a Christian, that again, I see as justifiable compliance. I also have a spirit within me that is stronger in its conviction than I was on my own beforehand. I guess then the question to ask is, what is justifiable compliance and who is willing to bear and discern the standard? Or, who is the voice of reason? Someone has to make some sort of rational judgment, don't they? If we were to truly define the word judgment and justice for that matter, and analyze how the justice system works and even how we justify ourselves and yearn for justice in the world around us, we'd come to understand our consciousness and the word judgement far more deeply and intuitively.

The Human Conscience

For instance, if I break the law but there's no police officer around to convict me, am I still guilty of breaking the law? Why do we turn our signal on in our car when there's not another car around for miles? Who am I guilty to if there's no one around to see me commit the offense and why do I experience regret or shame? I can't be guilty to myself because I'm the one willfully committing the act, but my conscience is condemning the act because it is bound to the truth and has been designed that way by God whether we admit it or not. Again, if I'm making the decision, then how is my conscience working within me outside of my wills desired intention? Now what if a cop breaks the law with no one around? If there supposedly is no God and they are the enforcement of the law, then who is their own conscience guilty to? He or she most certainly knows the law because they uphold it themselves and have affirmed and been trained to execute its principles. They should arrest themselves when they commit an offense but we somehow justify ourselves without God and live in contradiction of what we innately know is true. We're not only condemning ourselves in what we know is true, we're condemning ourselves in unbelief. Truthfully, we can shut off our consciences temporarily to appease our rebellion and feel a sense of liberty but again, the truth defines itself in the word rebellion because who are we rebelling against if there is no God and there's no one around to see us? So even though we think we are free to sin and at the time the feelings override our conscience, there's a universal and spiritual law at work that governs our mind unbiasedly and impartially that we can't escape from and never will unless we receive God's atoning sacrifice, because ultimately he is the one we are guilty too. I suggest to whomever reads this to read Roman's 2 and 3 and consider God's opinion on the matter of self vindication and justification. Romans 2:14-15 says, "When gentiles, who do not have the law, by nature do the things in the law, are a law to themselves, who show the work of the law written in their hearts, their conscience also bearing witness, and between themselves their thoughts accusing or else excusing them." Romans 3:20 says, "Therefore by the deeds of the law no flesh will be justified in his sight, for by the law is the knowledge of sin."

Concerning the conscience, I think of people that use cocaine and other hard drugs and how they are instantly elevated and stimulated euphorically in their senses but shortly after are driven into the ground by their own conscience and the devil who pounds away at the mind with shame and guilt. I know because I've done them and been there myself. It's called chasing the dragon with these heavier drugs because the only way to escape the condemnation is to continue in the high. My point is, where is the guilt coming from if there is no God to be accountable to and there is no satan to shame us? Is the unbearable guilt and shame in the actual physical drug itself? Of course not, there are spirits at work around us and within us that are imperceivable to the carnal mind, bearing down on our conscience regardless of our perception of them and ultimately we know it's wrong because of how we conceal the truth.

There's a huge straight away on the highway close to my house. One day I was driving that way and this Crotch-Rocket motorcycle came up beside me on the left. He kind of dropped back a little and I wondered what he was up to. All of a sudden he took off like a slingshot full speed and was gone. He must have hit over 150mph and then I caught up to him at the next red light. The question is why would he stop at the red light? There was no one else at the intersection except him and me and he just committed a worse criminal offense earlier by excessively speeding. What was stopping him from going through? It was his conscience and whether he wanted to listen to it or not was ultimately his decision to make. That's the free will that's been given to us by God, we just seem to have selective hearing at times. He justified the feeling and superseded his conscience even though he knew it was wrong, putting himself and anyone else in danger around him. It's interesting that the word "just" is based on or behaving according to what is morally right and fair and without justice our society falls apart. If it weren't true society would thrive in injustice but of course it's the complete opposite. It's even more interesting that the word justify is in accordance with what we consciously vindicate. Again, the problem with pushing God out of the realm of accountability is we're merely justifying ourselves outside of the eyes of God and the law and what ends up evolving is millions of people living in a crossfire of self condoned vindication. It's much like the actual laws of the road themselves that we are all conscious of. If everyone would adhere to them there wouldn't be millions of deaths and carnage all year round nor would there be a need for insurance companies to protect us or the law to implement justice. We all pay taxes for the law to execute justice so we can live free of the consequence of the offense. This is where defining freedom for people differentiates. If people would just listen to the road signs, be conscientious and respect the drivers around them, we'd all get home safe and sound. We'd also feel less fearful and a far greater sense of freedom trusting in those to do so. We don't realize that we actually yearn for justice for those who commit offences against us, but live in the vindicated hypocrisy within ourselves because we believe no one can see us. Whether the laws are there to convict us or not, the offense still has its consequences because sin is in accordance with the law. This is where our conscience and our will are continuously at odds with each other. We're at a time in history where the Bible is correct in saying people will call bad good and good evil because they're appeasing their narcissistic feelings of entitlement and these feelings are overriding their conscience. It's a dangerous and progressively problematic state of mind we're living to justify and is what is blinding us from the truth.

Contradictions of Ourselves

We live in complete contradiction of ourselves and how we've been innately designed to be free. In America they feel a sense of personal liberty because they can carry guns but here in Canada we feel a far greater sense of freedom knowing noyone is carrying them at all. Our whole lives are contradictory analogies like these that we gloss over all day long. Everyday the news and media outlets are littered with continuous personal attacks and accusations on the president and people in politics or leadership roles. They're under such a heavy weight of scrutiny and expectation but where does that expectation come from? Every move they make is under a microscope and being evaluated and scrutinized for moral integrity. We'll search for any minute sliver of ethical misconduct to condemn them whether it be sexually, racially, socially or economically to tear them down and incite an impeachment. This is the whole cancel culture we're living in. Hundreds of thousands of opinions and scrutiny flood the social media outlets and in the minds of people all through the country (speaking of Americans) over the conscious level of personal conduct we all yearn for from a leader, yet we live to disregard it ourselves whether it be in our own sex lives, moral conduct or even in filing our taxes. We are not perceivably acknowledging what we're generally condemning as a society. Every allegation points to a conscious moral standard that we're admitting to and acknowledging if we're condemning these offences. You've got tens of millions of people living in fornication and soaking every last second of it up on these television shows, movies, and porn sites, then the next breath they condemn it for people in positions of leadership. Our whole society is living in contradictory hypocrisy and in the condemnation of itself, even without the knowledge and admonishment of God. If we find someone guilty of adultery and we're tearing them down in dishonour then we've accepted and confirmed within ourselves that monogamy in a marriage is the appropriate standard to live by, as I was saying before. It's not necessarily even in a marriage, but in any relationship. If it wasn't true where would our anger, bitterness and hostility come from? If we catch someone lying or in an act of treason in any way we've defined truth and transparency as a desirable conduct to live by because of our disapproval. We're also defining loyalty, obligation, devotion, restraint, compassion and all sorts of other nouns that relate to conduct in our judgment. What's even crazier is we're all actually agreeing with so many values and virtues the Word of God is instilling and insisting upon for our sanctity of life. If common sense was a religion, Christianity would be the religion of common sense. Again, the commands are there to save us, not to enslave us. Good parents discipline their children out of love for their benefit and it's no different in how we should perceive God's commandments in accordance with us. They may feel convicting at times but just think if people would actually follow them, how much better this world would be. For instance, if we were all married and monogamous as the bible insists on us being, there would be no sexually transmitted diseases whatsoever. They're plausible in every aspect of life. Basic Instructions Before Leaving Earth are ironically the Bible's five letters. Ultimately, our complaints, and admonishment of others is continuous proof of the innate and inexcusable declaration within our conscience. The word innate actually is defined as the ability that one is born with and not one which we have learned. Intuition is defined as the ability to understand something immediately, without the need for conscious reasoning. The conscience is like a mirror and introspecting revelation simply in the obligation and expectation we desire from others. I'm looking for relatable synonyms for the word introspection and the word solipsism came up. It's defined as the view or theory that the self is all that can be known to exist. It says in philosophy, solipsism is an extreme form of subjective idealism that denies that the human mind has any valid ground for believing in the existence of anything but itself. It's interesting because that's exactly the contradiction I'm trying to prove within our own conscience. What a horribly neive philosophy and state of mind to live in. That word defines human ignorance and the disease of atheism in a nutshell.

If we expect a certain level of cordialism or ethical conduct from someone else then we should expect the same from within ourselves, otherwise we're in continual contradiction of ourselves. Even without acknowledging and submitting to God's Word and principles in our unbelief, we as a whole still believe ethical integrity is essential in an influential or leadership role and that those in them should be accountable to that conscious standard. We see that not only in politics but in teachers and principals in school. In management roles at work or coaches in sports. In babysitters, government officials and social workers. Police officers, mailmen, firemen, famous athletes and the list goes on. There's an integrity that we are all conscious of that's undeniable and is crucial to the safety and productive development of our interactive and impressionable society. If you aren't you're probably some sort of demonically introverted sociopath. Children walk to and from school every day all around the world and we all in majority defend and protect their innocence to the arrival of an ethically safe environment, especially parents. We yearn for justice and judgment in all these positions and circumstances, in fact we demand it and fortunately, so does God. God is even more severe concerning them than we are, therefore he's even greater in his forbearance to the standard of the cause.

This consciousness is in everything we do. We see it in sports when athletes use performance-enhancing drugs to inflate their careers. For years Barry Bonds, Mark McGwire and others were using steroids and hitting home runs out of the park at an alarming rate. The crowds would cheer them on, praising their heroics every time they rounded the bases. Years later they were all found guilty and subsequently stripped of their notoriety and shamed for their integrity much like Lance Armstrong in cycling. Their legacies have been forever tarnished for their willful defiance of the rules. It's such a strange contradiction in their denial of consciousness that they knowingly lived in for all those years, but the feeling of recognition and approval overpowered their own conscience to somehow justify the action until finally they got caught and then the guilt and scrutiny consumed them. It happened with the Houston Astros and how they cheated to win the World Series or when Ben Johnson used steroids to win the 100 metres. The craziest incident was when Tonya Harding got Nancy Kerrigan's leg busted to win the figure skating championships. It's incredible the lengths people will go for notoriety.

Much of the truth of our conscience is not only revealed in the expectation we desire from others but it is also revealed in what we are fearful of exposing, because what were these athletes hiding from if they didn't know it was wrong? What were they trying to cover up? What we do and don't do in front of children sometimes tells an even greater tale of what we innately know is right and wrong. It's not only what we do and don't do, it's what we intuitively protect them from. This is where we all stand guilty in so many aspects of our life. It's much like in our relationship to God. We seem to despise the convictions of God for confronting and exposing our own sin and injustices yet we yearn for the injustice to be exposed around us, especially if it's inflicted upon us. We'll throw the book at everybody else but won't open its pages unto ourselves as though his justice should be provisional and conditional. Again, we're actually in agreement with God in so many aspects of life except the one that convicts and brings to light our own sin. This is the spiritual mystery and enlightenment of our internal transparency that salvation in Christ is based upon. There isn't a thief in the world who enjoys being robbed and doesn't want its justice nor is there a violent offender who enjoys being beaten to a pulp. There isn't an arsonist that intentionally burns down his own house. There isn't a man living in adultery who wants someone sleeping with his wife nor is there a pathological liar who likes being deceived. Again, if we look at the judicial court system we all hold the hand of the judges gavel to the highest regard. They are a man or woman chosen for their own personal ethics and moral regard and we all hold them accountable to that standard. Our civil society doesn't discredit their authority or question the reason for their position, even as unbelievers, we actually depend on them to uphold our society in adherence to the moral law. The general masses in this modern Western World and in many countries around the world, when it comes to executing the law, pay billions of justified dollars in taxes for the law to be executed unbiasedly and depend on it for the safety and peace of mind of their families and communities. It's statutorily and intuitively been ingrained in our loins and no competent or rational coherent person can argue this otherwise, nor can a productive or compatible society function without this adherence to the law, yet as unbelievers, we smuggly disregard the perfect judgement and justice of God as though it's unmerited or should be conditional. The greatest contradiction is that in some countries, even in America, they still execute and justify the death penalty. We in a sense have become god justifying murder for those that do the same and with that are confessing that sin should be condemned and justice be executed with no exception.

More Contradictions

We are walking contradictions of ourselves in so many ways and I'm saying these things for us to see it not only from our perspective, but from God's perspective and to re-evaluate our ignorant disregard. Even convicted felons serving time in prison don't condone sex offenders especially in regards to children. It's something the general population does not tolerate and judges as inexcusable. They'll even take justice into their own hands which is a fascinating contradiction in itself.

A lot of these truths can be revealed simply in the innate and intuitive language we speak. We've defined so many words in the contemplation of our own conscious mind that conclusively tells the historical tale of a man's battle within the human will and propensity. What's even more contradicting is that many of these words we've defined ourselves without God's Word which more exposes our ignorance to them. Words like responsibility, discernment, accountability, sincerity, rationality, disposition, discretion, and condescending. Adjectives and nouns aren't proactive without us being conscious of them. Responsibility is the ability to respond or give a response and ultimately is rendering us responsible. Disposition is defined as a person's inherent qualities of mind and character and inherent is defined as existing in someone as permanent, essential, or a certain characteristic attribute. Condescending is defined as having or showing a feeling of patronizing superiority. You can't be condescending unless you're consciously aware of it because you're simultaneously contemplating it's outcome. My point is, where did these words come to be defined if we haven't consciously been in contemplation over them and resolved them in our mind? We say them before even thinking because we innately know their definitions are true. Other words like intrinsic, conscientious, refrain, restriction and restrained. If we're not conscious of something or previously aware of it, what are we restraining or restricting ourselves from? Where does our reluctance come from? Where does our apprehension come from? One of the most simple but telling words is considerate. It's literally breaking our will in half in one word, "to consider, it" and then act accordingly in the consideration of others. Another one is the word obligation. It's defined as an act or course of action to which a person is morally or legally bound as a duty or commitment. The list goes on and on of how we've innately recognized and acknowledged moral judgment, integrity and values in the language we speak and if we've come to subconsciously constitute moral judgment ourselves without God, how much more will a Holy God uphold his standard of moral judgment upon us and why should we condemn him and his Word for doing the same? It's like we're adamantly protesting for the justice we deny upon ourselves. We're like millions of perfect little judges running around hating a perfect judge. Another word that's interesting is the word identity and how closely it's related to the word identify. It's like our pride and identity in the world is holding us back from identifying with our own disorders and dysfunction. My whole point in all this is to try to reveal ourselves to ourselves by expelling our excuses and to help understand the conscious mind and the holy judgement of God. Yes there's a mystery attached to faith and to God, but so much can be answered merely in how we've been innately designed and to comprehend simple moral values and common sense. We come to know ourselves far more clearly when we come to know our designer because our conscience finds resolution and common ground with the source it's restraining itself from in noncompliance. The whole world is a continually evolving analogy of these fundamental truths in literally everything we do. A lot of the Christian faith is these truths being exposed and spiritually unraveling themselves to us in our willing transparency whether it be in the language we speak or the circumstances and contradictions that surround us. The more sin the Word of God and the Holy Spirit has convicted in me, the more I've admitted to its truth, relevance and the necessity for its unwavering justice. Unfortunately the world doesn't see its relevance anymore and merely snickers at it smugly as if it's all a fable or urban myth.

Chapter 4

Truth vs Error

Life has become full throttle these days to keep pace and God for the majority has merely become an afterthought or a word to appease ourselves and our position on life. We live moment-to-moment and second to second as our dopamine levels rise and fall. The idea of faith and of God has become so confusing nowadays especially with so many beliefs and opinions circulating the world and our accessibility to them through technology. It seems we can just pick one that appeases our immediate feelings or suits our current profile or portfolio, like opening a restaurant menu. We naturally don't pursue conviction for ourselves so Christianity seems too severe of a pill to swallow for most. We tend to formulate affirmations in our imaginations along the lines of serendipity or some universal karma based philosophy, as though the whole world revolves around us and gravitates towards us with our negative and positive energy. In some ways that can all seem wise and spiritually inspired but for me as a stubborn and skeptical person, much of it is superficial and vain faith to trust in and comply with. They'll call it the universal law of attraction but good people seem to attract a lot of negativity to themselves. I even had a guy the other day at work try to convince me to base my life on patterns of numerology. These are methods of faith in a sense but to me they're imbalanced forms of reasoning that leave us on extremely shaky ground. The old tenant upstairs from me one day said, "Everything happens for a reason and to trust in the universe," but that's a broad expectation in an unknown entity to entrust my entire life on. First of all, if everything happens for a reason I'd like to know that reason and if someone or something is being reasonable. Secondly, if I'm to trust in the universe, I'd like to know who I'm trusting in and what intentions they have upon my life and future. It's just common sense. It's like they're throwing a boomerang over a cliff in a windstorm and expecting it to come back every time with a pot of gold. To be honest, I like how I'm extremely stubborn and skeptical because I think God can use that to reveal to us the hidden mysteries of who he truly is in his Word. He's honest about life's challenges and afflictions and I'd rather have my faith test my will and be severe in it's declaration than be vain in its assumptions. Romans 11:12 says, "Therefore consider the goodness and severity of God: on those who fell, severity; but toward you, goodness, if you continue in his goodness." Notice how it says "in his goodness" and not in the goodness of our own.

Why God is Truth

At first when I became a Christian, I had no idea the journey I would embark upon but the more layers I've pulled apart, the more truth seemed to find its way to the truth and preeminence of Jesus Christ. I started researching religion after religion and all these different philosophies on life and views on God and faith and to be honest, it's a lot to unravel at first, but the truth is there and is undeniable if we persevere. This one supposedly fictional man has generated a lot of attention to put it mildly. I've been on both sides of the fence as an unbeliever and a believer, so I can see and relate to how people are skeptical and reluctant to pursue faith in God, and merely live accountable to themselves. I never viewed myself as a bad person or sinful at all and certainly wasn't searching to be convicted until I was confronted with the inferiority of eternal judgment. I became crushed by the power of truth and justice. As children we were rebellious at times but for the most part reverent to our parents, but as adults we seem to march by the beat of our own independent and impulsive drum. We feel a sense of independence from parental discipline but this lack of accountability and guidance as adults is the reason for our world's discourse. When I personally confronted my own sin through the revelation of Jesus Christ and the Word of God, I saw my sins as unforgivable. I just couldn't see it before seeing Christ for who he truly is. My mirror shattered at the reflection of my own sin. I was abrasive and full of bitterness and hatred. My mouth was filthy and full of manipulation, judgement, gossip, lies and ignorance. I had no forgiveness in me whatsoever and I cursed God and cursed the world as if it owed me something. I stole stuff all the time when I was younger and I treated women like objects of fornication and didn't think twice about it. Whatever affliction or trauma I was subject to in my past still didn't justify my actions. Sin still bore its influence and held its consequence no matter how justified my emotions seemed to be at the time. I wasn't this horribly violent guy but I hated this one arrogant guy growing up and I pushed him over in his chair at a pub one night. The friend he was with that evening who I also knew ended up blowing his head off the same night on the phone with his mom, high on cocaine. If I didn't push him that night in the pub, would that have changed the outcome? Probably. Me and a friend once came off the last ferry from Vancouver Island and just missed the last bus into town. We started walking home and I saw this massive boulder by the roadside so I rolled it into the middle of the road to be funny. We walked into a nearby town and then came back that way and broke into a motorhome to sleep for the night. On our way back there was a van all smashed in on the front end, broken down on the side of the road. They'd obviously hit the boulder, but the question is, what rippling effects did that actually cause in their life? I guess I'll never know but only through Christ could I turn the internal mirror upon myself and look back to see the collateral damage of sin and my own progressive dysfunction. Only in Christ was I compelled to do so. There's a revolving door in our conscience that seems to justify itself in its emotional release otherwise. Some will say then if my conscience doesn't condemn me then what am I guilty of and who am I guilty to? I would simply answer by saying that they're contradicting themselves and haven't dug deep enough into their conscience and turned their internal mirror upon themselves. A lot of our escapism and reactive emotions are the result of a broken childhood or hostile household growing up whether it be from divorce, abuse, rejection or abandonment. It's the root of alot of our pride as well. Some will even kill their conscience intentionally to hide from the pain and effects of the trauma. The tears and emotions that are triggered reveal to us the internal desire for a supportive, monogamous and united household, even before puberty. It's these emotional reactions from within us that actually reveal God's design in our consciousness and in our innate moral desires. These are congenital and instinctive attributes of humanity and if it wasn't true we wouldn't be so scared to face them and nothing would be severed. Where would our yearning for support come from if we didn't innately desire support as children and where would the responsibility and shame come from in parents in their neglect towards their children? If it weren't true, where would all this anger, unforgiveness and resentment stem from in so many of us? Why would we seek sympathy? Where would the maternal and paternal instinct come from in mothers and fathers? It all points to God's design in our contradiction. There's just so much truth that's revealed from the result of fornication and infidelity alone. I had a girlfriend in my early twenties who I was extremely attracted to. I fell in love with her head over heels but she kind of dragged me along and used me to get what she wanted when she wanted it. It was a strong sexual soul tie that I had never experienced before and she used it to tease and control me. It wasn't even the pain of us breaking up that bothered me, it was the fact that she led me on and had no concern or respect for my feelings. The trauma and rejection of that led me on a run of emotionless fornication for years that all stemmed from that initial rejection and the inferiority of being vulnerable and giving someone my whole being. It wasn't that I didn't want to love or be loved, it was that I was scared to give it and for it to be rejected and forsaken all over again. I feel this is where so much of our fear is based and why many of us are becoming so vulnerable and sensitive. We'd rather be alone and hide our love away for the fear of it being trampled on. I yearned for her reciprocating unconditional love and acceptance and my true desire was for a monogamous relationship with her. My point again is the emotions from the rejection don't justify the fornication and sin that followed. They just reveal my true internal desire to love and be loved. The affliction blinded me in my emotions and I lived in sin to try to find compensation but the truth of our internal design is found in the compensation we desire in the aftermath. It goes back to the title of the book and how we're "Blind in our afflictions."

Life's Illusion

Before Christ I didn't care about any of this stuff whatsoever. I was trapped in the emotional turmoil of life and consumed by all the pressures of society and the pressures I put on myself. I felt I had to be where the world was telling me I should be to find the acceptance I desired. It was a relentless and suffocating battle socially and financially to keep pace and to stay afloat. The idea of God to me was not a priority and totally irrelevant amidst all of my internal struggle and chaos and that's unfortunately become the state of this fallen world. It's a cycle that's nearly impossible to escape from within yourself because of how sensitive and manipulated the human mind has become. Some of us have been so traumatized and afflicted by our circumstances we just can't see through the trauma we've endured to live rationally or productively. There's just no forgiveness in our heart anymore and I don't blame people for feeling that way. It can be a cold, cruel world to say the least. It's horrible what some people have gone through and I would never want to minimize that. It's become a battle of self preservation that I was caught up in myself for so many years. It's like I had tunnel vision and become so deceived in the priorities of life. Navigating through this life can be so difficult when you're internally bound within your soul, contending in your mind with past trauma and over priorities, identity and purpose. It's like the world is dangling a treasure or fortune in front of your face that's always just outside your arms reach and you can hear the snickering in the background as though you're an inadequate failure. It can be an incessant struggle to overcome and the fear can be crippling especially when we put so much pressure on ourselves to succeed and affirm ourselves in the eyes and perceptions of others. We've subconsciously come to demand so much from life as we see it being lived out around us, but achievement and acclaim are comparable words that subconsciously destroy so many of us unknowingly. Faith, community and social interaction become secondary prerogatives and necessities in our yearning to establish our own bravado and control over our lives. It's not just in achievement, it's in the validation that drives our unsecured desires. I'm convinced it's this comparative and covetous spirit that's influencing and dividing our socially interactive unity and is what satan uses to puppet us around in our emotions and narcissistic objectives. I like the analogy of tunnel vision because it's so true in our society these days. It's been indoctrinated in us since we were children. 2 Corinthians 10:12

says, "For we dare not class ourselves or compare ourselves with those who commend themselves. But they, measuring themselves by themselves, and comparing themselves among themselves, are not wise." The comparison generates envy and that jealousy creates our inadequacy, fear, anger and desperation. It also generates the priorities within us that are most deceiving. The end of Galatians 5 says, "Let us not become conceited, provoking one another, envying one another." Titus 3 says, "We ourselves were also once foolish, disobedient, deceived, serving various lusts and pleasures, living in malice and envy, hateful and hating one another." There's just no unity in envy and with no unity, there's no community because the word community means to commune in unity. Again, if you break the word community down it's to be united in communion and the definition of communion is the sharing or exchanging of intimate thoughts and feelings, especially when the exchange is on a mental or spiritual level. In the Christian religion communion is simply acknowledging the sacrifice of Jesus Christ and communing in unity and in reverence of that sacrifice. Proverbs 14:30 says, "A heart at peace gives life to the body, but envy rots the bones." Job 5:2 says, "Surely resentment destroys the fool, and jealousy kills the simple." Proverbs 23:17-18 says, "Do not let your heart envy sinners, but always be zealous for the fear of the Lord. There is surely a future hope for you, and your hope will not be cut off." And finally James says, "Who is wise and understanding among you? Let him show by good conduct that his works are done in the meekness of wisdom. But if you have bitter envy and self-seeking in your hearts, do not boast and lie against the truth. This wisdom does not descend from above, but is earthly, sensual, and demonic. For where envy and self-seeking exist, confusion and every evil thing are there. But the wisdom that is from above is first pure, then peaceable, gentle, willing to yield, full of mercy and good fruits, without partiality and without hypocrisy. Now the fruit of righteousness is sown in peace by those who make peace. Where do wars and fights come from among you? Do they not come from your desires for pleasure that war in your members? You lust and do not have. You murder and covet and cannot obtain. You fight and war. Yet you do not have because you do not ask. You ask and do not receive, because you ask amiss, that you may spend it on your pleasures." These words are only too real in the world we live in today. I can feel it in me and the pulse of it around me everywhere I go and in every lens I see. It's literally the heartbeat and disposition of our society and the psychological and spiritual divide within and between us all.

I have a friend I've known for a few years now. He's done extremely well for himself financially and just finished building a house on a huge farmland property worth over three million dollars. The house is about 8500 square feet with an orchard in the backyard and a massive tree house built for his kids. He's got everything it seems that would make a person happy. He's got a new truck for himself and even bought a new Tahoe for his wife. There's a wrap-around deck and the front of their property is all gated with a driveway that wraps around to the back of the house with waterfalls and a hot tub. He phoned me the other day and told me that he just wasn't right in the head. He wasn't happy with his life and was on the verge of an emotional breakdown. I know him fairly well and being a Christian I can see through all the superficial materialism and pride much more clearly than he can. He just can't see past his impulses being his priority and sustenance. He's hiding behind and holding onto so much of what I've let go of. He's got an extremely aggressive personality and work ethic which has got him to where he is financially, but the affluence and success didn't necessarily bring him the happiness he expected and what is being advertised. His character has been molded and affirmed in its dependence upon them and he can't relate or communicate otherwise. His entire emphasis and philosophy on life is the pride he's supposedly entitled to by the equity he's established. He can be nice at times but it's very short lived. There's just no intellectual conversation in him other than the equity he stands behind. He did it by himself and on his own terms which is a commendable achievement but he's also an egotistical, abrasive and hostile over-achiever which has rubbed a lot of people the wrong way and has left him with few friends to share in his prosperity and accomplishments. At the end of the day he didn't do it to appreciate it as much as he did to receive the attention and validation for it, but when he finally reached his desired goal, there was no one there to recognize him for it. We've come to believe the more we achieve the more we'll find acceptance because of the attention we draw to ourselves but what we end up finding is that people simply feel envious. It's also a conceited approach to appreciation when all you're living for is to give thanks to yourself and your own accomplishments. I guess without believing in God there's no other alternative, you simply become your own god subjectively. That's why some people with seemingly everything are more lonely than people with nothing and deep down are envious of people with nothing in how they appreciate everything.

It's become a world driven by all this validation and impulsiveness. We've become so impressionable even as adults, but dying to our impulses and all these external influences is what God compels and teaches us to do. Some days I fail miserably myself amidst it all, but it's temporary and I'm learning to let go and trust God amidst all of these emotions and enticement. This is faith in its purest and most inclusive form. It's not to rely on the impulse of life to sustain us but to let go, close our eyes, pray and trust God through all of the contention and deceptive coercion that seems to have control over our hearts. I heard once that the longest journey in life is from the head to the heart and it's so true in the world we live in. When all we're focussed on is more and more, we are always two steps ahead of sincerity and appreciation and in that appreciation is where our soul has been designed by God for us to be at rest. We are just not at peace otherwise and that is where so much of our anxiety is rooted. God says about the Israelites in Hebrews 3, "Therefore I was angry with that generation, and said, they always go astray in their heart, they have not known My ways, so I swore in My wrath, they shall not enter My rest." God says that it is better for us to give than to receive and he means that in regards to the peace within our soul. We're just living in opposition and rebellion to him otherwise. It's a hard place to be for so many of us with the pride of man exalted so high and all of us wanting a piece of its supposed glory, but again, there's such a release when you can let it go and be in this relationship with God. These moments can be difficult but prayer is a powerful refuge and release for us to persevere and secure us in our vulnerability. It helps us to understand what appreciation is from the perspective of faith and God's creative hand.

Transparency and Surrender

Prayer brings us to a continual sincere state-of-mind and sanctifying maturity that is the foundational premise of our faith in Christ. God offers something far greater in Christ that the world can't offer. He offers an unconditional and uncontrived relationship where we don't have to be validated in everyone's eyes, solve every problem, prove every opinion, or accomplish every generic and impulsive goal every minute of every day. Faith helps us live independent of it all. There's an inclusive and personal acceptance in our transparency with God that dissolves all of the relentless expectations we perceive to be of importance. We don't have to look a certain way or dress in a particular attire. We can be nothing in the world's eyes yet be everything in God's eyes because his love for us is not based on the world's terms or perceptions of him. We've falsely defined love from a carnal sense when true love goes far deeper than a superficial benefit. God is who he is regardless of how we've perceived or represented him to be otherwise and is sovereign over our limited views and opinions of him. Isaiah 55:8-9 says, "For my thoughts are not your thoughts, nor are your ways my ways, says the Lord. For as the heavens are higher than the earth, so are my ways higher than your ways, and my thoughts than your thoughts." We can rest in who we are and who he's desiring each of us to be, outside of any religious pressure or comparison from the world. If the world rejects me, so be it, I push on with Christ. The challenge for us is simply in surrendering in who he is desiring us to be. Comparison and envy are infantile in God's eyes and the more experienced and mature we are in faith, the less these trivial and contentious diversions influence and affect us. The truth of God is that his spirit is there to draw the sincerity out of the human heart and again, he's unwavering in his efforts to do so, in fact he lives to intercede for this purpose through his Holy Spirit. All the petty nuances of self-affirmation and pride become so vain when compared to the bigger picture God instills in our hearts. He frees us from trying to prove ourselves and that's where so much of satan's deception is rooted. The greatest effect of our relationship with God is that we learn to forgive ourselves and accept ourselves for who we are and what we've done, releasing us from the judgment of others and the voices of comparison. The world doesn't realize that so much of it's bound up hostility and resistance towards God and the Bible is actually what he yearns to release us from in the world. Many of us are in pain and hiding in the shadows of inadequacy but God can bring us into the light with confidence knowing and believing we're a valued possession in his eyes because of how his love for us was displayed on the cross. John 3:16 says, "For God so loved the world that he gave his only begotten son, that whoever believes in him should not perish but have everlasting life. For God did not send his son into the world to condemn the world, but that the world through him might be saved." Through faith we come to realize that he offers the unconditional love, acceptance and peace we've desired all along and his Word and his spirit confirm it. He builds us up as the world tears us down, edifies us in our inadequacies and breaks down the barriers of resistance that are holding us from true freedom. The word encourage means to actually give courage and that's what the Holy Spirit does in the most disparaging of circumstances. This is another reason why I'm so incessant about prosperity preachers because they don't connect relationally or circumstantially with those in vulnerable positions where God's love is most needed. I know these words are relatable because I see it in the disposition of the world around me and I know it from within myself. We're torn in our identity and have misconstrued faith as some sort of religious oppression rather than a release into freedom and again, some just see it as a means for gain. Faith is a challenge and commitment like any other discipline to persevere through and is not how we carnally operate but the effects of the spirit of the world and our faith in it are undeniable and have become incessantly counterproductive and damaging, spiritually and psychologically. We are falling victim to a deceptive illusion that our faith reveals to us in Christ. The challenge in faith as I stated before, is the willingness to give up our control over our will and trust in an alternative directive for our lives and that's just not easy. It's difficult to let go and surrender, but I also see the outcome and intentions of those sincere in their faith and am continuously inspired by their maturity, perseverance and peace of mind. There's an internal deliverance within them where the world isn't wearing them down and filling them with anxiety. I see an authentic, genuine and more productive, family oriented objective than that of the world by far. People are united together, working for a common goal in support of one another and comfortable in their own skin. There's virtue, integrity and structure the world isn't recognizing in their misconceptions. People aren't hiding or scared to communicate their problems. They live in humility and transparency and take time to listen and pray for each other which is completely foreign to the secular world. They're living in faith and in its release and aren't being conformed or oppressed by it at all, as many perceive. They've been liberated from religion rather than being conformed or controlled by it and I'm the same way. Religion says that our strict obedience to the law defines our relationship with God, but the law is merely what convicts and holds us accountable to our conscience. Yes, conviction comes from our past offenses which we're all guilty of, but Jesus stands in the gap for us to move forward and be released from it all. Romans 5:20 says, "The law entered that the offense might abound. But where sin abounded, grace abounded much more, so that as sin rained in death, even so grace might reign through righteousness to eternal life through Jesus Christ our Lord." For me it's been a voluntary commitment since the day I believed and no one has influenced or deterred my progress otherwise. I've disliked people and their views and perceptions on faith and have even had personality clashes, but that's just a part of life and shouldn't dissuade us in our pursuit of the truth. It should actually draw us closer to Christ then push us away. Mature Christians have become who they've been created to be and have willfully chosen to do so. In all honesty, I am far too headstrong and stubborn to let any human control me or persuade me to be under their submission religiously. Only God has that respect in my heart and if I'm supposedly being conformed by something that is beneficial to me and to others then the discipline taught bears significant relevance and the product of faith, a viable conformity to comply with. I can only say it so many ways and so many times. Romans 8:29 says we are being conformed into the image of Jesus Christ and that to me is far more productive than being conformed by the sadistic powers of this world. If people are feeling oppressed in their faith they're probably being controlled by man's objectives and haven't defined faith inclusively for themselves because God isn't a tyrannical dictator who crushes us for every wrong move we make. He will convict you but he won't condemn you and he doesn't give the entitlement over to men to carry out our own objectives in a system of rules, especially in regards to finances. People are reluctant to believe due to the abuse of the tithe but nowhere in the Word are we forced to pay or give anything. It's such an unfortunate misconception of the unbelieving world. It's not only an unfortunate misconception in regards to the Word, it's unfortunate that entitled people and denominations have abused their position and the grace of God in their own lives. Romans 9:7 merely says,".. let each one give as he pleases in his heart, not grudgingly or of necessity, for God loves a cheerful giver." Jesus isn't the author of confusion, he is the God of peace and there's an internal release when you come to believe in salvation that far exceeds the spirit of religion that compels you to want to give to the cause. When the Word speaks of spreading seed, it speaks of contributing to the cause of salvation and spreading the gospel but unfortunately people have abused and misconstrued that for their own gain which will bear its severe judgment. Catholicism has claimed Christianity as their own for centuries, guilting people out of billions of dollars in their entitled religious hypocrisy and still hold that claim to this very day. They'd even murder people for disclosing the scriptures for fear people would come to realize their hypocrisy and have to relinquish their oppressive control. It's a complete travesty and religious tyranny and I challenge people who are skeptical in believing to read the scriptures and research history for themselves to conduct their own interrogation and analysis because eternity is a long time to ponder these misconceptions.

At the end of the day regardless of our views on all this, it's our choice to embrace life as a gift and appreciate the simple pleasures around us. It's our choice to love our neighbour as ourselves, swallow our pride and be considerate, selfless and charitable. It's our choice to be empathetic and compassionate. It's our choice to acknowledge the food on our plates in relation to the world and live in humility and ultimately it's our choice to believe in God, but again it's hard giving thanks, staying calm, being patient and finding joy amidst this world of scrutiny and comparative criticism, but that's what Jesus compels us to battle through in faith. We start a lot of our sentences these days with I would have, I should have or I could have, as if we're continuously devaluing ourselves and the process of life and the journey along the way. The world has deceived us into thinking that at every moment we have to reach some unrealistic pinnacle of gratification to keep pace, but in reality it's the pace that's killing and exhausting us in the process. We're putting such a demand and expectation on ourselves and it's become a detriment to our physical and mental health. It's a challenging opposition in front of us all, ourselves sometimes becoming the largest obstacle to overcome.

Chapter 5

The Battle Ensues

There's so much going on in my life and the world outside right now as I'm writing this. We're in an apparent pandemic with people freaking out and completely divided concerning vaccines. Trump has just lost the presidency which has completely divided America. There's pandemonium on the streets with protests, riots and looting over human rights. There's a black lives matter movement going on with people enraged and picketing. Australia is actually in complete lockdown where unvaccinated people aren't even allowed to leave their homes. It seems we're on the verge of world war 3.

When it comes to me, my grandpa fell, broke his pelvis in the backyard and died 2 days later. My grandma took her dog into the vet and they charged her 6,700$ for basically nothing, then said if she didn't give another 4000$ she wouldn't get her dog back, so she was forced to put it down. I just got grilled by an insurance lawyer for six and a half hours in my discovery for something I didn't do. Not only that, I just found out the drunk driver that nearly killed me, didn't even get charged. My friend's wife's sister and uncle just died of covid in Peru. My friend was just diagnosed with kidney cancer and another close friend has breast cancer. I found out my old sparring partner just died in a truck accident while he was moving. The old drummer in my first band died of throat cancer. My handicapped sister was basically locked in her bedroom and forced to wear a hair net by her caregivers for fear of covid-19, not allowing her to use the bathroom. There was an execution style killing at 9am in the ice rink where my boss's family works and apart from that, half the province has been set ablaze with forest fires.

It's like everything is falling apart around us but as a Christian I'm not going to react. Life has been revealed to me in scripture, so there's no reason to allow fear and anxiety to dictate my life and consume me. It's all painful and troubling but I actually see it as a good test for us all to evaluate where our faith lies and where we're investing our time and priorities. The question becomes who are we when these impulses aren't being gratified and these voids aren't being filled? Who are we when our hope in the world is fading away? Who are we amidst seclusion, turmoil, fear and persecution? Who are we without our TV on or our cell phone in our hands? Who are we without food or a drink in our hands? This is where true faith under the scriptures can be a crucial tool in navigating through all the voices in our head and the relentless pressures and temptations that surround us and impress upon our individual lives and identities. Unfortunately it's only going to get worse without faith as our refuge. Satan loves all of our impulses being met and drives it all forward because in times like these we're left unprepared, complacent and dependent upon them to sustain us, where God keeps us grounded, humble and prepared for any inevitable circumstances that may arise. Philippians 4:6 says, "Be anxious for nothing, but in everything by prayer and supplication, with thanks-giving, let your requests be known to God, and the peace of God, which surpasses all understanding, will guard your hearts and minds through Christ Jesus." There is a far deeper sense of security when we can die to our identity in the world whether it be how we look or how affluent or prestigious we are and embrace our identity in Christ. I feel success is still a desirable and applicable goal in faith but it's simply redefined in Christ maturely and not this continual gratified social and impulsive necessity the world has portrayed it should be, because we aren't going to always have that opportunity or accessibility. The world has just about run its course. Of course they're going to make it all a generic aspiration to create a general consumer but in faith we can see right through it all. Solomon was a man of infinite abundance and treasure but wrote of it all being vanity and was considered the wisest man on earth. It's much like the word abundance when attributed to faith. Success and abundance in Christ are defined in sincerity and in humility with productive relationships with friends and family and in charitable service to God and the community. I see that as a far more successful and abundant life than one you merely live and die to yourself and your possessions. I feel like I'm repeating myself, but again, disregarding these fundamental truths has become the world's downfall. The convictions we're denying and deeming irrelevant would have certainly saved us from much of the troubles that have compounded upon us.

Conspiracy or Reality?

Without faith or even a moral compass to guide us, we're prone to wander and react unwisely amidst our individual circumstances, perceptions and trauma. In fact, science itself proves all of this in the study of serotonin, dopamine and the endorphins in the body. Unfortunately, scientists have been paid millions of dollars for decades by luciferian societies, governments and pharmaceutical companies and are even in labs right now devising new schemes and praying on this design within us. They focus on our impulsive emotional tendencies and these chemicals in our bodies to enhance the consumer within us but we've just become too deceived and naive in the comfort and convenience of it all to realize it. What seems good at the moment usually has an ulterior motive attached to it. These aren't conspiracy theories, it's common sense and we are unfortunately all suffering and falling victim because of it without faith as our discipline and without God's spirit to guide us. The statistics and research proves our vessel functions far more productively in abstinence and in sincere faith because there's a conclusion to the internal cycle and chemicals in the body. There's a sustaining balance that suppresses our anxiety. It's as if the entire equilibrium of mind, body, soul and spirit align together for it's designed intention together in unison. It's in harmony with its directive. There's also a sense of belonging when we serve our purpose. When our conscience is clear we have no reason to allow fear to debilitate us in our confusion and desperation. It all points to a designer creating us to be in relationship with him whether we deny it or not. The proof and statistics are in the willful acceptance and obedience and in the willful denial and ignorance. Again, statistics don't lie. Without hope and faith we get anxious and volatile and these unsustained emotions compound into a degenerative generational imbalance and inoperative instability. Without emotional resolve we live to escape from the anxiety of it all and justify the escape in our unaccountability. There's a lot to be said and a lot of truth in being accountable to someone that loves you more than you love yourself. Instead of confronting the issues as faith in God compels us to do, we start eating, drinking, smoking or whatever else fills our immediate needs to ease the void and stress of it all, but in that we inadvertently invite satan into our lives. I did it my whole life but the anxiety grew and the cycle never seemed to come to an end. The chemicals never settled in my vessel and all my negative habits that I felt were sustaining me continued to escalate with my tolerance to them. This is far too real nowadays with almost a third of the population dependent on anti-anxiety pills. So many years of my life I blocked out with drugs and alcohol and I now see it was all just a temporary escape from a far deeper rooted problem in my soul from my disassociation with God. As I grew older the pressure to maintain balance and to succeed consumed me into a desperate state of frustration and anxiety. My personal health just continued to deteriorate physically, emotionally and psychologically amidst the desperation and I just couldn't see it. I didn't even know what I was living for anymore. I hope in this book to reveal the depth of God's love for us all and help release the pressures and strongholds people are facing and putting on themselves unnecessarily. I'm not writing it so we live for this life but we still have a life to live while we are here. There is a clarity and peace that resides in Christ that can help us live healthier, wiser, and more purpose-driven and productive lives without the religious oppression that dictates and scrutinizes our every move. Without him the world is lost because the world doesn't love itself as much as God loves the world and the only way we can see God's love for the world is in his sacrifice on the cross. The world without Christ is trying to put a massive puzzle together without the picture for reference and they don't realize heaven is in the picture and in the pieces.

The Devil At Work

Unfortunately as Christ's spirit is at work, so is that of the devil. 1 John 3:7-8 says, "Let no one deceive you. He who practices righteousness is righteous, just as He is righteous. He who sins is of the devil, for the devil has sinned from the beginning. For this purpose the Son of God was manifested, that he might destroy the works of the devil." So then the question is what are the works of the devil and what has God could come to destroy?

A lot of what I've learned since becoming a Christian is the power of the devil and how he's deceived us in our perception of reality and manipulated us psychologically through the media, movies and television. Again, conspiracy to me is an understatement in the highest degree because in a sense the entire world is conspiring against itself outside of Christ whether you think it's willfully being exercised or not. If you're sick of the word conspiracy then you need to wake up and at least research for yourself what people are conspiring to do because you will be severely compromised in the near future. If it's not in this generation it will certainly affect the next. There's just so much more going on behind the scenes that the masses are oblivious to and this coronavirus is no different. I'm shocked at how naive people are and how they'll even argue with you concerning such obvious collusion surrounding us. Conspire means to make secret plans jointly to commit an unlawful or harmful act. It's also defined as events or circumstances that seem to work together to bring about a particular result, typically to someone's detriment. What God's revealed to me is who and what they're actually conspiring to accomplish and how severely demonic it's all become. What's insane is how our taxpayer money and the interest on our loans actually pay the salaries of our government and these banking systems and secret societies to do so. It's not only in them, it's in Hollywood, the entertainment industry and wherever else there's an opportunity for money to be made and to conform and manipulate us psychologically. Harvey Weinstein is just a splash in the ocean to a far deeper progression of inflicted manipulation, perversion and telepathic coercion that has affected the way we view life and ourselves. There's a whole other dark and secret world of sinister evil that the general masses are blind to in their spiritual disregard. That's why they're called secret societies but what they've done in secret goes beyond what any of us can imagine. If we actually knew we'd be appalled. It reminds me of Ezekiel 8 where God shows him what the elders of Israel were actually doing in secret, behind closed doors. Ezekiel couldn't see it until God revealed it to him and when he did he was appalled.

There's weapons formed against us that are hidden in the compulsion of our minds and a spirit that transcends our carnal reasoning, bent on our demise. Google defines evil as profound immortality and wickedness especially when regarded as a supernatural force. Google is correct and in line with the biblical definition of evil somewhat, but even more crucial is that the Bible attributes the effects to its origin and exposes the directive. The carnal mind can see the negative outcome from the decisions we make to some degree, but can't see the spiritual impartation driving the procession or the magnitude of it all. As God reveals to us who believe what is pure and holy, he also unearths the spirit that is in opposition to them. As some die to their carnal flesh and surrender to God for his glory, there's also many others possessed by demons who live for their carnal flesh, against their conscience, to impose evil for satan's glory and to fulfill their own desire for impunity, control and power. It's all deeply hidden behind the veil of our carnal depravity and been willfully and cowardly imposed upon us all. We're compulsive vessels of spiritual inclination without even knowing it at times and our carnality drives their agenda. The problem is the spiritual world does know it and is progressive in accordance with our belief and unbelief. The Bible calls satan the deceiver of all the world and the father of all lies and he definitely has his hand in more areas that influence us then we realize. Him and his demons are like an unseen anthill underneath your house working feverishly without you even knowing it. We've become deceived and disillusioned in our perceptions of reality, following sin's illusive and seductive trail but it's fascinating how our perceptions change so dramatically when we simply believe in faith. It brings so much truth to light especially in a spiritual sense. Someone literally on the brink of suicidal depression can be radically transformed into a revived and rejuvenated pillar of strength and influence almost overnight. My life is a crazy testimony of this itself which I'll share later. Revelation 12:11 says, "They overcame him by the blood of the Lamb and by the word of their testimony," and Satan is who this is referring to.

The Book Of Life

Our lives are like an old rusty compass that is merely a degree out. We blindly trust it and go out on the journey of life assuming we're going in the right direction, but in the end we'll come to realize we were out from the very beginning. I now see the world has thrown out the moral compass altogether and vainly lives as a guide unto themselves. I also see a fake compass crafted to manipulate us as pawns in a false direction with a false incentive much like a blind man being led towards the edge of a cliff. An unbelieving world doesn't realize that God is the author of both directive and destination in this world and only the original author knows how the story ends and what direction to take. Hebrews says Jesus is the author and finisher of our faith and that he is the author of eternal salvation to those that obey him. Revelation and other epistles speak of the Lambs Book of Life slain from the foundation of the world and ultimately, we're all living within the pages of this book and need to take heed. Revelation 3:5 says, "He who overcomes will be clothed in white garments; and I will not erase his name from the book of life." Revelation 20:15 says, "Anyone not found written in the book of Life was cast into the lake of fire." Even the prophet Daniel wrote of the book of life saying, "There shall be a time of trouble, such as never was since there was a nation, even to that time. And at that time your people shall be delivered, everyone who is found written in the book."

We've naively trusted in the world's narratives and have become lost in them, meanwhile Gods are in procession and coming to their imminent conclusion. Anyone trying to be prophetic and rewrite his story with a different outcome is only leading themselves and their followers astray. Jesus Christ is this pristine and unwavering compass to follow and the source and origin to comply with. Jesus said, "I am the way the truth and the life" and the more I've learned of the elements of evil, his way isn't unreasonable considering the alternative.

The Glory of God

I feel through his Word God has revealed to us a relational intimacy that he himself shares with us outside of any four walls or any philosophy or intellect generated by man. If God were to exude his uttermost wisdom, love, and glory relatably and relationally to his creation, it would be through offering understanding and condolence in our deepest emotional grievances, and for me he has in his Word. It's like a gateway into his soul and he walks alongside us in the process. It brings truth in all the contention. It brings rest in all the anxiety and brings hope when hope seems to be lost. His Word is an incredible articulation to his true character and answers and confirms so many questions that the world doesn't provide answers to. Again, the world to me is simply perishing in it's blatant disregard and disassociation. The truth of it all is that God himself became a human being. The supernatural veil and divide we are separated from in our carnal limitations has been revealed to us in Christ. 1 Timothy 6:16 says, "He's the king of kings and Lord of lords, who alone has immortality, dwelling in unapproachable light, whom no man has seen or can see." 1 John 1:2 says, "That which was from the beginning, which we have heard, which we have seen with our eyes, which we have looked upon, and our hands have handled, concerning the Word of life, the life was manifested, and we have seen, and bear witness, and declare to you that eternal life which was with the Father, was manifest to us." He dwells in a dimension our minds cannot fathom or comprehend, nor are we able to access, but he made it accessible to us through Christ. John spoke of the lamb of God who would take away the sins of the world and Daniel had visions of one like the son of man coming to earth. Daniel 7:13 says, "I kept looking in the night visions, and behold, with the clouds of heaven, one like the son of man was coming, and He came up to the Ancient of days and was presented before him." Chapter 7:22 says, "The Ancient of days came, and a judgment was made in favor of the saints of the Most High, and the time came for the saints to possess the kingdom." Hebrews 7 describes a human figure that met Abraham returning from war and says, "Without father, without mother, without descent, having neither beginning of days, nor end of life but made like unto the Son of God." He existed before time existed and stepped out of his omnipotent realm into ours for us to behold his majesty and glory. He walked as we walk and faced life as we do by taking on the nature of a man. 1 Timothy 3:16 says, "God was manifest in the flesh, justified in the spirit, seen of angels, preached to the gentiles, believed on in the world, received up into glory." His spirit and will was in operation through an earthly human vessel and that is a fascinating revelation. He felt life through his hands and feet and through his eyes and ears and all the human senses as we do. He felt the emotions of joy and pain, and love and sorrow. He experienced the anxiety between spiritual consciousness and physical will. He was burdened and afflicted far more than we will ever comprehend but the glory of it all is how he conducted himself and persevered through the circumstances set before him.

It's an unrivalled pressure to overcome and that very pressure I see now as our greatest fear and weakness. He was sovereign over the predicament and saw the burden as an opportunity for the purity of his identity to be expressed and the true perception and depiction of God to be established and signified. Depiction means the true representation of something and this was Jesus Christ to the world. He's become the historical bearer of influence upon the world's moral and ethical standards and principles and he did it all voluntarily without a dime for compensation. Philippians 2:6-7says,

"Who, being in the form of God, thought it not robbery to be equal with God; But made himself of no reputation, and took upon him the form of a servant, and was made in the likeness of men." This becomes the fascination and mystery that compels us and drives our faith as true Christians. There was no superficial benefit in his motives other than to accomplish his set prerogative for the world's moral rejuvenation and salvation. He had a choice as we have been given a choice but with his choice he revolutionized the entire world. Revolutionary is defined as involving or causing a complete or dramatic change, or engaged in or promoting political revolution. I think Jesus takes it even further than the definition itself. It's the world's greatest historical paradigm shift in the potential of a human which can only be defined as inhuman. There is an initiative and intuitiveness in and about him that completely transcends our capacity. He claimed victory over so many of our failures especially relating to conduct and influence that so far exceed our level of righteousness and intellectual dexterity. He took the weight of it all upon his shoulders knowing all along he'd be tortured, rejected, humiliated, scrutinized and eventually murdered. Jesus faced our ultimate fears and endured the physical pain of those nails piercing his hands and feet. It's an awful and humiliating way to die but he disregarded his own life for ours as the ultimate demonstration of love and sacrifice. He didn't succumb to the fear of it all and hide from the objective. He wouldn't forsake us or his own identity even with the burden set before him to accomplish. There can't be more anxiety for someone to face considering the prerogative. He persisted through it for the world to be renewed and to perceive faith in him and the faith of him as justifiable and sufficient reasons and motivation for conviction, belief, compliance and change. I've said it before and I'll say it again. It's incredible to me. The whole ora of his being bears an incomparable equivalence and again, needs to be more cohesively evaluated. If I knew I had a set date I'd be brutalized and murdered and the reconciliation of the world's sin and influence rested upon my shoulders, I'd cower and be petrified every day leading up to it. I've lived in fear with no burden or influence to bear and certainly wouldn't live for it and the needs of it like Jesus did. He's the initial heavenly missionary and for me that's true love being defined proactively without a contrived or contentious motive behind it. It's so profound I haven't the words even to describe it's revelation. There's a providential maturity and divine celestial holiness in him beyond the spirit of humanity that again, can only be of God.

Then There's Me

For me (in futile comparison) my mind wanders and continually over analyzes situations and circumstances. I have some experience and head knowledge but even with the limited amount I have, I can't seem to get it from my head through to my lips with confidence and assurance. As I try, fears and doubts have always entered into my mind and I avoid the interaction. I get nervous and insecure and the words get lost in the process of contemplation, let alone attempting to formulate an irrefutable rhetorical guide and literary composition for the world to follow. I laugh at how ridiculous and inferior I am in comparison. I sometimes dwell on the most petty, insignificant things that my mind just won't let go of in my immaturity. To my defense my parents were both schizophrenics so I was born with systems of chemical imbalance like ADD and ADHD but I'm still fairly competent and coherent. I just get filled at times with anxiety, worry, resentment and unforgiveness and am easily offended by the reaction and perceptions of people towards me. Outside of Christ there is no natural propensity within me to selflessly act in a productive way when these feelings arise. In fact, when I'm interacting with people and the opinions become confrontational and abrasive or I sense a level of entitlement in someone, I want to react aggressively or again, I just shut off the interaction entirely. This hostility has always built up inside me especially before Christ. I've let so much of it go but there's definitely a part of it that's still there. I'll also admit, outside of faith, I just don't possess the empathy or compassion to care enough about the lives of others to invoke a change in them like Jesus. Nothing in me on my own has the desire to be influential or revolutionary. I also don't stand with enough formidable confidence to impose my own moral judgment or conviction upon another person's will. When contention or scrutiny come my way, I want to fight, I don't want to love at all. I've had moments where I've been charitable, kind and thoughtful and I've used good discernment under pressure in several situations but nothing that deserves honorability or praise. Those moments are few and far between. My bravery and courage are mediocre at best and I've fallen many times under the weight of scrutiny, maturity, responsibility and expectation. I've struggled my whole life with these common weaknesses and nuances in my character as we all do and haven't been unable to find a way to resolve them or even a reason to until I had faith. Jesus set the bar and our faith in him says I don't have to set it any higher. I give all the praise to him, a praise worthy of service and worship.

The burden upon Jesus's shoulders is something my mind can't even ascertain let alone exemplify so I've given that honor to him.

Law vs Grace

The human conscience is drawing further and further into its apex without resolution because again, at the end of the day, from an unbelieving standpoint, all it's guilty and accountable to is itself. We merely balance the scale in what we live to justify. We might have regrets at times but cannot find a proactive solution or purpose beneath the surface of it all. We seem to constitute more and more laws but all we're proving with them is that we're more and more guilty of them, even unto ourselves. I guess the question is, where is this refinement coming from and what is the outcome? 2 Corinthians 7:10-11 says, "Godly sorrow produces repentance leading to salvation, not to be regretted, but the sorrow of the world produces death. For observe this very thing, that you sorrowed in a Godly manner, what diligence it produced in you, what clearing of yourselves, what indignation, what fear, what vehement desire, what zeal, what vindication." The gospel message is that Jesus rectified this burden by accomplishing the consciences objective in himself to release us from the laws slavery and oppression. Through faith in Christ, God gives us his spirit and his spirit is extremely mature and wise in it's awareness and reasoning. True freedom is in the psychological and spiritual liberty and forgiveness within our conscious mind. If I have a conscience and I'm conscious of that, then the slate needs to be wiped clean for me to inherently exist in peace and grace and that's only through a relationship with God through Jesus Christ. 2 Corinthians 1:12 says, "Our boasting is this, the testimony of our conscience, that we conducted ourselves in the world in simplicity and godly sincerity, not with fleshly wisdom but by the grace of God." 1 Timothy 1:3-7 says, "Nor give heed to fables and endless genealogies, which caused disputes rather than Godly edification which is in faith. Now the purpose of the commandment is love from a pure heart, from a good conscience, and from sincere faith, from which some, having strayed, have turned aside to idle talk, desiring to be teachers of the law, understanding neither what they say nor the things which they affirm. But we know that the law is good if one uses it lawfully, knowing this, that the law is not made for a righteous person, but for the lawless and insubordinate, and for the ungodly and for sinners." Again, the power of His spirit exceeds that of our own and is far superior in its ability to persevere through all of the contention around us and is there to equip us with the tools necessary to push through. We know this because of what God accomplished through Jesus Christ and how he handled the severity of his life with grace.

How Faith Overcomes Our Conscience

It's so apparent these days how disillusioned and self-centered we get when the attention or praise is upon us and we're being edified or exalted, but Jesus never wavered in his prerogative. He was always aware of the thoughts of those he confronted and was wise to the influence he generated and projected upon the world. My failures are irrelevant now and don't produce the shame and inadequacy as they did before because I'm not trying to prove myself to the world anymore and ultimately, my faith is not in myself and what I do or have done, my faith is in him and what he did because what he did, I can't do. In our belief we now stand affirmed in his conclusive proclamation concerning us because he rectified satan's hold on us in the law. Any accusations that enter into our mind or condemn us in our thoughts, whether they be from within ourselves or satan get reverted in sincere faith because God has redeemed us in forgiveness to the condemnation and he is the overriding supreme voice of authority. Colossians 2:14-15 says, "He has made you alive together with him, having forgiven all your trespasses, having wiped out the handwriting of requirements that was against us, which was contrary to us. And he has taken it out of the way, having nailed it to the cross. Having disarmed principalities and powers, he made a public spectacle of them, triumphing over them in it." Notice how it says, "disarmed principalities and powers," as though that is their ammunition for accusations against us. Any other voice is a liar or an imposter and like I said before, has already been condemned. 1 Corinthians 4:3-4 says, "With me it is a very small thing that I should be judged by you or by a human court. In fact, I do not even judge myself. For I know of nothing against myself, yet I am not justified by this; but he who judges me is the Lord." The best thing to do in faith if we feel any shame or regret is to repent and move forward right away and not allow satan a foothold to torment our minds. God's not condemning us by the law, he's continually redeeming us from it in our repentance and in his forgiveness. 1 John 1:8-10 says, "If we say we have no sin we deceive ourselves, and the truth is not in us. If we confess our sins, he is faithful and just to forgive us our sins and to cleanse us from all unrighteousness." Philippians 3:12-13 says, "I press on, that I made lay hold of that for which Christ Jesus has also laid hold of me. Forgetting those things which are behind and reaching forward to those things which are ahead, I press toward the goal for the prize of the upward call of God in Christ Jesus." I see now that what Jesus has done is inconceivable for the carnal mind to articulate, mastermind or exemplify. It transcends human logic and reasoning and his Spirit continuously lives to intercede and deliver me and those who believe through the darkness of the world and our own souls.

The Power Of Letting Go

All of our minds have been darkened and jaded and they're becoming more and more jaded as we relish in our sinful nature and as satan's deception infiltrates our minds, but the light of Jesus illuminates the threshold of our will, spirit and soul. The challenge simply becomes letting go of all we're holding onto in this world and the glory and validation we seek for ourselves. Again, it's hard letting go and serving a purpose other than our own but when we do we see the world in a cyclone of its own pride, trying to claim every piece of the world's puzzle for its own. The more glory and praise the world seeks for and gives itself, the more the revelation of Christ becomes a relevant compliance to praise, honour and worship especially today amidst our modern-day narcissism and idolatry. Honouring God in worship is much like the world idolizing its favourite athletes or heros and living vicariously through their achievements and accolades knowing full well we don't possess their talent or skills ourselves. Worship is defined as the feeling or expression of reverence and adoration for a deity. The difference is this is God we're glorifying in worship and now he lives in us and his glory shines through us. It's not only through us, we can see his glory and influence shine throughout the world regardless of what we do ourselves. Whenever we or anyone around the world turns from their sin in faith, God is glorified. When we put our faith in action for the benefit of others, God gets glorified because living for our own glory dies to itself and will never turn us from our sin, nor will it benefit those around us because it's just not in our nature to do so and without conviction and direction, we don't change so the glory is all his. He is the ambassador of it all and even if we are inspirational or encouraging to some degree, the impact is insignificant in comparison to that of Jesus Christ. Our definition of glory is trivial in light of eternity.

Salvation and faith are a free gift that's been given to the world but we need to learn to receive it and apply it accordingly. God wanted nothing in return for his life except a heart for a heart, a soul for a soul and his love for our love. He did it voluntarily so there wouldn't be strife, contention or an entitled religious claim of possession and it's frustrating that people perceive him and his teachings otherwise. Romans 6:23 says, "The wages of sin is death, but the gift of God is eternal life in Christ Jesus our Lord." Ephesians 2:8 says, "By grace you have been saved through faith, and that not of yourselves, it is the gift of God, not of works, lest anyone should boast." There was a man on the cross next to Jesus being crucified for his sin. While everyone was mocking Jesus and scourging him, this man saw Jesus for who he truly was. He simply asked him for forgiveness and even defended Jesus as the onlookers berated him on the cross. In his confession and defense, God forgave him and simply said, "..today I will see you in paradise." This man was condemned to death and minutes from his last breath. He never paid a tithe or performed a religious act of any kind to please God whatsoever. He was no part of any denomination or religious organization. He had probably never been in a theological debate his entire life let alone won one. Catholicism wasn't founded yet nor were Protestants, Baptist, Eastern Orthodox, Methodist, Pentecostals, Armenians, Calvinists or Lutherans. There weren't Jehovah Witnesses, Mormons or Seventh-day Adventists either. Martin Luther was born 1500 years later with no influence to the initial premise to salvation. This man had never been to Bible College, in fact the Bible hadn't even been fully inscribed yet in the New Testament. He simply believed in faith and that belief saved him, negating so much of our religiosity and systematic theology. God accepted him without religious partiality and that is what becomes so liberating in defining faith.

Religion vs Faith

The thing about a gift is when we don't receive it as a gift, we attribute it as a debt and are forever working to pay it back to get back on level terms and regain control or get compensation. Unfortunately sin is not a debt we can pay back in what we do or theorize. If that were the case we'd all stand justified in our sin by our own conditions. This is where religion and the transformation and regeneration of faith are in severe conflict because we have nothing we could ever do or offer in return for what he's given us and he's not asking for us to pay it back. Colossians 2:20-23 says, "Therefore, if you died with Christ from the basic principles of the world, why, as though living in the world, do you subject yourself to regulations…. Do not touch, do not taste, do not handle….which all concern things which perish with the using, according to the commandments and doctrines of men? These things indeed have an appearance of wisdom in self-imposed religion, false humility, and neglect of the body, but are of no value against the indulgence of the flesh."

There were no stipulations in place for his voluntary sacrifice then, or any foreknowledge generated by man, in fact the ones that claimed to know God the most in Jesus time in their supposed adherence to the law, were the very ones that killed him. The favour of God wasn't earned then and it can't be earned now because it takes away from the idea of selfless, sacrificial and unconditional love. God sees through our contrived entitlement and opportunism and came to free those enslaved by it. Religion becomes a contrived nonrelational expectation that precedes our actions that unfortunately produces a position in the mind of man. This is how so many religions base their relationship with God upon. They don't see the expectation of reward from our moral confiance as a form of narcissism but he does because there's an action of mercy on his end in response. Those consumed by religion won't allow God to work in and through them or receive him as a gift because they feel they are in control of the relationship, fulfilling the law in their conscience. They're merely rewarding themselves in what they do and faith is merely subject to their own moral reasoning. Unfortunately for so many, it's become a constant battery of inadequacy, anxiety and condemnation that satan uses to suffocate us in every minute task we do and it never takes the monkey off our back. I've been there myself ensnared in fatalistic condemnation and it can be exhausting and debilitating, but again, God has given Jesus Christ as a free gift to whomever believes, whether you're in Africa or the Antarctica, or whether you're in prison or on the Hollywood hills. Galatians 2:16 says, "A man is not justified by the works of the law but by the faith of Jesus Christ, even we have believed in Jesus Christ, that we might be justified by the faith of Christ, and not by the works of the law, for by the works of the law shall no flesh be justified." Chapter 4:9-11 says, "Now after you have known God, or rather are known by God, how is it that you turn again to the weak and beggarly elements, to which you desire again to be in bondage? You observe days and months and seasons and years. I am afraid for you, lest I have laboured for you in vain." In chapter 3 Paul also speaks of how frustrated he is with the Galatians and says, "Did you receive the Spirit by the works of the law, or by the hearing of faith? Are you so foolish? having begun in the Spirit, are you now being made perfect by the flesh? Have you suffered so many things in vain, if indeed it was in vain? Therefore he who supplies the spirit to you and works miracles among you, does he do it by the works of the law, or by the hearing of faith? These scriptures destroy religious control, oppression and entitlement all together. All the religious entitlement and voices in our head that persistently nag away at us get silenced at the embracing of our faith and our transparency with God. In Isaiah 9 it says, "The people who have walked in darkness have seen a great light, those who dwelt in the land of the shadow of death, upon them a light has shined. For unto us a child is born, unto us a Son is given, and the government will be upon his shoulder. And his name will be called Wonderful Counsellor, Mighty God, Everlasting father, Prince of Peace. Of the increase of his government and peace there will be no end. Upon the throne of David and over his kingdom, to order it and establish it with judgment and justice from that time forward, even forever. The zeal of the Lord of hosts will perform this."

Wonderful Counselor

God has many attributes but that one in Isaiah 9 states that he is a wonderful counsellor. I feel so many of these moments of uncertainty we battle with in life can be resolved simply by closing our eyes in prayer and conversing with God. A relationship isn't formed without reciprocating interaction and this is what God desires from us all through prayer. Prayer is an extremely misunderstood and devalued practice and discipline to the unbelieving world. It's also misunderstood from the religious lens and perspective. The world's narcissistic pride and greed has severed and disregarded its own internal desire for unconditional love and acceptance and that's who God is to his creation through prayer. It's how we communicate with him. It's more of a coexisting deliberation as you would a good parent, friend or counsellor deciphering the tasks at hand and the emotions and circumstances in everyday life, however minimal or severe they may seem. The difference is God's providence and unwavering love, along with his empathy and restrictions to time. He is an omnipresent spirit of refuge outside the restrictions of religion and time and is consistent in reciprocating our transparency. Prayer is a powerful way of meditation to secure our standing and identity in our faith and to keep perspective through all our circumstances. It also secures us in our vulnerability and strengthens us in our weaknesses. Merely relieving the emotions of life is transformational in of itself and helps us endure the process and stay focussed in affliction. This pandemic has become a severe test for people being subjected to confined and isolated situations and without faith and prayer I see a disastrous result transpiring now and in the near future with mental health. It's so easy getting hung up and trapped inside the emotional courses of life and we suffer without perspective and a place to release and vent it all. That's what a good friend or father offers to those they love and God is no different in his capacity. There's times where the world's empathy just doesn't meet our emotional needs or our desires for condolence and may never do so. There's trauma and vulnerability so deep inside some of us that is too hard to verbalize or be trusted in the hands and minds of others. There are valleys in life and times we're at a loss where our hearts are grieving and in need of deep internal refuge and hope, and this is what God offers freely in relationship with him through prayer and no four walls can ever take that away from us. If that were the case Christians would be falling apart because churches have been shut down for over a year. Ultimately, Jesus can relate to it all through what he endured in his own life and on the cross.

I'm going through it right now as I write this book, not only with what's going on with the world outside but within myself. I'm an adopted kid who has had no support from my parents emotionally or financially. I have a handful of friends that have given me some support through this accident, but for the most part I've been in isolation and it's been a true test in resilience and dependence upon God to sustain me in my emotional and physical trials. I'm in continual chronic pain as I write this and I can only sit for so long until my neck and back seize up completely but my faith strengthens me through it all. There's a persisting objective regardless of my circumstances that compels me to endure and bear the initiative. My physical limitations aren't restricting my mind's spiritual fortitude as they would without faith. All I'd do is dwell on my circumstances otherwise.

Being An Example

The world is suffering for the lack of hope and emotional endurance therefore some of us are called to endure life's afflictions however difficult they may seem for the world to see faith as a means for refuge and perseverance. I guess if faith were merely about health and prosperity the broken world would have no reason to relate and this book would be an irrelevant testimony of unfaithfulness, along with the Bible itself. 2 Corinthians 6 says, "We then, as workers together with God, also plead with you not to receive the grace of God in vain..... We give no offense in anything, that our ministry may not be blamed. But in all things we commend ourselves as ministers of God. In much patience, in tribulations, in needs, in distresses, in stripes, in imprisonments, in tumults, in labors, in sleeplessness, in fastings, by purity, by knowledge, by long-suffering, by kindness, by the Holy Spirit, by sincere love, by the Word of truth, by the power of God, by the armour of righteousness on the right hand and on the left, by honor and dishonor, by evil report and good report, as deceivers, and yet true, as unknown, and yet well-known, as dying, and behold we live, as chastened, and yet not killed, as sorrowful, yet always rejoicing, as poor, yet making many rich, as having nothing, and yet possessing all things." Sometimes God will break us down and use the most awful of circumstances for us to realize our need for him and for our testimony to reach out to the world who is in need of emotional refuge and not just some open checkbook to prosperity, because why would God make us all healthy and wealthy before repenting of our sin when salvation is the final outcome of faith. It would defeat the purpose of his sacrifice and merely enable us to continue to live in sin without repentance. He would defeat his own purpose and live contrary and in contradiction to himself in sanctifying us. 2 Corinthians 1:8-9 is an eye opener in many ways concerning faith but especially to prosperity preaching. It says, "We do not want you to be ignorant, brethren, of our trouble which came to us in Asia; that we were burdened beyond measure, above strength, so that we despaired even of life. Yes, we had the sentence of death in ourselves, that we should not trust in ourselves but in God," In Paul's letter to the Thessalonians he says in verse 4:3, "This is the will of God, even your sanctification," and in closing his letter in chapter 5 he says, "Now may the God of peace himself sanctify you completely; and may your whole spirit, soul, and body be preserved blameless at the coming of our Lord Jesus Christ. He who calls you is faithful, who also will do it." When that previous scripture says making many rich and possessing all things it speaks of spiritual awareness and deliverance in faith and that only happens for those who've endured sanctification. It speaks of God's selfless love, mercy and forgiveness, not some shallow and vain materialism. Proverbs 3:11-12 says, "My son, do not despise the chastening of the Lord, nor detest his correction; For whom the Lord loves He corrects, just as a father the son in whom he delights." Sanctification is defined as the process of being freed from sin or purified, and that's not easy. It can be relentless and it's only through the Word of God and prayer that I can even process life and evaluate it all productively and relatively. I'll admit prayer is difficult as I stated before and I struggle with it myself, but when I swallow my pride in humility and pray

I find true strength, clarity and peace. It's also difficult to admit I need to be sanctified but I feel like I'm held hostage otherwise in the worries and impulsive tendencies of my mind. Acknowledging God snaps you out of bad habits, complacency and even the condemnation of the devil. Proverbs 3:6 says, "In all your ways acknowledge Him, and He will make your paths straight." Also, Peter says to cast all your anxiety on him because he cares for you.

God's Persistence

I can see now how so many turn to escape with food, drugs, alcohol, or prescription pills and why I did the same for so many years before I had faith. It's because again, there's no release from these bondages and bound up emotions of life and these emotions can be severe and unrelenting. It's like we're bound in between the two, the unrelenting pressure of the world and the relentless love of God. If we were to admit our deepest yearnings in life they would be for someone to listen to us and accept us in our most vulnerable state and for people to acknowledge our circumstances and sympathize with them, but this is rapidly fading away as the world's narcissistic spirit drives into its climax. We all live vicariously through our idols but our idols don't hold our hand while we are drowning nor do they visit us or give us hope on our deathbed. The majority of us will never have a personal relationship with those we idolize whatsoever. This is why faith doesn't evolve alongside the world and why God doesn't change in his character or in compliance with us. He remains that loving father regardless because this is his true character and his ears and arms are open all day long, 24/7. It's okay to come to him with any concern or inclination, or however broken or angry we are because he doesn't judge like the world judges. Of course he judges sin and keeps us grounded and humble but he doesn't judge the emotions, in fact, he welcomes the most severe emotions because in him they find resolution (as long as we're seeking resolution) and he knows it's the reaction to the emotion that causes us to sin. Hebrews 12-9 says, "Furthermore, we have had human fathers who corrected us, and we paid them respect. Shall we not much more readily be in subjection to the Father of spirits and live?" Ultimately, God is so deep in his understanding of the emotions because of what he faced and endured in Jesus Christ. He understands anxiety, scrutiny, isolation, depression, humiliation and fear. He understood it then and he understands it now because the world curses his name on every corner of the globe all day long. There is no other name that has been cursed at more than God in all of history. He was and still is the centerpoint of all the world's derision yet he remains faithful to his Word. People that don't even believe in God curse the name of Jesus Christ. It's on the end of their lips all day long. They'll spit the word out with every hiccup or misstep during the day. I hear, God dammit, Christ almighty, for the love of God, Jesus Christ, for Christ sake, and many others all day, every day whether it be in everyday life or in movies and television. We get offended and even kill one another for the most petty of offenses in our insecurities but God is being mocked every second of every day. Ultimately, God wants us to be aware of the ramifications that follow the emotional reaction and we all can agree that is a justifiable perspective to comply with. If we don't we're just being ignorant. There's a deeper psychology to faith that I don't think people are aware of and I'm trying to put in relatable words. The religious perception and misconception of it is deterring people from its saving grace. I'll agree, at times it's hard to see God in this light especially with the state of the world and all the questions and contention that arise concerning him, but he's steadfast in his mercy towards us and is patient to guide us to the truth of his Word. He's not this generic or systematic religious entity that some of these religious denominations portray or perceive him to be. He's personal and deeper than that, but we can't see him this way until we put all things into perspective and see it through his eyes. We are biting the hand that's feeding us and expecting him to reach down for more but how do we feel when people take us for granted and curse or mock us? The world lives in a way that's completely ignorant towards God and even reviles him and for him to suffer and be patient through it for our sakes along the way, is a testament to his sovereignty and true forgiving nature and character. There's a new Christian song out that describes this love so well. Some of the lyrics go,

> The overwhelming, neverending, reckless love of God,
> It chases me down, fights 'till I'm found,
> leaves the 99,
> And I couldn't earn it, I don't deserve it,
> still you give yourself away
> Theres no shadow you won't light up,
> Mountain you won't climb up,
> coming after me
> There's no wall you won't kick down,
> lie you won't tear down, coming after me…

That song has brought me to tears many times. Again, his name is probably cursed over a million times every minute of every day but he's not shaken or offended enough to where he's not willing to forgive those who sincerely come to him in repentance and I was no different. That to me is a greater miracle and of greater importance than all the health and prosperity ever given unto man. It's not only our faith in him that's revolutionary, it's his faith and mercy towards us and how he stands on his Word that is revolutionary and mind-altering. He's big enough to see through to our trauma and to where all of our anger and frustration stems from and forgives it all when we come to him in faith. We live in a deceptive world with a diluted sense of reality that he's selflessly committed to saving us from. Hebrews 11:6 says, "Without faith it is impossible to please him, for he who comes to God must believe that he is, and that he is a rewarder of those who diligently seek him." I would say it's impossible to diligently seek God if all you're living for is an expectation from him. For him, there has to be a sincere acknowledgement there, especially in regards to sin. This is where mercy defines itself because imagine God struck down each person who cursed the name of Jesus around the world. There would be millions of dead corpses scattered throughout the globe within seconds. I think about 50% of the western world would probably be dead within 24 hours. It reminds me of this video I saw years ago with this man getting struck by lightning. You can still find it on YouTube if you search for it. There was a surveillance camera up high looking down on a residential street. Eventually out from the bottom of the screen you'll see a couple walking hand-in-hand across the street towards their car in the evening. A few seconds later another man walks up behind them seemingly to rob them but gets struck down by a bolt of lightning. After he gets hit he slowly gets to his feet all groggy but seems to be going back where he was headed before to rob them. He then gets struck down again by another bolt of lightning. There's so many analogies to work with here, but it's amazing how he kept going as if getting struck by lightning wasn't warning enough of his sinful desire and pursuit. My point is, imagine God struck each of us down not only for cursing him but for every unseen, hidden thought or sin we commit. I think the world would probably last about 10 minutes or less. We'd be all living in a petrified state of fear every second of the day. The world doesn't understand God's mercy nor his love or his hatred for sin because to love righteousness is to hate sin.

Why God Hates Sin

God has to hate sin to love us. I love how one preacher put it, he says,"...for us to love we have to hate in righteous indignation because to love is to hate sin...If you love Jews you must hate the Holocaust. If you love African Americans then you must hate slavery. If you are truly good, righteous and love all that's pure and beautiful, then you must hate." We reserve that right for ourselves but won't give that right to God. For God to love and bless a marriage and family he has to hate fornication and adultery. He has to hate homosexuality to love family because not only does it go against his design, their is no family generated in homosexuality. There's no mother, no father, no sisters or brothers and no generation to follow. We want it both ways but that's where common sense and tolerance are destroying us. For God to love homosexuals he has to hate the STD's and sexual promiscuity that's killing them. Ultimately, he doesn't need our approval to exercise his right and we've come to a point where we've pushed his mercy to its limits. 2 Corinthians 5:10-11 says, "We must all appear before the judgment seat of Christ, that each one may receive the things done in the body, according to what he has done, whether good or bad. Knowing, therefore, the terror of the Lord, we persuade men, but we are well known to God, and I also trust are well known in your consciences." The Bible in a nutshell is God saving us from his own righteous judgement in Christ and there's some pretty weighty scriptures that testify to that. 1 Thessalonians 6-10 says, "It is a righteous thing with God to repay with tribulation those who trouble you, and to give you who are troubled rest with us when the Lord Jesus is revealed from heaven with his mighty angels, in flaming fire taking vengeance on those who do not know God, and on those who do not obey the gospel of our Lord Jesus Christ. They shall be punished with everlasting destruction from the presence of the Lord and from the glory of his power, when he comes, in that day, to be glorified in his saints and to be admired among all those who believe, because our testimony among you was believed." There are many more heavy scriptures that definitely make us question our moral tolerance and complacency. The truth is, that God is not in contemplation with himself and isn't wavered or persuaded by our futile allegations concerning him either. He's compelling the world by the Holy Spirit and through the Word of God to change its heart and turn from its sin, and in that willingness a relationship with him begins. A good Father forgives the mistakes and nuances of his children and is there to teach and guide them through the process of life without compromising in his convictions and God is no different when we become his children through faith in Jesus Christ.

More Of Defining Faith

He is the God of truth and holds us to the truth he proclaims for our own benefit. He doesn't sugarcoat life as though it's a complacent pass through or carpet ride like many of these false teachers are promoting to us. They're merely selling faith out and abusing grace with every word from their mouths. Faith is a responsibility and a test through circumstances and over earthly priorities and at times there isn't an immediate prosperous benefit to our faith as there isn't in any genuine relationship. God isn't a vending machine or some credit card we rack up debt with, then pay back at our own leisure. Faith is a commitment and an unwavering consistency that is about confronting reality and truth head-on. It's about abstinence, patience, forgiveness and perseverance. I heard once that adversity is an opportunity for ministry and that's a great way of perceiving faith. In Paul's first letter to the Thessalonian church he sent Timothy to establish and encourage them concerning their faith. He says, "No one should be shaken by these afflictions, for you yourselves know we were appointed to this." There's a destination to faith and that isn't necessarily defined by the result of it in this world. As we hold on to our belief in our most grievous seasons of life, faith continues to be defined through the process. The truth of faith is it is about suffering at times and about learning and exercising persistence. Forgiveness and abstinence can be painful attributes of our character and disciplines in faith and that's the painful reality of it. Abstinence is defined as a self-enforced restraint from indulging in bodily activities that are widely experienced as giving pleasure. The truth is that it is extremely difficult especially in regards to our hormones and money. We all want the pleasures of life but without maturity and restraint, pleasure has its consequences. Dangling prosperity and health in our faces is cruel and arrogant and through this pandemic these kinds of heretical teachers look like complete monsters. I've needed someone to confide in, not someone to bribe me or tease me from the position they've gained by attributing their prosperity to faith. It's been depressing going through this pandemic and the aftermath of my accident to be completely honest. The world outside doesn't skip a beat concerning me. I've felt like an anti-social cave-dweller coming out of his lair some days and I know many are feeling the same way but I'm fighting through it all in faith and learning millions of people face these struggles, internal fears and insecurities in their lives and have throughout history. People have been through far more than this pandemic in the course of history and we haven't done anything in our generation to deserve any favour from God otherwise and only faith reveals that to us. Nevertheless, this is the generation with an opportunity for ministry and an influence to uphold. We are of the living and we need the wisdom and maturity of faith to transform us spiritually and psychologically. Proverbs 2 says, "My son, if you receive my words, and treasure my commands within you, so that you incline your ear to wisdom, and apply your heart to understanding; Yes, if you cry out for discernment, and lift up your voice for understanding, then you will understand the fear of the Lord, and find the knowledge of God. When wisdom enters your heart, and knowledge is pleasant to your soul, discretion will preserve you."

My fear is that this generation has been so psychologically manipulated that it's impossible to convince or persuade otherwise. I feel faith can heal and resolve this and the emotions within us simply with the hope and refuge it generates for the soul, but again, as we've digressed in our ignorance and unbelief, satan's deception has progressively infiltrated our minds and households without us even knowing it.

Our Impressionable Minds

Hundreds of opinions, perceptions and diversions can consume and cloud our thoughts simply being idle at home and being bombarded by the influences on TV and social media. It's hard to pick up on without the Holy Spirit as our guide of discernment and now with this pandemic, it will get even worse. It's troubling how we've succumb to fear, and how deeply they have impacted our compatibility and self-esteem. We've become extremely self-conscious, disillusioned and jaded in our cognitive interaction before even walking out the front door in the morning. We've all bought into satan's methodical plan and been conformed subliminally and subconsciously by our own fears and impulses. He is a psychological psychopath and become the god of our impulses, derailing us in our lack of discernment, restraint and discipline. I just watched the Super Bowl where the halftime show was Shakira and Jennifer Lopez lip syncing and dancing around for 15 minutes as onlookers cheered them on. Shakira gyrated her vagina like she was having an orgasm on stage and Lopez slid up and down a stripper pole in her lingerie the whole time. We just don't realize the influence and impact this kind of entertainment has had on us spiritually and psychologically. 50000 sets of eyes in the audience and hundreds of millions around the world are drawn to the derrieres and vaginas of two mothers in their underwear. It's so demonic and demented but we embrace it and cheer them on as though the entertainment is worth the lustfilled repercussions. The men are filled with lust, the women are jealous in envy and the kids are influenced by our justification of it all as adults. As true faith peters out so does intolerance, compliance and conviction and we grow more and more desensitized and immune to moral and spiritual relevance. Our moral standards and discernment have become completely desensitized in the last few generations and our minds have become vicarius, fantasy driven vessels of depravity. Vicarious is defined as being experienced in the imagination through feelings or actions of another person and that is the overriding power and influence of entitlement and idolatry these days. These two women are obviously physically beautiful to the eyes but are just being used as pawns for satan's plan of conformity and don't realize the influence and rippling effect it causes in the hearts and minds of men and women all over the world.

The allure of fantasy and fictional tales are dangerous gateways for the imagination to lose focus on true reality for adults and children but especially children because they are so impressionable and vulnerable to adult influence. They create an illusion through sensationalism that methodically broadens the gap from true reality. Sensationalism is defined as the use of exciting or shocking stories or language at the expense of accuracy, in order to provoke public interest or excitement and that's exactly what's taking place around us through these lenses even in the simplest of commercials or advertisements. Those words "expense of accuracy" are more detrimental to us than we think. We stare naively at these screens thinking they are resolving our emotional needs but they have become strong mechanisms for satan to enhance our emotional dependency and coerce, divert and control our minds. How many men have taped that halftime show around the world and masturbated to it? If we truly knew, I think the numbers would be alarming. We're becoming addicted to the show and to the experience, but all it's showing us is our true colours.

It's not only on television, we're becoming enslaved screen hounds to these cell phones, iPad devices and whatever other distracting lens of technology impresses upon our time and attention. Baywatch was the number one show on television for years but it's only an illusion that's enhanced the lust within men all over the world. They pay dozens of extras to walk back and forth in the background with the camera focussed on their rear ends, vaginas and breasts. It's a false reality they create that merely enhances the expectation and desire within us all. We forget that we are all one click of a button away with television and these handheld gateways from being an impulsive consumer and drawn into an alternative motive and agenda. They are extremely dangerous dependencies and without spiritual discipline and discernment we are so gullible in our insecurities to the sinister and diluted intentions behind them.

Satan is a mastermind at accentuating it all and creating social unrest and insecurity through these lenses. The world can't see how he does it especially if they don't believe he exists from a spiritual perspective and in his biblical identity. Many see the devil as this little red cartoon character with horns and fangs and I'm sure he loves that alias or depiction of him, but it goes far deeper than that in cause and effect. He causes it by enhancing the carnal desires and emotions within us, which in effect cause the reactive implosion. It's incredible what we can't recognize without God and how impressionable we are even as assumably mature adults. 2 Corinthians 4:3-4 says, "Even if our gospel is veiled, it is veiled to those who are perishing, whose minds the god of this age has blinded, who do not believe, lest the light of the gospel of the glory of Christ, who is the image of God, should shine on them." They're all calculated diversions and sophisticated strategies to implode our society and are part of satan's global domino effect for totalitarianism and he knows that faith in Christ is the greatest opposition to his plan. It's much of the reason for this book and what concerns me more than anything as I see the effects in their procession around me. For instance, daytime soap operas draw the viewer into these vindictive plots of sexual fantasy and betrayal, specifically targeting women alone during the day. Their minds get lost in the drama and fantasy of it all and then get filled with thoughts of adultery and sensuality, getting hooked into the storylines. They then start questioning and devaluing their own lives, dedications and obligations to their partner or family. If they're married, their husbands come home to a negatively influenced despondent mind and attitude that's been coerced into believing in their own unfulfillment. Their husband then turns to their own emotional escape on television or their cell phone feeling unappreciated, to combat the rejection. Meanwhile, in the divisive separation from the influence, the kids are left to their own devices being subject to manipulation themselves from the lack of attention, affection, unity and discipline in the home, murdering people in video games to appease and justify their own emotions. Here's a family divided simply by the coercive influence of a lens. It can be so subtle to the faithless, complacent and untrained heart and eye but when you see it, it's like a blueprint of terrorism unveiling itself before your very eyes. Terrorism can be psychological as well as physical, dont kid yourself. Subtle is defined as delicate or precise as to be difficult to analyze or describe and that's what's subconsciously infiltrated our minds. Again, it's subtle and has been a generational progression of desensitization for decades. It's a curse word here, a raised skirt there or a set of breasts to enhance our subconscious desires, slowly desensitizing us and lowering our standard of morality, increasing the expectation and demand within us all. The halftime show, Baywatch and soap operas are just three of the avenues satan uses to influence our society. Sets of eyes and ears come in all ages and emotional ranges and he aims to negatively influence them all. It's sad to see how the years of desensitization have turned into a twisted state of rebellious liberation. All the hits and likes are revealing proof of how sinful we are and what our desires and emotions are drawn to. Every time we hit the subscribe button or enhance the ratings to a show or movie, we further incriminate and victimize ourselves. The statistics don't lie and each click gives satan the glory over our will. I was flipping through the channels the other day and there was a full-blown anal sex scene going on in a movie. The two actors were just going at it with no shame, for the whole world to see. There's still discretion on some channels but you can find it if you want to and these kids are better with technology these days than any of us adults. It's no-holds-barred these days and all we're doing by watching this garbage is fueling its intended purpose more and more. There's a station I found while flipping the channels that is even worse. There's a show called naked attraction where five men and women are naked with their heads hidden until the end of the show. The one lady or man picks off each contestant one by one while the camera focuses on each of their genitalia, then at the end when he or she finally decides which one they like, they get completely naked themselves on the stage and walk off into the sunset together. The show right after has two complete strangers meet, strip each other's clothes off and get into bed right away with a voice in the background daring them to proceed further. Then the show after that is called popup porn which has a transvestite narrating actual real life homosexual porn with different storylines of men giving other men anal and oral sex. We've come a long way from Mister Dressup and Sesame Street these days. We've become infatuated with sex, violence and shock value and haven't understood the accumulative effects and impact they've had generationally on all of our minds. There have been discretionary institutions pleading for the moral cause but nearly everything has become accessible or been bought out by satan's minions over the years to carry out the agenda.

I watched a YouTube video a while ago called "Out of Shadows," about a former stuntman in Hollywood who broke his back doing a crazy stunt. He started researching the occult and their luciferian dialect and found out how real it all truly was behind the scenes. He said he didn't come to know God from going to church, he came to know God from how real the luciferian society and occult world truly were and it scared him. He said there's a very small group of people that influence all of the companies that we watch whether it be Disney, Marvel, Lucas Studios or many others. This small group of people control the narrative and content we all watch. It makes you think you have all these choices but you actually don't. The question is who's telling them what to put on those channels and movies and what is their agenda? They are a very sophisticated and collaborative coalition of entrepreneurs that the common simpleton is oblivious to, who are possessed by the spirit of satan. Unfortunately we've been seduced and fallen victim to their influence and entrapment. Discretion has become a thing of the past for the most part, and is actually used now to define our freedom of rights and democratic liberation in tolerance. Some of the storylines these days are purely evil and deeply rooted in sorcery and the occult, which reflect the psychology of satan and how perceptive he is to our carnal nature, but we seem to be affectionately mesmerised by it all as though the fantasy hasn't influenced or affected our reality. Even if we do, we don't care because that's become a basis to our human rights. This is a dangerously naive perception we've accepted and we need God to open our eyes before truth and virtue are completely consumed. I took some notes down on a few movie introductions that say it all. "Patient zero" is a movie about a super virus that has turned humankind into highly intelligent, streamlined killers, and an asymptomatic victim that can communicate with the infected must lead the last survivors on a hunt for patient zero and a cure. "Here alone" is a movie about a young woman named Anne who struggles to survive after a mysterious epidemic decimates society. She leads an isolated life and battles the threat of the bloodthirsty survivors who were infected and lurk outside the forest. But when her supplies run low, she must make the desperate journey into town to forage for any remaining food.... "Pandemic" is a movie about a devastating virus outbreak that plunges the world into a state of chaos. Zombies roam the streets while survivors fight to stay alive. They aren't just movies about viruses and pandemics either, there's countless movies about demons and supernatural forces these days. The movie "Legion" is literally psychotic with all the biblical references which trailer reads,

"A group of strangers in a diner suddenly find themselves surrounded by demons. Their only hope lies Michael, an archangel, who wishes to protect the unborn child of the restaurant's waitress." The entire movie these demons are bent on stabbing the baby to death in her stomach as it's apparently the last hope for humanity. The movie Constantine is about a detective who comes to Constantine who is an exorcist to help her investigate her twin sister's death. As he digs deeper, he realizes a dark conspiracy which could threaten the world. I could go on and on but these scripts are so intricately demonic and written to increase the paranoia within us all. They're also ironically timely in relation to the world's events weather it be viruses or terrorism. These aren't coincidental but we've come to see everything as a fantasy or some sci-fi reality, until true reality comes knocking at our door, our phone rings about a loved one or we ourselves are laying in a hospital bed. I'll never forget the day I got the call that my best friend was murdered in front of his house. It's an emotion I saw as fictional until I was forced to deal with the reality of it all myself.

No Excuse

As adults and especially as parents we should be ashamed of ourselves. All the vulgarity, promiscuity and violence going on before our eyes is daunting and horrific. These horror movies are full of demonic torment with women and children being subject to their cause. There's women being beaten and raped in the storylines and men possessed by murderous rage. They are so realistic and graphic these days and have shed more blood in these scripts to fill an ocean but we again seem to be infatuated by it all. It's one thing to make documentaries and non-fictional reenactments of historical events for us to learn and grow from but these new movies are inspired by the spirit of demons. They're appalling, atrocious and despicable and

I wouldn't want to be the writer's, producers and directors of these movies when they'll have to face God. They want to produce horror for us to see but the horror will most certainly be turned on them far worse than anything their imaginations can generate. Regardless of them, we are a horror unto ourselves with what we allow into our minds and homes and even though it's being imposed upon us, we're still willfully subjecting ourselves to it and embracing it more and more, in fact, we're relishing in it. Satan is literally mocking God's creation and watching us succumb to his influences in our ignorance and complacency. You can see how it's all being implemented now as millions are isolated at home and drawn to the deception of fear and depravity, glued to these lenses with their faithlessness and unsecured emotions. Instead of purifying and glorifying what's good and ethical as faith compels us to do, we've come to purify and glorify what's evil and feeding and fuelling the devil's sadistic machine.

We all love to point fingers at societies increasing depravity but we are all embracing it internally to some level. What we approve in our eyes sometimes reflects what's going on in our heart, whether it be jealousy, envy, resentment, anger, lust or revenge. Whatever the emotions are, satan is there to enhance them in vicarious outlets that somehow justify their temporary emotional release. Don't get me wrong, movies and television are at times incredible works of art and again, can be extremely creative and inspirational when used in a positive way to influence us or recreate qualities of mind and character but they're few and far between these days and most are devilish containers of subliminal and telepathic wrath. Telepathy is defined as the capability of transmitting thoughts to other people and of knowing their thoughts and this coalition of hollywood psychopaths I speak about has accumulated knowledge through profiling for years. Profiling is defined as the recording and analysis of a person's psychological and behavioral characteristics, so as to assess or predict their capabilities in a certain sphere or to assist in identifying a particular subgroup of people. They'll goat us in with sympathy for the main character, targeting our own emotions and then use the sympathy to justify his or her revenge and murderous vindication. They've even gone so far as turning the villains into cult heroes. Everything is a dramatic climax within our emotions and they use suspense to draw us into the storylines. We get mesmerized by the music, cinematic beauty and drama of it all but hidden behind it all are coercive plots of deception. Again, somehow we justify it all as entertainment in the satisfaction and stimulation it brings our unresolved emotions. Our selfish way of thinking is that if it doesn't affect us personally then we disregard the general influence and impact on the world as irrelevant. We also attribute the success and affluence of the actors, producers and directors as justifiable means to the work presented to us because we naturally justify the pursuit we're on and striving for. It's seductive and all hidden behind the escalating power of fame and idolatry. Again, these are the ramifications of a Godless world living to appease its impulses and disregard its conscience. I'll never forget a line in a movie I was watching that said, "To deny our impulses is to deny the very things that make us human." This is one of the greatest contradictions I've ever heard but it's what these psychopaths use in these scripts to manipulate our subconscious. Unfortunately this mindset has severe accumulative repercussions that individually we just can't see unless we look at life beyond ourselves and our own needs, and see it all from an eternal and influential perspective. Sometimes we not only justify our priorities but we justify the hostility we're being subject to through the lens due to the hostility within ourselves but when we become wise to our own personal hostility, we become wise to the implosion around us and the illusion and agenda the world is subjecting itself to through these lenses. What influences us naturally compels our decisions but without God's spirit we can't seem to refrain ourselves from the enticement of the world's influence in our carnal propensity. We have no source for reference to expose it or be accountable to and we just react according to our feelings. Unfortunately this is where the wool has been pulled over our eyes and where the spiritual realm is holding us captive in its power over our impressionable will. This is why faith in Christ holds a far deeper significance than merely from a religious or superficial perspective. This battle is real and affects us emotionally and psychologically and unless we are spiritually inclined and regenerated, we fall victim to it's deception. The ramifications are everywhere with people committing suicide and getting murdered and raped every hour of the day. There's infidelity, divorce and fornication running rampant and for what? It's all for a piece of the pie and in the pursuit of social validation and of what's being promoted. Our identity has been defined for us and we're destroying ourselves trying to attain it.

Chapter 6

Celestial Beings

The word spirituality has evolved over the years in it's carnal definition and has widely expanded throughout the world in its interpretation. Unfortunately that's part of the deception in of itself because spirituality doesn't evolve at all. Google defines spirituality as a broad concept with room from many perspectives. It says, "In general, it includes a sense of connection to something bigger than ourselves and typically involves a search for the meaning of life. As such it is a universal human experience. Something that touches us all." I'm sure that is satan's favourite definition of spirituality in its disassociation to him and God. It sounds like the writer is trying to appease everyone's individual perspective and not to be prejudiced against a certain one, which I can understand secularly, but as a Christian I understand far more than they do spiritually and I know that plays right into satan's plans of complacency. If I were to rewrite that as a Christian I'd say, "Spirituality isn't a broad concept at all because a concept is much like a theory and doesn't solidify or define anything. Spirituality is evidence through faith and there's one perspective. In general, it involves the connection to God who is bigger than ourselves and involves the meaning of life."

Spirituality in the world gives no prevalence to an actual entity at work in the field, whereas Christianity defines and identifies with them and their intentions. I see them as unseen spiritual forces or angelic beings that exist between physical matter and the properties within the air much like the humidity in the air and how it's actually water but we can't see it or how we see stars as solid mass in our eyes but are actually made up of gases. I speak in simpleton terms because when it comes to the properties or substances that form these beings it goes beyond my area of expertise or any of our scientific capabilities. These entities do exist though regardless of how we can scientifically prove it otherwise and are conscious of our consciousness and the influence and impact over our decisions. How they restrictively coexist between realms is beyond me outside of the biblical explanation. In 1 Corinthians 15 Paul says, "There are also celestial bodies and terrestrial bodies; but the glory of the celestial is one, and the glory of the terrestrial is another." Prophets of the Old Testament like Ezekiel speak of angelic beings in visions and describe them intricately. Ezekiel 1 says, "The appearance of their workings was, as it were a wheel in the middle of a wheel. When they moved, they went toward any one of four directions, they did not turn aside when they went. As for their rims, they were so high they were awesome, and their rims were full of eyes, all around the four of them. When the living creatures went, the wheels went beside them, and when the living creatures were lifted up from the earth, the wheels were lifted up. Wherever the spirit wanted to go, they went, because there the spirit went, and the wheels were lifted together with them, for the spirit of the living creatures was in the wheels. When those went, these went, when those stood, these stood, and when those were lifted up from the earth, the wheels were lifted up together with them, for the spirit of the living creatures was in the wheels. The likeness of the firmament above the heads of the living creatures was like the colour of an awesome crystal, stretched out over their heads. And under the firmament their wings spread out straight, one toward another. Each one had two which covered one side, and each one had two which covered the other side of the body. When they went, I heard the noise of their wings, like the noise of many waters, like the voice of the Almighty, a tumult like the noise of an army, and when they stood still, they let down their wings. A voice came from above the firmament that was over their heads, whenever they stood they let down their wings." This is an incredibly detailed description and in Isaiah 14 he even describes satan himself saying, "How you are fallen from heaven, O Lucifer, son of the morning! How you are cut down to the ground, you who weakened the nations! For you have said in your heart, I will ascend into heaven, I will exalt my throne above the stars of God, I will also sit on the mount of the congregation, on the farthest sides of the north, I will ascend above the heights of the clouds, I will be like the Most High. Yet you shall be brought down to sheol, to the lowest depths of the pit. Those who see you will gaze at you, and consider you, saying; is this the man who made the earth tremble, who shook kingdom's, who made the world as a wilderness and destroyed its cities?" The New Testament speaks of angels and demons as well. It even speaks of demons as fallen angels. In Revelation 12:7-9 it says, "A war broke out in heaven, Michael and his angels fought with the dragon; and the dragon and his angels fought, but they did not prevail, nor was a place found for them in heaven any longer. So the great dragon was cast out, that serpent of old, called the devil and satan, who deceives the whole world, he was cast to the earth, and his angels were cast out with him. In Jude1:6 it says, "The angels who did not keep their first estate, but left their own habitation, he has reserved in everlasting chains under darkness for the Judgment of the great day." It goes on in Jude with that specific angel again named Michael arguing with the devil. There's many other scriptures that speak of demons. James says, "If you believe there is one God, you do well, even the demons believe and tremble." Matthew says, "When an unclean spirit is gone out of a man he walks through dry places, seeking rest, and finds none." Matthew also says God gave his disciples power over unclean spirits, to cast them out, and to heal all manner of sickness and diseases. Peter reiterates Jude's words and says that God didn't spare the angels that sinned but cast them into hell and delivered them into chains of darkness to be reserved unto judgment. Mark says when the unclean spirits saw Jesus, they fell down before him and cried, "You are the son of God." Luke says that Mary Magdalene had been healed of seven evil spirits. Mark says a demonic spirit threw a boy into convulsions and made him foam from the mouth and gnash his teeth. In describing angels Hebrews says that humans are made a little lower than the angels and that they are ministering spirits sent to serve those who will inherit salvation. It speaks of thousands upon thousands of angels in a joyful assembly much like it does in Revelation. Hebrews 13:1 says, "Let brotherly love continue. Do not forget to entertain strangers, for by doing so some have unknowingly entertained angels." Matthew speaks of angels concerning children and says to take heed because their angels always see the face of God who is in heaven. He says the Son of Man will come in his Father's glory with all his angels and give reward to each person according to what they have done. He says in chapter 24:3, "He will send his angels with a great sound of a trumpet, and they will gather together his elect from the four winds, from one end of Heaven to the other." Luke says that there is rejoicing in the presence of the angels of God over one sinner who repents. There's many more but Revelation speaks of them the most in the bible. One of them is Revelation 14:6 that says, "I saw another angel flying in midair, and he had the eternal gospel to proclaim to those who live on the earth, to every nation, tribe, language and people." In Revelation 4:8 it even reiterates some of Daniel's visions from the Old Testament and says, "Each of the four living creatures had six wings and was covered with eyes all around, even under its wings. Day and night they never stop saying, holy, holy, holy, is the Lord God Almighty, who was, and is, and is to come."

When it comes to angels and demons I think we like to create what we think they are in our imaginations and through these Sci-Fi movies but there is an actuality to them outside of our dimension that we're unaware of in our biblical illiteracy. I actually saw one myself years ago above my bed. It was as if the air closed inside itself and formed into a being like the movie Predator. It actually entered into my ex-wife at the time and she screamed bloody murder. It was somehow interconnected within her dreams because before I saw it she was being tormented over and over in her dreams as soon as she'd fall back asleep. Ironically it was the night of her baptism which is a whole other story. I also heard one speak through a drug dealer's money collector while doing street ministry that I'll mention later in the book. Whatever we call these spirits even as unbelievers, whether they be angels or demons, ghosts or paranormal activity like these new shows seem to suggest, they're real, and the presence of them seems to be everywhere. If we can't necessarily see them, we can feel them either around us or within us. Some people have an ora or presence about them as if they were encompassed by a spiritual entity that again, goes behind physics. My neighbor gave his life over to Jesus in his mid thirties but before that he was a major drug dealer on the downtown eastside here in Vancouver. He's told me crazy stories of murder, even by the cops but more eery is the stories of demons he'd see all the time down there. His stories were very descriptive and he had no reason to lie to me. In speaking of a spiritual entity, Job 4:15-16 says, "Then a spirit passed before my face, the hair on my body stood up. I stood still, but I could not discern its appearance. A form was before my eyes."

The truth of it all is that if we're being impacted, affected or influenced by something outside of ourselves then it gives claim to spiritual significance and prevalence in ourselves and the world around us. Many people feel they're being tormented especially those with mental illnesses like schizophrenia but noyone would willfully or consciously torment themselves therefore it has to be from an external source. A spirit is alive and present especially if it's voice is being heard in our mind and impacting our decisions, but unless we identify with the source and its purpose we can't discern the persuasion of the voices' claim. There are many convicted felons that have said, "The devil made me do it," but what was actually being transmitted within them is the truth and mystery behind the spiritual claim. Again, I suggest people read the screwtape letters by CS Lewis and see how involved these spirits can be in our minds and their intentions.

Discerning Spirits

An old saying is that satan's greatest lie is for us to believe that he doesn't exist and that's exactly what's happening around us in society without the revelation the Bible is meant to expose. Demons are running rampant attaching themselves to any false prophecies, heresies, doctrine or carnal premonitions that arise outside of Christ. 1 Timothy 4:1 says, "Now the spirit expressly says that in latter times some will depart from the faith, giving heed to deceitful spirits and doctrines of demons, speaking lies in hypocrisy, having their own conscience seared with a hot iron..." Interesting how it says doctrines of demons insinuating how intelligent they are in literary composition and in the manipulation of our minds. They also love our religious entitlement and biblical illiteracy because they live to deceive people into the worship of themself. They thrive in resentment and bitterness and they relish in our pride, ego and gossip, but what holds them powerless is forgiveness, love, support, and faith. 1 Peter 5:8-10 says, "Be sober, be vigilant, because your adversary the devil walks about like a roaring lion, seeking whom he may devour. Resist him, steadfast in the faith, knowing that the same sufferings are experienced by your brotherhood in the world. But may the God of all grace, who called us to his eternal glory by Christ Jesus, after you have suffered a while, perfect, establish, strengthen and settle you." Somewhere in the unseen world and dimension our carnal liberation is in severe conflict with God's sanctification and salvation. As we strive for our carnal aspirations and destiny in this world, God's selfless mercy is drawing us to the destiny of our souls. Demons and angels are at war over disassociation and sanctification and between them our conscious will is being drawn to both. The bible says that angels are ministers for those who will inherit salvation therefore demons are the opposing spirits to convolute and derail their objective and satan is the mastermind behind it all. They've severed their opportunity to serve God eternally for their impudence and insolence, and are now spirits of mischief who live for nothing except the downfall of the world and the ignorance and disregard of salvation. Angels on the other hand live in service to God and have held their vow as ministers of truth, perseverance and patience through faith and sincerity. In John's vision in Revelation 22:9 he fell down to worship the angel who showed him the visions but the angel then said to him, as in other scriptures, "See that you do not do that. For I am your fellow servant, and of your brethren the prophets, and of those who keep the word of this book." All these opposing spirits know the Word of God and know the outcome for themselves and for us in our free will to choose. So much of life from both sides of the spiritual veil has been built on holding on or selling out on the promise of things to come and the whole world will soon see how drastic of a mistake that was in our unbelief. Evidently, if even one claim to a spiritual entity or impartation of any kind has taken place in history, where does that leave atheists or agnostics? Where does that leave evolutionary science? It leaves them dead.

Heaven and Hell

If we only knew what surrounds us in the heavenly realms and what these opposing spirits are compelling us to conform to or abide in. If we felt hell for a split-second no one would want to go there, and if we experienced heaven for a split-second we'd all want to be there, but without faith none of it bears significant relevance to us anymore. Heaven and hell have merely become vain slang words in our language, but God's word most certainly declares otherwise. Again, people see the Christian faith as too black and white and too severe or rash of a decision to make, but for me the declaration is far too severe to simply be disregarded as irrelevant. In fact, the Bible warns us of hell far more than it speaks of heaven. The very last words of Isaiah in chapter 66:24 say, "They shall go forth and look upon the corpses of the men who have transgressed against Me. For their worm does not die, and their fire is not quenched. They shall be an abhorrence to all flesh." Psalms 9:15-17 says, "The nations have sunk down in the pit which they made, and the net which they hid, their own foot is caught. The Lord is known by the judgment he executes, the wicked is snared in the work of his own hands. The wicked shall be turned into hell, and all the nations that forget God." Revelation 21:7-8 says, "He who overcomes shall inherit all things, and I will be his God and he shall be my son. But the cowardly, unbelieving, abominable, murderers, sexually immoral, sorcerers, idolaters, and all liars shall have their part in the lake which burns with fire and brimstone, which is the second death." In Matthew Jesus says that hell is an everlasting fire prepared for the devil and his angels and for us who don't repent, it's a place of everlasting punishment. In Matthew he also says to not fear those who kill the body but cannot kill the soul. He says to fear Him who is able to destroy both soul and body in hell. In speaking of heaven 1 Corinthians 2 says, "No eye has seen, nor ear has heard, nor has entered into the heart of man, the things which God has prepared for those who love him." In Isaiah 25 it says

God will swallow up death forever and wipe away the tears from all faces and remove his people's disgrace from all the earth. Revelation 21:4 says, "God will wipe away every tear from their eyes, there shall be no more death, nor sorrow, nor crying. There shall be no more pain, for the former things have passed away." There's many more scriptures concerning heaven and hell but Luke 16 explains them in greater detail with Jesus's parable of the rich man and Lazarus. It says, "There was a certain rich man who was clothed in purple and fine linen and fared sumptuously every day. But there was a certain beggar named Lazarus, full of sores, who laid at his gate, desiring to be fed with the crumbs which fell from the rich man's table. Moreover the dogs came and licked his sores. So it was that the beggar died, and was carried by the angels to Abraham's bosom. The rich man also died and was buried. And being in torment in Hades, he lifted up his eyes and saw Abraham afar off, and Lazarus in his bosom. And he cried and said, Father Abraham, have mercy on me, and send Lazarus that he may dip the tip of his finger in water and cool my tongue, for I am tormented in this flame. But Abraham said, son, remember that in your lifetime you received your good things, and likewise Lazarus evil things, but now he is comforted and you are tormented. And besides all this, between us and you there is a great gulf fixed (or chasm), so that those who want to pass from here to you cannot, nor can those from there pass to us." Ultimately, we can incessantly disregard it all in unbelief as much as we want, but satan still exists and so does God, and angels and demons don't cease and desist their work in the spiritual realm on our conditions. Our unbelief doesn't change the outcome no matter how hard we want or feel it to be true. The judgment of God is inevitable.

Chapter 7

Satan's World

Ramifications of Sin

Again, the imminence of biblical Christianity is an unavoidable and impending certainty I wish people wouldn't take so lightly. Our faith teaches us to refrain from all these compulsive tendencies satan is enticing us into. Ephesians 4:26 says, "Do not sin, and do not let the sun go down on your wrath, nor give place to the devil." 1 Peter 4 says, "We shall no longer live in the flesh for the lusts of men, but for the will of God. We have spent enough of our past life time in doing the will of the gentiles, when we walked in lewdness, lusts, drunkenness, revelries, drinking parties, and abominable idolatries. In regard to these, they think it strange that you do not run with them in the same flood of dissipation, speaking evil of you." Without faith the world is our oyster in impulsive and sensual liberation and demons flourish as we are their hosts in our fleshly desires.

They've got every corner of our impulsive mind targeted and again, these lenses are the most influential gateways for them to operate. If we're angry or resentful we can watch the UFC, a homicide show or mass murder and bludgeon people to death in a video game. If our hormones are racing, we can watch a Miley Cyrus video, old reruns of Baywatch or watch a porno on the internet for hours on end.

Whatever our feelings or impulses are these days, moment-to-moment, the emotion can be temporarily stimulated through these lenses with one click of a button, but unfortunately the feelings merely intensify as we become more and more impulsive, desperate and jaded, sinning against God's design within us. The enticement increases the craving and impatience in our lives as our dopamine levels rise and fall, which ultimately leads to an unbalanced level of discontentment and dissatisfaction. We yearn and crave these pleasures in life especially from a sexual perspective because that's what's being advertised to us, but it generates an emotional and chemical imbalance and despondency within us that satan feeds on outside of our obedience to God and his objective for our lives. The definition of despondent simply says, "In low spirits from loss of hope or courage" and that's exactly how many of us have become without faith as our refuge and dissuader. 1 Corinthians 6:18-20 says, "Flee sexual immorality. Every sin that a man does is outside the body, but he who commits sexual immorality sins against his own body. Or do you not know that your body is the temple of the Holy Spirit who is in you, whom you have from God, and you are not your own? For you were bought at a price, therefore glorify God in your body and in your spirit, which are God's." Of course this pertains to believers but it's in the context of his design for each of us and where we've come otherwise. Ephesians 3:16-19 says,"...that He would grant you, according to the riches of his glory, to be strengthened with might through his spirit in the inner man, that Christ may dwell in your hearts through faith, that you, being rooted and grounded in love, may be able to comprehend with all the saints what is the width and length and depth and height, to know the love of Christ which passes knowledge; that you may be filled with all the fullness of God." The discipline of abstinence in faith has far more benefits than we realize. It's not only satan enticing us, we are to blame as well and have to take far more responsibility for our own vessels. Unfortunately we're not, we not only devalue ourselves sexually, we naively fuel our bodies with sugar, caffeine, energy drinks and garbage food all day long to supply our own demand for stimulation. The more we depend on these temporary fixes the more it shows how insecure we are without them. We ingest so much poison into our bodies I can't believe it's resiliency whether it be from food, alcohol, cigarettes, drugs, prescription pills or even salt and sugar. Until some sort of disease hits us we feel like we're invincible as though everything being advertised to us has our best interests in mind, without any repercussions. It's like being in a candy store and shoving everything we see into our mouth for hours and then wondering why we end up sick to our stomach. We're not designed to handle all the sugar and other chemicals they load in there, but we justify the initial feeling regardless of the outcome. It's much like how we've been created emotionally, we're not designed to handle the continual impulsive behaviour and pleasures of sin without consequence, especially from a sexual perspective. We're just burning out and yearning for more and more of what's tearing us apart and we're fuelling the fire and need ourselves. Again, it's our own sinful nature alongside satan's enticement that's destroying us. James 1:14-15 says, "Each man is tempted when he is drawn away by his own desires and enticed. Then when desire has conceived, it gives birth to sin; and sin, when it is finished, brings forth death."

Exposing Conspiracy

I see many have become wise to the physical manipulation in our foods and ingestion through growth hormones, GMOs, preservatives and manufactured chemicals which is great, but aren't aware of the spiritual and emotional manipulation that precedes much of our compulsion and physical dependencies. Satan and his minions have cornered every market of our cravings and have conspired to combine the two. Alot of our ingestive habits and obsessive disorders are triggered by the impact on our emotions and trauma. It's the root of almost every addiction whether it be alcohol, cigarettes, drugs or eating disorders and again, they've been in chemical labs around the world with this knowledge and intention to do so. We become very gullible in a weakened, insecure and vulnerable state of mind. They target our self-consciousness and self-esteem which trigger our impulsive and compulsive behaviours and dependencies. It's all a malicious game we're falling victim to due to the illusions and perceptions they've indoctrinated and used to deceive and control our minds by enhancing our fear and social anxiety. They've become our refuge filling the voids in our lives, replacing our relationships with each other and with God. When I say "they" as we hear so regularly from people these days, it's because there are people behind the scenes in these secret societies willfully and consciously implementing and orchestrating these vindictive practices. I mentioned conspiracy before, but don't be deceived, it's been their emphasis for decades and satan's progressive plan since the fall of mankind and the American dream now drives the incentive and agenda. Impulse makes profit, emotion molds the consumer and a consumer's dependency pays for an alternative agenda. These people are malicious opportunists and entrepreneurs. Without knowledge, obedience and restraint through faith we're prone to succumb to the practices they implement because the effects aren't recognized in our ignorance and blindness to it all. I just can't repeat that enough. For them to sell antidepressants, common sense would say, make the world more depressed. To sell cancer medicine and suck patients' bank accounts dry, common sense would say to lower our immune system and cause more cancer. The world is truly this evil behind all of our perceivable knowledge and if you don't think so, you're naive. Ephesians 4:17 says, "You should no longer walk as the rest of the gentiles walk in the futility of their mind, having their understanding darkened, being alienated from the life of God, because of the ignorance that is in them, because of the blindness of their heart; who, being past feeling, have given themselves over to lewdness, to work all uncleanness with greediness." The words "have given themselves over" struck me the most from this scripture. We just see comfort and convenience as justification to our emotional cause and the procession of life and that's as far as we take it. We've even come so far as attributing that all to God. I know I'm repeating myself in trying to reveal this stuff but I see it as the literal heartbeat of our imbalanced world and it bears repeating. We merely escape from our emotions instead of facing them but satan and his minions know how to make a door for each emotional escape. It almost has to be a continuous reminder these days with our minds in such an impulsive state of dependency.

Thankfully, God's spirit is this saving grace and his Word is unmatched in exposing and confirming it all. The effects are meticulously and maliciously hidden behind the forefront of our minds and sub-conscience. These are very devious and sophisticated practitioners in psychological and chemical warfare. They've mapped out every move in our households from the cupboards to the refrigerator and from the couch to the remote control. They've also mapped out every orifice of our bodies in what we ingest, from our oesophagus through our intestines and from our trachea through to our lungs. The weapons are pointed at us in almost everything we touch biologically or psychologically that poison us or trigger an impulsive response and we're sucked into it all by the power of advertising and the media. Whenever a product goes through a set of hands, there's an opportunity to alter its narrative. It's a world driven by supply and demand therefore they create the demand and own and regulate the supply. Even my last sentence has been affected by them because our memory partially triggers and influences our conscious decisions and without repeating some of my points, whoever reads this will register it, but probably forget it soon after due to the effects of the poisons in our air, food and water system. People think this stuff is conspiracy theory but again, they'd be surprised what length people will go and have gone for money and power. They're professional instigators and antagonists and have infiltrated every system and aspect of science, government and technology. They create a problem with the only solution to solve it. What's even crazier is we'll give them praise as though they're our saviour, much like with these vaccines. These people are lunatics. Interesting in defining antagonism it says to provoke hostility but is also used in reference to biochemistry and says antagonism, in ecology, is an association between organisms in which one benefits at the expense of the other. Ultimately, the opposite of independence is dependency and dependency is what makes profit and conforms our minds into a regulated and entrapped state of imperialistic socialism. This is their end goal and how they monopolize the world.

We're Being Poisoned

My book isn't necessarily a book on conspiracy but we've definitely been intentionally dumbed down into a complacent and naive state of mind, because again, if our conscience affects our rationality and restrains us from our impulsive decisions then their control and profit margins are less. It's basic mathematics. When you actually start studying some of the chemicals we're ingesting in our food, it's appalling, not to mention from a pharmaceutical standpoint. It's no wonder so many are becoming diabetic and dying of cancer and autoimmune diseases. Sodium fluoride is a chemical produced as a waste byproduct of phosphate fertilizer and aluminum production. It is highly toxic, contaminated with arsenic, mercury and radionuclides and has been shown to leach lead from pipes into the water supply. A Harvard researcher found that the consumption of fluoridated water lowers our IQ, memory capacity, causes bone cancer, kidney damage and various other severe health effects. We believe the false front that it's for our teeth by the government, but how much fluoridated water actually impacts our teeth when we're drinking it and when has the government actually cared or been concerned for our health? What is it doing within us after we ingest it is the real question. Unbenounced to the majority, it's also used in pesticides and rat poison. Unfortunately, the poison sits in our systems and each effect gives them the revenue intended. I'll admit our healthcare system is beneficial in some respects, especially here in Canada, and there is safe medicine but much of the science and technology we think is working for us is actually working within us for its own designed intention. Again, sometimes the end of that needle or that pill we swallow hold truths and narratives far more sinister than what we realize. Conspiracy to me is also in withholding information from the public, especially if it's affecting our health and well-being. People have been prescribed painkillers like Advil and Aspirin for decades but are now seeing the effects in kidney and liver damage. Talcum powder has it's benefits and is used in dozens of products but is now being linked to various cancers. In 1980 the FDA banned aspartame from use after having three independent scientists study the artificial sweetener, finding that it came with a high danger of inducing brain tumors. Somehow it has passed through the FDA since then and is used in all sorts of products like diet soda, gum, sugar-free candy, ice cream, low calorie yogurt and fruit juice. It's now said to cause headaches, dizziness, seizures, depression, ADHD, Alzheimer's, multiple sclerosis, cancer, lupus and congenital disabilities, yet it's still being mass produced and on the shelves of grocery stores around the world. The FDA has approved several food dyes that manufacturers add to candies, sport drinks, baked goods, salad dressings and even medications. Research indicates these dyes contain carcinogens that cause cancer in lab animals. As these dyes do not enhance the nutritional quality or safety of foods or medications, scientists continue to argue that they should not be added to food products. The question then is if these effects have been proven, why are they not banned and how do they pass through the FDA's hands? Why is aluminum in food additives like salt when it's been directly linked to Alzheimer's? How is microwave popcorn still on the shelves when it's directly linked to cancer? The lining of the microwave bags contains perfluorinated compounds to resist grease and prevent leaking but are a severe risk to our health. PFCs also exist in teflon pans, pizza boxes, and sandwich wrappers. These are products that are mass produced and used by millions every day. The FDA is funded by taxpayer money and is responsible for protecting the public health by ensuring the safety, efficiency, and security of human and veterinary drugs along with biological products, etc. My question is, are they actually fulfilling their obligations and what moral compass and standard are they living by? It seems many pets die of cancer these days as well. The World Health Organization has named both BHT and BHA as cancer causing compounds so how on earth do they get in these pet products? Beginning in 2007, there was a wide recall of many brands of cat and dog foods due to contamination with melamine and cyan uric acid. The recalls in North America, Europe, and South Africa came in response to reports of kidney failure in pets. My own dog had cancer in his jaw that spread through to his brain. Are we and our pets merely commodities and test subjects until these effects are publicized? Do they merely justify the mass production of these chemicals with the money that's generated? There's also been hundreds of recalls on corn-based pet foods that have contained elevated levels of aflatoxin which causes tiredness, vomiting, reluctance to eat, yellowish tints to the eyes and gums, diarrhea and even death. I thought we were being protected from these toxins but they seem to be taking their effect, even if the amounts ingested are minimal and unpublicized. The problem is 99% of the public don't have access to these laboratories or the discretion being implemented. We just blindly put our faith in science and the nobleness of humanity as though they're obligated to disclose all their knowledge and information. Sometimes what we assume is most detrimental to our health. Naturopaths are booked weeks ahead nowadays and are revealing so much of this kind of stuff. When it comes to cancer, science itself has proven cancer cells thrive in acidity or low pH levels but not in alkalinity or high pH levels, but we never see commercials or advertisements warning the public. They certainly aren't coming from our government. A diet high in alkaline foods like fruits and vegetables that limits acidic foods, such as those from animal products, will raise blood pH levels and create an environment in the body that discourages cancer growth, meanwhile we devour fried food, pop, dairy and coffee all day long. There's also processed meats and other foods with preservatives added that are dangerously acidic and carninegetic. The list is endless of these types of conspiracies but the longer products stay on the shelves, the more money they make. It's collateral revenue all the way down to the pharmaceutical companies. The government and these big corporations make billions on alcohol, firearms, cigarettes, prescription pills and lottery tickets, so we'd have to be asinine to think their primary concern is for our health, let alone our teeth. This same fluoride is in our mouths millions of times across the planet, every second of every day in our water supplies and in our toothpaste. The powers-that-be hold so much data and information from public knowledge it's insane, and again, we naively go about our lives as though they have our best interests in mind. The government are professionals at projecting empathy and being attentive in finding solutions and strategies for our needs but it's all a false front in balancing a severe deficit and ulterior motive. They're trapped in a contract and mandated themselves and doing whatever they can to lie their way through it and balance the budget, even if it's detrimental to our health. They put warning labels on cigarettes now but they sure aren't arguing with the revenue they take in. It's just another opportunity for them to lie, cheat, and steal. Science and technology is simply being promoted to optimize revenue and further our dependency upon it and them. In the wrong hands it has become chaostrophic to the welfare of our health and our planet. People think science will save us moving forward but just remember, science made the atom bomb and the outfit that made the chemicals for the atom bomb now makes the GMOs and herbicide for the majority of the world's agriculture. I suggest whoever reads this to look into Monsanto's history and see what you find.

There's obviously benefits to science in the right hands, don't get me wrong, but science also makes handguns and automatic weapons. Science and technology made asbestos and the ships that delivered millions of tons of garbage out to New York's harbour and dumped it. It then took the same brilliant bunch of scientists to realize this destroyed the ecosystem and they now need to find a scientific solution to save it. Seems to me a lot of brain power goes into blatant ignorance and stupidity. We spend a lot of time and money on science to save us from what it's already destroyed. Scientific devices detect pollution in the air that it's caused itself, along with mercury levels in the ocean. Brilliant. They say reaching the moon was science's greatest achievement but what did it actually achieve? A false hope and greater financial deficit? How brilliant. Again, my book isn't all about conspiracy theories, that is for each one of us to research on their own, but when you start lifting the dominoes of the pyramid, the truth of evil unveils itself before your eyes in a way you'd never expect. We've become like habitual sheep to these sinister plots with satan as the composer as we blindly and complacently trust the carnal process and go about our lives indifferent and oblivious to it all. Christianity is his adversary and what he aims to destroy not only from an eternal perspective but because it's the highest moral standard of abstinence, restraint and discernment that confronts the real issues and exposes these objectives. It reveals his true identity and the deception of evil into which the world will be consumed outside of salvation in Christ.

Perilous Times Will Come

Regardless if the world realizes it or not, from a spiritual perspective, Christianity is actually the only belief restraining the world from its complete implosion, in fact it's all foretold in the Bible and in place to do so. 2 Thessalonians 2:6-10 says, "Now you know what is restraining, that he may be revealed in his own time. For the mystery of lawlessness is already at work, only He who now restrains will do so until he is taken out of the way. And then the lawless one will be revealed, whom the Lord will consume with the breath of his mouth and destroy with the brightness of his coming. The coming of the lawless one is according to the work of satan, with all power, signs, and lying wonders, and with all unrighteous deception among those who perish, because they did not receive the love of the truth, that they might be saved." When God's Holy Spirit detracts from the scene, the possession of the demonic realm will take over like a cloud of death and the mercy and intercession of God will be gone forever. 2 Timothy 3:1 says, "Know this, that in the last days perilous times will come. For men will be lovers of themselves, lovers of money, boasters, proud, blasphemers, disobedient to parents, unthankful, unholy, unloving, unforgiving, slanders, without self-control, brutal, despisers of good, traitors, headstrong, haughty, lovers of pleasures rather than lovers of God, having a form of godliness but denying its power. From such people turn away!"

We have been fully warned and are getting very close to these prophecies coming to fruition. Satan knows his time is short and you can see how brazen he's become disclosing his identity and intentions through these lenses. There's movies out there these days that reveal the events in the near future that will prophetically unfold, but the onlookers are too naive to see how it's a reflection of themselves, mocking them in their unbelief. They're watching their own outcome unfold as though it's merely fictional entertainment and even endorsing and funding it. We become entertained and even become the encouragers to our own demise. There was a movie released in 2011 called Contagion by Steven Soderbergh, that made 135 million dollars in the box office. The trailer reads, "The death of Beth Emhoff and her son leads to the discovery of a deadly virus. While the US Centers for Disease Control struggles to curb its spread, a worldwide panic ensues." Point being is there are preemptive agendas behind these scripts that are far more than coincidental. The entertainment industry has been used as a tool for psychological conformity weather it be in viruses, terrorism, justification for war, sex, idolatry or whatever other form of manipulation precedes the agenda. It all forms justification to their cause and effect. The question behind all this apparent conspiracy theory I'm professing is who are these people and what is so far up their derrieres that they'd want to do all this? There's many answers to why in my opinion, of course the allure of money is one, but another is the discontentment in willful defiance. They stand with an infinite overhead of finances and impunity but they live in a cowardly state of dissatisfaction and emptiness. They have to hide from the knowledge they possess and from what they feel they've achieved financially. They live in a lie and all that's left to live for is themselves and the demise of the world, much like the demons that possess them. They've been lured into the trap themselves and been confined to its chains. It's impossible to be proud of something that they're forced to conceal in secrecy, especially if it's harming people. They are all pathetic cowards and they know it and they hate it. Their innocence is gone along with all the sanctity and purity of life, so they merely live to compensate for it. Again, much of their pathetic world is sworn to secrecy so I'm sure many minions are trapped in the extortion of the agenda into which they wish they'd never become involved initially, but the effects are transpiring regardless. It's amazing the power of idolatry and what sociopathic and psychological oppression it generates in the heart of man. It forms these diluted idiosyncrasies not only in these societies but in serial rapists and murderers as well. We grow in resentment and live for retribution. People will sacrifice so much of themselves for so little in return and these secret societies are an outlet to express that resentment. It's like being in an extremely sophisticated gang without ever having access to or knowledge of its leader's identity. You just get sold into the initial allure of its power, impunity and privileges, meanwhile selling out your soul as your knowledge supposedly increases. I'm going to talk more about these luciferian lunatics in the next few pages and in the conclusion of this book but to be honest, until you repent of your own sin and receive Jesus as Lord and Saviour, it's impossible to truly see the depths or extent of it all.

Ultimately, I want people to receive salvation for their soul as the primary reason behind this book so the truth doesn't alarm them into a deeper state of fear and anxiety as it encroaches upon them. 2 Timothy 1:7 says, "God has not given us a spirit of fear, but of power and of love and of a sound mind," but unless you receive his spirit the truth of the world's collusion will consume you into fear and paranoia. It's a good thing to die in Christ but you have to know him and the atonement he made for your sin first. I'd rather trust him over my soul than our government any day of the week, let alone these psychopathic monsters.

Sodium fluoride is the sole ingredient for rat and cockroach poison. It's MSDS sheet says it's corrosive and not for human consumption and the EPA classifies it as a pesticide, but our government who supposedly funds and oversees these organizations for upholding a standard of ethics, pour it into our drinking water for everyone to consume. I think people need to take a far more urgent approach to the salvation of their souls especially with this coronavirus pandemic going on, before death comes knocking at their door or the door of their loved ones and these poisons take their effect. I see it all as conspiracy and merely birth pains to system dependency and a precursor for them to implement justifiable monitorization and interrogation which will lead to forcible compliance. I know these things are hard to bear, but sometimes it's the depth of evil and the revelation of it that scares us into the reason for salvation, much like my own testimony and the Hollywood stuntman I mentioned earlier. I'm an extremely stubborn and skeptical person myself, but when I started pulling back the pages of time and researching the depth of evil, I assure you conspiracy is no theory. Again, what God wants to expose, satan imposes upon us all and in this insurging struggle the war rages on in the heavens and here on earth. Until we come clean with God and acknowledge the issue of sin within us, his plans monopolize and the murder and suicide rates rise, depression and anxiety escalate along with drug overdoses, sexually transmitted diseases, rape, cancer, violence, addictions to prescription pills and food and unfortunately the destruction of our planet. Interestingly the word monopoly is defined as exclusive ownership through legal privilege, command of supply, or concerted action. It says a monopoly exists when a specific person or enterprise is the only supplier of a particular commodity. This contrasts with a monopsony which relates to a single entity's control of a market to purchase a good or service. This is the desired goal of totalitarianism into which we're all falling victim. The goodness of the carnal mind cannot keep pace with the evil of the spiritual mind because the spiritual mind is cunning enough to use the carnal mind against itself. He'll even use our own sympathy and compassion from a carnal sense to shame those who understand the lie, which much of the division from the coronavirus vaccines is based upon.

Covetousness

For me the element of evil that seems most discreetly disguised is envy and comparison that's generated through these lenses. I cannot emphasize this enough to how damaged we all are because of it. It's the fuel they use to initiate so much collusion and why it's so crucial to understand God's Word and warnings. 1 Corinthians 13 says, "Love suffers long and is kind; love does not envy; love does not parade itself, is not puffed up; does not behave rudely, does not seek its own, is not provoked, thinks no evil." Galatians 5:22-26 says, "The fruit of the spirit is love, joy, peace, long-suffering, kindness, goodness, faithfulness, gentleness, self-control. Against such there is no law. And those who are Christ's have crucified the flesh with its passions and desires. If we live in the spirit, let us also walk in the spirit. Let us not become conceited, provoking one another, envying one another." The world has attached itself to a false reality it's been subject to but it's inadvertently the reality it's accepted for itself. We've allowed its influence to define life for us and to become our teacher. I see so many people discouraged with no self-worth as though validation and social acceptance is their only key to joy and happiness. It's like we're born into self deprecation as soon as idolatry influences our psyche. It's psychotic how disillusioned we've all become to envy and comparison. It's literally the heartbeat of our disposition in the majority of our interactive society. It generates psychological desperation in both men and women along with anxiety, eating disorders, plastic surgery, liposuction and even worse, the sexual pressure and expectation that's generated. The mirror is sometimes our worst adversary especially with women because of the unrealistic expectations we all put on ourselves for acceptance. It's just part of this pristine bar and comparative illusion satan enhances that we're all falling victim to that compounds our desperation and insecurities.

The impact affects us deeper psychologically than we all realize and is one of satan's most principal focuses. Whether it's a commercial with Cindy Crawford selling hair products and makeup or runway models selling lingerie, it drives the obsession for acceptance forward, but it has its reverse effect in rejection. For years runway models were presented close to anorexic but all it's done is set an unrealistic bar of expectation for acceptance and driven the value and dignity of women down. It's not just women and how they are presented and perceive themselves, we're all feeling this incessant pressure to acquire more and more and to achieve greatness in every opportunity that presents itself, like those we idolize, but all it's doing in a general sense is producing regret and inadequacy. Again, you can see its influence in almost every decision people make these days. The percentage of people living these glamorous, lavish and affluent lifestyles is so small in the big picture but we're drawn to its mirage through satan's lens of influence. It's incredible how empty and vain it all looks now amidst this pandemic. It's like we live with the belief that the more secured opinions and praise we receive from our achievements, equity or appearance the happier we'll be but it's just not true reality. It's all so temporary, in fact, the more opinions we draw to ourselves the more scrutiny and envy comes alongside because judgement tears down our perception of ourselves. At the end of the day, everyone is entitled to their own opinion and it's impossible to be affirmed in everyone. Also, the more we promote ourselves and create an identity, the more is expected of us to uphold it. All we end up doing is drawing people to our own internal fears and the insecurity within us. If all we're doing is living for acceptance then we have not accepted ourselves for who we are apart from it. I'll admit, some people thrive in it with their ego elevated and with the attention they receive, but the majority succumb to the pressure and expectation they put on themselves. If that's our ultimate goal in life, all we become is a slave to the opinion and we are never truly secure within ourselves outside of the attention or acceptance we receive. All the world does in its own insecurity is present a false impression of itself and life just becomes a circulating and dissatisfying proving ground. Satan has illuminated the glory of man and the pride within our ego to draw the attention of the world to ourselves to be recognized and validated, but in the process he's drawing us into our greatest fears and it's our fears that consume and destroy us. It's very deceiving but if you notice, there is no second place anymore in these lenses. Everything is about being the best whether it be in sports, music, acting or in business. Anything less isn't credible or praiseworthy because again, our priorities have been manipulated to desire the credit that's due. The Tampa Bay Lightning just won their second Stanley Cup in a row and in an interview with one of the players he said that only now he will be validated because they'd won two Stanley Cups in a row. It's become such a selfish and vain existence these days on so many levels. It's all about award shows, record books, paychecks, red carpets, trophy cases and the legacy you leave behind. The thing about being the best is what that says for all the rest. We think it's inspiring us but it's actually devouring and degrading us all in the covetousness that's generated. It's no wonder it's one of the ten commandments and mentioned 19 times throughout the bible. Jeremiah 6:13 says, "From the least of them even unto the greatest of them every one is given to covetousness; and from the prophet even unto the priest every one deals falsely."

I remember watching a pregame football show one Sunday and the whole hour's focus was on Peyton Manning and his career as a quarterback. All these announcers bantered about the whole hour was how unfulfilling and insufficient his legacy was by only winning one Super Bowl and whether he'd be inducted into the Hall of Fame or not. They literally tore him apart about not being the best of all time and continually compared him with those with better numbers. They presented all the statistics and records to the viewers and concluded their opinion about him being a failure and what a mediocre legacy he would leave behind. Here's a little boy who's innocent little dream was to have fun throwing a football. He pursues his talent and sees it as a career option. He then succeeds financially and plays the game he loves. He buys a house with millions in the bank for him and his family to enjoy and retire on without worry or concern for generations to follow. He donates his time and money to philanthropy and charities around the world and even ends up in movies and on Saturday Night Live. This guy has accomplished and experienced more in his life than 99% of the world's population yet his greatest fans are his greatest critics. It just goes to show that it doesn't matter how much you've achieved, how much attention you draw to yourself or how validated you are in your own eyes, someone will always be there to tear you down and they may be the ones closest to you.

It's the aftermath of it all that's the problem and why it says in Philippians 2:3- 4, "Let nothing be done through selfish ambition or conceit, but in lowliness of mind let each esteem others better than themselves, but each of you look out not only for his own interests, but also for the interest of others. Let this mind be in you which was also in Christ Jesus." The world has set the qualifications for us and this has made us all feel unqualified. It's also determined life for us which has wired our determination. 1 John 2:15-17 says, "Do not love the world or the things in the world. If anyone loves the world, the love of the father is not in him. For all that is in the world, the lust of the flesh, the lust of the eyes, and the pride of life, is not of the Father but is of the world. And the world is passing away, and the lust of it; but he who does the will of God abides forever."

Salvation At Hand

The first step in processing all of this as an individual, no matter your position in life is to admit it to yourself. Whether you are someone in retirement or a teenager in high school. Whether you're a wealthy entrepreneur or a housewife. Whether you're a young athlete chasing his dream or a dishwasher in a restaurant, we all need to stop, evaluate and forget ourselves and our own immediate needs and motives for a moment, especially amidst this pandemic, and ask ourselves, why do we as a whole generate such a problematic social dichotomy? Where is all of this anxiety and social unrest coming from? How have we become so system-dependent, who controls the system and do they have my best interests in mind? If there's any psychological insecurities within me then where are they coming from, and what is true security? We need to breathe, take a step back and not allow external influences to dictate and direct our own self-analysis and spiritual awareness. Again, we've unfortunately allowed the world to define and teach us life instead of God and we're living in the repercussions of that. God knows what's best for us because he created us. We're living three steps ahead of his calling upon our lives and God doesn't entice us into anything sinful, confusing or emotionally destructive. The spirit of the world convinces our minds to deny and detract the confrontational questions of eternity and our moral consciousness to appease ourselves into a continual benefit. The problem with that is if all we're living for is the benefit of ourselves then who else benefits? Galatians 5:13-15 says, "Brethren, you have been called to liberty, only do not use liberty as an opportunity for the flesh, but through love serve one another. For all the law is fulfilled in one word, even in this, you shall love your neighbour as yourself. But if you bite and devour one another, beware lest you be consumed by one another."

How is this scripture not relevant in today's society? I should write another book and just repeat that scripture ten thousand times to get it through our thick skulls. I speak to myself as well in how imperative it is to know and study God's Word. I guess the question pending for the world is do we truly believe in God's Word and are we willing to abstain from sin, bear faith's initiative and hold on for the promises to come? Do we truly love God, and what does that mean to actually love God? I don't think we even contemplate what that means in this day and age. It took a voluntary action on God's behalf in the person of Jesus Christ and we need to be thankful of that and careful of asking for more and more in this life from a God who's given it all. Jesus says in John 8:23-24, "You are from below, I am from above. You are of this world, I am not of this world....if you do not believe that I am He, you will die in your sins." We need to take this seriously, release our identity in the world and surrender it to God. We also must repent of our selfishness and pride and ask him for his forgiveness. He suffered the punishment for the sin we deserve and only when we acknowledge this, a relationship with him begins. Accountability is the initial stepping stone to salvation and seeing the world's inevitable course, again, I don't see the cross as an unreasonable option. It even goes deeper than that for me. The word option somehow cheapens his grace for me. I feel a sense of gratitude for what he's done and the mercy he's shown me. I'm eternally grateful and indebted to him and that compels me to want to serve others. I'm struggling with words to even articulate the severity of all this. We don't have the power within ourselves to save ourselves from death but Jesus claims that he is the resurrection and the life. I say it facetiously but that's a fairly profound statement to say the least. Our time is so short here in relation to eternity and if we could see where we would be now, again, we wouldn't hesitate, but that's what faith is in Christ. It's the belief in a better life to come and trusting in that promise regardless of our circumstances and not compromising God's convictions for the sake of our best life now. This is why satan's entire emphasis is to instill into our hearts, our best life now, so we live to claim it all for our own in every moment and kill ourselves and each other trying to attain it. We become faithless and selfish in our gluttony and the resources of the world rapidly dissipate in our narcissism and entitlement. It reminds me of the old Beatles song, "Live and Let Die" and that's exactly what we're doing marching to the beat of our own drum without God. The problem is deep down in our souls we know the truth God has instilled in our hearts, but we're just too scared to trust him enough to release our lives into his hands. The pride within us has become too strong and we hate the idea of relinquishing it. We feel like we need to hold on to something or see it with our eyes to prove it's real, but again, biblical faith is the substance of things hoped for, and the evidence of things unseen. In many ways living for our best life now is proving our lack of biblical faith. Ironically the famous prosperity preacher Joel Osteen has a book titled "Your best life now" but it's such a drastic and convoluted misrepresentation of God and faith on every level. Hebrews 11 defines those who lived in faith and says Moses chose to suffer affliction with the people of God rather than enjoying the passing pleasures of sin, and esteemed the reproach of Christ greater riches then the treasures in Egypt because he looked to the eternal reward. Faith is not only abstaining from sin and bearing its initiative which is hard, it's also living amongst sin knowing hell awaits the ungodly, and that is not an easy burden. It's exhausting and opposes everything the world's trained us to live for. 2 Peter 2:5-8 says, "God did not spare the ancient world, but saved Noah....a preacher of righteousness, bringing in the flood on the world of the ungodly, and turning the cities of Sodom and Gomorrah to ashes, condemning them to destruction, making them an example to those who afterward would live ungodly, and delivered righteous Lot, who was oppressed by the filthy conduct of the wicked; for that righteous man, dwelling among them, tormented his righteous soul from day-to-day by seeing and hearing their lawless deeds." When you become a Christian you start to see sin in everything and it can be a debilitating and depressive state of mind to live in.

The Word Will Come to Pass

The world is closing in around us spiritually and economically and even if we've found some sort of temporary solace and tranquility as individuals outside of Christ, don't be fooled, his words will still come to pass regardless. Jesus himself says, "Heaven and Earth shall pass away but my words will not pass away." I guess it goes back to the question if we believe these words of his are true. Not only in the promises to come but what we are living in right now. If it weren't true we wouldn't be in this disparaging internal struggle and fight within ourselves like we are. It's like the more we try to justify and liberate ourselves outside of God the worse everything gets. Ironic isn't it?

If we're living in such a supposed state of personal and spiritual liberty without Christ, then the question is why are we so progressively and exceedingly angry, bitter and incompatible? Why is the news and shows like Live PD and Cops on everyday telling the tale of our dysfunction and depravity? Why are the courts and prison systems increasingly overwhelmed with new criminals? Everything we're watching on TV is living proof of the truth of God and the fall of mankind. Why do counsellors have a never ending client base these days? Why are tens of millions of people dependent on painkillers and antidepressants to balance their instability? This willful liberation we've devised and defined for ourselves should bring us joy, peace, sustainability and satisfaction shouldn't it? The truth is that it's not, the world's a total disaster because we're defying our creator, defining life our own way in noncompliance and impeding his intention and calling for our lives. We're deceived otherwise and our indulgences aren't bringing the satisfaction desired or advertised. In the very words of Mick Jagger himself, "I can't get no satisfaction," and he's lived in the laps of luxury with promiscuous gluttony as his motto every day.

The thing about being called is whether we answer the call or not and by refusing to do so, we're failing to adhere or comply to the voice on the other end, severing his merciful hand in the process. God has called each of us to many things but he's called all of us to awareness through his Word. He repeatedly warns us of the deception of the world and the deceitfulness of sin. In 1 Peter 5:6-9 it says, "Therefore humble yourselves under the mighty hand of God....casting all your care upon him, for he cares for you. Be sober, be vigilant, because your adversary the devil walks about like a roaring lion, seeking whom he may devour. Resist him, steadfast in the faith, knowing that the same sufferings are experienced by your brotherhood in the world." It brings me back to the title of my book and how from a carnal sense, we're "blind in our afflictions" and don't see the conspiring evil of the world. I hate giving these psychopathic lunatics any more attention then they deserve, but we literally have more faith in them than we have in God, who sacrificed his own life for us. We put more trust in those poisoning, manipulating and murdering us than the one who was martyred for us and gave us his Word as a warning for us to follow. It's like God is pleading with us through every available lens of technology to recognize the ramifications of sin. It's staring us all right in the face and all we seem to do is welcome more, but the more we welcome it, the less justified we are in our excuse not to see it. 2 Timothy 3:12-15 says, "All who desire to live godly in Christ Jesus will suffer persecution. But evil men and imposters will grow worse and worse, deceiving and being deceived. But you must continue in the things which you have learned and been assured of.... you have known the holy scriptures, which are able to make you wise unto salvation through faith."

As I mentioned before, the scariest revelation in his Word and what I see coming is when God's patience reaches its limit and he refrains his voice, detracts his hand of mercy and gives us over to our reprobate mind. He's done it before in history and carnage ensued but in these end days it will be a catastrophic climax to the symphony of satan's final song. In defining reprobate Google says they are selfish, unprincipled, depraved, disreputable, and not known for their inner goodness. That's Google's definition but God's Word goes even further in defining a reprobate and says in Romans 1:18-32, "The wrath of God is revealed from Heaven against all ungodliness and unrighteousness of men, who suppress the truth in unrighteousness, because what may be known of God is manifest in them, for God has shown it to them. For since the creation of the world his invisible attributes are clearly seen, being understood by the things that are made, even his eternal power and Godhead, so that they are without excuse, because, although they knew God, they did not glorify him as God, nor were thankful, but became futile in their thoughts, and their foolish hearts were darkened. Professing to be wise, they became fools, and changed the glory of the incorruptible God into an image made like corruptible man and birds and four-footed animals and creepy things. Therefore God also gave them up to uncleanness, in the lusts of their hearts, to dishonor their bodies among themselves, who exchanged the truth of God for a lie, and worshiped and served the creature rather than the Creator, who is blessed forever. Amen. For this reason God gave them up to vile passions. For even their women exchanged the natural use for what is against nature. Likewise also the men, leaving the natural use of the woman, burned in their lust for one another, men with men committing what is shameful, and receiving in themselves the penalty of their error which was due. And even as they did not like to retain God in their knowledge, God gave them over to a "reprobate" mind, to do those things which are not fitting, being filled with all unrighteousness, sexual immorality, wickedness, covetousness, maliciousness; full of envy, murder, strife, deceit, evilmindedness; they are whisperers, backbiters, haters of God, violent, proud, boasters, inventors of evil things, disobedient to parents, undiscerning, untrustworthy, unloving, unforgiving, unmerciful; who, knowing the righteous judgement of God, that those who practice such things are deserving of death, not only do the same but also approve of those who practice them." God's definition sure makes us all take a longer look in the mirror. Apart from reprobate, the words that stand out to me most are "those who profess to be wise." Unfortunately, this is the world that surrounds us with people claiming their wills destiny as their own, right to the grave without any apologies to the life left behind. They disregard their sin and allow the world to deceive them into appeasing every desired feeling or emotion without any fear of consequence or judgment of God to come. Titus 1:15 says, "Unto the pure all things are pure: but unto them that are defiled and unbelieving nothing is pure; but even their mind and conscience are defiled."

It reminds me of a trick I learned catching fruit flies in the kitchen. If you put a little apple cider vinegar in a bowl, cover it in saran wrap and poke one little hole in the top, all of the fruit flies in the kitchen will gravitate towards it. One by one they fall victim to the enticement of their impulses. You'd think they'd catch on seeing so many die before them right before their eyes, but the enticement is just too strong. They fly through the little hole, get trapped and can't find their way out, then they panic and drown. It's like they're torn between impulse and discernment and that's exactly like satan's spiritual vacuum in the world and what the gospel saves us from. The gospel opens our eyes to the world's sin and the sin within ourselves and diverts our intentions and compulsion. When we become born again God's Spirit dwells within us who believe and his spirit is not an impulsive or sinful spirit at all. We are only truly liberated when we're not being controlled by our impulses or being enticed by them and can restrain ourselves. There's that old saying "everything in moderation" but God has us take a closer look at the word everything. When we listen to God through his Word, we start seeing the black hole the world is being sucked into. It's like a preemptive voice of confirmation as you navigate through life's choices and circumstances. There's also a sense of joy and liberation living inconspicuously without the need for acceptance and affirmation. When you're not being deceived you can live relieved. The last little fruit fly can save himself with a little discernment and carry on to battle another day, or it can proceed further and die like the rest. There's a choice there as there is for us, but again there's just so many angles satan has a hold of our attention and emotions these days. He bates us into his snares and without discernment and the revelation of God through his

Holy Spirit, it's a fierce struggle to overcome, especially in our own strength and wisdom. It was for me my whole life. Nothing the world offered resolved the problem and it became a never-ending emotional hangover. I can see now why so many people become paralyzed with social anxiety and depression and don't know where to turn to deal with it all to end the vicious cycle. Again, this will all be tested through this pandemic as people are being confined and isolated in their homes, forced to contemplate life, faith and their circumstances without impulsive stimulation and optimism as their refuge. I see a dangerous calamity ahead. Even optimism itself can be a deadly trap that a democracy and universalists get drawn into by satan. We seem to tolerate any belief or justify any philosophy that pushes our optimism forward. Unfortunately the world has taught us and supposedly scientifically proven to us that we've merely evolved from a rock and that there is nothing outside of ourselves to save us from ourselves. It's also taught us that we don't need saving. We've blindly and naively trusted that there's a progressive continuum to life and to our future and that science and technology will answer all of our problems moving forward. Unfortunately, much like the biochemistry we think is saving us, the technology we think will save us will be used as a concealed ambush to destroy us and completely entrap the world. It reminds me of a show called "rising tides" where dozens of towns and even entire cities are being swallowed up by water around the world. You'd think these brilliant scientists and governing powers with all their knowledge and access to technology would warn millions of people before these catastrophes occur, but they don't. They see it all through their lens but don't say a word. They have absolutely no care or consideration whatsoever for the well-being of the world and just live for the benefit of themselves.

We've been convinced that there is no reason for faith and hope beyond this world or a relationship with our creator because the theory of evolutionary science says that there isn't a creator. It's indoctrinated to little kids in kindergarten and has been ingrained in our schools curriculum and subconscious for decades. Of course satan wants us to believe that because we self-destruct without hope and accountability. It's an emotional and reactionary deathtrap believing that garbage. I've been there myself and it can be debilitating especially for those hypersensitive, self-conscious and insecure. We can come to a state of unrelenting fear in our own dependence where we feel trapped in our own vessel and identity and the only refuge is to escape from it through drugs and alcohol or hide from it all together in introversion. The person we see in the mirror isn't the person we want to be because again, the world has defined life's purpose and self-worth for us and we've believed it.

Chapter 8

"Many Are Called, Few Are Chosen"

For me personally, that's not all I've contended with over the years. A darkness has always loomed over my soul as though I've been selected or targeted for a deeper purpose or some sort of anointed calling or fate. Everything the world taught me was in complete contrast with what I felt was going on inside of me and the presence that was around me but I couldn't grasp what that was as an unbeliever. The word fate is defined as the development of events beyond a person's control and regarded as determined by a supernatural power. The word destiny is very similar and defined as our preordained path in life. Point being is that destiny and fate or even the word preordained can't exist outside of a predetermined course of action and these words should never be uttered by an atheist or even an agnostic for that matter because they're in complete contradiction of themselves and in the intuitive language we all speak and in the meanings they define. It's much like the word soul. Soul is defined as the spiritual or immaterial part of a human being regarded as immortal. The definitions vary because the word and properties of the soul are such a mystery but it also says the soul is regarded as a distinct entity separate from the body, and commonly held to be separable in existence from the body. My point is, what entity is this if it holds no physical properties? I guess you could go on with words like premonition, omen, harbinger, intuition, impartation, angels, ghosts, demons, spirits, or being immortal as well. These are words that can only be defined in faith because we cannot physically hold on to them or conclusively determine them carnally. Without God everything behind us or ahead of us is strictly coincidental and by chance and that to me is extremely naive.

Regardless how I perceived it all at the time, something existed outside of myself and it was bearing down on me heavily. The presence I felt around me growing up was outside of matter and was again, conscious of my consciousness and prevalent alongside my affairs. It was like the presence of fate was moving alongside me in the forbearance of my will. The darkness I felt was partially genetic I feel, because my birth parents were both mentally ill with schizophrenia, especially my mom who was a tormented demoniac, but I also see a calling upon my genetics as a desired interest in both God and satan and I was somehow caught in between the two. Even 20 years before coming to Christ I felt this severe inclusive presence and pressure upon myself externally which somehow coincided and affected me internally. I never considered myself a spiritual person nor did I really care to question it, but regardless of my perceptions, the surrounding presence was still there and fixated upon my life. In regards to spirituality, I felt that karma was the persisting result and justification to our actions but that's as far as I'd ever take it. I just didn't care otherwise. I'd even take karma to such a degree it would cause an obsessive compulsive disorder within me but I didn't necessarily link it to God or a supernatural force of any kind. I guess I could say that I intuitively knew there was a God but just never pursued him. I look back and wonder myself, to be honest.

Regardless, the circumstances at times we're just too coincidental for them not to be directed or appointed from above in the supernatural realm. It wasn't just me, there were situations and circumstances happening around me that confirmed the same intuition.

One of my best friends growing up who has now passed away, was drinking and driving around an ess turn on a country road in the middle of the night. He misjudged one of the turns and then careened into the forest of someone's property, hitting a tree and flew through his windshield. The owners of the property phoned the police because they heard a loud bang as my friend lay there mangled and bleeding to death. The police ended up coming but he was so far into the forest they couldn't see him and left. Shortly thereafter the same owner phoned again hearing a similar sound. Ironically, a guy in a stolen car came around the same turn, flew into the forest and hit the back of my friend's car. The police then came for the second time and found my friend lying there bleeding to death and saved his life. Some of these stories are unexplainable in our lives outside of the supernatural but for me I couldn't determine whether they were for me or against me. It was a heavy and suffocating presence of darkness at times that I just couldn't bear on my own but then I also seemed to be shielded just enough to get through it. It's like there were two opposing spiritual forces contending over my footsteps, my mind and the destiny of my life and soul. One that wanted me dead and eradicated from the earth and one that was imploring me to trust in them ethically and let go. Now I can see it was God's mercy drawing me to himself but I was just too naive, stubborn and "blind in affliction" to realize it.

Once back when I was around 19 or 20, I was packing some lumber back and forth on a job site. I remember being so bound up with frustration and anxiety over my life and circumstances that I could hardly function, the pressure was so intense. This darkness I speak of had consumed me and it was almost like I was hyperventilating in my mind. I then remember bending over to grab another load of lumber and seeing a black cassette tape laying in the mud by the lumber. The first thing I did was smash it with the heel of my work boot about three times. I then bent over to pick up it's mangled remains and the title of the tape said, "Let go, let God." As soon as I read that and the words registered, almost simultaneously a spirit of some sort launched me onto my back. It was completely supernatural and was obviously to get my attention but my mind was just too preoccupied, confused and in pain to understand that. I do remember taking it all in for a second and then throwing the tape towards my car as though it mattered but ultimately I was just too stubborn and disgruntled to pursue the incident any further. Like the majority of us, I was bound to my own pride and self-determination. It was like I was on a collision course of self destruction within my own fears and emotions and I just couldn't see it. I felt an even deeper grievance that I couldn't figure it out and accomplish the objective within my own strength. I felt lost and alone and the weakness of it at times was too much to overcome. I also would never admit it to anyone which left me feeling even more introverted, reclusive and isolated. I'll admit my footsteps have been on shaky ground over the years to say the least. I felt weak and inferior to it all and there were years I would put up a wall, block it all out and bury myself into drugs and alcohol to escape the burden. I knew there was a purpose and calling on my life but I was just too young and unwise to identify with the source behind it.

I was also too emotionally traumatized to see a reason for change. I had no faith or spiritual awareness to draw from nor did I have anyone to confide or trust in. I had no mentor or father figure to turn to for guidance to embark on any kind of influential journey and eventually I fell victim to the pressure I put on myself. It's life and it can be consuming but thankfully, those days are in the past as a distant memory and that weight and burden has been lifted. (I would even say it has been shifted.) I can now see myself in a different light and can see the source for all my trauma and the reasons for all my confusion and have come to terms of deliverance with it all. This is God's supernatural grace. I am now compelled by God's Spirit who instills in us a greater purpose and calling outside of our own and the worlds. The calling and objective still hold a heavy burden and can be extremely challenging at times, but the burden isn't so intensely fixated upon my own identity and vessel anymore. It's like I'm set free from the world's opinions of me and the pride behind my old objective has been completely released. There is now a set objective in spite of myself that I don't have to generate from within myself. The result has been accomplished and my faith is in that accomplishment.

Calling of Christ

Christ's identity is what lifts the burden off our shoulders and releases us from our own because his calling or shall I say the calling that was set upon him set the precedence in our world and in the unseen world. That's why he says in 2 Corinthians 3 that where the spirit of the Lord is, there is liberty. If I were to die an hour from now, or anyone else for that matter, the imminence of the Bible continues on and the call and objective doesn't change for the world, nor in the spirit world, therefore why would we put all the pressure on ourselves with these objectives in motion either way? We can all make a proactive difference to some degree but the overriding burden is just too heavy to bear. Jesus said, "I have overcome the world," and all we can do is contribute to the cause of faith to the best of our abilities and keep moving forward. John 16:33 says, "These things I have spoken to you, that in Me you may have peace. In the world you will have tribulation, but be of good cheer, I have overcome the world." 1 John 5:3-4 says, "This is the love of God, that we keep his commandments. And his commandments are not burdensome. For whomever is born of God overcomes the world. And this is the victory that has overcome the world; even our faith. Who is he who overcomes the world, but he who believes that Jesus is the son of God." It's the good fight of faith as Paul says in his first letter to Timothy and is a progressive continuum as the Word of God unravels and closes into its climactic end in eschatology. God faced what we can't bear with his objective to be the guide in and through our vessels until the day of salvation. What he delivered himself through is our redemption and restitution. I looked up restitution and it's defined as the restoration of something lost or stolen to its proper owner or a recompense for injury or loss and that was exactly God's objective for the world in Christ on the cross.

We're lost without him and the enemy has stolen the truth from within our hearts. He's also damaged and jaded us in the process but God came to redeem what's been lost and renew and rejuvenate us again. This isn't some derived fallacy of man, this is a true rejuvenation of the human soul and spirit. Titus 3:5 says, "Not by works of righteousness which we have done, but according to his mercy he saved us, by the washing of regeneration, and renewing of the Holy Spirit." God releases us from the pressures we put on ourselves by placing all the pressure on himself in Christ. All the pain within our hearts and all the strongholds that are bound within and upon the human vessel were placed on the vessel of God as Isaiah 53 so prophetically and descriptively indicates. It says, "He is despised and rejected by men, a man of sorrows and acquainted with grief, He was despised and we did not esteem him. Surely He has borne our griefs and carried our sorrows; Yet we esteemed Him stricken, smitten by God, and afflicted. But He was wounded for our transgressions, He was bruised for our iniquities, the chastisement for our peace was upon Him, and by His stripes we are healed. All we like sheep have gone astray; We have turned, every one, to his own way; And the Lord has laid on Him the iniquity of us all...He was led as a lamb to the slaughter...." There's no other scripture in the Bible that can better articulate what I'm trying to convey in my book. It's all right there, written hundreds of years before Christ. God in the flesh, reconciling the world back to himself. Through faith, he draws us to himself with that truth for us to deliver and that truth is the release people need whether they believe it or not. It frustrates me that people are so stubborn that they won't even consider opening the pages of the bible anymore. It's a literal travesty. Matthew 13:15 says, "For the hearts of these people have grown dull. Their ears are hard of hearing, and their eyes closed, lest they should see with their eyes and hear with their ears, lest they should understand with their hearts and turn, so that I should heal them." He's not speaking of a physical healing as these new health and prosperity teachers emphatically insist, he's speaking of the brokenness within the human heart.

I have an old friend that struggles with depression and severe alcoholism. He has succumbed within the fear of his mind and identity and lives isolated from the world and from the perceptions of others. I've tried to share my faith with him but he's taken it personally as though I'm judging him and has cut me off from any communication. I bought him a Bible years ago and it sat below his TV for years collecting dust. I remember visiting him once years after giving him the book and tried sharing more of my faith with him. He was in such pain and needed help. This certain scripture came to mind about my yoke being easy and my burden being light but I couldn't remember where it was in the Bible. I then looked under the TV and saw the bible I gave him and went and grabbed it. Incredibly, the first page I opened was where that scripture was in Matthew 11 and not only that, my right thumb was directly on the scripture! We were both dumbfounded, especially him because he heard me uttering the words beforehand. He said, "How'd you do that?" And I just said, "That wasn't me, that was God!" I think it registered for a second but he was partially intoxicated and merely fell back into his escapism not realizing the truth that could set him free. I share that because I feel the majority of us are the same way regarding the Bible and I was no different. Matthew 11:28-30 says, "Come to me, all you that labour and are heavy laden, and I will give you rest. Take my yoke upon you, and learn from me, for I am meek and lowly in heart, and you shall find rest for your souls. For my yoke is easy, and my burden is light." Unfortunately, nothing has changed within his stubborn and prideful heart and he continues to fall deeper and deeper into addiction and into the perceptions and fears within his mind and those generated by the world. God's mercy was right there at the end of my thumb but he could only recognize it for a split second. All he wants is rest for his soul but he continues to turn away from the source of it. Some of us are so scared of letting go for fear of what's on the other side but with God, there's peace, sanctity and freedom.

God's Creation

Jesus is the precedence of existentialism. The word precedent is something done or said to serve as a rule or example and precedence is the condition of being considered more important than someone else or the priority of importance. The word existential is self-explanatory but is basically two words combined being essential and existence and we all need to ask these pivotal and crucial questions in life right now of what is essential for our existence now and in the life to come? What is the meaning and purpose of life? If it's moral fortitude or compliance then what's the standard and reason why? What does existence beyond this life look like and how do I get there? We've all become deers in the headlights of complacency, especially in this western society, but these questions bear far more urgency and relevance than ever before. For me, Jesus is the substance and substantiator for all philosophical, intellectual and spiritual contemplation. Substantiate means to provide evidence to support or prove the truth of something and we're surrounded by the evidence in everything we do and see. There's so much there that the world is neglecting to discover in Christ and won't inquire about in their misconceptions and insinuations. You get to a point in life when you've processed all the questions of existence from a carnal perspective and realized there's just nothing new under the sun that man hasn't been in contemplation over. You've thought through life's circumstances where they are good or bad, right or wrong or past and present. You've processed it all, justifying karma along the way to some extent, but reconsidered it due to unbalanced circumstances. You've contemplated inductive and deductive reasoning to find answers, even subconsciously but nothing seems to add up. You've dismissed chance or coincidence as ignorant denials of pre-motivated concurrence. You've contemplated all the evolutionary theories science has proclaimed but the fact is they're theories and something remains unresolved within us attempting to solve it all within ourselves. Ultimately, it's all just too vast and complex for us to solve and there's just no proof in a theory. Life and especially nature is a continual metamorphosis happening before our very eyes every day. It's incontinuum and we didn't push the button to set it in motion nor can we pull the plug. So much of life is a mystery and beyond our comprehension and with all the answers we supposedly have now, we're still at the mercy of it all regardless of our trivial claims. It's God's incredible creation before our eyes and we need to accept that and be in reverence and awe. The world will perish before anything gets scientifically resolved and even if we hold a claim to something, what real difference does it make? Time is of the essence and our internal clock only has so many years on this earth. I always thought it was amusing looking at it from God's perspective as this little spaceship feverishly attempts to get to the first planet with literally trillions of stars and galaxies beyond. What a false hope and waste of time and money. We're trying so feverishly to find something else out there when he's right there in his book. To me they're all futile efforts in showing how inferior we are to the power of God. The moon orbits around the earth and the earth orbits around the sun creating an impeccable 24 hour 365 day seasonal cycle and the only explanation the greatest scientists have is that a big bang happened. Brilliant. I speak facetiously but that is one extremely creative big bang. How does a massive explosion create such perfect balance when no explosion has ever generated balance, especially an entire universe? How does it generate a gravitational pull inclusively fixated to one planet? It's like a hurricane making a computer out of a junkyard. Again, it's all just too complex and intricate for us to create or solve and if we could, we'd do it ourselves. If we could save ourselves from death, we'd have done it by now but death is inevitable and the only one with that saving power is Jesus Christ. We don't understand the intricate properties that make up the stars and trillions of them look down at us in four corners of the globe every day and night. We've put all matter under a microscope and focussed in on all of space through a telescope but there's an inevitability to life that seems predetermined and unavoidable. All the greatest minds in history and even presently haven't held the answers to the origin in their hands. Every theory is undetermined therefore they all theorize their belief in faith regardless of their denial of faith. It's beyond our comprehension no matter how insatiably we dissect it.

There's something within the seeds of life that are preordained and have nothing to do with us and our creative hand yet we are completely dependent upon them for our survival. Everything in our natural world seems to have a purpose and designation and there is no designation without a design and there is no design without a designer. Evolution calls it natural selection but if that's true, who selected it. If everything serves a purpose then who proposed it? If there's an order in life, who ordered it? A minuscule redwood seed grows over 200 feet high and through the process of photosynthesis pulls in carbon dioxide and water. It then uses the energy of the sun to convert the chemical compounds to feed itself and produce oxygen in the atmosphere. Trees actually breathe out what we breathe in and clean and refine the air through the process. It's incredible, and not only that, they create more seeds from within the initial seed because that's their designed intention. These mysteries in life are incalculable and beyond reason, they're of God. The problem with evolutionary science is it bases its entire theory on coincidence and chance, which again to me is merely ignorant and adolescent. The word determined in any context has a conscious and contemplative thought process behind it and that comes from determining a purpose for it that can only come from a designer. A caterpillar destroys the entire theory of evolution within only a few days. It transforms into a butterfly with a completely different form and colours, with the ability to fly through the miraculous phenomenon of metamorphosis and we have no idea how, it just happens. The whole world is an incredible array of intricate design and balance whether it be in nature or within our own anatomy and all God is saying is that we are the pinnacle of his creation and he desires a relationship with us all.

I've personally come to peace realizing I can't solve it all and don't have to. I'm completely at the mercy of the procession of God's design and I'm okay with that. What infuriates the pride in man is how powerless we are in not being able to dictate or control it. When we try to, we compromise and destroy it. Human beings create human beings inside of human beings that grow inside of human beings and each one is diversely different. Children are born with all sorts of innate giftings and characteristics generated from the same testicles and in the same uterus. Some are male and some female and we had no preconceived blueprint of our own determining the outcome. Some are even twins or more of different sexes! It's miraculous and it takes me more faith to believe what science has undetermined than to believe what God proclaims in his Word and what he reveals to us before our very eyes every day. Our body produces melatonin to align itself with the 24 hour cycle of light and darkness and we don't know how, it just happens. The gravitational pull is perfectly aligned with the equilibrium of the human body and we don't know how, it just happens. If it was one degree off we'd be floating in mid-air or be sucked into the core of the earth. Science is bearing so much more on coincidence than they even realize. There is no other alternative to their evolving theory. Everything has to occur progressively by chance and coincidentally, including every God given item you buy at the grocery store that aligns with our brain's recognition and digestive system. That includes salt, pepper, chocolate, coffee beans, vanilla, caramel, apples, oranges, bananas, wheat, beef products, chickens, and thousands of others. It's all just too miraculous of a convenience. I just bought a butternut squash a couple days ago along with a spaghetti squash. They were side by side in the vegetable aisle. My question to an evolutionist is why and how did two differentiating choices of squash evolve? When did the seed branch off to form its diversity from the other and where did these seeds originate when it takes a seed within these fruits and vegetables to form them? Much like there's diversity in the same animal species. I don't see how any gardener who's in their right mind could watch their fruits and vegetables grow and believe it all occurred by chance. Our bodies are dependent upon them to survive. It's the same supposed coincidence with natural resources like oil, coal, natural gas, iron, phosphorus, copper, lumber, stone, sand and soil. These are essential for the existence of life. Regardless of what we believe, a big bang doesn't create something that creates something within itself especially if nothing was initially created and if there's seemingly a pre-determination or pinnacle biologically to evolution as presumably theorized then who determined it and what are we evolving towards? What is the final outcome to the metamorphosis happening within me and how is the metamorphosis refining or correcting itself within itself without me being conscious of it? It's a contradiction in of itself because it's in a supposed process of reaching its designated intention and conclusion. If that's the case then who intended it and who concluded it in their mind? Natural selection is defined by Charles Darwin as the process in which an organism adapts to its environment through "selectively" reproducing changes in its genotype. If this is the case, who selected it? The word select is a proactive verb. It just makes no rational sense.

If humans are the pinnacle of evolution then so many attributes and characteristics of preceded nature would've had to devolve and degenerate to reach our limitations, much like apes and chimpanzees are actually stronger per pound than humans. Dogs smell better, birds see better, moths hear better and many have stronger digestive systems. Where did evolution stop in generating these attributes in humans when these characteristics would benefit us? There are amphibious creatures along with nocturnal species and endless other characteristics that far exceed that of humans. How do life expectancies differentiate between species if we all originated from the same source? When and why did apparently prehistoric species like crocodiles stop evolving? Some animals even hibernate for months at a time, which would be nice to be honest. I'd love a long five month nap after writing this book. Not only that, how do they preserve themselves and not starve to death? Honestly, evolutionary theory explains nothing and again, it takes contemplation to determine anything and there's a mind to contemplation and determination. Species may adapt to their surroundings to some extent, as do humans, which is common sense but nothing is evolving in our DNA or they'd see the metamorphosis taking place through a microscope in everything. Humanity has adapted more in the last 100 years than any other time in history yet we haven't evolved biologically whatsoever. There are endless discrepancies in evolutionary theory and even as a non Christian I would never have concluded in my mind that there was no God or creative entity. How can intuition or instinct coincidentally and conveniently evolve so diversely when there's a distinctive individual purpose behind each entity much like how dogs and horses compliment humans. How could anyone not see how these animals aren't designed specifically by God to adhere to the needs of humans? It's not only dogs and horses with humans, almost everything in nature seems to compliment each other for survival and dependency whether it be predator and prey or the balance of the ecosystem. I watched a documentary recently on how they eradicated all the wolves from Yellowstone National Park for 70 years. They then found the ecosystem was increasingly delapitating and decided to reintroduce a small pack of wolves to the park in 1995. The narrator said what happened next was one of the greatest scientific discoveries in the past half century. Brilliant. They call it a trophic cascade which is an ecological process which starts from the top of the food chain and tumbles down to the bottom. Without the wolves controlling the deer population their numbers grew rapidly even with attempts by humans to control them. Eventually over time the deer grazed most of the vegetation away. The scientists found that not only did the wolves start killing the deer after being reintroduced but it started changing the character of the deer completely. They started avoiding open fields and valleys which allowed the vegetation to regenerate five times faster than it did otherwise. Within a few years forests of cottonwood, aspen and willow started forming which subsequently brought in all sorts of migratory birds. Beavers started coming into the park which the narrator says are like ecosystem engineers, creating niches for other species. The dams they built from the rivers provided habitats for otters, muskrats, ducks, fish, amphibians and reptiles. The wolves would kill coyotes and as result, increased the numbers of rabbits and mice which brought more hawks, weasels, foxes, badgers, and ravens. The carrion the wolves would leave behind from their kills brought in more bald eagles and helped provide food for bears along with berries from the bush being regenerated. What was even more fascinating to scientists is they realized the wolves actually transformed the behavior of the rivers. They stopped meandering and with less erosion, the channels narrowed, forming more pools which were perfect for wildlife habitat. They found the regenerating forests stabilized the banks so they collapsed less often which caused less erosion. Wolves not only transformed the ecosystem, they transformed the physical geography of the entire park. How someone can not see a design in that, is baffling to me. The point is nothing adapted or evolved whatsoever. They took out an element to the design and it all fell apart.

There's so many holes to evolution, it's like a water strainer in the kitchen but if I'm supposedly evolving or adapting to my surroundings to better my survival then we should all be growing dorsal fins to swim and wings to fly, especially those living in higher altitudes or along the water. I should be developing snake venom to ward off the contention in the world. I speak as a facetious simpleton but there are supposed adaptations in nature far greater than within myself if I'm the presumed pinnacle of it all. My digestive system should be that of a crows and my eyesight that of an eagle and so on. How can adaptation differentiate so vastly and reproductively when thousands of species have lived in the same climate and terrain geographically for centuries? There can't be diversity to the theory of evolution or procreation for that matter because it's supposed origin initializes it's theory with only one evolving embryo and it takes two to reproduce. Its chance upon chance upon coincidental chance upon chance, just like there's a tiny pocket of air in a chicken egg for it to breathe and break through its shell. Has it conveniently evolved for this purpose or was it the designed purpose of God? To be honest, it's all infantile and asinine and all these psychopathic puppeteers have done by supposed carbon dating is pay off scientists with their supposed credentials to stretch the registered time so far to where we all think the gradual change is occurring too slowly to see the evolutionary effects within us and around us. There should be billions of scattered skeletal remains from the evolutionary metamorphosis that's supposedly taken place, not only in humans but in all species, but there's not and mankind has excavated half the earth. Did they just disappear? If we were to open up some of these freemason books from the past they would reveal all of these secrets in their sadistic narratives and agenda. If I look at a painting on a wall I know intuitively that someone painted it, it's common sense, but the whole world is an open canvas to billions of people everyday and for us to think there isn't a designer is just mere ignorance. Epheshians 4:18 says, "Having their understanding darkened, being alienated from the life of God, because of the ignorance that is in them, because of the blindness of their heart."

Confirmation in the Word

The scriptures testify and reveal to me a mind that is intricate and articulate, outside of time and space that loves us deeply and intimately and is in constant willingness to reconcile and absolve our ignorance in forgiveness and draw us to his dominion for our own good. There is a clarity and resolution in Christ that provides me enough trust, proof and release for my conscience to establish it's peace of mind. There's nothing left for me to prove or solve anymore. If I'm trusting in the world to substantiate my faith then all I'm subjecting myself to is the limitations and capacity generated by it and that is a scary faith to depend on, especially in this day and age. The truth is that if someone is continuously trying to prove their point or be affirmed in their opinion or theory, they haven't found the resolution within themselves. So many of the mysteries of life find resolution and are conclusive in Christ that excuse and nullify the world's contention, and at times, even my own mind's incessant banter. We just don't generate the wisdom from within ourselves to solve it all and that's okay. My faith is confirmation that he has and does. He carried it all on his shoulders to take the weight off our own. It's like God masterminded a universal redemptive plan for us to confide in his resolution and to serve one another in unity, by serving us. Hebrews 10 is incredible in explaining the power and supremacy of Jesus Christ and it does it with only a few words. "Therefore, when He came into the world, He said, "Sacrifice and offering you did not desire, but a body You have prepared for Me. In burnt offerings and sacrifices for sins you had no pleasure." Then I said, "Behold, I have come, in the volume of the book it is written of Me, to do Your will, oh God."

There is no resolution in human intellect, philosophy or science outside of Jesus Christ because he is the author of the designated resolution. We're trying desperately to find another escape hatch but there is no escaping the truth of God. At the end of Paul's first letter to Timothy he says, "Oh Timothy, guard what was committed to your trust, avoiding the profane and idle babblings and all oppositions of what is falsely called science, by professing it some have strayed concerning the faith." Science is defined as the intellectual and practical activity encompassing the systematic structure and behavior of the physical and natural world through observation and experiment. That all sounds great but my Bible says Jesus Christ is the Alpha and Omega, the first and the last, and that everything was made through him, and without him nothing was made that has been made. If this is true then without him science would have nothing to observe or experiment with. End of story and end of philosophical discussion.

Answering the Call

Ultimately, it's our choice whether we want to answer his call upon the world and turn the internal mirror on ourselves. I've done it and I'll admit it's extremely humbling, but it's also revolutionary in resolving the conflict within us all. He inevitably left us with the responsibility to evaluate our own conscience and battle through our pride and skepticism to form our own inclusive opinion concerning sin and salvation. This is his call upon the world whether we're a jew or a gentile and whether we like it or not. Acts 11 specifically says that God has granted the gentiles repentance to life and salvation is the life God grant's us in repentance. Wherever we stand and whatever pain, hypocrisy or trauma is holding us back, his ears and arms are always open for us to confide in along the journey, and his spirit is always there to provide confirmation. The spirit draws you to the Word and the Word confirms what's going on in your conscience. This unrelenting persistence is the love the world is disregarding and where religion has missed its mark in representing God's true identity. Sin separates us from God and the only way to see him for who he truly is, is to repent of our sin. The more the world has put its faith in science or made faith about circumstance the more it's become justified in its irresponsibility and that's not God's intention in his Word for our lives. He went to the cross for the sin because that's the underlying problem and curse of the world. Until we confront that, nothing can change. Galatians 3:13 says, "Christ redeemed us from the curse of the law by becoming a curse for us."

Jesus is not some mythical being nor is he this passive aggressive hippie that he's been portrayed in movies and on television over the years. He came to show us true grace and reveal to us the truth and severity of our sin, but more importantly he came to atone for it on the cross. He didn't mix words then nor is he mixing words with the world right now. Again, I realize it's very difficult to trust in anything these days but where has trust got us in the world? We can't trust politics and the government for obvious reasons. It seems everything they say is a fabricated lie. We can't trust the FBI, FDA and CIA or whatever other three letters form these corrupt organizations. We can't trust the medical system or pharmaceutical companies. All they seem to do is diagnose us with more deficiencies to sell us products that cause us more harm. The medical symbol ironically has two snakes running through the middle of it. We can't trust the chemicals in our food or water supply anymore. We can't trust the news outlets or media. We don't trust most religious affiliations and their intentions. Some of us don't even trust our friends and family anymore. In fact, I guarantee most of us can only count on one hand the number of people we can trust sincerely in our lives. There was a time where you didn't have to lock your car or the front door of your house, but those days are long gone. Everything's alarmed now with cameras and motion detectors everywhere. Trust has almost become foreign in our world nowadays, but this is the true empowerment of our faith in Christ. He never leaves us or forsakes us. Hebrews 13:5-6 says, "Let your conduct be without covetousness, be content with such things as you have. For he himself has said, I will never leave you nor forsake you. So we may boldly say: The Lord is my helper, I will not fear. What can man do to me?"

Sharing our Faith

Growing up I felt such an emptiness in my soul. It was like I was all alone and I despaired life and the loneliness of it everyday. It never seemed to leave me until the day I came to Christ. It's been almost ten years and that feeling has never returned. He's the foundation to base our life upon. He's a friend, a father, a counsellor and a support system until our time comes and we need to share that trust, hope and faith with others who have grown callous and are in need of the same grace and refuge in their lives.

There's a patched member of the hell's angels who's started coming to our church recently. You can tell he's broken and torn but he's coming to the knowledge of Christ and can see the love, maturity and acceptance of God in the congregation. We need to grow in this redemptive unity, maturity and knowledge and live as an example to others and not fuel the contention and greed of the world. It's a challenging objective to follow, don't get me wrong, especially with the pride and stubbornness of man these days. The great commission in the gospel of Mathew is to make disciples of all the nations but it's not a simple task. The heart of man is chained to its own pride, fears and ego and is seemingly unresponsive to any contemplative evaluation. The lack of trust and faith has generated a smug, selfish and bitter spirit that drives our culture in this generation that's hard to penetrate, as I stated before. The gospel can certainly ruffle some feathers and bring us back down to earth attempting to evangelize. People are repulsed by anything that may oppose or confront their opinions or will's intention. It's like we're standing in the way of their pursuit of the world and it can be awkward and uncomfortable trying to persuade or convince them otherwise. It's like trying to save a porcupine that's tangled-up in a thornbush. Evangelizing is a gift of God and a serious transition in humility and maturity that only the Holy Spirit can guide us in and through. I've certainly had some backlash along my journey, especially with family and friends. I mentioned my faith to my brother and he hasn't spoken to me in years. My adopted mother is completely repulsed by anything to do with the bible or Jesus and my best friend growing up thinks it's all a joke and hasn't called me for a decade. Even those who don't take offense simply say, "I'm glad that's working for you," and continue on their pursuit of the world. It's so hard because of the pride people carry from the journey that brought them to where they are. It comes to a point where evangelism becomes so difficult that we either give up, shut up or simply make faith about ourselves. I know because I've been there and have to fight through it every day. I naturally want to live for myself even with God's commission laid on my heart. The gospel is a contentious subject that leaves me frustrated at times especially while I'm battling through life's afflictions myself, but it's what we're called to persevere through.

I remember a story I heard of this older street evangelist who was ministering to the addicted and homeless. He was approached by a street thug who berated and mocked him about being a Christian. He then smacked him across one side of his face saying, "Jesus told you to turn the other cheek." The old guy fell down, then picked up his glasses and got to his feet. The thug then smacked him across the other side of his face putting him to the ground again. He humbly gathered himself up and the thug broke down in tears in front of him and surrendered his life to Jesus right there on the spot. It just goes to show that God can work in ways that we'd never expect if we hold on in faith and persevere for the greater cause of salvation. It doesn't mean we all have to minister on the streets to thugs but we all interact with people everyday and they all need a saviour even if they don't realize it. Some people are more gifted at interacting and evangelizing than others but we can all fight through our fears and play our part even if it's setting an example or serving in the church. It's hard because an opinion entices controversy, confrontation and resentment which at times we're not all equipped or mature enough to handle especially to those who are passive aggressive, but we still can't compromise our opinions and stay silent. I'm guilty of this myself but the more silent we are the more the world grows in its complacency, tolerance and self justification. Romans 10:13-15 says, "Whoever calls on the name of the Lord shall be saved. How then shall they call on him in whom they have not believed? And how shall they believe in him of whom they have not heard? And how shall they hear without a preacher? And how shall they preach unless they are sent? As it is written, how beautiful are the feet of those who preach the gospel of peace, who bring glad tidings of good things!" I'm not going to lie, im preaching to myself here because I struggle with this confrontive interaction myself but I'm learning not to take offense to anything because people are merely reacting in their carnality as we would have and it's not necessarily the person I'm confronting, but the carnality within them. People assume Christians are judging them from a position of entitlement but we're trying to help them escape the judgement of God and that's an extremely difficult message to deliver. Without God's spirit our minds don't generate the grace or wisdom to diffuse all of the accusations, insinuations, contention and justification the world and it's voice has compiled for itself. Only through God's spirit and the knowledge of his Word can we become effective in making a dent in the armour of the world's pride. It's distinctive and revolutionary in unearthing the carnal propensity within us. Hebrews 4:12 says, "The Word of God is living and powerful, and sharper than any two-edged sword, piercing even to the division of soul and spirit, and of joints and marrow, and is a discerner of the thoughts and intents of the heart." It's just so difficult to transfer this message because until man sees a reason to confront their own sin it doesn't see a reason for the sacrifice of God.

Stubborn Man

It can be such a war at times because the more God reveals to us our own carnal propensity to sin, the more we come to realize the severity of it in the world around us and the desperate need for God's patience and mercy to be realized in the heart of man to invoke a change and conversion. Some teachers have called it sacred schizophrenia with all that goes on in the mind of a Christian. It's insane what God sees us do and what goes unpunished but without this intercession and regeneration from God, philosophical discussion of any kind just becomes a reverberating appeasement of men and women who love and live to hear the sound of their own voice and affirm their own position or opinion. It's just vanity bouncing off other voices of vanity. Only God can truly revolutionize the conversation through his spirit and when he does the whole world becomes an unlocked veil and mission field of broken glass with pieces facing every direction. The world seems to be holding onto what's destroying it, when all God wants us to do is let go and confide in him. It's incredible the power of pride and how destructive it can truly be. We're actually living and fighting for the pride and entitlement that's destroying us and we just can't see it. It's like me smashing that tape into the ground when I was younger. It actually said, "Let go, let God," but I just wouldn't do it. It also reminds me of being addicted to cigarettes. We know deep down it's harming our bodies and will eventually kill us. We cough and gag our lungs out. We're irritable, smell awful and waste our money away on it. We know all the statistics and health risks concerning it, yet somehow we justify it in our conscience. We'll use that one person who smoked till they were 105 to justify our means, yet millions more die every year of smoking related cancer and heart disease. It's unfortunate that it takes the effects and consequences of it to eventually initiate the reason for us to change but we're just that ignorant and stubborn. Before we come to realize it, the damage has already been done. We just can't let go of our pride and impulses in these mundane voids of life where we have to be patient, creative or improvisational so we continually feed them in our weakness with these habitual and compulsive contradictions. It's in these mundane voids that faith fills and sustains us that people don't realize. God instills a purpose and commission within you that drives you to abstinence. The Holy spirit within a believer takes away the desire because again, he's not an impulsive spirit. God's spirit is a loving spirit driven to save us from ourselves. He's a spirit of peace, joy, humility, understanding and tranquility. It's not only cigarettes, it's the same with food and alcohol or whatever else is within arm's reach of our minds' apparent sanctity and escape. I know because that's what I used to escape my whole life. The system satan has devised is not only to control us physically but to manipulate and conform us emotionally and psychologically in every little facet of our lives in how we respond in the void. That's the whole plan of his elite regime of degenerate psychopaths because we're unsecured in the faithless void which has created the impulsive consumer within us. We literally embrace their poisoning and have become addicted to our own demise in so many aspects of our lives. Just like that last little fruit fly looking down from the top of the bowl. We've been given a free choice in life but our own pride and afflictions have blinded our rationality. As we play the victim role in our afflictions we justify these substance abuses and get more and more conformed to their control, allowing the poisons to take more of their effect. I can hit myself with a hammer and say the hammer hit me as much as I want, but I'm still the one swinging the hammer. Again, these are the ramifications of this self-willed world who are unaccountable to God and who live by the standards it sets and the philosophy it justifies.

It's become a world puppeted by consumer-driven dependency and again, without God's conviction and discernment, nothing can change. It's a difficult position being a christian these days with it all unfolding around us yet still desiring the pleasures and common graces of life. I'll admit, at times I'm completely torn in between myself. Self preservation has been ingrained in my soul since I was a kid and I have to pray every day to let that go. It's that sacred schizophrenia again that we war with as believers. I hate that it's the truth sometimes to be honest. I hate what the world has done to itself and how selfish it's become. I hate what people take for granted and it's easy to get bitter and emotional with all that's transpiring. I even hate what I take for granted and the resentment that builds up within myself. I feel like I'm trapped in between the call and commission upon my life, and the desires of my flesh. It's not only my desires, it's the compensation I feel I'm entitled to from what I've endured in life. The world definitely has its way of inciting a sense of retribution within us but however justified we feel, these emotions are what faith calls us to persevere through. The problem with sin is that it feels good at the time. It's what Paul struggled with in Romans 7 and what we're delivered from in Romans 8. Romans 7:22-25 says, "For I delight in the law of God according to the inward man. But I see another law in my members, warring against the law of my mind, and bringing me into captivity to the law of sin which is in my members. O what a wretched man that I am! Who will deliver me from this body of death? I thank God through Jesus Christ our Lord!" This commission of God is unrelenting and even though I know it's the truth, it's still hard to submit to it. You work so hard to get ahead and to a point of pride and accomplishment in life but realize our freedoms, opportunities and accessibilities will soon be taken away. It can be demoralizing and doesn't seem fair to those who are sincere and live with integrity but that's the imbalance a sinful world has generated for itself and we're unfortunately living in the outcome of it. I wish I could be optimistic for the future but that's just not true reality. I desire the blessings of life and of God's creation as much as the next guy, it's only natural, but I also see contentment and moderation sustaining our minds and resources with prosperity and gluttony destroying them. It's become all too real in these last days and we can see how needy, impulsively dependent and fragile we are in the midst of this global pandemic.

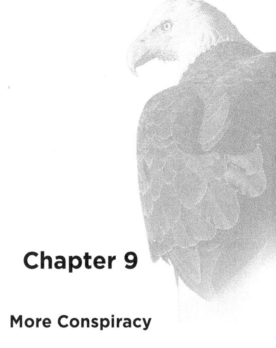

Chapter 9

More Conspiracy

We've become consumed by our own consumption because, again, attainment is the carnal intent of the faithless mind. The global elite are sucking the resources out of the world and bankrupting countries in the process for profit and control as we all blindly indulge as though there's an infinite supply. Now anxiety will increase even more as inflation rises with the supply in their hands and compulsion and entitlement in our minds. Even our government is blinded by their patriotic pride and economic optimism, living beyond their means with no idea what or who their dependant upon and their intentions. Much like the masses, in their denial of God they can't see the depth of evil and the extent that it reaches. I watched a speech with our Prime Minister Justin Trudeau recently where he repeatedly spoke of investor's over and over as though that was his entire hope and initiative for our country's future. It's such a deceived world we're living in on every level. Proverbs 22-7 says, "The rich rules over the poor, and the borrower is servant to the lender." Christianity is not only the enemy of satan but has also become the derision of the consumer because we're pleading for the world to abstain from the impulses that it feels are sustaining it and that it's entitled to. They see our warnings as criticism or judgment but the warnings are of the extortion and entrapment we're blind to and falling under. We're growing further and further in debt but we don't realize that the lender has no obligation towards us and can pull the plug at any time especially when our deficit is in the trillions. Just think if the oil distribution stops or our access to wifi abruptly ends. Not only that, just think if the tap on our cell phones stops working. It's going to reach that level of extortion sooner than later. They're living for their cause as we are for our own, but theirs will be a devastating reality none will be prepared for, especially with the demand so high. This pandemic is merely part of an extracting monopoly and imperialistic way of furthering that enslavement, just like that rock that's thrown in the water. The ripples circulate but the ones who are affected down the line don't know who threw the initial stone or why. We also don't know how deep that rock falls.

I Googled extortion to find its definition and it took me on some interesting roads. It's defined as obtaining benefit through coercion, whether it be through threats, violence, or intimidation. (I would personally add manipulation to that). It's punished by criminal code 346 of the government law but is actually what they use to control our society, much like mobsters in the protection racket. You're basically subject to the control and regulation of hypocritical lunatics with an ulterior motive of their own. It's extortion with every opportunity that presents itself to them. Even in a democracy they'll offer a protective security or shell as though you're unsafe and vulnerable without them as your dependency by promoting fear, then they feed on your vulnerability by extracting your resources as compensation. The entire world from an imperialistic standpoint is actually the victim of this kind of global extortion and blackmail on a bigger scale if we were to see it from the top of that illuminati pyramid. Every collateral ripple from the initial narrative can be used for an alternative agenda or expenditure, so they initiate the affliction whether it be wars, rumours of wars or terrorist attacks. They've done it psychologically and economically for centuries from buying out resources and fluctuating the stock market. It's all a pre-motivated, multi-level lending scheme through insider trading and secret narratives that create this massive domino effect like we're seeing now.

911 is probably one of the greatest hoaxes on the grandest stage ever in history. I can't believe people are so naive to think it was a terrorist attack as the government and media have insisted. To me it shows just how indoctrinated and dumbed down society has become relying on the media and news outlets to supply us our information. We've become so gullible and disillusioned in trusting the media driven narrative, especially in America through their patriotic pride. Even without being a Christian, it's pretty obvious the whole 911 fiasco was an inside job. A massive one at that, I'll admit, but still an inside job. The whole thing was a complete sham. The facts just don't line up from the top to the bottom. I don't call it a conspiracy theory, I call it analyzing common-sense. These types of incidents send narratives in motion and hold variables people don't realize in the resources, economics and markets of the world. We've got to look at who stands to benefit from them and 9/11 and this pandemic are no different. Again, the dominos that are still standing haven't been implemented yet and hold the keys to who's behind the ones that have already fallen. The owner of the properties surrounding 911 signed a 3.2 billion dollar, 99 year lease weeks before their collapse with a 3.5 billion dollar insurance policy specifically covering terrorist attacks. Coincidence? I don't think so. There was massive insider trading and fluctuation in the stock market minutes before the towers fell as though many had advanced knowledge. There was also apparently the largest depository of gold in the world stored there with over a hundred billion dollars worth but only 200 million of it was apparently accounted for. There are so many variables that

are underneath the surface of the public eye that certain people stood to benefit from. The proof doesn't end they're either, because every witness whether they were firemen, reporters or citizens on the street claim to have seen and heard consecutive explosions proceeding the towers collapses, much like a controlled demolition. I've seen the videos and you can see a row of explosions plain as day as they fell, along with the adjacent buildings. The list goes on and on of false information put out by the media that don't line up with the facts and the eyewitness accounts of what truly happened. Again, it just goes to show how powerful the media can be in manipulating and deceiving the public in staging and presenting these false fronts and flags much like a Hollywood movie. It reminds me of the movie "Wag the Dog" with Robert De Niro and Dustin Hoffman where everything is staged and two steps ahead of public knowledge to further implement the procession of the agenda. They use these illusions and diversive tactics for their end result of totalitarianism. They'll use staged exercises and imaginary crisis situations as smoke screens to divert our attention and for responses to alternative variables. 911 unfortunately wasn't imaginary and cost thousands of people their lives including over 300 firefighters, but that's how evil and sinister these people are in implementing their objectives. Everything else surrounding 9/11 was a complete hoax as well. There was no plane that hit the Pentagon or landed in a forest in Pennsylvania. There is no proof, eyewitnesses or surveillance footage of either one. It was a cruise missile from a plane that eyewitnesses saw leaving the area shortly after. All the passenger numbers and their identities are fraudulent and don't line up. The cell phone calls were staged and pre-recorded that were supposedly made seconds before impact, plus cell phones didn't work at that altitude back then. The majority of the identified hijackers have ironically been found alive. The black boxes were conveniently destroyed upon impact and never found from the Twin Towers yet a passport from one of the hijackers was miraculously found in perfect order. The cockpit voice recordings were undisclosed along with the firefighters records, and the ones that finally did were all manipulated. The list is endless if people would open their eyes and dig a little deeper but unfortunately the majority continue to trust the system as though it has our best interests in mind. The crash site at the Pentagon was a 16 foot wide hole in the front wall with the surrounding windows still intact but a Boeing 757 that supposedly crashed there is 124 ft wide. People apparently felt a shock wave consistent with that of a cruise missile. I could go on and on as many have in writing books on conspiracy but no plane has ever been vaporized as they suggest and ironically there was another 16 foot hole in an adjacent wall further into the Pentagon. These were inside jobs that the public has complacently disregarded in their patriotism and the pursuit of the American dream. Skepticism is disregarded and in the shadow of humanistic determinism. You can see how they hype up the public with the illusion of terrorism through Hollywood years before, to justify the cause for retribution and revenge. That's the psychological aspect that's so blinding. They also hype up patriotism to justify the funding of the army. They both work together to implement the narrative. Even the military is fighting an alternative war they don't realize because they've been disillusioned by the promotion and propaganda of liberty, patriotism and pride themselves. These sinister lunatics actually use the taxpayers money and the interest on loans to pay for a military to take over the world for their own purpose and agenda without the public even knowing. If that's not a conspiracy, I don't know what is. I've seen interviews with soldiers who have stated it's all a fabricated lie and that they've just served as pawns to an ulterior motive. They're literally fighting a war against weapons their own government sold to their enemy that are firing back at them. What a contradiction that is. For them it's a game of impunity outside of the law for money, power and control and over stocks, oil, resources and our accessibility to them. This is where the Rothschilds and Rockefellers of the world have focused their attention. The problem is they own and know the quantities of resources and they don't provide us with the information because information yields control. The truth is in who withholds the lie. In many ways, it's the outcome of capitalism and free enterprise in this supposed free world that we've all succumbed to. It just gives them free reign in regulating the markets. These global elite entrepreneurs amass so much wealth in a capitalist system they can overthrow and manipulate even the government. The government gets trapped in justifying capitalism from the income and taxes they receive to balance their budget but then get sold out to the resources they don't own and need to survive. They're simply forced to comply with the narrative to keep the economy moving. The economy may seem to be moving forward but all it's becoming is further in debt and sold into the illusion. Unfortunately, even our government has to sell out to the narrative and that's where we all find ourselves amidst this pandemic and where the truth is hidden. I'll never forget the video of President Bush's security guard whispering in his ear in a children's classroom as the twin towers went down. He didn't express any emotion because he knew exactly what was going to happen. He's been ordered to comply and that's when you know there's powers far greater in charge unbenounced to the masses. Unfortunately even he himself has been deceived and these lunatics have the whole world mapped out along with its resources. They've got calculated timelines orchestrated for each domino to fall and carry out its objective and for those who think the Bible is irrelevant in our day and age, again, they should read it's parallels concerning 911 in John's visions in revelation. It's a global allegory of our world's systems and economics reaching their end. It's so sad to see and the more aware you become, the more you've got to overcome the righteous anger that builds up inside you. These people are like pimps prostituting the world away for advantage with money they never earned. Being a Christian makes it even harder to endure because as you get to know God personally, you start to take it personally, which can be a depressing inferiority and realization.

Holding on till the End

The state of the world and the human condition can be an overwhelming revelation in of itself to overcome let alone trying to change it. I feel so meek and irrelevant compared to everything I just wrote down. I can't believe these people do what they do, but it's still being done and needs to be recognized in the heart of man. I wish all these lies would be exposed for people to see and believe but apart from writing a book, I don't know how to relay the message. We've become so brainwashed. I want to reach through the television while the news is on and help but I feel helpless sometimes. Again, we are falling victim to a propagated illusion but this is why the biblical worldview is so relevant and introspective. It's the analogy behind the cover of my book and what is so blinding. Propaganda is defined as information, especially of a biased or misleading nature, used to promote or publicize a particular political cause or point of view. That's its political definition but it also says propaganda is information, ideas, opinions, or images that give one part of an argument, which are broadcast or published in order to influence people's opinions. It's not only being broadcast through movies and television but the narratives are also being ghostwritten through publishing and any other outlet that can manipulate our minds. We are selling ourselves out and selling ourselves short by buying into this plethora of lies and deception. I remember a show I watched on global warming and alternative fuel solutions. The beloved Barack Obama was endorsing a new conservative fuel refinement solution that would supply us with over a hundred year supply. Thousands of onlookers cheered him on for his uplifting speech and supposed concern for the environment. The truth years later was hectares of empty waste land

and resources being sucked dry with a tenth of the initial promises he suggested. He lied and he knew it and all he is like many others seated in these elite luciferian societies are trained speakers carrying out an undisclosed agenda for deception and profit. He's a puppet presenting himself as a politician when his true identity is hidden behind an arrogant veil of malicious coercion and ironically, he's the number one twitter follower in the world right now. He's more like an actor playing a part in a live movie who follows the director's script. The truth actually lies in who's writing the script and pulling the strings behind the teleprompter. Obama won't disclose the director's identity because he's under contract and so far in the game himself. Very little of what we see doesn't happen these days without a conspiring narrative or agenda attached to it. Money is truly the root of all evil. We've become a product to extract revenue from, from the day we're born to the day we die. We're like sponges that get wrung out and thrown in the trash to these psychopathic lunatics. Anything that extracts profit can be considered a commodity and sold as a product and that is what the masses have become. Every impulsive decision we make as a population is an escalating digit for gain and gross revenue. As we progress to the end of supply and resource, again, the world will turn into a frantic state of panic and wonder why as we cling to our dependencies, disillusioned by a false sense of security. It's a hypnotic trance we've fallen victim to and will render us helpless and unprepared when these imposed dominoes begin to fall. The Bible even says that there will be a falling out from those in faith because many will not be compromised and will become so blinded by their impulses and pride that they'll take precedence over the true fundamentals of faith. Even many pastors and church leaders will be compromised in regards to their salary and status in life.

1 Timothy 4:1 says, "The spirit expressly says that in latter times some will depart from the faith, giving heed to deceiving spirits and doctrines of demons, speaking lies in hypocrisy, having their own conscience seared with a hot iron." Jesus says in Matthew 24:24,

"False christs and false prophets will rise and show great signs and wonders to deceive, if possible, even the elect. See, I have told you beforehand." Many people's faith will be worldly and come to be defined by either stimulation, optimism, expectation, recognition or benefit. Unfortunately, they are all contrived appeasements that hold no eternal foundation. That's why I'm so adamant about the dangers of these delusional prosperity teachers because it's unrelative to the dispensation of prophecy in the Bible and the revelation of the spirits around us. The truth has become extremely difficult to discern for many people but the ones with true faith will understand and dig their heels in deeper as things start to unfold and won't be alarmed as the domino's take effect. In this, faith will be defined around the world in what people had faith in, the world or the world to come. Some theologians feel we'll be raptured out of the world as the Bible indicates but I feel things will get far worse before they get better and it's hard to pinpoint that time in eschatology.

There's so much contention in Christian circles concerning the subject that has even divided churches and formed separative movements and denominations, which to me is just irresponsible and immature. It's a grey area in our faith that I haven't completely solidified nor has anyone else because I don't see God giving us any more of a reason to justify our complacency. In a sense it would contradict the definition of biblical faith. We are complacent enough as it is. In Matthew 24 it says, "Heaven and Earth will pass away, but my words will by no means pass away. But of that day and hour no one knows, not even the angels of heaven. Watch therefore, for you do not know what hour your Lord is coming. But know this, that if the master of the house had known what hour the thief would come, he would have watched and not allowed his house to be broken into. Therefore you also be ready, for the Son of Man is coming at an hour you do not expect. Who then is a faithful and wise servant... blessed is that servant whom his master, when he comes, will find so doing." Again, the projected difficulty I see ahead of us in faith, is being patient and not yielding to the system's dependencies, not only physically but psychologically and holding on to the scriptures promise of salvation. I realize it's a helpless feeling seeing the effects unfolding and not being able to make a significant impact but that is part of the burden we bear in faith. The truth hurts especially concerning those around us who aren't saved. Again, people just blindly trust the governing system as though it's obligated to serve their best interests. The problem is that the system we're entrusting our lives upon holds no credibility whatsoever. The opposing government parties are like little children fighting over a box of cereal. They argue and gossip about each other like it's a fraternity frat house. Do we really trust them with our future?

It's a crazy dilemma we're living in that will only get progressively worse on the horizon as urgency and dependency escalate from the promotion of impulse and access to resources. I can't express enough how soon this will overtake our civil liberties. Time to wake up and be vigilant because our faith will be tested. The world will literally be falling apart outside of our front doors and the commercials will still be advertising their products, blockbuster movies will still be made and Joel Osteen will still be preaching prosperity. In fact, that's exactly what's going on through this pandemic. The commercials don't change their course and Joel Olsteen's exact words were, "You will prosper in this pandemic." It was actually his message for the entire half hour of his sermon a few months ago. People are totally delusional. Years ago his Lakewood megachurch in Houston Texas was surrounded by rising flood waters from tropical storm Harvey. Thousands were being evacuated throughout the city and he got a lot of flack for not opening his doors to those in need. Regardless of that, it was the fact that he kept preaching prosperity even amidst a devastating flood outside of his front doors. I'm not trying to pick on him exclusively (although it's fairly easy to do regarding faith) it's the spirit within him that is so uneducated and blind to the elements of evil around us. It reminds me of a picture I saw of several golfers on this beautiful golf course enjoying their day with a raging forest fire in the background. It's such a contradiction in true reality. Luke 17 says, "As the lightning that flashes out of one part under Heaven shines to the other part under heaven, so also the Son of Man will be in his day....And as it was in the days of Noah, so it will be also in the days of the Son of Man. They ate, they drank, they married wives, they were given in marriage, until the day that Noah entered the Ark, and the flood came and destroyed them all. Likewise as it was also in the days of Lot: They ate, they drank, they bought, they sold, they planted, they built, but on the day that Lot went out of Sodom it rained fire and brimstone from Heaven and destroyed them all. Even so will it be in the day when the Son of Man is revealed."

Back to the Illusion of Envy

The rich can't see the truth of God because they're stationed in a position and posture of pride, entitlement, achievement and recognition, absorbed by the complacency within their impulsive accessibility. The poor for the majority are blind to God's truth within their circumstances and trauma, weighed down by their identity and afflictions, struggling and envious to obtain the position of the wealthy but consumed by regret, blame and inadequacy, usually substance dependent. Then there's the majority somewhere in between, at least in this Western Society, who seemingly drive and fuel the whole economic system, who can see both sides but still can't see God because their time and priorities are being enslaved by the interest driven banking system and are usually living just beyond their means, trying to get ahead, but always falling a bit behind. Wherever we are on the social or financial scale, satan seems to have a hold of our priorities, impulses and emotions in all the carnal spectrum. There's a commercial endorsing a company called "Credit Karma" that is a perfect example of the propagated deception of our world. It's a 30 second commercial that starts off with a girl looking down on her luck, living in a run-down apartment with her friend. She then checks her credit score on Credit Karma and sees that it's only at 550. All of a sudden it changes to 702 and simultaneously her apartment transforms into a bigger, more comfortable setting with a whole new layout in the room. She then swipes her phone screen once more and it magically goes to 823 with the room transforming even better into a lakeside house on the water. There's so many manipulative narratives here but my point is how deceiving they can be and how they create the desire and illusion so we all become further and further enslaved to the lender economically and psychologically. They orchestrate it all through envy, pride and social acceptance and our blindness to it causes so much turbulence, divisiveness and disdain within the heart of man towards one another and within ourselves. It's a daunting truth and satan knows it and escalates the divided emotions by enhancing and enticing us through the world's level of achievement and affluence. We become so affected by the illusion projected upon us. If you create a race with a prize at the end, everyone burns fuel to win the race, risking their lives in the process, but in the analogy of the world, the ones putting up the prize are the ones who own the resource of the fuel. We are all like mice to them in our own individual running wheels. The psychology behind it all is to allow the carnal ego and prestige of man to rise and inflate itself and the admiration and accolades to grow increasingly and unrealistically through our idols to create the feeling of inadequacy and desperation in the common man. This is where the majority of pressures we put on ourselves are actually rooted. We want what we can't have and the illusion of it becomes an obsession, especially as it's continuously promoted and advertised to us day in and day out, in our eyes and ears. It's been ingrained subconsciously in almost every culture around the world, especially now with everything so accessible through technology. The desire for recognition, social acceptance and acclaim become an insatiable thirst for our emotions and impulses to abstain from and we exhaust ourselves in the process from uncontentment in the comparison. We've come to not even live for the moment anymore, but to prove and claim that moment as our own. It builds up a massive inferiority within us and that's why we see these athletes making hundreds of millions of dollars nowadays. It's a psychological investment for these elite puppeteers and not necessarily due to their worth as an athlete or inspiration in the community. There's another directive behind it all people can't see in consumerism. It's actually the idealistic framework and influence narcissism generates through idolatry and the profit they draw from the consumer that drives the economy forward. It creates an inflated persona and a presumptuous, ego-driven and vicarious state of mind to live up to and follow. Vicarious is defined by living as if through someone else or something experienced in the imagination through the feelings or actions of another person and that's where our own identity can get so lost and deceived. The more they invest in the affluence and adoration of the idol the further it divides society as the inadequacy, mediocracy and unfulfillment increases. The carnal man sees an idol as inspiration but God sees it all as psychological manipulation and debilitation especially from a spiritual or financial perspective. Year after year these contracts get higher and higher. A football player for the Dallas Cowboys was just offered 30 million dollars a year and turned it down wanting 40 million. A basketball player also turned down an offer for 50 million a year. It's just more appalling proof of man's self-centered, egotistical mindset. Interesting how as the percentage of contracts have escalated, the percentage of suicides has escalated alongside. Another baseball player signed for over a quarter billion dollars recently. It's a ludicrous amount of money to throw a baseball, football or basketball around when the world is crumbling around us. In the big picture it's all a vein distraction satan uses as an illusion and diversion to draw us away from salvation and the priority of our soul. These shows like Big Brother, Alone and Survivor are also perfect examples of the lengths people will go with the priority of money set before them. People will lie, cheat and steal their way to gain money or recognition. His minions work behind the scenes to implement more and more of these divisive narratives as we're drawn to them by our trivial complacency. The psychology of it forms an idealistic separation and divide between fantasy and reality in how it influences our culture, especially children in a severely detrimental way. The impact becomes so innately ingrained into our subconscious from such an early age because we attribute everything we do as a means for personal and financial gain. We've been taught that every action is for the benefit of ourselves otherwise there's no purpose to it. The mindset that has developed in our culture and throughout the world from this idealistic American dream is a contrived approach in our intentions, purpose and meaning of life. Children have come to attribute the love of sports to the affluence received from it and not necessarily for the joy and camaraderie of it. The fame, fortune, and prestige become the inspiration more than the appreciation for the talent and relationships developed along the way. The effects are deeper than people realize in how we coexist and interact with each other as a community in society. When there's a continual narcissistic desire for gain, self-promotion and self-preservation we naturally don't reciprocate selflessness and kindness to people, we merely use it and them for our own advantage. We start seeing everything as an opportunity and use people and the world anyway we can for our own benefit, no matter who we hurt in the process. Every interaction becomes a contrived opportunity to win the race and reach the goal being advertised. It becomes an expectation and demand into which we feel we're entitled to receive. It's much the same effect in prosperity preaching. Everything we see as a justifiable opportunity for ourselves to be stimulated or prosper whether it be in our actions, our sexuality or in our relationships. Mathew 6:24 is so true in saying, "No one can serve two masters, for either he will hate the one, and love the other; or else he will hold on to one and despise the other. You cannot serve

God and money" He says this in regards to money which is so true but it's the same in regards to self exaltation and attention.

My friend is going through it right now with his mother-in-law. She's sat there for the last decade watching Joel Osteen every day and feels she's entitled to every bit of stimulation the world offers. She's become a selfish and insecure glutton and has completely torn apart the family in her entitled narcissism without even knowing it. She whines, gossips and complains about every little detail in life and blames everyone close to her for the lack of service to her. This is the outcome of idolatry and how it generates an inflated perception of ourselves and who we desire to be. Google defines idolatry simply as the worship of idols or extreme admiration, love, or reverence for something or someone. Narcissism is defined as an inflated sense of our own importance and a deep need for excessive attention and admiration. It's also defined as causing problematic relationships and a lack of empathy towards one another. They definitely go hand in hand but the lack of empathy in the definition hit a nerve with me because that's the overriding problem with our world today, humility and empathy. Again, the world sees idols as inspiration but satan uses them as an impressionable tool and a dividing valley of influence between prestige and inadequacy in the common man, especially when attributed to money. Interestingly, the antonyms for narcissism are charitable, generous, self-sacrificing, philanthropik, humble, pleasant, gracious and merciful. That pretty much explains it all because these are the sustaining attributes of love and peace in the world and what it is obviously lacking. It's not just in sports either that causes this mindset, it's anywhere an idol can be formed in our minds desire but especially in actors and musicians. They're provided a lofty paycheck for their talent to be expressed but the talents are used as a product under a contract to carry out their own agenda for mind control and revenue. Actors are simply acting out all of our desires in these scripts that we can't in reality because we're under the law and they're free outside of the law for the sake of art and entertainment. This is where satan can take over the flesh and implement his strategies because somehow we feel empowered in the vindicated freedom they're living out in our imagination. It's very similar in music because the incentives and recognition become the detractors to our moral conscience in the illusion of the fictional fantasy. I can see talents and passions as justifiable means for inspiration and influence but fame, fortune and prestige are desires that have poisoned the world and infected us into a deflated sense of mediocrity and desperation. It's unrealistic and unattainable for the general population but the desire seems to fuel our intentions and has developed into our desired persona and purpose in life. I can't help but comment more on some of the reality shows on TV today like Cops, First 48 and Live PD these days. The cops and investigators are always baffled and scratching their heads at why these rapes and petty murders take place over and over again. These young men are literally executing people in the most heinous of crimes for what seems like nothing. It's because they're infatuated with an elevated perception of themselves and they feel everyone and anything is in their way to reach or attain that desired goal. They're consumed with inferiority over the idolatry that's being projected upon them and it forms a root of bitterness and envy. They hate themselves before even coming to know themselves. What's so sad is when reality hits them and they realize it was all such short lived vanity. The battle for a few extra dollars and social acceptance ends up to be a life sentence to where their identity in the world is lost forever. There's just so many psychological implications to the unfulfillment that get lost in the tail wind as we all push forward to the mirage and illusionary goal that's been projected upon us. People fall victim to the measure of success and at the realization of their own inadequacies and imperfections trying to be someone they're not and it demoralizes them. They ultimately victimize themselves and the world around them for nothing. Again, idols can form inspiration if it's used productively and in humility to some degree, but it can also form figments of our imagination which can form an unrealistic expectation especially exalting people who only have their own needs in mind. You think of all the autographs ever given by idols over the years, but very few of us have ever known them personally, yet we worship them. The carnal mind doesn't analyze what's eternally productive, it just perceives the influence as the justified cause to the desired outcome. Michael Jordan is not only idolized but has been literally worshipped for his accolades in basketball and business. His success may have inspired millions to play basketball which is a positive outlet, don't get me wrong, but it's his dream they're chasing and his dream has already been accomplished and fulfilled by him. His dream is a worldly desire and bar that's been set to which he's received his worldly praise, but is actually a deterrent to the truth of spiritual reality and the reality of God that has had its reverse effects. He's now retired basking in his adulation as though that's the inspired goal for the world to pursue. Unfortunately, that's the whole deception of idolatry and why Jesus' own words in Matthew 20:16 say, "The last will be first and the first will be last: many are called but few are chosen." My point again is that the pursuit of fame and fortune is blinding and causes such a ripple effect psychologically in how we accept ourselves and each other. It consumes people in self-deprecation and forms this narcissism within us all. It also averts us from the destiny of our souls which is salvation in Jesus Christ.

True Heroes

Personally, I see desiring to be someone else as devaluing who we were created to be and blinds us from our own individual gifts that God has inclusively given us and called us to in our lives. Ephesians 4:7 says, "To each one of us grace was given according to the measure of the gift of Christ. Therefore he says, when he ascended on high, he led captivity captive, and gave gifts unto men.... he who descended is also the one who ascended far above all the heavens, that he might fill all things. And he himself gave some to be apostles, some prophets, some evangelists, some pastors and teachers, for the equipping of the saints for the work of Ministry, for the edifying of the body of Christ, till we all come to the unity of the faith and of the knowledge of the Son of God." It's amazing when we live to serve our gifts and callings how at peace we are with God and how much direction and purpose we have intuitively in our lives. Without God we live in a vicarious state of unrest and in a convoluted perception of ourselves and our identity. The true heroes in life and pillars of inspiration especially through this pandemic, are those who don't seek praise or recognition for their actions. They are policemen, firemen and military personnel who risked their lives and serve in the line of duty for the freedoms we share. They are those who aren't deterred because of their circumstances and live selflessly to serve others. Any athlete, actor or musician relies on them when they're in trouble or injured. They're also paramedics, nurses and doctors in hospitals battling through the emotions of injuries and deaths and facing the consequences of true reality everyday. They are conservationists and people who instill fundamentals and moral values in everyday life. They are counsellors, school teachers, coaches and volunteers in shelters and charity organizations. They are healthcare and social workers for the mentally challenged and handicapped. Those that grieve and feel the brokenness in the world and want to help. They are people that are patient and compassionate and don't compromise their morality for their own benefit. They are tradesmen and housewives who work hard for their families and stand united in marriage for the greater cause and not for the cause of themselves. These are the heroes that sustain our communities and interactive world. They are people selflessly on their knees praying for this lost and broken world. Unfortunately the heroes and idols we've been subject to and built up in our minds are just too far-fetched and non relative to the circumstances that surround us and are used as a deceptive tool to impact our perceptions of true reality. The effects have taken their course from the years of methodological, meticulous desensitization and have caused severely destructive ramifications. Even if the majority don't act upon their feelings, the inadequacy and resentment within us all is still real and impacting our judgment and rationality. It creates a bitter envy and comparative spirit in our world that grows as the glory of our idols escalates and as our eyes stay glued to these lenses.

Ramifications of the American Dream

The problem is more and more are acting upon their feelings. We see through the lens what we can't attain and it becomes a debilitating inferiority whether it be in acceptance or affluence. We want the money, sex, fame and prestige for ourselves as we see it being exemplified but unfortunately our hostility becomes reactionary and the outcome of it causes much of our problematic society. We've become viciously jealous and violent especially in America. 39773 people died from guns in America last year alone and over half-a-million since 9/11. Terrorism isn't the problem nor is racism as we've been deceived into believing, in fact these are the least of America's problems. These are obvious issues that need attention and rectification but the problem is far more severe than these. We have become a terror unto ourselves in fornication, unforgiveness, envy and idolatry. They are calling covid an unprecedented global pandemic but there's a far deeper pandemic spiritually and psychologically taking place around us. The American dream is like a seductive snake charming the carnal flesh of the world in its promotion of stimulation and self-liberation. The rippling effect is wherever the lens and promotion can be seen for the seduction to implement its objective and our emotions and feelings can be drawn into its coercion. I'm a few kilometres across the border here in Canada and I can see the influence taking root all around me. We've become far more of a sexually driven and violent society in the last couple decades then we truly realize. We've also become far more fearful and introverted. Three blocks away a man was stabbed to death next to the market on the corner. Another man was riddled with bullets from a targeted shooting about a mile away, close to my friend's house. Another man was burned alive at a gas station in an apparent arson murder case that's on my way to church and there was a drug-induced lunatic that ran a Cadillac Escalade through traffic that killed someone a block up the road. There's a cross with flowers surrounding it and a picture of a young teenage boy that unfortunately died in the accident. This was all within a five-block radius of where I live and I live in one of the safer communities in the city. I forgot to mention the time about four blocks from my house where I saw a big tall lanky guy staggering across the street. At first glance when I drove by him, it looked like he'd been shot or stabbed in the stomach so I drove around the block to see if he was okay. He told me he'd been attacked by a machete in a home invasion and that the cops would be after him and to leave him alone. Eventually another samaritan phoned the cops and within five minutes we were surrounded. My point is that I live in Canada where we don't have crime and gun violence nearly to the degree of that in America or around the world but the desperation and entitlement seems to be escalating everyday. It's far more psychological and spiritual than people realize and has become an unsafe and unstable world to live in with so much of our minds being influenced and the pressure of our identities under scrutiny. We've become socially dependent on a world that's being controlled by deranged and vile men with extremely bad intentions for our lives physically, emotionally and psychologically who are possessed by satan himself. They're closing in on us with every form of technology much like The Truman Show so boldly illustrates. That movie is a perfect example of the complex psychology of satan above the perceptions of our minds and how he's ensnared the world like a spider's web. What's incredible about The Truman Show is through all the lies and psychological manipulation his acting wife continues to promote products through the process as part of her contract just as Jim Carrey plays his role as a part of his contract to the viewer. We think we're watching him within the context of the movie but it's really about us in the context of satan and how he puppets the world. It's crazy how bold these actors and producers are in actually re-enacting the reality that's taking place around us. A spider's web is a perfect analogy because of how unassuming it seems at first until you complacently get caught up in the web and the more you fight to get free the more you entangle yourself, until eventually, you're consumed. Unfortunately, when it comes to the world, they've cornered every market for revenue in their insatiable thirst for power and control and watch as we react and fall victim in our blindness to it all. Ironically much of their deceptive conformity lies in the world wide "web" or the "internet" as though we're being trapped in them both. It's also ironic that we have a social security number and card to establish and secure our identity in the system to which I feel holds very little security. It's impossible to feel secure in a system of conformity and now we're seeing the effects. The truth is we're all feeling the conformity and oppressive pressure of the system whether we believe in conspiracy or not. It's not if we believe that conspiracy is a theory, it's what those in independent impunity are conspiring to do and what their identity is. That's where everyone is so lost and divided in their opinions on conspiracy. Again, they own the supply and generate the demand therefore they can inflate and control the entire system economically and psychologically through social unrest. We can ignore and deny it all we want but the evidence is in everything we see. There's hundreds of mass shootings a year now as if it's the norm in society. Life has become like an illusionary video game to vent our hostility. Again, until blood is actually shed we don't realize the severity of true reality because the illusionary fantasy has become our minds reality. I saw an episode of First 48 where a 16 year old was bullied by a bunch of kids in front of his girlfriend. Him and his friends then made a hit list and started shooting each one of them one by one. There were surveillance cameras around a convenience store that finally caught the 16 year old chasing one of them with an Uzi, shooting them multiple times and killing them. It all goes back to that root of bitterness and entitlement that idolatry generates. It's just so sad to see it in younger and younger ages.

These pathetic hellbound minions have used people as lab rats to conduct decades of chemical, psychological and social experiments without us even knowing to cause this division and delusion within us all. Delusional is characterized by holding idiosyncratic beliefs or impressions that are contradicted by reality or rational argument, typically as a symptom of mental disorder. It also says a delusion is a false belief that is based on incorrect interpretation of reality. A delusional disorder, previously called paranoid disorder, is a type of serious mental illness called "psychosis" in which a person cannot tell what is real from what is imagined. Again, I feel the whole world has become delusional without Christ and is under the cloud of misconception and conspiracy in everything we do. Everything I see is ingenuine or fabricated, especially the news and media outlets.

More Conspiracy

If flies on the walls of time could produce literature we'd all be shocked at how evil, evil truly is. I watched a documentary a while ago on these three identical twins that were purposely separated at birth in an adoption clinic. They ended up finding each other miraculously in their late teens. The story was on the news and they actually became quite famous after being on talk shows in the following years. They started doing research to find their original birth parents and discovered they were used as a social experiment unbenounced to anyone. They were divided into different homes as a social experiment with researchers documenting their emotional conduct and habitual tendencies throughout their childhood. There were other stories very similar that leaked out with one involving two twin sisters by the same organization. It was so morbid and demented watching it, I could feel the evil through the television. So much of this stuff has gone on without the general population's knowledge and like I said before, we'd be appalled at how interconnected it all is to the ones we're dependent upon and have entrusted our lives to. We'd be shocked at what the taxpayers money has been invested in over the years. These aren't mere conspiracy theories as people perceive them to be. Sometimes the greatest evil is the evil that affects us the most and is the hardest to see. It can be in plain sight, right behind the veil of perception but almost impossible to recognize. It's the collateral procession of the original lie and in the secrecy that evil manifests itself the most. We are definitely being poisoned physically and psychologically and their greatest tactics are to hide the lie or else divert or pay off the insinuations. We can never catch up with the narrative as it's set in motion. They'll also murder the insinuation if it endangers the progress of the lie. The lie is the ultimate tool of extortion because it holds the truth of the objective. This is part of the global elite's elusiveness hidden behind their all seeing eye. They see what we can't see because they own the 360 degree lens of innovation that videos the world and with it they're always two steps ahead of every move or insinuation we make. There's a show on the history channel called, "America's book of secrets." The commercial reads, "Which holds more secrets, the Illuminati or the Freemasons, Fort Knox or area 51, the FBI or the secret service? What deeper history is lingering in the shadows?" It's definitely interesting but they're far more elusive than what a new TV show will disclose to the public. It's all part of the narrative that's hidden in the archives. It's a lie covering a lie behind a lie, covering a lie and no one outside of their round table other than God of course can truly see who is on top of their demented pyramid scheme. They've quite simply mastered the lending scheme from an economic perspective and collapse each system as it generates any sort of self-sufficiency or independence. It's like playing musical chairs with the invisible man. You know he's in the room but his identity is unknown.

A lot of their identity has come out to the public but much of what we assume to know are the dominoes they've used in extortion to fulfill their agenda and divert the blame whether it be in politics, secret societies or religion. Each one is behind the eight ball of their own greed and entitlement. Again, if you are discerning enough you can see how they fulfill and monopolize their agenda and objectives through scripts in movies and television but the majority of the population is oblivious and consumed by their pursuit of the world. Movies like the "Hunger Games" are a perfect example of all of this going on. It's a merciless and ruthless evil they're inciting and provoking to the public. I watched another crazy movie called V for Vendetta that reveals much more than the untrained eye can see. The main character is an anarchist or so-called freedom fighter who attempts to ignite a revolution through elaborate terrorism against the government. There's so many intricate narratives and extortion through religion and the occult in the movie but what struck me was when V the main character set up a massive set of dominoes that fell down to spell his name as though he was the puppet master and supreme conductor to the game. I'll mention too, like I was stating before in the book, how seductively we've come to admire and sympathize with these cult heroes and characters because of course, he's praised in the movie as a modern day pied piper.

What concerns me is how much knowledge they hold, how much power of discretion they possess in broadcasting these scripts and how integrated they've come to influence and affect our society. It's become an incredibly blatant mockery of our intelligence on every level and they know it and relish in their sense of empowerment because of it. Satan in his own sick way is being worshipped by us unknowingly. We're giving him all the praise for fulfilling all of our hearts desires and these men are the dealers in his sick game of cards. It's like a rabbit trail trying to pinpoint these perpetrators like taping together the remains of a paper shredder. Even the main character V in the movie wears a mask throughout, never revealing his true identity. There's of course the CIA, Freemasonry, the Illuminati and all sorts of interconnected secret societies. There's the so-called global elite, banking systems, the New World Order and many other syndicates and aliases who are in cahoots behind the deception but even they in all their perceived impunity, intelligence and amalgamation are sadly deceived by satan himself. You can put a name behind it and call it what you want but at the end of the day they're just evil self-serving men with nothing better to do with their pathetic lives than to destroy ours. I'm not going to write too much more about these pathetic hellbound lunatics because it just irritates me and gives them more of the glory and attention they don't deserve but I also think people should become aware and do some research for themselves, especially during this pandemic because soon we'll see how deeply they've impacted and infiltrated our freedoms socially and economically. It's formed and shaped so much of our culture's state of mind and complacency that with only a little research, would help us to become far more aware and wise. More importantly, it confirms the biblical world view on so many levels and aspects of our lives. These people are psychopaths not only for what they are imposing upon us but how psychotic they are in their blatant irreverence to the eternal judgment of God.

Warning

They will all die and be petrified in a state of permanent torment and shame for eternity without a hand to hold or an ear to listen. Their actions will be an irreversible judgement that will never leave their soul and satan will laugh as they themselves will be seen by themselves as the greatest pawn and most deceived. This is what 2 Timothy 3:13 means when it says evil men will grow worse and worse, deceiving and being deceived because even they themselves are deceived by the greatest adulterer and deceiver of them all. My warning to anyone involved in the occult or societies who think they hold a wisdom or awareness to what's going on in the world as it dictates society is to be careful in what you claim to know because all you are is an over-stimulated puppet being used for another agenda unbenounced to you that's a degree further up the pecking order than yourself. If it wasn't true, what are they withholding from you and why don't they reveal it to you? You yourself have been deceived in the oppression of your identity since you were a child by demonic spirits and the outfit you pursue and now you justify your procession in the compensation, but all that is, is a part of the deception. You're just being used for the insecurity within you. I suggest you reevaluate your involvement and the destiny of your soul. I promise it won't be worth it. There's still time to repent and accept Jesus, even if it costs you your life. Those who don't will feel like they were sandwiched between two eternal beds of nails and wish they never pursued or did what they'd done. Imagine being in a crater in space all alone in full awareness of your past, with a strong gravitational pull holding you in a permanent paralyzed state of conscious deliberation and shame. That's hell, and that's where these people are all going. The world isn't worth it, nor are the secrets they hold. Mark 8:36 says, "What will it profit a man if he gains the whole world, and loses his soul?" This being true, they stare straight at God's word and warnings and willfully proceed with their objectives and rebellion. That's what satanism is at its core, is rebelling against God's Word and pursuing what you consciously know is wrong. It's seeing the effects and still implementing them and more. Their flesh has become possessed by the insatiable spirit of power and irreproachability and it consumes them into a continual state of immoral liberty and wilful defiance. They think they know satan personally and inclusively because they are his hosts in their wills desire but satan knows the outcome of God's word and these men who think they are allies in compliance to him, again, will realize the joke was on them all along. He'll step over them like every other deceived corpse he's manipulated in history. The Bible says satan disguises himself as an angel of light and he's even disguised himself to them, even though they're possessed by him. Satan craves the feeling of being glorified and exalted over God therefore he mocks his creation by turning us against ourselves, who are the image of God. It's his obsession in his fallen state of jealousy and envy towards God. The glory lies in our decision to impulsively abstain in reverence to God or to indulge in iniquity, and for some the spirit of iniquity becomes an obsessive liberation and empowerment over their conscience.

Chapter 10

Sexual Contradiction

It's insane to me what lengths they've gone and how intricate the degrees of evil have intertwined. I guess that's why it's called organized crime but this is a whole nother level of sophistication. They've influenced so much of our world but the most damaging I see is from a sexual perspective. It's one of satan's primary objectives to pervert and manipulate because of the damage it causes when practiced outside of the biblical standard. Sex can temporarily feel good through our senses but it also makes babies and babies don't thrive in broken, ununified and unnurturing environments. Children grow up much like myself, in all sorts of vulnerable and unfortunate scenarios and react according to their environment and circumstances. We've come to justify the stimulation of sex over the responsibility and accountability that precede and proceed the action. This is why it's so imperative to understand the spiritual psychology of satan because he's accentuated the desire and acceptance through these lenses to such a degree until we can't suppress the impulse and then he relishes in the aftermath of both pregnancy and post orgasm emotions. Unfortunately it's in the aftermath of the orgasm that the truth of God's design and standard are revealed. Satan is the father of the one night stand and uses every residual emotion in the outcome whether it be rejection, expectation or irresponsibility to further destroy God's creation. It's not just him enticing us either, it's our own naive and perverted ignorance that obviously causes the damage as well. We've come to sacrifice our dignity for social acceptance because our identity in the world has become our priority outside of our identity in God. My birth parents were two drug-induced hippies without a care in the world who had random sex on the hill of a mental institution without any concern or obligation to the repercussions. I was this little helpless child that was taken away from my mom at birth as she was deemed unfit and irresponsible and then was subsequently given over to the foster care system. We don't realize that God's standards and convictions are there to save us from these devastating repercussions. We also don't realize that the conviction in us is actually him fighting for our dignity and virtue when we give it away so easily ourselves. I still suffer from childhood trauma like rejection and separation anxiety forty years later and it's no different for so many others that are born in these irresponsible, unplanned pregnancies and circumstances.

I have a friend that moved to Mexico 15 years ago that just had a baby. She's there basically alone with very few friends or family but decided to have unprotected sex with her new boyfriend as she wanted a baby. I'm sure at first he played the role and seemed to fill her desire for acceptance but as soon as the baby came he was gone. He just used her for sex and now she's left as a single mom, raising a baby all alone. What's also interesting is that now that the baby is born and her maternal nurturing characteristics have kicked in, she hates him for his lack of responsibility and obligation towards her and wants a godly man of virtue, integrity and responsibility. She thought because he was having sex with her that she was being accepted but really the dignity in her and respect of her was being rejected. It's not just random sex causing these unfortunate pregnancies nowadays, they are people with their own intentions in mind and not the intentions of the baby. People just want a baby to have a baby as though it's a social trend without any care, welfare or consideration for the baby's safety or future. We certainly can't blame God for all of this especially if he's given us strict warnings and instructions otherwise. In my situation I was lucky I was born in Canada where there are social services in place for these unfortunate situations but around the world there's not and a lot of the suffering we're seeing is due to our own repetitive unaccountability and ignorance throughout the generations. It's become a generational curse for many nations. You look at these countries with thousands of children living in poverty and disease and we all wonder why and even blame God but common sense would tell them to stop having sex. They're bearing children in a situation that they can't bear themselves and where there's little to no opportunity. It's even more of a revelation now through this pandemic with people still conceiving babies as though they're optimistic of a promising future. It's just a selfish and blatant disregard for true reality on every level. Again, it's extremely selfish to conceive a child into circumstances that are poisoned and without resources or opportunity especially if you're living in them yourself. It's not just in poor countries, it's anywhere where the environment is unsafe or toxic. Even in my sinfullist days of fornication, I never finished my orgasm inside my partner for fear of pregnancy. It's just common sense. It's become a catastrophic epidemic of ignorance the world is undeniably responsible for. Whether we are enticed by satan or not, we are still conscious of our actions and living in the consequences of them. I don't see the stimulation and climax of an unprotected orgasm being justifiable to this catastrophic aftermath. Millions of abortions happen around the world every year with such an ignorance to the consequences. It's amazing that the world hates a God that has designed us and all our senses for the purpose of love and all these emotional implications are proof of that. He's designed sexual intimacy to be sacred in marriage but unfortunately the world seems completely liberated to practice sex with whomever it wants, whenever it wants, without any concerns, accountability or reverence to God and satan entices us along the way to every degree of justifiable fornication.

I came in contact with an old neighbour from over 20 years ago on Facebook a while ago. She's grown into quite a beautiful woman now and I could hardly recognize her to be honest. We communicated back and forth for a few months and then decided to go for a walk to catch up. I figured I'd share my testimony about coming to Jesus when the time was right and just have an innocent and harmless conversation. We exchanged numbers and I finally texted her to schedule a time and she texted me back simply saying "I am horny" with a picture of her bare legs up to her underwear in her bathroom. I was like huh? I hadn't seen this girl in more than 20 years and hardly knew her back then, yet she was willing to have sex with me wherever and whenever and show me pictures of her almost naked. It's insane how demented that is and how little she respected herself and her own dignity and also how little she respected mine. If that's our world nowadays, that's painting a big brush to the norm of sexual expectation and insinuation. Sex is the greatest physical intimacy and emotional release you can have with someone yet she was willing to release it all without any emotional connection and regardless of the consequence, but that's how our world is these days. We give so much of ourselves away for so little in return. What troubles me more is without Christ I was the same way. I probably would have followed through with her advances as most men would in the world. If we're not emotionally attached or fear transmitting diseases or pregnancy, we can just wear a condom and there's no apparent harm done. The action is somehow justified or edified in our masculinity as men but unfortunately the effects are deeper than just physical because that's not how sex was designed to be. 1 Corinthians 6:18 says, "Flee sexual immorality. Every sin a man does is outside the body, but he who commits sexual immorality sins against his own body." It's a spiritual soul tie and there's a severe effect on our dignity that compiles over the years of denial, especially with women who yearn deeply for acceptance, intimacy, trust, emotional refuge and security in a man. I guess it kind of goes back to our conscience because if we know to wear a condom, what are we protecting ourselves from if we aren't aware of the consequences? Either way we're contradicting ourselves in justifying the temporary pleasures that sex brings. Of course I didn't follow through with her advances and texted her back sharing my faith and convictions about the issue. I understand because I lived that lifestyle before Christ so I didn't judge her, but what's interesting is a few weeks later she texted me back apologizing and sharing how confused, insecure and lonely she's been in her life lately. I feel deep down these young women aren't even thinking about the actual act of intercourse as much as they're so bound up with peer pressure and yearning for acceptance that they're willing to sacrifice whatever it takes to gain that social acceptance and attention. It's like they put themselves out there to gain the attention like their friends and idols and then have to live up to the identity and expectation they promote of themselves. To me it's just more ramifications of this idolatrous and envious world. The truth again is that we're living against the design within us and it's breaking us down emotionally and separating us from the love of God and our relationship with him. These are the exact implications celibacy and monogamy in faith save us from. Even after masterbation the design of God is revealed because we feel empty, bitter and unfulfilled as though acceptance and love are the designed intention within us. It all points to God's principles on sex being the foundation for us to follow and when we don't these severe implications transpire and escalate. Abortion is the norm these days with over 25% of women having the procedure done in Canada. I can't believe we're this irresponsible but the statistics don't lie. It's just become a form of birth control nowadays. The women seem to get the hardest criticism but it's extremely selfish and irresponsible for a man to finish his orgasm inside of a woman without a condom and without concern for the aftermath, like I was saying before. It's such a contradiction and act of negligence because much of our own trauma, anger and pain in our lives come from a broken home and lack of support as a child which many times is from an unplanned pregnancy. We've come to a point as men where we don't even remotely consider the feelings or emotions of women in intercourse anymore, we're just doing it for ourselves to get off and brag about it to our friends. Sex to men is for control and validation and has become a perverted demonization of women on every level. We've become perverted heathens, void of any moral or ethical dignity anymore.

Outside of love and marriage women have merely become objects of fornication to men because that's how they've been presented to us and that's how they've come to represent themselves. The two sexual combatants' intentions are in complete contrast to each other to the desired result and satan has drawn both together for his cause and effect. A man's erection lasts until his orgasm and nine times out of ten his orgasm happens before a woman's so the actual sexual climax of a woman is rarely satisfied nor is it appreciated or even considered. This being the case, why are they even having sex? It's all hidden behind social acceptance and this is where we've become so insecure and vulnerable. Its not just abortion that's the problem with fornication where millions get murdered in the womb every year, single parenting is the norm these days along with an overloaded foster care system where all sorts of problems and trauma occur. Over a half a million kids are in the foster care system along with tens of thousands given up for adoption in North America every year. Another problem that people don't even consider anymore is that these relationships and pregnancies weren't ordained or sanctified by God and so many genetics have intertwined inadvertently all over the world with God's mercy as the only savior to our carnal definition of sexuality. There's so many generational curses and demonic oppression in seeds intermixing that have created such a collateral dichotomy. I have to define the word dichotomy in describing what I'm trying to say. Dichotomy is a division or contrast between two things that are or are represented as being opposed or entirely different. It says a dichotomy is a partition of a whole into two parts. In other words, this couple of parts must be jointly exhaustive: everything must belong to one part or the other, and mutually exclusive, nothing can belong simultaneously to both parts. Such a partition is also frequently called a bipartition. Finally it says a division into two especially mutually exclusive or contradictory groups or entities. Fornication and sanctified marriage is the wall between God and man and how we define conception. He's reconciled it all to himself through Christ but how much mercy do we expect from him especially to those willfully defying the obvious consequences. These aren't issues we should complacently disregard any more, these are paramount to the sustenance of our world and that we've totally abused and taken it for granted. Random sex or any fornication is not bringing us the joy as advertised. Kids get conceived and grow up lost and vulnerable without love, structure and proper discipline, then get addicted to drugs or alcohol and lash out on the world from their lack of support and guidance. We're just not connecting the dots anymore and live in a world of its own contradictions and hypocrisy, standing guilty as charged.

More Contradictions

We give all sorts of premise to protect the innocence and vulnerability of babies the second they exit the womb with medical aid, social services, resources and maternity leave in this Western world, yet we fight and bicker for the liberty to kill and dispose of them two seconds before while they're in the womb through abortion. People are even trying to pass legislation now to execute babies in their final trimesters and even after birth. I'm at a complete loss for words how insanely irresponsible and demonic these issues have become. For these to even be issues to the extent that they are, there has to be a such a massive amount of unprotected sex going on around the world. I can see how abortion could be an option in some unforeseeable circumstances such as rape, severe health complications or disease but for two competent and willing individuals, there is no excuse. If you're competent enough to do it and get yourself to the abortion clinic then you're competent enough to understand the consequences. If you were to ask any coherent, competent person if at any point in their lives, they were an embryo, they would say yes. It's irrefutable. The question then is what difference does it make if you kill me now or kill me then, if in your answer you identified with yourself? You've murdered me either way. Abortion activists will argue that we're too young to be conscious of it but I guess murdering people unconscious or in their sleep should be justifiable then now as adults? Any abortion activist will admit to having a soul so I don't see how they can justify killing one. Ultimately, they're all trying to escape the shame from the design within us to justify their own liberty to defiance. Their lives are the result of a heterosexual conception and somewhere down the line there are broken pieces that have bound them in seeking compensation but the truth reveals itself in the emotional compensation they desire. Regardless, we suck lives and souls out of wombs like a vacuum and sell the body parts for profit. That's where our society and government has come in all its scientific brilliance and philosophy. I remember watching a Planned Parenthood interview where one of the co-founders didn't know she was being filmed by a hidden camera. She went on agreeing to terms of purchasing tissue from abortions and even advocating prolonging the trimesters for the increase in tissue so she could eventually buy a Lamborghini. Call me simple-minded but to me, human tissue equals a human being being formed in the womb. You could tell she was leery about sharing the information of what she was doing but that is the contradiction in of itself, because if she thinks there's nothing ethically or morally wrong with it, then what is she leery about revealing? Again, this has become our world without God and living in its own vindicated sense of liberation.

It's not just concerning abortion or sex either, there are so many other aspects we've obscured and defined about life, death and the afterlife that we live in contradiction to ourselves and our conscience. We live so irreverent and complacent to any sort of eternal judgement nowadays as though just because we don't believe, it won't happen. My best friend growing up despises my faith. He's repulsively ignorant towards the Bible and Christianity all together and won't talk to me anymore. He used to snicker and mock me thinking it was all a joke and even mocked God with every word from his lips. He's said things about God and the bible that I can't even repeat in this book they're so despicable. His mother, who I was very close to when I was younger, died recently of cancer. She was an awful mother in so many ways, smoking, drinking, doing drugs, committing adultery and abusing her kids physically and verbally along the way causing the family years of emotional trauma and pain. I actually visited her in the hospice days before she died and it scared me to see the emptiness and grievance in her soul. You could feel the spirit of death around her in the room. A year later after she died my friend posted on Facebook how happy he is that she's in a better place, looking down from heaven and even praising her and her time in this life.

I just shook my head in disbelief and wonder. This guy literally hates the idea of Jesus Christ and the bible wholeheartedly, let alone contemplated salvation, yet he believes she's looking down from heaven? Huh? How does he suppose she got there and what heaven does he suppose she's in? Are we really this delusionary because it's most certainly not the heaven of the Bible? Unfortunately we are delusional with how passively we entertain the inevitability of death and judgment, because I hear that all the time from people. It's such a contradiction. It's like we're pleading for there to be a God to reward us for our good works in this life but that's where it ends. It's become some sort of vain expectation without any accountability, moral reverence or acknowledgement of God or his judgment. We don't balance the scale or understand perfect judgment and reject God due to his perfect and holy judgment of sin.

Kobe Bryant died recently in a horrific helicopter crash that claimed several other lives. I don't want to make light of the incident especially due to the children being involved but as a Christian you see the reactions of people after his death and it makes you concerned for how uninformed and oblivious we are to the severity of the bibles declarations concerning life and death, much like my friend and his mom. His fellow players, friends and fans praised him for months after his death for all his accolades and contributions on and off the court and would point to the sky in full assurance that he was in heaven looking down in a glorious shrine of all his achievements. I could write a book on this subject alone, but my point is, what in people sets this innate expectation without the acknowledgement or confirmation from God? We're denying the only heavenly relevance yet we're expecting to go there when Jesus himself says that he is the resurrection and the life and that unless a man is born again he cannot see the kingdom of God. What other heaven are we referring to? Acts 4:12 says, "There is salvation in no other, for there is no other name under Heaven given among men by which we must be saved." I watched a documentary about Mohammed Ali that was much the same. He simply figured that his good works outweighed his bad in this life and that there was a place waiting for him in glory. On his headstone was engraved a quote that he was regularly heard saying that read, "Service to others is the rent you pay for your room in heaven." The problem much like Kobe Bryant is he was a womanizing adulterer who fathered many children while he was married and even got secretly married while he was still married to his wife. He rejected Jesus Christ as his savior and was devoted to Islam his entire life. Again, the question becomes which heaven is real? The one we formulate to justify our sin or the heaven that God delivered us to from his atonement of our sin? We've become far too vain to the destiny of our souls and have put our faith in our own moral fortitude to establish our justification for eternal reward, but at the end of the day we have no power within ourselves to save ourselves or go anywhere outside of ourselves therefore we are completely at the mercy of God. We've tragically got things backwards and have obscured them in a way I don't think we even realize anymore. This is the heaven of our own imagination, not the heaven of God.

Singing our Way to Hell

Much of our generation has sung along to these songs like "Highway to Hell" from ACDC as though hell is some sort of extravagant party for sinners but what are we really singing about? The words themselves are telltale evidence to the complete disregard and complacency to God's word and providential authority. The lyrics and guitar solos get our souls rocking and singing along as though these bands are heroes of our generation but I look at it as satan literally writing the lyrics himself. It's like we're singing the praises of his glory to our own demise. The lyrics read,

Living easy, living free, season ticket on a one-way ride,
Asking nothing, leave me be,
I'm taking everything in my stride,
Don't need reason, don't need rhyme,
Ain't nothing that I'd rather do,
Going down, party time,
My friends are going to be there too!
I'm on a highway to hell, I'm on a highway to hell
No stop signs, speed limits,
Nobody's going to slow me down

Like a wheel, going to spin it,
Nobody's going to mess me around,
Hey satan, paid my dues,
Playing in a rocking band,
Hey mama, look at me,
I'm on my way to the promised land…

There's a lot to be said here but I'll let the words speak for themselves. They're acknowledging hell and so are we by singing along which is a contradiction in itself for a culture that doesn't follow the Bible and they even address satan as their master by paying their dues to him. The problem is that the hell of the bible most certainly isn't going to be a party for rock and roll singers, nor will it be for those who praise and idolize them. I keep reading the lyrics over along with some of their other songs and am shocked at how brazenly pompous they are as if God is a complete joke. It's blasmephy and shows how satan can become the host in the sensation of our flesh and how he increases our stimulation to build our egotistical complacency. The truth is the world is on a highway to hell, in fact it's more like an autobond but there is no promised land when you get there. The promise is you will go there without the saving power of Jesus Christ. Hell is a place of eternal torment and punishment for those who transgress against God and especially for those who willfully mock him in irreverence. Galatians 6:7-8 says, "Do not be deceived, God is not mocked, for whatever a man sows, that he will also reap. For he who sows to his flesh will of his flesh reap corruption, but he who sows to the spirit will of the spirit reap everlasting life." The end of Isaiah says the worm will never die and the fire will never be quenched so I'm not sure what hell they're referring to or suggesting. There will be no living easy or any free ride. There will be no friends and I guarantee their mom will not want to see them there and vice versa. In fact the original singer died choking on his own puke and the one brother who played rhythm guitar all those years recently died of lung cancer and I wonder if they think their influence on the world was all worth it now. If they knew where he was, I guarantee they'd stop playing their music, especially that specific song and the world would stop singing along. That's the spiritual chasm we cant see but if we could we'd be astonished and petrified. The end of Hebrews 12 says we should serve God acceptably with reverence and godly fear because he is a consuming fire. I don't think they took this scripture seriously. They have another song called "Hell's Bells" which is much the same idea. The first verse speaks of satan and reads,

> I won't take no prisoners,
> won't spare no lives,
> Nobody's putting up a fight,
> I got my bell, I'm going to take you to hell,
> I'm going to get you, satan get you,
> Hell's bells, satan's coming to you...

We are completely delusional spiritually singing along to these songs. It's like we know the truth deep down in our heart, but we hate it and the contradiction of it is our place of sensual rebellion that we love to embrace and in that rebellion satan gets glorified. One song that I naively sung along to on the radio for years myself was "Sympathy for the devil" by the Rolling Stones. I didn't even realize what I was singing about, but now I read the lyrics and can't believe how seductive they are. The whole song speaks of satan and reads,

> Please allow me to introduce myself,
> I'm a man of wealth and taste,
> I've been around for a long, long years,
> Stole million man's soul and faith,
> And I was around when Jesus Christ,
> Had his moment of doubt and pain,

Made damn sure that Pilate,
Washed his hands and sealed his fate,
Pleased to meet you, hope you guess my name,
But what's puzzling you, is the nature of my game,
So if you meet me, have some courtesy,
Have some sympathy, and some taste,
Use all your well-learned politeness,
or I'll lay your soul to waste…

That song is literally psychotic in the spiritual reality that surrounds us because satan certainly won't have sympathy for you when you die. It's incredible to me these passive contradictions that we complacently sing along to in pop culture much like "Hotel California" by the Eagles which is all about the church of satan to which the world adores and even worships. It even speaks of how seductive the spirit is and has actually just surpassed "Thriller" by Michael Jackson as the number one selling album of all time. There's other songs like "Running with the devil" by Van Halen and even songs about heaven like "Stairway to Heaven" by Led Zeppelin. There's actually over 40000 lyrics in all genres of music with reference to the devil and dozens of band names and albums. A lot of these analogies relate back to our conscience revealing itself before our very eyes and ears but we aren't evaluating these contradictions in a conscientious way, especially biblically. What are we professing to and what are we condoning? It just doesn't make sense. We are so blinded by the afflictions of man that we've merely come to embrace the outlet in our pain, further afflicting ourselves in the process. We'll support any outlet that we can relate with no matter what it is or who it harms in the process but all we're relating to is the effects from denying God.

The worst mockery of God that I even remember singing to growing up was "Jesus Christ Pose" by Soundgarden. The lyrics are viciously antichrist and read,

And you stare at me
In your Jesus Christ pose
Arms held out,
Like you've been carrying a load
And you swear to me,
You don't wanna be my slave
But you're staring at me,
Like I need to be saved
In you're Jesus Christ pose
Thorns and shroud
Like it's the coming of the Lord…

These guys are really pushing the envelope to spite God. The music video is an even worse mockery of God and starts by saying, "And God so loved Soundgarden he gave them his only song." The video goes on with the band singing and hanging upside down with flashes of Jesus's skeleton on a cross as the centerpiece. It's kind of repetitive throughout with a heavy drum beat and guitar riff until finally the lead singer Chris Cornell starts driving nails into the skeleton on the cross while screaming at the top of his lungs. It's shocking watching it now as a Christian at how ignorant and aggressive they are towards Jesus Christ. I'm not sure I even know what to say. The album went platinum and sold millions of copies worldwide which brought the band fame, fortune and acclaim for decades. Cornell went on to other bands and made a solo career of his own until finally he committed suicide a couple years ago. The question again is where is Chris Cornell now as I write this? His lyrics mocked Jesus as though he didn't need saving but now he's dead, or is he?. I don't think his song back in 1991 would have gotten him many brownie points with God right now, nor during his life. I would say he's in a bit of a dilemma. I want to say, "Lord have mercy on him, he didn't know what he was doing," but the video seems to suggest otherwise. What excuse does he have and what excuse does the world have singing along to this garbage? He gambled with eternal damnation which is far more severe than he ever thought he realized and he even influenced the world to do the same.

These heavy metal bands like Metallica and Slayer are much the same in their supposed love of satan and hatred toward God in their music but completely contradict themselves in so many ways. They are fierce in their anger towards politics and all sorts of social conformity and injustice from religion and the government which definitely shows their awareness and intelligence. Their lyrics are their outlet and again, are full of hatred towards our government and its misuse of power and money but what are they really saying? In every note they play and lyric they scream to the audience they're acknowledging their own awareness of moral conduct and the expectation of it from those in influential positions. They're voicing the results of its effect on them with their audience but merely enhancing its objective and influence from their own platform. Every creative loin in their soul is united together in vengeance for the evil impunity and oppression that is being afflicted upon them and that we're all being subject to, but all they are is reacting in sin to its cause and effect themselves, further enticing and influencing the culture. They say they're satanic but oppose the oppression satan afflicts upon them. They have no idea who satan is whatsoever. If they knew the satan of the bible they'd understand all of this, but they are oblivious. My point again is, who are they even identifying with in regards to God and satan? They've misidentified both. Ultimately, it's a win-win for satan and his demons either way in the resentment, division and hostility that ensues.

He manifests himself through all of these outlets and is a deceptive angel of light just as the Bible indicates. Whether it be in heavy metal, rock and roll or gangster rap, wherever the desires of our carnal flesh are exalted and can influence a culture through an outlet, ideology or stereotype, he is there to supply the need and becomes a vicarious source of escape for our emotions and feelings. Again, we seem to live in a deceptive chasm of these delusional contradictions all day long. There's a popular American singer named Lil Nas X who gives satan a lap dance in one of his videos and has teamed up with a company called MSCHF to release a new athletic Nike shoe dedicated to satan complete with a pentagram and supposedly a drop of human blood in each shoe. I also noticed an upside down cross on the tongue and the number 666 inscribed on the side, along with the scripture Luke 10:18 in which Jesus says, "I saw satan fall like lightning from heaven." This kind of stuff is just blatant mockery and ignorance of the biblical and spiritual truth that surrounds us all. I could go on forever with these paradoxes in our culture. These people don't have a clue what influence they're generating and what they're inflicting upon themselves.

There's a new show on TV that's simply called "Evil" on CBS. The storylines are all about demon possession and the supernatural in almost every episode. There's exorcism, murder and all sorts of sociopathic dialogue involving children and serial killers. An unbelieving audience is glued to their screens of these shows watching episode after episode of something they adamantly deny in their perceived reality, yet the reality of it is staring them back in the face manipulating and implementing its directive. The question is, are demons a fantasy or are they real and if they're real, are they associated with the bible? This is my point in all this because if they're not, what demons are we referring to and why? People say they have demons in their head all the time. It's just become an expression we say nonshalontly, but are they truly real? In one of the most popular country songs out right now, the singer speaks of fighting demons in his head. There's also a rap song by BMike that's actually called "Fighting demons in my head" that's extremely graphic in all that he wars with in his mind. So are they real? That's the dilemma we're in here. Many of these people are professing atheists and agnostics so again, I'm not sure what they're associating with. I even saw a commercial for H&R Block the other day with a representative on the phone with a client nonchalantly referring to satan and hell. The phone clerk says, "I see your job status is now working from home?" He then answers jokingly by saying, "You know hell isn't all lakes of fire and tickle fights with satan, sometimes it's a three hour video call." We're denying the supernatural defined in the bible even though it's our only source for it, but in that denial and neglect of it, the spirits are constantly at work in our subconscious minds without us being cognitively aware of it. The word cognitive is defined as relating to, being, or involving conscious intellectual activity such as thinking, reasoning or remembering but somehow in our ignorant complacency we've become cognitively impudent as though it's all fictional irrelevance. The supernatural is no fictional fantasy and there's many other shows now that involve these sorts of scripts that we're all growing infatuated and mesmerized by. We just don't realize how satan deceives us psychologically and subconsciously without defining his biblical identity and having the spirit of God to teach us. It's beyond our carnal capacity to see how he manifests himself, like a permeating death cloud that you just can't see. For many, television has become an escape but we're being drawn into what we should be escaping from. You'll notice almost every script these days involves betrayal, vengeance or murder. It's like everything we watch has a drastic and suspenseful conclusion to enhance our fear and anxiety. Every second commercial seems to be about a new drug to save us from a new disease or else a new app to enhance our credit rating. The word circumscribe is to constrict the range of activity or for someone's power or freedom to be limited or restricted and that is his eventual goal for all of humanity physically and psychologically. If you think of it like a farmer's field of potatoes. They lay dormant and unseen under the ground until the first rainfall and then they all start to bud together under the soil in every corner of the farmer's field and that's what satan is doing through all these outlets simultaneously.

More Contradictions

It's not only the supernatural, there's many more contradictions I see everywhere within our society. I was at a freedom of rights rally supporting a friend of mine who likes evangelizing a while ago. To be honest I don't like getting involved in contentious or volatile confrontation but I thought I'd take in the experience just to see what takes place at these events and rallies. There was a bunch of stuff going on but for the most part it was several groups battling over human rights and free speech against a few Christian speakers. There was one group up in arms screaming, "My body, my choice!," protesting for the right of abortion. There was another group that was even more volatile contesting their lesbian and transgenderism rights for equality and there was also many marijuana activists mixed in together with them all. It finally got so hostile, dozens of police had to form a line to barricade them off from the speakers who actually had security guards surrounding them as they were on the microphone. This one lady was so irate she was spitting in my face and violently ripped my friend's testimonies out of his hand, throwing them on the ground and screaming for her voice to be heard. It actually got extremely hostile for about an hour or so but as I stood back and assessed the situation, I saw so many contradictions in our emotional awareness and consciousness. The speaker's weren't even condemning their actions, they were merely stating their own opinions on free speech and equality. All these groups formed together in a united front against these Christian speakers who were actually quite peaceful and reserved, but to me they're living in such contradiction to themselves on every level. First of all if you're gay you will most certainly won't ever need an abortion, therefore these two groups are contradicting each other. Secondly, here in British Columbia they're all in complete liberty to smoke dope and live and marry however they feel justified sexually. We're one of the largest producers of marijuana in the world and even paint the crosswalks like rainbows in support of the gay and lesbian community all over the province. For me unbiasedly assessing the situation, from a neutral perspective, if they were confident and at peace within themselves and secured in their identity and in the opinions they hold, why were they incessantly seeking affirmation from the people they adamantly disagree with who weren't even condemning their lifestyle? They're trying to force Christian's to believe in their lifestyle but they're contradicting themselves in the freedom and tolerance they desire and that's all the Christian speakers were standing up for. To me, if they were at peace within themselves they wouldn't have to prove it and there wouldn't be such hostility within them towards the community they are trying to convince and receive acceptance from. They're actually confirming the dissatisfaction and shame within their own conscience by their unsecured emotions and in how they seek affirmation, assurance and acceptance. They're proving that all they're living for is acceptance and that there is no fulfilment in the lifestyle they're adamantly contesting for. There was a spirit in all of them that was so furious and full of hatred as though they're opinion is all that mattered, but that's the whole point because they aren't secure in their own opinion or in their perception of themselves. Everyone seems in support of gay pride nowadays but it's a scary thing when all you're living for is your own pride, no matter what your identity is in the world. What's even worse is when you're trying to prove it. James 4:6 says, "God resists the proud, but gives grace to the humble," but our culture is actually fighting to establish it. That is a selfish and self absorbed philosophy on life that lives on unsecured grounds. Again, if we're living for the affirmation from the world around us, we'll always be lost because everyone is entitled to their own opinion. That's what freedom of rights and civil liberties are in a democracy therefore it's impossible to ever fulfill that desire. Essentially, nobody's obligated to condone anything as tolerance becomes our defining stance on liberty. We're fighting for freedom against an obligated philosophy or opinion yet we're infuriated when our philosophy or opinions aren't heard. It makes no sense, and to me, this is our evolving contradiction.

We've become so delusional and immature in these issues because homosexuals should thank the heterosexual intercourse for their gift of life and for me it's impossible for them to say they were born that way because no one has ever being born that way. The gay men produce sperm and lesbians have their menstrual cycle, therefore their minds desires are in contradiction of their own bodies. Ultimately, a homosexual world has no mother, no father, has no children and has no next generation. The family dies in their cause and with their philosophy, yet they hate God for upholding these principles and convicting the world of these actions. Our common sense has deteriorated into a shallow grave of mindless stimulation and emotional vindication. We are so deeply searching for social acceptance outside of God, that we will destroy our bodies and minds by any means necessary to find it and this is much of the deception satan has inflicted upon the world. If all their identity is based on is sex, then what I see is people lost outside the identity they're trying to affirm and hold onto because there is so much more to life than just the stimulation of sex. Again, the truth of it all is who we are in the fulfillment when the orgasm is finished, whether we're homosexual or heterosexual. We're experientially being conformed by our own feelings and sensuality but it's not providing us a productive and sustaining resolution, it's actually increasing our dependence upon it in our dissatisfaction. Again, I see so much of it being rooted from the compounding effects of idolatry. I feel many women compare themselves to the women presented on television and movies and in their inadequacy and fear of rejection from men attempting to live up to the standard, they gravitate to an identity that is accepting and supportive. There's so much pressure on women to be sexually active these days and many claim homosexuality to relieve that expectation. I also believe much of it stems from abandonment or the abuse and fear of a male figure in their lives which is completely understandable.

When it comes to men and homosexuality, I see the pressure of masculinity being so strong that they not only embrace the sexual lifestyle to relieve the pressure, they change their character entirely to where they aren't pressured to live up to the standard at all. It all stems from idolatry and the fear of rejection. Anywhere we feel acceptance, we'll conform ourselves to that identity even if it's not who we truly are. Again, if it's who we truly are we wouldn't have to prove it.

Ultimately, we're broken without a safe and supportive family core and I feel if people were to truly examine the root of their trauma and pain and what they yearn for, it would be to go back to their childhood and grow in a more secure, supportive and structured environment full of love and acceptance from their parents. Our society is lost without these fundamental truths. Even with that as an anchor, the pressure from the world is so severe nowadays that people are lost and crumbling in their perception of themselves. It's all so sad. I've worked in street ministry off and on for years and their stories are always full of abuse, neglect, abandonment and rejection. Much like my own story, two people decided to have random sex and the outcome is a lost and broken vessel without support and love, left to fend for ourselves in a search for an identity and for acceptance.

The statistics don't lie and common-sense reveals a lot to those who have it and seek for it but the impulse and gratification these days seems to override the conscience and the influence seems to persuade the impulse more and more. My point in repeating this is because this is where spiritual relativity is defined and where the truth of God can be seen in how we progressively and emotionally react in our afflictions. There's an origin to our discourse that God re-establishes where discretion and abstinence reveals to us the truth within us all. The bible is not religious, it's practical and relevant teaching for our souls to this very day. Proverbs 2 says, "If you receive my words, and treasure my commands within you, so that you incline your ear to wisdom, and apply your heart to understanding....then you will understand the fear of the Lord, and find the knowledge of God... when wisdom enters your heart, and knowledge is pleasant to your soul, discretion will preserve you, understanding will keep you, to deliver you from the way of evil." In denying the Word, we're denying exactly what he says will transpire and cause our pain. We then try to carnally redefine what he's defined, somehow blaming him for the outcome. This is another part of our evolving contradiction and where so much of our anger and resentment stems from.

I was in the community pool a few months ago sitting in the adult hot tub when I saw a young mid-twenties girl walking towards me. She looked like she had a skin coloured bikini on from a distance but as she got closer I realized she was naked from the waist up. It startled me at first and I motioned to the lifeguards for her to go back to the changing room and put a top on. She then started bickering contentiously with me about her rights and freedoms. It caused a bit of a scene because there were several people around but it's interesting the narratives surrounding it. It was a busy Saturday afternoon and there were two other guys in the hot tub who were on her side, obviously because they enjoyed the scenery. I was frustrated and actually worried for her and her safety. The more frustrated I was the more they all got frustrated with me. I stated to the one younger guy that the bible says if anyone looks at a woman with lust he's committed adultery in his heart and he replied, "Who gives a s*** about the Bible." I then got even more upset and told her there's children and the elderly in the pool and that she should have more respect for them and for herself. The lifeguard finally came by and stated that there's a new law allowing her to be topless in the pool. I finally threw my hands up in the air and said "You're all crazy!" Before Christ I wouldn't have cared so much and probably enjoyed the scenery myself but he opens our eyes and hearts to a deeper moral consciousness, not only for the concern of others but the concern for her and her own self-dignity and well-being. I told her she's putting a target on her back with that kind of mindset but she just got more incessant about her rights and freedoms. We are pushing the boundaries of tolerance for the sake of our entitled feelings but there's definitely repercussions to the boundaries we're crossing. From a male perspective it's a fine line she's crossing because perverts and pedophiles are allowed in public pools as well and many of us struggle with these issues far more than women realize. All she's doing is enhancing the lust within us but if anything were to happen to her she'd be scarred for life and blame the man for acting upon his feelings. She's drawing and enticing all the men's attention to herself but holding us accountable to any sort of violation towards her. It's like a young deer strolling through a pride of lions in spite and blaming them for being hungry. It's so blatantly ignorant and naive to the surroundings and reality we live in. There used to be a serial killer that actually lived in the area surrounding the pool named Clifford Olson who raped and stabbed his victims to death. I'm saying this not for us to live in fear but to be cautious of the attention we're drawing to ourselves because we don't know whose eyes are upon us or what they're struggling with. Again, she's purposely triggering men's impulses and hormones for her own selfish and sensual desires for attention and acceptance but meanwhile regarding their restraint and conduct as a means to her own liberty. It's a complete contradiction. I'm not trying to justify men in our actions in any way but we need to respect and analyze these things from all perspectives. Women do not know what goes on in the minds of men and vice versa and we need to respect that in a God fearing way because if women knew, they'd dress far more appropriately, guaranteed. What's even more of a contradiction is that a few months before this happened, a man was caught videotaping a lady over top of a change room wall in the same facility. The story was even on the news and headlined in the local newspaper. The same Community Center then spent thousands of dollars extending the walls to the ceiling in every bathroom and change room, meanwhile they allowed this young 20 year old to walk around half-naked and even defended her right to do so? It makes no sense to me. It's like we're justifying and appeasing to every individual feeling and not using common and rational sense anymore. She's just a little girl trying to prove her worth in the world but doesn't realize it's a dark world full of dangerous men with bad intentions. If that's all she feels she's worth, it's imperative someone informs her otherwise and I'm glad I did so.

Sexual Contradiction Again

All of this desensitization has definitely affected how we all perceive ourselves and how we define and tolerate liberty interactively. If sex is so glorious, essential and liberating in our culture as it's presented to be in the media, movies and television, then why don't the actors reveal their own personal sex lives? They should disclose every little detail to the world. Why don't we document the lifestyles of pornstars and their own personal sex lives? Porn stars have sex all day long, releasing endorphins with good-looking men on camera for everyone to see and even get paid for it. The same goes for prostitution. We should look behind the scenes into their lifestyles and find the peace and sustenance we're all looking for shouldn't we? That's what's being advertised but all we are is lying to ourselves because again, when the orgasm is finished the truth of who we truly are is revealed in the unfulfillment and shame. Deep down these people are jaded, lost and broken, living in regrets too deep for words, chasing it all away with the feeling of sex as though it's defining acceptance for them but internally they're degrading themselves and growing further and further into dependency, sinning against the design within them and what God puts in all of our hearts. Sex is about private intimacy and love and anything else is a detriment to our wellbeing. We all know it's wrong or we wouldn't be ashamed when we talk about it or when we watch it and again, these pornstars would be respected pillars of influence in our society. If we've justified porn as being acceptable in our own conscience then why don't we share our habits and obsession with our family or in front of an audience of people? Why don't we talk about masturbation? Even the slightest glance in public at a woman's derriere brings shame to us as men because we all know it's wrong and if we didn't we wouldn't turn away for fear of being judged.

Porn is a 50 million dollar a year industry that destroys whoever it touches whether we think nobody's watching or not. The actual voice response system I'm using to transcribe this book won't even print the word p*** because it's considered derogatory. It's a vicarious outlet of satan like so many others that jade our perceptions and virtue, demoralizing the creative design of God. We all need to repent and ask Jesus for his forgiveness; however we've fallen victim to satan's lies and whatever sins we've committed. If you feel offended or convicted, let it be from God's Word and not my own because I was as guilty as anyone before Christ opened my eyes. I'll admit p*** isn't my weakness nor has it ever been even before Christ, but I still suffer with lust myself. I'm human. I hope for those reading this that they realize I'm writing this as a general consensus and not attacking anyone personally. There are many who do live genuine, wholesome and God-fearing lives to which a lot of this doesn't apply but for the majority, I feel it needs to be addressed and are in need of God's forgiveness and reconciliation.

It's a powerful and seductive spirit that's overtaking this world and the only weapon to fight against it is the Holy Spirit of God. It's an interwoven tapestry of evil that the world is falling victim to as I was and only by God's grace can I comment otherwise. It's just so frustrating and deflating sometimes trying to communicate these truths without offending people. The reality of evil is so overwhelming, I feel trapped in the knowledge of it. It's like warning that guy on the train tracks that the train is coming while he's got his headphones on. He's just walking at the beat of his own drum, feeling stimulated without a clue to the danger that's coming. The world is walking into all these snares of the enemy like blind doe in a field of landmines. I think deep down people know there's trouble on the horizon but chase the concern away through these impulses. It's just so confusing to find truth and purpose in life with so many opinions, theories and options circulating the information superhighway. I don't blame people for wanting to escape from it all. It's so much easier to lock the windows and doors, close the blinds and shut out the interactive world outside pretending everything is okay but it's not and sooner or later we all have to face what's on the other side no matter how well we hide away and camouflage ourselves. The world causes so much anxiety within us that God's truth and acceptance releases us from. He gives us a justifiable purpose to live for him and not for the world.

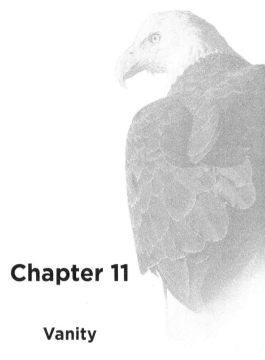

Chapter 11

Vanity

There's an ex NHL player who wrote a book recently about his life and career. (You can tell I'm Canadian because I use many hockey references) Anyways, he stated that his whole dream in life was to do whatever it took to win the Stanley Cup. Ever since he was a kid that was his only goal and priority in life. All the workouts and practices, the thousands of miles travelled and money spent by his parents were all to reach his dream and everyone around him was working for the same goal. The problem was when he finally achieved it, he said the next day was the most depressing and deflating day of his life. This supposed achievement and climactic experience seemed so vain in retrospect. He could only watch the video back so many times but that experience was gone. It was his whole identity and life's ambition but when it was reached he came to realize that it was his only identity and the next day he didn't even know who he was. That short little skate around the ice holding a trophy with his teammates was a temporal experience and a distant memory that couldn't sustain him in the presence of the aftermath and of true reality.

I'm watching documentaries on wrestling stars where it's much the same story. They get to the pinnacle of their careers with fame and fortune and then true reality completely consumes them in the expectation and vanity of it all when they're done. They live to create a false identity and then for the rest of their lives they're lost trying to find their own.

It's amazing the cycle every year of these dreams, aspirations and emotions being fulfilled and unfulfilled whether it's in sports, award shows or Hall of Fame induction ceremonies. It's become our whole culture's infatuation. It's just so incredible the build-up satan has orchestrated in our carnal aspirations and optimism every calendar year to enhance our idolatry and complacency. To him it's just another revenue cycle and diversion to condition us in our compulsive dependencies. Hundreds of thousands of fans spend billions of dollars vainly cheering on their teams and idols year round for nothing but a moment of pride and adoration. I'll admit, I love sports myself but the priority of it seems so vain and trivial in light of the gospel because an experience is only that, an experience. The instant it's fulfilled it becomes a memory. It just all seems so vain in light of the bigger picture of the world and salvation, especially right now. I was never famous or in the public eye so I can't relate to the level of winning the Stanley Cup other than to express an opinion but I was in several garage bands over the years and have a similar perspective. There was always so much time and energy spent driving and preparing to play. It was a buildup of emotions to get there and then this exhilaration would consume you as you play as if you're on top of the world, living your dream. The problem is that was my whole emphasis but there were 23 more hours to the day with many other responsibilities that got none of my attention. We lived for the escape from life but could never find our way back to it. It's good to be passionate and have hobbies and goals but there are responsibilities that should be paramount to our priorities. All of our lives in the band were falling apart outside of this temporary release that we were feeling and living for. My drummer got a DUI and then overdosed on my birthday one year. The bassist's wife was hammered and flipped her car over in the ditch outside of my house coming to tear a strip off him. Ultimately, the beer and dope would wear off and the temporary euphoria of the music made the rest of the life seem so mundane and depressing. My life had no balance and everything I was living for was actually what was destroying me. The last song would end just like the hockey game ends, along with all our favorite movies and TV shows with their credits. They are all unsustainable experiences and indulgences that our senses can't supply our soul the resolution it needs to sustain itself. It's merely releasing the emotion but not sustaining or resolving the emotion which has become much of our imbalance in society spiritually and psychologically. They just come back and the cycle never ends. They actually escalate in our desperation to regain them. I feel like im sucking the fun out of life but you see that in so many famous figures like musicians over the years how they are highly exalted and then they burn out, overdose or commit suicide like Cris Cornell, Chester Bennington, Kurt Cobain and so many others. They reach their desired goal but when they get there they'd rather die than stay there. It reminds me of Jim Carrey saying he wishes everyone would get rich and famous and do everything they ever dreamed so they'd see that it's not the answer. When it comes to me and my band, I finally broke down in the emptiness of it all which I'll share more in my testimony but that brokenness is what many of us need to come to know our need for God. It also brings so much relevance to the truth of God's Word.

What Changed Me

What finally delivered me through all the desperation and anxiety as I look back now was when my perception of reality and truth registered clearly. It's like my intuition was being generated from a higher level of moral discernment outside of myself. God supernaturally interceded and there was a spirit continually revealing these foreign epiphanies and confirming my inquiries towards them along the way. A spirit entered in that was not generated by me the day I saw Jesus Christ as the incarnation of God. It struck me as such a revolutionary phenomenon the world seemed to disregard as irrelevant and the fascination of it consumed me. The pages just came alive as if they had a life of their own and as the pages came alive, this spirit came alive within me. Certain scriptures were so profound to me that I couldn't just pass them by as fictional or irrelevant. It's as though the foreknowledge within the Word justified its own relevance. There was a time just after coming to Christ that I was in our jam room with the band, ready to start our set. I remember being torn between God's truth and the music. Regardless, I had a couple beers and tokes of a joint as we usually did, but something had completely changed. About three songs into the set I knew I was finished. We were generating a devilish spirit that was not conducive to the spirit that was now within me. I could feel the presence of death in the room and in the air around me. I stopped that day and haven't been drunk since. That was 10 years ago and I haven't even had the urge or temptation in me to do so. My awareness had miraculously transitioned into a deeper enlightenment and my intuition and directive almost instantly was compelled for a greater purpose and hope. God's spirit knew I was authentic and genuine in my persistence towards him and continued to reveal himself to me unconditionally. It was hard on my relationships with my friends in the band but I knew it was the right path to take. It wasn't a hope generated by the world, it was a confirmation and hope secured through his Word that seemed preordained, vastly exceeding my own propensity. It's like it was from another world. When you read this next passage in Hebrews ask yourself if this could be generated by the carnal intellect within man. Hebrews 6:17-19, "Therefore God, determining to show more abundantly to the heirs of promise the immutability of his counsel, confirmed it by an oath, that by two immutable things, in which it is impossible for God to lie, we might have strong consolation, who have fled for refuge to lay hold of the hope set before us. This hope we have as an anchor for the soul, both sure and steadfast, and which enters the presence behind the veil." Scriptures like these left me dumbfounded to the origin of them all. The words are so powerful and deep and whether I understood them or not in the beginning, they started to transform me and regenerate something within me supernaturally. It was and still is a pure spiritual conduit unraveling itself to me, in me and around me, exposing to me the carnal mind. Without God all of our trust, faith and dependency falls solely on the limitation of the carnal mind and the carnal mind is what God came to expose, redeem and regenerate. Romans 8:5-8 says, "Those who live according to the flesh set their minds on the things of the flesh, but those who live according to the spirit, the things of the spirit. For to be carnally minded is death, but to be spiritually minded is life and peace. Because the carnal mind is enmity against God, for it is not subject to the law of God, nor indeed can it be. So then, those who are in the flesh cannot please God." I'll admit the Bible is very convicting but there is truth to conviction and in the Word of God lies this spiritual conduit and truth and where truth claims victory is when it unveils all the lies and deception that mislead us and affect us in society. Spiritual truth claims victory not in what we experience or in what we benefit superficially but when we're transformed and regenerated into productive, compatible and discerning vessels that are wise to the deception of the enemy and the situations and circumstances that surround us.

Another Jab at False Teachers

The spirit and allure of the world has misguided us in our inclinations and initiatives and we've all progressively contributed to the depravity and consequences we're facing. The problem with truth, comes personal accountability in which people don't want to confront. We just don't see the need to as mortal beings because we've been convinced by science that that's all we are. People again, would rather ignore the imposing and confrontational questions of immortality and sin and live to justify themselves, trusting in science's claims. They'd rather take their life's pages to the grave than to come clean to God with their sin, but I'm warning whoever reads this, that is a grave mistake. The root and underlying problem with the world is sin no matter what science, Oprah Winfrey or spiritual gurus like Eckhart Tolle are teaching it otherwise, but we seem to be embracing and tolerating it more and more. All they are and supposed spiritual advisors like them are money seeking attention hounds in the embracing of it and of more tolerance. They are all about "the moment" and "the now" but the moment is slipping away and they give no answers to why because it doesn't sell their product. A few of Eckhart Tolle quotes are deadly to the realization of sin and to the hope and salvation of God. He says, "Realize deeply that the present moment is all you ever have…...Being spiritual has nothing to do with what you believe and everything to do with your state of consciousness….People don't realize that now is all there ever is, there is no past or future except as memory or anticipation in your mind…...Always say yes to the present moment. What could be more futile, more insane, then to create inner resistance to what already is? What could be more insane than to oppose life itself, which is now and always now? Surrender to what is. Say yes to life and see how life suddenly starts working for you rather than against you." And finally he says, "Life will give you whatever experience is most helpful for the evolution of your consciousness. How do you know this is the experience you need? Because this is the experience you're having at the moment." These words are satanic, self-appeasing garbage that make me cringe. They completely oppose faith and the salvation of God through Jesus Christ. These people have literally no spiritual awareness whatsoever to the reality that surrounds us. They're completely oblivious. The problem with the evolution of the world's consciousness is that it's not bringing itself to the repentance of sin and the only consciousness there is, is the consciousness of that. The emptiness in our soul is the hope we've generated from within it and these people sell the world out to that false hope. They remind me of 2 Peter 2 that says, "There were false prophets among the people, even as there will be false teachers among you, who will secretly bring in damnable heresies....many will follow their destructive ways; by reason of whom the way of truth will be blasphemed. By covetousness they will exploit you and make merchandise of you." Eckart Tolle's words are shallow puddles of vanity as the imminent spiritual reality of the world closes in on itself. These types of teachers claim we're all innately good and without sin but these are sinful words of death from people that are spiritually dead. If our greatest fears stem from the judgment of others and in ridicule and scrutiny, then the basis for our fears are in the sins of others towards us. Sin is the effect and cause not only in scrutiny and judgment but in lying, cheating, stealing, abuse, neglect, divorce, violence or in gossip. If it wasn't true, talk shows like Oprah Winfrey wouldn't have any dialect. Everything in life is from cause and effect and they can define it however they want but God defines it as sin. It's impossible not to believe in sin when it's sin that causes so much of our world's calamity and personal trauma. It's just so deceitful how it encroaches upon us like weeds in a flower bed. Satan is so elusive and inclusive to each of our weaknesses and trauma but we just can't see it in our denial of God. These new age teachers think by being inspiring and optimistic they're being spiritual but they're merely masking the problem with vein band-aids and false prophecy while the demonic world uses them and takes its hold upon us all.

Psychologically of Satan and His Minions

Again, satan's affected us subconsciously behind the forefront of our minds through these outlets telepathically and subliminally to where we don't even realize it. It's like we're in some sort of illusionary psychosis or trance. Psychosis is defined as a condition that affects the way your brain processes information. It causes you to lose touch with reality. You might see, hear or believe things that aren't real. It says psychosis is a symptom, not an illness and that mental or physical illness, substance abuse, or extreme stress or trauma can cause it. Welcome to our world as science itself defines it. Subliminal is defined as something that is not easily perceived but maybe remembered due to constant repetition. Subliminal influences or messages affect your mind without you being aware of it. It means below the threshold or surface of your conscious mind, and you don't even notice that you're being controlled. The word "controlled" is what stands out to me. They've used this stuff for decades slowly and methodically imprinting and conforming our ideology psychologically, with technology alluring us into complacency by its apparent convenience. These supposed spiritual teachers are victims to its seduction as well attempting to define spirituality as the spirits of death coincide. I read an interview on 60 Minutes about the deception taking place before our eyes that wrote, "Other examples highlight a more deliberate effort to monopolize your time. Consider Instagrams implementation of a variable-ratio rewards schedule. Instagram notification algorithms will sometimes withhold likes on your photos to deliver them in larger bursts, so when you make your posts, you may be disappointed to find less responses than you expected, only to receive them in a larger bunch later on. Your dopamine centres have been primed by those initial negative outcomes to respond robustly to this sudden influx of social appraisal. This use of a variable reward schedule takes advantage of our dopamine driven desire for social validation, and it optimizes the balance of negative and positive feedback signals until we've become habitual users." Just for reference algorithms are defined as mental processes which relate to how people understand, diagnose and solve problems mediating between a stimulus and response. These things have far more bearing on our lives than we realize. It's like a concealed form of conformity in computer programming and the database system.

It's incredible how obvious these computer programs and other conspiracies have become yet how unaware the general public are of them. I'll admit some of it is hard to detect subliminally and subconsciously but it's gotten to a point where some of it is so disgustingly blatant that we just have no excuse anymore, especially in regards to Hollywood and the entertainment industry. Miley Cyrus is one of satan's little pawns of influence. She's in a music video that has her rolling around in little white underwear half the time then molesting a sledgehammer the other half. It's a completely vulgar display of perversion and promiscuity that the world has come to tolerate. Not only do we tolerate it, we embrace and validate it. Over 1 billion people have viewed that video. There's no positive message or influence in it whatsoever. It's just her butt naked molesting a sledgehammer but she's become a cult hero to so many young women and Oprah Winfrey and Ellen will have her on as their number one guest, praising and glorifying her for her success. You can see that with idolatry as the ploy and success as the emphasis in our culture, our dignity is sacrificed along with the influence that's generated. It's a cruel game and pawn of satan in a magnified war over the human will and soul. Something about degradation and sin entices and invigorates our stimulation to where we buy into its enchantment and satan and his minions know it and use it against us by paying her and others royally to impose it upon us all. She knows what she's doing but with a check dangling in her face she's willing to override her morality. As long as she stays silent and selfish to her own cause, she gets glorified being in compliance with their agenda. It's favorable extortion in a way and just another script she's paid to act upon much like Barack Obama and many others. Those who try to expose their agenda, especially under contract, get silenced or murdered much like JFK. One of JFK's speeches before he died was a heart cry to expose these secret societies and their narratives and agenda. It was on April 27/1961 and I suggest to anyone reading this to read it in its entirety. He says in part of it, "The very word "secrecy" is repugnant in a free and open society; and we as a people are inherently and historically opposed to secret societies, to secret oaths and to secret proceedings. We decided long ago that the dangers of excessive and unwarranted concealment of pertinent facts far outweighed the dangers which are cited to justify it….today no war has been declared--and however fierce the struggle may be, it may never be declared in the traditional fashion. Our way of life is under attack. Those who make themselves our enemy are advancing around the globe. The survival of our friends is in danger. And yet no war has been declared, no borders have been crossed by marching troops, no missiles have been fired...no war has ever posed a greater threat to our society." This is a bone chilling reminder of the evil that infiltrates our world. JFK was behind the veil where he could see its severity and was courageous enough to expose it. Unfortunately, there's thousands that have sold their souls and fallen under their control realizing it's inescapable, much like being in a street gang. I'll never forget a Bob Dylan interview where he was asked, "Why do you still do it, why are you still out there?" Dylan says, "It goes back to the destiny thing, I made a bargain with it a long time ago and I'm holding up my end." Interviewer, "What was your bargain? Dylan, "To get where I am now." Interviewer, "Should I ask who you made the bargain with?" Dylan, "With the chief commander." Interviewer, "On this earth? Dylan, "On this earth and the earth we can't see."

Money pays for the mouth's zipper to uphold the driving procession of a global lie. There's thousands of different agents in all facets of our lives around the world that are living with this secretive knowledge but fulfilling and executing the objective and narratives. The contracts vary in sizes and in degrees of importance. Tom Hanks and his wife had apparently caught the coronavirus but what's interesting is how his son did a quick interview confirming it on utube. His interview to me seemed staged as he had his shirt off with his whole chest tattooed with the Illuminati pyramid and "all seeing eye" as the centerpiece, as seen on the American dollar bill. These are all little contracts that push the agendas procession ahead as these agents gain promotion. I remember Amy Winehouse in her last video formed a triangle symbol in reference to the Illuminati and soon after she was dead much like Michael Jackson and many others. You sell your soul to their contract and if you don't uphold your end of the bargain, like Bob Dylan stated, they'll take you out of the picture. They will not relinquish their control over our compulsive minds because awareness produces restraint and like I said before, restraint opposes impulse which is satan's power over our flesh. Another video with Miley Cyrus is just her mouth and tongue extracting and ingesting a jizz like fluid over and over with a snake's tongue caressing her face while satanic symbols are flashing around her. She's literally simulating a male orgasm all over face for the whole world to see. It's so repulsive I can't even go back and watch it to comment on it anymore for this book. If that's not bad I don't know what is, but again, we buy into it and embrace it with millions and millions of likes and views on social media and the internet. Even if the majority aren't watching it, it's still out there pushing the bar of toleration, desensitization and perversion for the next generation.

I remember watching the Grammys a couple years ago and this fairly overweight hip hop artist came out with a group of dancers in their thong underwear. They danced around and shook their derrieres like it was hump day at the horse corral. It was appalling and for those reading this think I'm racist or judgmental, all of the dancers were of different ethnicities and were just out of control. If that wasn't bad enough, on the stage behind the dancers was a massive inflated bum in a thong that was as wide as the stage and about 25 feet high. I couldn't believe my eyes and I thought to myself, "that is a bold statement in depravity that we all seem to be embracing." The most intimate and sensitive part of the female anatomy that has been designed by God to make love and give birth is being demoralized and desecrated right before eyes and the whole audience cheered her on for it much like the Super Bowl halftime show. This stuff has become society's fascination these days and satan just keeps pushing the bar of depravity more and more as we keep proving our love for it alongside with all of these views and likes, giving praise to these idols. Again, they elevate the affluence and success for justification over the moral discernment and influence. We don't consider the lust and desires of men being enhanced and the intimacy and privacy of women being degraded and devalued. They just see the influence as an empowerment to the means of success meanwhile abuse and rape esculate all over the world due to the lust and expectation men are being influenced by and subject to. It's not only in sexual influence, it's in violence as well or wherever success takes precedence over moral influence. We're proving how sinful we are by the attention we're giving them in our responses. Archaeologists have literally discovered Noah's Ark on Mount Arafat in Turkey and have made several documentaries for YouTube. The one I saw had only 1.5 million views. This is one of the greatest archaeological discoveries in history and no one seems to care or give attention anymore. We're proving to God within ourselves where our desires gravitate to. We're staring right at it all in every piece of technology as I was saying earlier but satan is like a puppet master behind the scenes enhancing and enticing our propensities. It's come to a point now to where it's reached its intended purpose and the collateral damage will now bear its fangs. I remember a few years ago an R&B singer named Chris Brown was caught and convicted of abusing his girlfriend Rihanna. Her face was beaten so bad she was barely recognizable. At first he was shunned by the public but only a little while later he was a headliner at the Music Awards being lifted up by cables and thrown all around the stage to be praised and glorified. For me, I feel much of these incidents are staged plots to condition us and dumb down our convictions and consciousness. We're just not seeing the implications of all this illusionary fantasy and how these narratives impact the justification in our conscience. Satan himself and his pathetic minions confess to there being a moral consciousness or they wouldn't be so hell-bent on influencing us to oppose it. One of the worst I've ever seen is a Superbowl Bowl commercial for the website Ashley Madison. Their primary slogan is "Life is short, have an affair." It has 17 million clients and has become a 90 billion dollar business around the world. I watched an interview with the cofounders wife on "The View" and she herself stated that it was destructive to cheat on your spouse and that she lives in a monogamous relationship with her husband and would be devastated if he were to commit adultery on her. In her own words and confession she says the website is not creating cheaters but simply supplying a need for the public. Again, their success is a contradiction and overriding their own admittance to moral consciousness and discretion. Does the public really need any more adultery? Do children need to suffer anymore from divorce? Millions of people are subject to these outlets and it shows their seniority and how powerful they are behind the scenes in the authority to broadcast them unmolested. That's why democratic tolerance is so dangerous in regards to influence and desensitization. Satan has infiltrated and come to own the power of discretion even over the government. He knows how to monopolize every facet of our lives. The advertisements themselves are seducing to the eye and even if people are discerning enough to turn away, the impulse is still triggered and questioned in their mind especially with these beautiful women stripping down to their underwear or bikinis on screen. It's like a relentless battering with every commercial and advertisement in technology these days. We've grown to have selective hearing and tunnel vision in what we prioritize. Again, we've become addicted to shock value and our eyes are drawn to what pushes the bar but it's become such a depraved, impure and evil source of entertainment. It's these demonic spirits of lust that weaken men and build up their unfulfilled resentment towards women that are the most dangerous. It's all a painful reality that needs to be exposed to the masses and within our hearts for a significant change to occur. We don't consider the painful effects of adultery or the rippling effects and emotions in the family with these influences being inflicted upon us. This all hits home for me because my ex-wife committed adultery and had a baby with some guy on her baseball team and all she did for 5 hours every night was watch reruns of the Bachelor and the Kardashian's. I'm afraid it's becoming too late for so many because of how separated and disillusioned we are from God's truth. His truth is encroaching upon us prophetically like a biblical glacier. It's an immovable, inevitable and inescapable formality the world is unsuccessfully pushing up against. We're like millions of rebellious and stubborn children punching and kicking away at a hundred foot tall glacier that doesn't change its course or timeline. There's a bigger universal picture taking place that the majority is blind to that far exceeds science and human philosophy. It's amazing how a tiny little beaver will work feverishly night and day building a dam. It's tiny little teeth relentlessly gnaw away at all the surrounding trees and branches as he drags them around for his intended purpose. When he's finally finished only a trickle of water gets through and he basks in the pool of his glory and works. The analogy is similar in how satan works behind the scenes and suppresses the truth of salvation from flowing through by implementing all these strategies and diversions through our impulsive minds. 2 Corinthians 4:4 says, "The god of this world has blinded the minds of them who do not believe, lest the light of the glorious gospel of Christ, who is the image of God, should shine upon them."

Salvation is laid out for us as a free gift for this dam to break and this river to run through and release us into true liberty but we so desperately want to push it away and be conformed and enslaved by the weakness of our carnal mind. If it feels like I'm repeating myself, believe me, this stuff needs repeating. We perceive freedom to be our carnal flesh being in complete liberty to gratify every impulse but these two liberties are continuously opposing each other in the light of consequence and salvation. One liberty that saves and one that destroys. The liberty in forgiveness through God's sacrifice and the liberty to do "what thou shalt wilt" as famous satanist and occultist Aleister Crowley once stated and Jay-Z so boldly displayed on one of his T-shirts. My question to Aleister Crowley now, much like my question to Chris Cornell and the bass player for ACDC is, was it worth it? I guarantee they'd give it all back. Every sensation, every sin, every word published, all the exaltation and influence they generated along with all the confidence and liberation they ever thought they had. They'd give it all back for one chance at saying sorry to God, but they gave up that chance in this life and now are forever condemned in eternal damnation. Right now as I'm writing this Aleister Crowley is infused in a permanent state of darkened claustrophobia due to the wilful conscience he opposed and imposed on the world. The satan he claimed to know is nowhere to be found and no help to him now. Hebrews 2:14 says that satan holds the power of death, not the power of life, but Jesus says in John 14, "I am the way, the truth and the life," and unfortunately outside of him, we're choosing our way, the lie and death. I guess the question to whoever is reading this is, is it worth it to you? What way are you going to choose? The way to everlasting life promised by Jesus or the way to death also promised by Jesus? What excuse does Aleister Crowley have? If he didn't believe in God then who did he so insatiably oppose? What spirit possessed and inspired him if satan doesn't exist and he lived to deny his own conscience? Nobody truly understands or realizes the gravity of sin and what they're imposing until the effects are felt in hell and they're left to ponder it for eternity with no way out. This inevitable destination should snap us all out of our complacency and into a place of repentance and humility but we just don't seem to care anymore. Our ignorance has become our bliss. The majority of us are obviously not taking wilful defiance to this degree but there's still something in us that's hanging on to the world and our impulses as though they're sustaining us. The truth is they're not, they're destroying us. If there were no voids in life we wouldn't continually be trying to fill them. Much of what we're escaping from is what we're chasing after and that's the whole mirage of satan. There is an emptiness inside of us all without God that only he can fill and all of this division, confusion and hostility is proof of that. We need the reconciliation from our creator to experience the release of truly being forgiven. If we saw God as a father over his own house we'd understand that he's trying to maintain order through his spirit and Word to save us from his own righteous judgment. It's not that complicated. Through repentance and God's sanctification comes understanding and appreciation but a faithless, gluttonous and impulsive spirit produces greed, envy and dissatisfaction. There is no arguing these facts. We are literally pushing away the only name that can save us. Jesus Christ again, has become a curse word instead of a word of praise and appreciation even though we depend on everything he's created to sustain our lives. Everything is from the hand of God and all these ignorant devil worshipping lunatics due is bask in the gluttony of God's creative hand, spitting in his face in the process. Even atheists and agnostics do the same all day everyday but if they could only see how great of a contradiction they are truly living in.

More Vanity

We can only truly understand the revelation of God when we ourselves bear the influence of God, until then we just live to justify our means. Again, we need this reconciliation from our creator to experience this release of truly being forgiven. Not in an experience the world promotes to stimulate us, but an experience within our heart that supernaturally transforms us in our spirit. This is the spiritual rebirth of being born again. Romans 8:13-16 says, "If you live according to the flesh, you will die, but if you through the spirit mortify the deeds of the body, you will live. For as many as are led by the Spirit of God, these are the sons of God. For you have not received the Spirit of bondage again to fear, but you received the Spirit of adoption by whom we cry out, Abba, Father. The Spirit himself bears witness with our spirit that we are children of God."

This generation has more at its fingertips to satisfy its impulses than any other time in the history of the world. Everything is about innovation, convenience and amenities everywhere we look. It's created the desire within us. Everything is an experiential drive of fulfilment and stimulation in everything we do. Stimulation is in the forefront of our minds impulsively and socially to keep pace with the status quo. It's become impulse after impulse after impulse. We've got remote controls for every electronic device and even for our cars to start in the morning. There's even temperature controls for our seats and steering wheels nowadays to keep us comfortable. We have every recipe online for food and every drink concoction imaginable. We've got malls, theme parks and cruise ships to cater to our every need. We've got video games and 3D simulators that look so realistic, it's like you're living inside the screen. There's even robotic lawn mowers with GPS coordinates so we don't have to physically mow our lawn anymore. We've got massage chairs, hot tubs, steam rooms and saunas for our aching bodies. Every idea has been patented to benefit us for our convenience in every aspect of our lives. We've even got Siri and Alexa to help us when we need something but the problem is we've become completely spoiled in the continual conclusion of it all. If impulsive stimulation was bringing us joy, we'd see it everywhere but it's actually becoming the opposite. It's made us weak and vulnerable and merely increased our craving for it and our dependence upon it.

We scroll through our cell phones and change channels on the TV more times during the day than we breathe it seems. God forbid we lose our phone or the TV remote, It's like the end of the world. I see far more joy in children with access to nothing than in adults with access to everything but that access has unfortunately reached the minds and hands of younger and younger generations as satan influences our lives. We need to learn the simplicity of life again and enjoy its natural process in appreciation and humility instead of continually seeking the outcome because when the outcome is achieved the process is finished and we just become addicted to the transition from outcome to outcome, especially when the outcome is attributed to acceptance and success. Life just becomes a self-promoting reward system of action and result over and over again. We've come to identify the outcome as our key to happiness, and success and validation as our only priority so we can hopefully sit back one day in a retired chair of our own accolades and pride. Unfortunately it's a mirage we're chasing. Joy and happiness hold two vastly different meanings in the light of God's salvation. I have more joy simply in the assurance of my salvation than I ever did living for impulse. I have more joy in the pain of being sanctified for that matter because I know God's real and that's such a greater joy and hope to live for. I saw a documentary recently of Garth Brooks in the pinnacle of his career much like the hockey player I was talking about earlier. With all the fame and fortune reaching its climax and all the attention he was receiving, he internally fell apart. His marriage and relationships with his kids all crumbled, along with his joy and peace. He got to the pinnacle of the American dream and when he got there it was all emptiness and vanity. It's like we become partners with satan in our own self-serving narcissistic determination but it's made us all hostile, anxious and desperate. Satan loves over-emphasizing the outcome of achievements and accomplishments in our music idols and sports heroes. He loves us drawing attention to ourselves and basking in our own glory and pride, making each moment over dramatic so we forget to enjoy the process of life in humility and thankfulness. When we make it about us, we forget about God. Again, it all generates a stereotype in the mind for attention, acceptance and affirmation. We see that through social media outlets like Facebook, Instagram and snapchat how every moment of people's lives needs to be documented as a constant exaltation and affirmation for others to witness as though life has become a proving ground. It's no wonder there's so much insecurity when that's become our security and it's no wonder there's no spiritual awareness or independence when that has become our dependence. All we're doing is exposing our inferiorities and emotional insecurities along the way, creating this disunity and interactive instability. Instead of loving God and loving each other, we've become haters of God and haters of each other. There's no contentment in the void anymore or time to meditate and appreciate the provisions laid before us. Even though we see ourselves without God as progressively evolving through innovation, the core needs of our hearts aren't being met and are rapidly dissolving. There's so much more joy in the appreciation of life and of God than the self exaltation of our own life. 1 Peter 1:8-9 says, "Though you have not seen him, you love him; and even though you do not see him now, you believe in him and are filled with an inexpressible and glorious joy, for you are receiving the end result of your faith, the salvation of your souls." Facing the truth of our sin is what God wants and compels us to do. He says in 2 Peter that he wishes that none should perish but all should come to repentance. When we believe, repent and accept the sacrificial atonement God made through Jesus Christ, our eyes are truly opened spiritually. Until then we are spiritually dead and the spirits in the other realm are at work to either draw us to God or steer us away into our desires. Any other spiritual premonition or inclination is a result of our own carnality that lives to appease and justify itself in its own determination and destination.

I went through quite the situation with a close friend of mine from high school a few months ago. He's an agnostic as many of my friends are growing up and is still plotting away in the world and claiming it all for his own. You can call it agnostic or atheist but I just see people living indifferent to anything philosophical or spiritual. I don't see the point in being over analytical in categorizing what people believe. They simply believe in themselves and live for themselves. Some are just more selfish than others. Regardless, he has no concern or reverence for God whatsoever and simply lives by the entitlement he creates for himself. He was recently divorced and struggles heavily with alcohol addiction but seems to live to justify it all with the lofty paycheck he receives. He has no appreciation for life whatsoever and just lives to serve his own needs. There's also two young kids involved that are torn in between it all but as long as he's feeling stimulated, nothing affects him. Actually, all that affects him is the amount he pays in child support. His selfish impulses are paramount over any accountability, emotional responsibility or obligation to his family or friends. He was called to go out of town for a few weeks and needed someone to dog and house-sit while he was gone. I agreed and showed up one evening to go over everything. Ironically, he was pulling into the driveway at the same time as me in his Nissan 350Z sports car. He then got out completely hammered, slurring his words and stumbling everywhere. I confronted him about drinking and driving and being an ignorant idiot, especially considering my own accident but he got mad at me for confronting him and calling him out. He actually thinks that I got in the way of his life as though I was the problem for interrupting his path in life. He had no concern or consideration for me, the other people driving on the road, his dog or his kids whatsoever. He just made excuses for his own selfish needs while putting everyone else's in jeopardy. Being of a sober mind, I started getting more and more angry as he argued to justify his ignorance. This righteous anger built up inside me with every word that came out of his mouth and made me think of the mercy of God in such a sobering light. Sin puts more people at risk then we realize whether it be drunk driving or other sins, however small they are. The cross is God's own declaration to the severity of sin for us to see his personal plea to its implications. My old friend is becoming another casualty to pride and self-entitled justification much like the rest of the world without God.

While editing this a close pastor friend of mine's son was murdered and burned up in a car fire. He knew of the gospel but wasn't willing to surrender and it cost him his life. I also had another acquaintance who died of an overdose recently. He also knew of God but wasn't willing to surrender. He put posts on Facebook all day but lived to be affirmed in the eyes of people and not the eyes of God. It ended up consuming him and cost him his life as well. Hebrews 3:12-13 says, "Take heed, brethren, lest there be any of you an evil heart of unbelief, in departing from the living God. Exhort one another daily, while it is called today; lest any of you be hardened through the deceitfulness of sin." I realize the writer is speaking to believers but he's even warning us who believe in the deceitfulness of sin therefore how much worse does sin deceive unbelievers?

In regards to my friend, we've been close since high school but I have to pray that he literally hits rock bottom and for everything to be taken away from him for him to come to his senses and see the consequence of his actions. He's totally blinded by his pride and in the afflictions that he inflicts upon himself. His older sister just died of a drug overdose and he has her initials on his car's license plate, yet he still doesn't get it. It's just like the majority of the world's relationship with God. What is it going to take for us to see? My friend's two little kids are so vulnerable and impressionable and all they want is a good dad that spends time with them, loves them and is there to guide them, but he could care less. It's all about him and everything else is a secondary burden to his own path and indulgences. When I was in the kitchen arguing with him there was a gross empty feeling of death in the house. The place was a disaster with marijuana and beer cans everywhere as though he hadn't a care in the world. All his needs were apparently being met but his life was falling apart around him. He's got a new truck and sports car, a nice big house with a massive stereo system. He takes home $8,000 a month and drinks beer and eats out every night. He sleeps with girls whenever he wants and drinks every night away like it's a party but unfortunately the party ends, the beer wears off, and the one night stand is only that, one night. His kids still need a dad in the morning and reality continues to bear its fangs. He's got the worst anxiety and is so full of bitterness with all of his impulses being met. I'm not saying everyone is as bad as my friend but it's an illustration of how far we can get out of balance without a heavenly Father to guide us and be accountable to. Romans 6:19-23 says, "I speak in human terms because of the weakness of your flesh. For just as you presented your members as slaves of uncleanness, and of lawlessness leading to more lawlessness, now present your members as slaves of righteousness for holiness. For when you were slaves of sin, you were free in regard to righteousness. What fruit did you have then in the things of which you are now ashamed? For the end of those things is death. But now having been set free from sin, and having become servants of God, you have your fruit to holiness, and the end, everlasting life. For the wages of sin is death, but the gift of God is eternal life in Christ Jesus our lord."

God as a Father

God wants to bring us back to our innocence where we experience true joy in the simplicities of life. Where life was full of elation in the discovery and wonder of our surroundings. Where life was pure, new and vibrant and we weren't so affected by external influence and bound in our selfish indulgences. When life wasn't so attainable and in excess. Where we had proper discipline and were at the mercy of our parents. Again, it's in this family structure where this is most exemplified, with trust, dependability and protection. It's just so frustrating because I think deep down we all realize this but we're so blinded and trapped in the materialistic consumerism of it all. Life was so much better when we were young and our identity wasn't in question or this incessant revolving mirror of comparative reflection every waking moment of our lives. I realize many of us didn't have a good father growing up but I know many of us wish we would have. I've been a Christian for almost ten years and I have a hard time saying Father myself because of the trauma and brokenness in my own childhood. I have a hard time giving over the reins and trusting in a father figure especially in relation to my own but the character of God is so good behind all of our fears and misconceptions of him. If we'd just get to know him we'd come to realize how merciful and loving he truly is because we're all like this in relation to him whether we admit it or not, or whether we like it or not, and his convictions are proof of this.

I personally didn't have the most memorable childhood with my parents but the times I do remember that were good were at my grandparents little farm, messing around in the back 40, hitting golf balls everywhere and playing with the dogs. There was structure, trust and safety and they truly cared for me and my sister unconditionally. There wasn't all this incessant pressure and concerns of life beating down on my brain. Of course maturity, responsibility and accountability grow as we age within the natural progression and design within our being, but we still need to hold on to this relationship with God as a father and us as his children however old we are. We get in serious trouble when we start dictating life's choices, circumstances and principles ourselves, disregarding God's standards and guidance for our lives. This is the danger of detachment and dissociation from God. We need God's level of maturity and responsibility to guide us no matter what age we are or position we are socially or financially. Nowadays kids want to grow up so fast and experience life as they see their idols and peers doing as though we hold so much of life's joy in our hands in our adult independence.

Unfortunately, they just aren't wise enough to see what a disaster we've made this world as adults and how many of us would love to go back in time and be in their position, making different choices along the way and experiencing life anew again. Children are the future of our world but they are following in the destructive and jaded footsteps we've left behind. Kids just don't go outside anymore like the old days to socialize and interact. Their characters and personalities are being conformed through these poisonous and idolistic screens at home and they're not being challenged or challenging themselves to create in the innocence of their imaginations and developing life skills or giftings. They've become lazy and inept in the perseverance and interaction of life. There were three kids upstairs where I lived for the past few years and I never heard a peep from them or saw them in the backyard playing at all. They just go in their rooms and shut their creative minds off, entering into their fantasy world without developing any commutative or social interaction. Unfortunately, none of them will realize what hits them as true reality overtakes this world and persists alongside their illusion of true reality. They're forced to question their identity in the world before even reaching puberty through these impressionable screens of depravity and adult influence. It's disheartening because their minds just aren't mature enough or equipped to process it all rationally and unfortunately it deeply affects them psychologically in the fears that are generated in what they're being subject to. 12 and 13 year old girls will be innocently enjoying life and within only a year or two become pregnant and on the verge of suicidal depression. In my generation sexual activity was generally around 18 to 19 but now it's as young as 13 to 14. It's an awful reality that we're seeing at younger and younger ages. It's like as soon as their minds question their social identity comparatively to what they idolize on television or through social media, they spiral into a frenzy of acceptance and approval, willing to sacrifice all their innocence from the peer pressure. These girls are seeing their adult idols sacrificing their identity for the sake of money and admiration, attributing the empowerment of women to their sexuality. It's so bad on so many levels and causes such a rippling effect from generation to generation and through all ages and sexes. I felt it in my generation but these kids have it even worse with access to technology. They've come to attribute their sexuality as their means of confidence and empowerment but it's merely created an insatiable, perverted predator in the spirit and heart of man that's actually devaluing women as objects of pleasure, instead of objects of respect and appreciation. Again, that's all I saw women as growing up because that's how they represented themselves on television but now the bar has been set so much higher. The question again becomes who is being empowered when rape, teenage pregnancy and sexual abuse percentages escalate as well as the fear that's generated in women's minds. Much like the young women in the pool, they just don't understand the reverse effect because the more they supposedly become empowered and draw attention to themselves sexually, the more men are driven to the obligation and expectation they are generating. Women are actually fuelling their own fears by enhancing the enticement in their desire for acceptance. 90% of women seem to be wearing these yoga pants nowadays that are perfectly hugging the outline of their lower torso to draw attention to themselves. They leave very little to the imagination and definitely fuel the lust in men far more than they realize. I was in the gym doing rehab the other day and this girl was in front of me stretching and exercising. No word of a lie, she looked at her own derriere and vagina in the mirror at least 50 times in about 15 minutes. I see it all the time there. They're working feverishly to sculpt their bodies into these pristine vessels of acceptance to draw men's attention their way but it's dangerously superficial psychologically and so far separated from the true sustenance of who they are and who they're created to be. I guess the question is where is the empowerment in these young suicidal and depressed girls who see sexuality as their identity? Sometimes their first sexual experience completely destroys them. It's like they're staring acceptance in the mirror with every glance as though that's the only purpose to life. I know personally how it affects men because I obviously am one and have my own struggles with lust. Fortunately I have a lot of restraint and can't even imagine what goes on in the minds of some men with that as their weakness, especially without God's convictions. These are more of the implications of idolatry from the acceptance and rejection it generates. Our philosophy has come to be established through stimulation and acceptance and with our accessibility to them and our reception of them. It's all counterintuitive but we're so deceived by it regardless of what our conscience is telling us. Counterintuitive is defined as something that goes against what you believe would be logical, or something that goes against common sense. It's just so deceiving how the spirit of the world compels our decisions and what our desires should be.

From a carnal sense, our ego has established our confidence and self-esteem when true confidence is established by God through faith, humility, restraint, mercy, grace and the appreciation of life. Outside of these is merely the abuse of common grace because who can humbly communicate or interact productively with someone with an ego? It's impossible because the entire basis for the self-esteem of an ego is to put you secondary and demoralize you comparatively. I have more confidence knowing I don't have to portray or prove myself as being confident.

Again, the idolatry and stimulation of the world has created this disillusion and imbalance within us all. It's turned us into depraved, despondent, violent and lust-filled predators especially with our eyes being glued to these lenses all day long. For instance, if I were to watch 3 hours of the UFC where the combatants beat each other to a bloody pulp, then play two hours of Resident Evil on Xbox, then watch a horror movie, then close it off with a Miley Cyrus video and some porn, how do I suppose to commune peacefully and effectively being subject and subjecting myself to all of this depravity? When do these thoughts and influences erase from my mind? The truth is they don't, they affect us spiritually and subconsciously, desensitizing us without us even being aware of it, opening gateways to torment us in the demonic realm. I watched a movie the other day with Michael Caine where he was this old retired military veteran who ended up taking vengeance and murdering all these hoodlums that were ransacking his neighborhood. They built it up at first as they do in so many of these movies to justify his vengeance but one of the scenes was absolutely horrific and had him in one of the hoodlum's underground lairs where the hood was repeatedly raping an unconscious girl, injecting her with heroin, videotaping it then watching it over and over while she lay on the couch beside him puicking up vomit. Caine eventually shot him and his accomplice but what the hell is this crap? How is this stuff even tolerable? My God in heaven. I was so full of rage and darkness after watching it. I hated everyone that took part in making the movie. The actors, director, producer and anyone else should all die, I thought to myself. That's what lingered in my head afterwards. These people are sadistic, perverted sociopaths. What a sick world we live in to broadcast this stuff. This goes far beyond advising viewer discretion. The problem is these thoughts persist and linger, elevating the fears and desires in our minds and influencing our perceptions of true reality and fantasy, then true reality hits us even harder when we're faced with it because we've become unprepared and so far separated from it. In 1 John 4:18 it says, "There is no fear in love, but perfect love casts out fear because fear has torment." Interesting how it says torment as though this is how we're being influenced and conformed spiritually through our fears, but unfortunately, true reality continues to persist alongside like that immovable glacier alongside the disillusion of fantasy in our imagination and we fall victim to its lie, whatever age or gender we are. There's an old saying that "perception is reality" but if I perceive something to be true when it's not, I've fallen victim to the lie within the perception in my mind and this is how satan deceives us through our desires and perception. These are the pre-emptive narratives and zionistic methods to progressive psychological mind control and subjectivity that I'm obsessive in trying to explain in words. Those with discernment are now seeing these psychological narratives take effect through this pandemic. People are at home now isolated with no clue to the future that lies ahead. All the optimism and securities they thought they had will now enhance their insecurities with their dependency on man.

It's a vicious battle over our souls and I hope to expose and bring this battle to the light as I share my testimony to hopefully help those in chains, who are confused and struggling for answers themselves. I also want to plant a seed in those who are overconfident and complacently rolling through the paces of their own entitlement, moral fortitude and vindication, not seeing a need for faith or God in their lives. Many people are financially secure or are just decent, upstanding citizens and don't see a need to evaluate or define the word salvation. It just seems too complicated of a subject to ascertain and we merely live indifferently, leaving it up to our own justified balances and scales of morality. Many of us have just come to trust the governing system and are now left in fear through this pandemic, wondering what's in store for the future. Deep down I think people realize that things aren't lining up concerning this pandemic but they still can't grasp why and merely trust that the system will regain its balance and is designed and obligated to proceed for the general public's benefit. The truth is it's not and in so many aspects of life we've succumbed to our own faithless and naive complacency. I think we hate the fact that we have to believe it and take it seriously as well. So many people are in debt and have invested into the system and that's left them forced to believe and be optimistic of it. The problem is that's the whole trap and why optimism can be so blinding. It draws us into its illusion while another objective works alongside. There's a lot of uncertainty and opinions circulating in the trust of our governing system right now, but just remember, that it's impossible not to believe in conspiracy when all our fears and distrust are based on those conspiring against us. I saw a commercial the other day promoting a new vaccine that prevents various types of cancers. How is that not a conspiracy when they haven't apparently found a cure? Again, if conspiracy wasn't a reality you would live with no fear or skepticism and again, you wouldn't lock the doors of your house and car at night. Not only do we lock our car doors at night, we press the lock button on the keyfob two seconds after we close the door. If we didn't believe in conspiracy, there wouldn't be a better business bureau and we wouldn't choose to eat organic food. The same people who say they don't believe in conspiracy and trust in science and technology won't hold their phone to their head for fear of radiation, all have protection software for their computers and again, will not eat genetically modified foods. These same people that trust in the theory of evolution and natural selection do anything for their children or family when they're ill or compromised, yet they're complete liabilities to them. They're only lying to themselves and living in contradiction of what they believe in and have faith in.

Chapter 12

Perseverance

I pushed all these questions aside as irrelevant myself but I now see that as a critical error in judgment on my part. I realize it's a contemplative struggle on both sides of the faith spectrum but in Christ the struggle is totally different. My old deceived and self-deceived identity has been released and now my struggle is to grow in knowledge and maturity and to communicate God's truth so others don't suffer anymore or progress any further in the lie. Hence the purpose and title of the book "Blind in affliction". I'll admit it is painful persisting forward in faith with such a critical message to deliver through the pride and contention of man. It's part of our suffering as Christians, but again, in Christ the contention of man and the opinions and perceptions of others don't matter anymore. We can't take offense because the carnal mind outside of faith is continuously being exposed to you and we can see them as we once were in our own blindness. We actually grow and mature through this process and become far more patient, resilient and merciful interactively because it's like we're staring back at ourselves in the mirror before our own enlightenment. This is a part of how we come to forgive ourselves and why self-righteousness or entitlement can't exist in the comprehension of God because, again, we don't generate this level of maturity and wisdom within ourselves. It's all part of the ministry and revelation of Christ and the sanctification behind his redemptive spirit. I'm in the process of sanctification as we all are as Christians and that can definitely be grievous at times. 1 Peter 4:12-14 says, "Do not think it strange concerning the fiery trial which is to try you, as though some strange thing happened to you, but rejoice to the extent that you partake of Christ's sufferings, that when his glory is revealed, you may also be glad with exceeding joy. If you are reproached for the name of Christ, blessed are you, for the spirit of glory and of God rests upon you." I've been so lost through the mountains and valleys of life and faith but the truth of the Word compels me to persevere. It's infectiously sovereign and gives me the wisdom and strength to carry on through all of my circumstances because the need outside of myself remains the same. The spirit within me continues to supernaturally confirm his authority and persistently clarifies and delivers me through the thoughts and bacteria ridden contention of my mind. When reluctancy and doubts set in, truth in the spirit override them in redemption. It's a growth and a cycle in the journey of faith outside the carnal world, equipping us to be battle-tested warriors of faith. The same afflictions were faced by God head-on in Christ and what he delivers us through now as we face our challenges in the world. This is the redemptive power of the Spirit of God in Jesus Christ. There's a deep internal struggle within the human mind and soul he delivers us from battling ourselves in faith. It definitely can be a war and burden for those destined for the higher callings in Christ and all will attest to that. The Word says that we've been created in Christ Jesus and are being conformed to the image of his son, therefore the sanctification process is being drawn to a set standard and precedence, and that isn't easy. The more we're drawn to Christ, the more inferior we are to his power and glory and that's hard for our pride to let go of. There's a call in Christ to be holy and blameless through persecution and affliction that can feel impossible to uphold and personify but that is what faith is and how it's being defined within you. Phillipians 3:14 says, "I press toward the mark for the prize of the high calling of God in Christ Jesus." That's why the bible is so compelling to me because it opposes our own will and pride on every level. It's a heavy weight to bear that only God has the wisdom and strength to exemplify but it's what compels us in faith. It's a pressure valve we can't release into grace in our humanity. I most certainly do not have the capacity without faith. It's so easy to get ahead of ourselves seeing the need but then getting overwhelmed, being immature and unprepared spiritually. I've been there and all I can say is, "yikes." Some burn out or even abort the mission all together with the spiritual and emotional toil and scrutiny that comes from being followers and proclaimers of Christ. The devil is sophisticated and crafty and that's why in 1 Timothy in regards to leadership Paul says, "Must not be a novice, lest being puffed up with pride he fall into the condemnation of the devil. Moreover he must have a good testimony among those who are outside, lest he fall into reproach and the snare of the devil." It's not only that we're spiritually and morally weak and immature, we lack influential wisdom in seniority and formidable positions. Our ego grows with the attention it receives and in the acceptance we desire and that narcissistic spirit can take us over forming a sense of empowerment and control. We are also prone to fail as our wallet sees increase and again, faith becomes a contrived opportunity for our own credit. A part of us wants to escape into the pleasures of the world and justify our position by claiming the wisdom to be of ourselves much like these prosperity preachers. The accessibility to money becomes too enticing and they avert the initial premise to faith in regards to their circumstances then begin to define faith in regards to circumstance and their salary. Others get self righteous and others get way too ahead of themselves in head knowledge and theology and become spiritually abusive over-analyzing every little detail as though God is some sort of cosmic kill-joy. Then there's many of us who again, are overzealous in our good deeds and optimism but don't establish a secure doctrinal foundation and get emotionally exhausted and again, get swallowed up by the never-ending need. I've been through it all and it's a challenging journey for anyone comprehending the Christian faith because ultimately, we are not God. I've completely burned out trying to save the world and so have millions of others. All of these failures again point to Jesus Christ, no matter how strong our faith is or how indifferent we are to faith in the world. All have fallen in history with Christ's standard magnified upon them. Our intentions always become either entitled or self-absorbed outside of Christ's. He's like a refining fire. Philippians 2:20-21 says, "I have no man likeminded, who will naturally care for your state. For all seek their own, not the things which are Jesus Christ's."

It's a war over two wills. Our carnal will and the selfless will and spirit of God, but the glory is in how his spirit isn't shakin or overcome by anything I just listed. He's seen it all before and if we were wise we'd understand that historically and put ourselves in those peoples shoes who have struggled in faith before us. We can learn from not only our own mistakes but from the mistakes of others, if we're wise. We're not called to save the world, we're called to point people to the saviour of the world. We can obviously learn from the genuine faith and persistence of others as well which is far more optimistic and encouraging. Regardless, he's consistently faithful and unaffected and continues to teach inclusively through all of our character flaws and complacent tendencies, especially to those who comprehend this level of love and mercy and are willing to humble themselves in repentance and learn. Again, sanctification can be a trying and grievous process with satan enticing us along the way back into the sin and impulses of the world, playing his games alongside our journey of faith. I'm naturally stubborn, so it's a challenge for me every day to be honest. He'll expose all of our weaknesses and attachments to the world whether they be in our identity, lust, money or in our past trauma or mistakes to trip up our progress and maturity. I'm not writing this to deter anyone from believing in God, in fact it becomes more of a reason to believe as the truth is revealed to us and within us in our faithful persistence. Satan's persistence is enough proof in of itself to believe as far as I'm concerned. The evidence becomes undeniable when you witness it within yourself from a spiritual perspective and this is the spiritual war we're losing erasing God from the picture. The intensity of it all can become overwhelmingly real, especially as a Christian with a powerful testimony and a gift for evangelism. We are all given gifts from God that can be used to expand the kingdom and for edification and support in a community of believers and the enemy targets them and our faith prodding away at how we define it all in our minds and use them. He's the relentless accuser as the bible indicates in Revelation 12. It says, "Now salvation, and strength, and the kingdom of our God, and the power of His Christ have come, for the accuser of our brethren, who accused them before our God day and night, has been cast down. And they overcame him by the blood of the lamb and by the word of their testimony, and they did not love their lives unto death. Therefore rejoice O Heavens, and you who dwell in them! Woe to the inhabitants of the earth and the sea! For the devil has come down to you, having great wrath, because he knows that his time is short." Satan will use any emotional tactic to doubt or waiver our security in faith to deter our confidence. He does it to deter others from believing themselves and is why he influences us to define faith circumstantially. The world looks at us as the influence unto faith and when we are wavering or compromising in the slightest degree, satan sees his opportunity to voice his condemnation and divisive persistence. James 4:7 says, "Resist the devil and he'll flee from you," but that resistance is our responsibility in faith and perseverance. It's saying resist because of how persistent he can be. He loves disunity and veering our faith in convoluted directions. He loves when we're all arguing contentiously and debating over petty principles and doctrines. He loves it when we base our faith on circumstantial evidence. He's the manipulation within our entitlement and feelings and aims to stunt our progress, growth and scriptural maturity in Christ to silence our voice unto salvation. Titus 3:9 says, "Avoid foolish disputes, genealogies, contentions and strivings about the law; for they are unprofitable and useless." Proverbs 13:10 says, "Only by pride comes contention, but with the well advised is wisdom." Unfortunately what's even worse is it's become an experience driven world so many new age teachers attribute faith in God with a continual emotional experience through music, healings, speaking in tongues or whatever else they conjure up in their false interpretations or anticipation. We're slaves to anticipation in the world so we can easily become deceived by it and for me, if you're not experiencing all these manifestations, it's actually God protecting you from them. They call them gifts of the spirit in reference to the bible but are used way out of context and not for the intentions originally emphasized for the edification of the church and proof of God's power. So much of it these days is heresy and derived for the edification of ourselves in our lack of faith and actually becomes a gateway for demons to possess us through the anticipation of false prophecy and the expectation that's generated. These exalted teachers are the hosts of demons to feed upon our biblical illiteracy, emotional insecurities and stimulation and all they've done is divide the church. I've seen it first hand. Far more knowledge, understanding and spiritual discernment is obtained through obstinance rather than experience and prosperity. This is a reason we fast as Christians where there is no stimulation or experience in the natural realm to deceive us in our complacency. Abstinence develops patience and appreciation for God and allows the confirmation of the Word to register clearly, without distractions. When we fast it gives no opportunity for the enemy to have a foothold over our impulses or emotions. Our faith is our overcomer so we need to focus on what we're overcoming from a biblical perspective rather than fixate our motivation on trivial and temporal irrelevance. These teachers are divisive heretics who aren't willing to confront or bear the eternal objective of salvation and are destroying the world's perception of faith in the process. Again, the problem with feelings and emotions is they're temporal and unsustainable. It's all based on adrenaline but the song will end, the healings will cease, and the gibberish tongue will bear no purpose or relevance. In fact, that's exactly what's happening amidst this pandemic and where true faith is being defined around the world. We can call it all spiritual in the present moment but true spirituality in faith maintains itself through trial and in the aftermath. I see people in these new-age movements just making it up as they go along to prove their spirituality or to be a part of something and feel a sense of belonging but inwardly they're exhausting themselves from the anticipation and the unsustainability of the temporal experience. I feel it can cause even more depression because of the false hope and expectation that's generated and how they perceive the love of God for them in its opposition to the cross. It's a godforsaken burn out to be completely honest and without biblical discernment I feel many are being sucked into the worship of demons. Again, much like prosperity teaching, it's impersonal and contrived. They're abusing grace, depending on what they can see to establish their faith for proof of assurance, when biblically this is no faith at all. Jesus even addresses this issue to those in his generation in Matthew 16 by saying, "Only a wicked and adulterous generation seeks after a sign." Ultimately, that's because that's all they wanted from him but there's so much more to life and there's so much more to faith in him. Hebrews 11 defines faith quite extensively but the end of Hebrews 10 is its precursor and says, "Knowing in yourselves that you have in heaven a better and an enduring substance. Don't cast away your confidence which has great recompense of reward. For you have need of patience, that, after you have done the will of God, you might receive the promise. For yet a little while, and he that comes will come and will not tarry; Now the just shall live by faith, but if any man draws back, my soul shall have no pleasure in him; But we are not of them who draw back unto perdition, but of them that believe to the saving of the soul. Now faith is the substance of things hoped for, the evidence of things not seen. For by it the elders obtained a good report." These scriptures are amazing contradictions in how we perceive faith nowadays. The end is amazing how it says the elders obtained a good report because ultimately, they experienced nothing but suffering for the truth in faith.

I was driving home from church a few years ago and pulled alongside this old Honda Accord with its hazard lights on. The car was in pretty rough shape and looked like it was full of camping gear or garbage at first glance. I rolled down my window and asked the girl driving if she was okay. She said it was something to do with her brakes and kept saying she was fine over and over again, but I finally convinced her to pull over so I could take a look in the Tim Hortons parking lot. The car was a disaster with garbage all over it as if she was living in it. She was a gorgeous mid twenties woman who looked to be a hippie or some sort of free spirited gypsy by the way she was dressed. I pulled one of her wheels off and realized she had a major leak in her brake line. Little did she know there was a massive hill just past the Tim Hortons. In chatting with her she disclosed her faith as a Christian and that she was a flagger in her church and a prophetess. We went in for a coffee at the Tim Hortons and she started speaking in this unknown gibberish as she communicated with me. I was a fairly new Christian at the time and had heard of some of the charismatic stuff going on but this was my first experience of it one-on-one. I was kind of confused by her mannerisms and demeanour but continued working on her car. We ended up getting it to a garage close by and I paid for it to get fixed a couple days later without her even knowing as she stated she was completely broke. There's many variables around the incident but I remember her saying that God would have helped her if I didn't get her to pull over. What she doesn't see being wrapped up in all these signs, miracles and charismatic wonders is that God did help her and show her a miracle by an actual Christian pulling up beside her and helping her fix her car, saving her from careening down the hill with no brakes. It just shows how experiential premonitions can blind us from the actual prevalence and sovereignty of God in the present moments of life. If she was a born-again believer or not is between her and God but for me, it's just so far from a productive basis for relative thinking and proper interpretation of reality. I saw her as giving her whole life over to some faze or experiential movement rather than actually giving her life over to God in faith and sincerity. Unfortunately so much of this stuff is going on in supposed Christian communities these days with divination and presumptuous anticipation for signs and wonders, that are in complete contrast to mature hermeneutics in scripture. So much of it has to do with our impulsive generation and its inability to appreciate life and be still and patient throughout the mundane moments of the day. The very last thing God would do is create more of an impulsive dependency and histeria within us. God still heals but he wants to heal the heart first. I don't want to sound like a prude because there is a lot of joy worshipping and praising God but there has to be a balance as well. I understand it's extremely difficult at times to die to the human flesh and our impulsively dependent minds but that's what we're called to do in Christ. Christianity isn't for the faint of heart or for wimps, especially as we progress closer to the end of the world and satan's power and deception surfaces and is elevated to its climax. I've felt it all myself at times on several occasions throughout my journey in faith. I've felt tempted, dejected and discouraged evaluating all the premises surrounding the Christian faith as we all have but it's the real battle that's worth all of the emotional scars along the way. The scars actually become the truth of the scriptures' relevance and prevailing relativity. People will separate themselves from you and persecution will come as the scriptures indicate. It can be a trying test of maturity and faith in what you actually believe in.

I did a lot of street ministry in my early years as a Christian and got completely massacred spiritually and emotionally in my immaturity. I thought I was strong in my own will from my good deeds and works but got too far ahead of myself and didn't realize the target I was putting on my back. I took the weight on myself as the ministry grew and became more productive but my lack of knowledge and experience in faith gave the enemy an avenue to completely destroy and derail my life. I wouldn't say I became arrogant but I was just not seasoned in spiritual warfare enough to handle it and didn't realize the sacrifices and costs of faith treading on enemy territory. He suffocated me and choked me out to where I was dejected and demoralized, unable to speak at times in my weakness. If anyone doesn't believe in spiritual warfare, especially atheists or agnostics, they should get involved with Christian street ministry for a few months and I guarantee they'd change their views on spirituality and the demonic realm. There's murderous and tormenting demons running rampant in the hearts and minds of lost and troubled souls everywhere. It's incredible the presence of evil as the sun goes down and the drugs start taking their effect. It's as though the demons come alive behind the shadows of our sensory perception and start possessing the air around you. I've heard demons speak through people and seen manifestations several times that are most certainly not from this world. I once heard a voice come from a man who was a drug dealer's money collector that was literally from the depths of hell. It's a sobering reality when you see it first-hand that only the Bible gives prevalence to and is not only manifesting itself around you but it's happening within you and within the ministry team. I've even seen demon possession manifesting itself in their pupils as they talk with you. I saw a young girl overdosing in front of me once while the paramedics were around her and you could see a spirit in her as her eyes rolled back in their sockets, tormenting her and sending her into convulsions. The manifestations are even more prevalent around safe injection sites where people are walking around possessed like it's the zombie apocalypse. That is an eerie and sober reminder of the other side. It's scientifically explainable but it's severe and it's real in the air of these areas, especially in the slums where people have given up hope and given themselves over to the devil. The spiritual presence is undeniable. The east-end of Vancouver BC is one of the most prevalent hot spots for drug addiction in North America. There's about five city blocks of complete demon manifestation and torment everywhere you look. It was the area where the worst serial killer in North American history would take his victims and feed them to the pigs on his farm. We bumped into the main drug dealer on the corner one day trying to bring people into the church for dinner, and the look in his eyes was of murderous death. There was a controlling force within him and around him so evil and wicked that was certainly not from this world. It was so eerie the hair stood up on my arms as we talked with him and I wanted to get out of there. My point is that there's rulers of the darkness of this world and spiritual wickedness in high places as Ephesians 6 indicates and without the revelation of God and his spirit, we're doomed in our carnal mind to overcome it.

The Good Fight

The war rages on and I've groaned within myself for eternal peace, yearning to be released from it all into heaven's glory where my thoughts are unabated and where the despair and effects of the world aren't weighing me down, but it's not my time yet. I must soldier on in faith as we all should as Christians. We're not called to be complacent gluttons, we are called to fight the good fight of faith and sometimes that's being in the trenches of life and abstaining from life's temptations. 1 Peter 1:6-7 says, "In this you greatly rejoice, though now for a little while, if need be, you have been grieved by various temptations, that the genuineness of your faith, being much more precious than gold that perishes, though it is tested by fire, may be found to praise, honour, and glory at the revelation of Jesus Christ." 1 Peter 2 says, "I beseech you as strangers and pilgrims, abstain from fleshly lusts, which war against the soul." They'll be a time when we will experience a release into euphoric grace and peace, much like an eagle stepping foot off a cliff's edge but until then the war still rages on and there's work to be done. 1 Peter 2 goes on by saying, "When you do good and suffer, if you take it patiently, this is commendable before God. For to this you were called, because Christ also suffered for us, leaving us an example, that you should follow his steps." You see how it's not one or two scriptures that faith is being misconstrued and misrepresented from these false teachers but literally the whole bible? Romans 8:20-26 says, "We know that the whole creation groans and labors with birth pangs together until now. Not only that, but we also who have the first fruits of the Spirit, even we ourselves groan within ourselves, eagerly waiting for the adoption, the redemption of our body. For we were saved in this hope, but hope that is seen is not hope, for why does one still hope for what he sees? But if we hope for what we do not see, we eagerly wait for it with perseverance. Likewise the spirit also helps us in our weaknesses." We must soldier on in faith and I'm doing the best I can to write this book but I know there's people with far more gifts and resources than me who can contribute to the cause. Our eternal salvation is sealed in Christ and we need to let our ties in this world go and partner with God for his cause. I guarantee the greatest experience in this world will pale in comparison to the worst in heaven.

I'm finishing writing this amidst this pandemic and people around the world are living in fear, not necessarily the fear of the virus itself but the fear and uncertainty of losing their dreams and aspirations in this life. So much of our fear is based on us placing our hopes and optimism in this world and not in the world to come. Cruise ships are being held at port and airlines have been closed down around the world. There's evacuations, forced confinement, confusion and pandemonium all over the world with the apparent death toll rising in every country, and whether they're false flags of deception and conspiracy or not, the end is on the near horizon and we need to awaken from our global complacency and get our souls right with God and accept his offer of salvation before it's too late. If we truly believe with all of our hearts the promise of salvation, we'll invest ourselves to it's cause because the more we invest our time and money in this world the more it will be flushed down it's deceptive drain. Again, biblical truth is imminent and a daunting and encroaching revelation like that unavoidable glacier but it's so much closer to overtaking us then we realize. Jesus even foretells the end of the world in Matthew 24 by saying, "You will hear wars and rumours of wars. See that you are not troubled, for all these things must come to pass, but the end is not yet. For nation will rise against nation, and kingdom against kingdom. And there will be famines, pestilences, and earthquakes in various places. All these are the beginning of sorrows. Then they will deliver you up to tribulation and kill you, and you will be hated by all nations for my namesake. And then many will be offended, will betray one another, and will hate one another. Then many false prophets will rise up and deceive many. And because lawlessness will abound, the love of many will grow cold. But he who endures to the end shall be saved. And this Gospel of the Kingdom will be preached in all the world as a witness to all nations, and then the end will come......Then there will be great tribulation, such as not been since the beginning of the world until this time, no, nor ever shall be. And unless those days were shortened, no flesh would be saved, but for the elect's sake those days will be shortened." Jesus isn't mixing words and again, I don't see what's so grievous about admitting your sin to God and asking for his forgiveness, considering the alternative. There's no one more stubborn or sceptical as me but I'm not ashamed to admit I'm sinful at all anymore. Sin actually comes quite naturally to me to be honest and if there's a judgment to come, I most certainly need a saviour.

1 Peter 1:13-14 says, "Gird up the loins of your mind, be sober, and hope to the end for the grace that is to be brought unto you at the revelation of Jesus Christ, as obedient children, not fashioning yourselves according to the former lusts in your ignorance." Again, it's all justifiable compliance to me and all that will happen upon salvation is you'll pass through death into life by your admittance and repentance, where the world outside of Christ won't. Jesus himself said, "Unless you believe that I am He, you will die in your sins." The question is, what do you have to lose especially in a world with nothing more to gain?

I see life as a journey, a raging river with its ups and downs and emotional highs and lows along the way without knowing when the waterfall is coming. The difference for those in Christ is as soon as we careen over the waterfall's edge, he'll hold us up into his arms where the world will be in a never-ending freefall. Some people feel it's unfair and two black and white but we're sure limited and struggling to find an alternative solution otherwise. I actually just heard on the radio that the attempt of science to prolong life is a 110 billion dollar industry. The truth is there isn't an alternative solution, death is a formality and we're trapped in our sin until we release it unto God and accept his sacrifice for it. It grieves my heart that people don't know God in this powerful and intimate way and struggle and suffer like they do without hope and without faith. I'd rather my belief tell me the truth of my sin and the formality of the world than to lie to me and lead me astray.

The struggle for us all even in faith is the battle between optimism and pessimism. It's like we're all torn between the two. Even the majority of Christians won't venture into the pages of revelation because it's too ominous of a reality to accept. It takes us out of our comfort zone and compromises our hopes and plans for the future. Again, we think we're being positive and inspiring by being optimistic for the future of the world but it can also blind us from the truth of pessimism foretold in the Bible. Unfortunately, there is no future for the world and people just don't want to accept that nor do they want to hear it. It's literally impossible as a born-again believer in Jesus Christ to be optimistic for the world's future. In Matthew 24 Jesus himself warns us of the end days and states that there will be an end to this world. Pessimism is defined as a tendency to see the worst aspect of things, believe that the worst will happen, and a lack of hope and confidence in the future. Scientifically it says pessimism is a negative mental attitude in which an undesirable outcome is anticipated from a given situation. To an agnostic or an atheist this all seems like a negative kill-joy but with salvation as an alternative solution, pessimism becomes far more relative and optimistic especially since redemptive science isn't keeping pace with the elements of evil. It's scary to me how naive people are just coasting along in life and feeling justified as that same waterfall approaches ever so near. They have no idea what's on the horizon and their preconceived notions concerning the bible are holding them back from the salvation of God. My adopted mother is much the same. She despises even the thought of the bible and rejects it wholeheartedly but she doesn't even realize what she's rejecting. She's never even opened it. She's too stubborn to give thanks or pray and when questioned about God she curls up her lip in disgust and just blames him for her circumstances. That's the extent of her analysis as far as theology, spirituality or salvation takes her. She has no fear or concern over her soul whatsoever. She adamantly denies the existence of God but blames him for everything as though if he exists he should have been there at her every beckon call along the way even in her unbelief and ignorance of him. I know I've mentioned it before but I've met so many others along the way who have felt the same way concerning God. As soon as something goes wrong or they're faced with difficult circumstances, they blame the god they don't believe exists. They just vainly and complacently regard him as insignificant because he wasn't right there in every moment of their lives even in their ignorance of him. We expect so much from a God we adamantly deny and that will unfortunately be the world's greatest contradiction that it will have to ponder for eternity. The truth about my mom is she's miserable and much like the world, she's living in her own contradiction. She's extremely judgemental and gossips about everyone. She has no empathy or sympathy for anyone and sits back in a chair of her own entitlement, blaming everyone for the world's problems without lifting a finger herself to help anyone. She even judges the lives of her own kids and looks down on them as though we're worthless failures as she lives alone to dwell on her own. Her three favourite passions and hobbies in life are knitting quilts, gardening in her backyard and walking her dog. Here again is someone who depends on the God she despises for everything she loves, from the second she wakes up until her eyes shut in the evening. The whole world's the same from the water tap to the fridge door and from the air we all breathe when we walk outside to the gas we put in our cars. It's all from the hand of God. Like many of us, my mom is trapped between her own pride and her own regrets and needs to be released from it all through the redeeming power of God through the Holy Spirit.

Deep down she's bitter with the world and the choices people have made that have hurt her. She's also bitter with the choices she's made along the way, but wherever the blame lies in her heart, God has given each of us a will to choose and that can be seen as a blessing or a curse. The will to choose can be seen as a responsibility or a chance to be selfish and irresponsible and unfortunately many choose the alternative. I chose the alternative my whole life and it nearly killed me. These are the truths of this fallen world but somehow we take such offense being confronted by them and revert it all back to blaming God. My mom doesn't see my love for her in sharing the gospel. It's an offense to her own perseverance in life but what's amazing about God, and this goes for whoever is reading this, is the second we acknowledge Him in any way he's there with an ear to listen and forgive us. Even a twinkle of belief or recognition he'd be there and she can't see that as his patient love towards her all the way through her life. Again, we just don't put ourselves in God's shoes and see how he and his angels unselfishly suffer for our sake. Romans 2:4 says, "Do you despise the riches of his goodness, forbearance, and long-suffering, not knowing that the goodness of God leads you to repentance? 2 Peter 3:13-15 says, "We, according to his promise, look for new heavens and a new earth in which righteousness dwells. Therefore, beloved, looking forward to these things, be diligent to be found by him in peace, without spot and blameless, and consider that the long-suffering of our Lord is salvation." The last few words say it all. We also never consider angels who are selfless servants for our good and never get glorified or praised for their work. Hebrews 1:14 in reference to angels it says, "Are they not all ministering spirits sent forth to minister for those who will inherit salvation?" These are things we don't even consider anymore in the secular world and even too many in faith. Much like demons, we write about angels in secular songs but have no association to them biblically. Regardless, it's our wall of pride that is so difficult to penetrate. We use apparent contradictions as an excuse when we are walking contradictions in of ourselves. Our footsteps are overloaded with hypocrisy with every stride. The majority of us have had three square meals a day our whole lives in this western world and haven't given thanks for one. We're lucky a grain of salt or sugar has touched our tongue with the amount of ignorance and blasphemy that's left our mouths and I'm no different. It just shows how merciful and patient God is with all of us along the way, especially in regards to our emotional trauma and circumstances. That's ultimately what the entire storyline of the Bible is about, it's our complacent and wilful disregard, followed by his discipline, then his forgiveness and mercy over and over and over again. We just aren't seeing how truly godless and evil we are collectively. There's pockets of kindness and productivity in areas and aspects of life around the world but overall we're a disaster. We're attention-seeking gluttons, living for ourselves and our own self-preservation. We fail to realize the consequences of these accumulative actions and aren't carnaly prone to hold to any sustainable or unified level of accountability within ourselves therefore the consequences are just and truth continues to bear it's biblical claim.

I can see it all now in such an affirming clarity that I was oblivious to before my conversion. My afflictions and trauma were blinding me and all I did was react amidst it all without any guidance or direction but God had mercy on me and opened my eyes through Christ. It wasn't religion, in fact the word religion makes me cringe. It was by his spirit and his spirit alone that delivered me. It wasn't by any wisdom or human philosophy derived by man, nor was it generated from within myself. It was by the revelation of Jesus Christ. In Galatians 1:10-12 Paul says, "Do I now persuade men, or God? Or do I seek to please men? For if I still pleased men, I would not be a servant of Christ. But I make known to you, brethren, that the gospel which was preached by me is not according to man. For I neither received it from man, nor was I taught it, but it came through the revelation of Jesus Christ."

I was lost, empty and confused and my mind was growing progressively volatile, jaded and problematic and this generation is no different. I couldn't even process or operate outside of dwelling on my past and present circumstances. I wanted so desperately to find comfort and support but it wasn't there. I needed someone to sympathize and relate to my grievance and pain and affirm my own perseverance in life, but no one cared. There was no mature deliverance from it and the people around me were just self-medicating through their own trials and trauma and we merely enabled each other even more in the process.

Thankfully now I have a saviour and his spirit is within me, guiding me through my life especially after this accident. My mom and dad have offered no support whatsoever, like I said before. My brother hasn't called or text to see if I'm ok. My best friends growing up consider empathy as a burden to their own selfish needs and people who should care have just petered out. We live in such a narcissistic world now where people just don't reach out and I write this book to sympathize with those in pain who need a deeper hope than that of the world. This is my opportunity to reach out because in Christ we can live independent of it all. As Christians we are to hate the world and the spirit it generates because it doesn't offer a solution to the needs of the heart. To be honest, I've found far more support from my church than my own family and friends growing up. Of course it hurts but I don't give in or take offense because I have faith and have seen God work through it all bringing me new friends, support and a renewed hope each day. He will ride this world out in each of us who are believers wherever we are and in whatever state our societies are in. In Hebrews he says, "I will never leave you or forsake you," and in Philippians 4:6-7 he says, "Be careful for nothing, but in everything by prayer and supplication with thanksgiving let your requests be made known to God. And the peace of God, which passeth all understanding, shall keep your hearts and minds through Christ Jesus." Our ears in this world have become reverberating drums for our own causes and I've learned that chasing sympathy around is a black hole of incompassion. Our faith is our refuge and reassurance as Christians to bear these sufferings and be strengthened for our testimony to be a witness to others for proof of deliverance and perseverance. It's a supernatural joy and assurance that's foreign to the world. James1:2-4 says, "My brethren, count it all joy when you fall into various trials, knowing that the testing of your faith produces patience. But let patience have its perfect work, that you may be perfect and complete, lacking nothing. If any of you lacks wisdom let him ask of God, who gives to all liberally."

It's still not easy but there's a confidence and a hope in the Word that resonates within your soul. 2 Corinthians 1:3-6 says, "The God of all comfort, who comforts us in all our tribulation, that we may be able to comfort those who are in any trouble, with a comfort with which we ourselves are comforted by God. For as the sufferings of Christ abound in us, so our consolation also abounds through Christ. Now if we are afflicted, it is for your consolation and salvation, which is effective for enduring the same sufferings which we also suffer. Or if we are comforted, it is for your consolation and salvation."

The world is in a mad frenzy over this supposed pandemic (or scamdemic as I've heard it called) but it's showing how vulnerable and dependent we all are and how fragile life can be without faith. People were selling packs of toilet paper online for $75. Alcohol sales are up 40% and the divorce rate has skyrocketed 150%. People are consumed with fear from what they're being told through the media. This has completely blindsided the secular world but again, as bible believing Christians, this is all in the back of our minds with what's been foretold to us in the Bible. It's unfortunate but I don't let it emotionally derail me. I feel it's a mercy call of God for us to wake up and not only that, to open up his book. The time is now to evaluate all of this inclusively and independently and to question our eternal destiny instead of our destiny in this world because the world is closing in on itself rapidly.

Misconceptions Again

Again, the world sees religion and Christianity as some sort of cosmic kill-joy or domineering oppression for control. What they don't realize is they're totally right about religion but have combined the two and misinterpreted the Christian faith wholeheartedly, somehow seeing it through a religious lens like catholicism (which is a complete disaster.) I was much the same growing up. I saw Christianity as either catholicism or televangelism on TV as I'd scroll through the channels and that's it. The truth of Christ is in complete opposition to man-made religion and what he came to expose. Apart from Jesus rebuking the religious leaders in his time, the bible only references religion once in James 1. He says, "Pure and undefiled religion before God and the Father is this: to visit orphans and widows in their trouble, and to keep oneself unspotted from the world." These are pretty simple instructions that have no religious oppression or attachment to them whatsoever. Man-made religion has prostituted the name of Jesus to shame people for the empowerment of themselves. They manipulate and convolute the gospel for their own profit and control and it's a shame that people see it that way, but the scriptures adamantly oppose all of this hypocrisy, especially money hungry televangelists. There are many legitimate missions and charity organizations raising money for the cause but the bad ones have caused so much damage to the perception of christian philanthropy to the world. The Word is clear and doesn't pull any punches on the fierce judgement of these imposters and false prophets. John 12:48 says, "He who rejects me, and does not receive my Word, has that who judges him, the Word that I have spoken will judge him in the last day." The bible doesn't say anything about following a specific religion or denomination instituted by the entitlement of man nor does it justify laundering money. In Matthew 23 Jesus absolutely hammers these types of heretics and self-entitled religious organizations. He says, "Do not according to their works, for they say, and do not do. For they bind heavy burdens, hard to bear, and lay them on men's shoulders, but they themselves will not move them with one of their fingers. But all their works they do to be seen by men.... they love the best places at feasts, the best seats in the synagogues, greetings in the marketplaces, and to be called by men, Rabbi Rabbi. But do not be called Rabbi, for one is your teacher, the Christ, and you are all brethren. Do not call anyone on earth your father, for one is your father, he who is in heaven... Woe to you, scribes and Pharisees, hypocrites! You cleanse the outside of the cup and dish, but inside they are full of extortion and self-indulgence..... you are like whitewashed tombs which indeed appear beautiful outwardly, but inside are full of dead men's bones and all uncleanness. Even so you also outwardly appear righteous to men, but inside you are full of hypocrisy and lawlessness." Jesus doesn't stop there and let's heretics have it in many more scriptures as do the rest of the epistles. 1 Thessalonians 2:5 says, "As we have been approved by God to be entrusted with the gospel, even so we speak, not as pleasing men, but God who tests our hearts. Neither at any time did we use flattering words, as you know, nor a cloak of covetousness, God is witness. Nor did we seek glory from men…." I'm writing this, pleading with people to reevaluate their misconceptions. The true gospel is an independent and personal relationship with God through the revelation of Jesus Christ. When we take our last breath it won't be the power of the pope or a some ordained priest who saves anybody, it will be the resurrection power of Jesus Christ. It even irritates me transcribing this because the pope automatically gets a capital letter as though he holds some sort of religious hierarchy in the Christian religion and the world. Hebrews 7:15-16 says, "There arises another priest, who is made, not after the law of a carnal commandment, but after the power of an endless life." This scripture speaks of Jesus Christ.

Wake Up Call

Wake up call world, now is the time because tomorrow isn't promised. He's giving each of us a responsibility to seek truth through his Word to better clarify these questions and find the answers ourselves. Dust it off and read it or else go and buy one from the store while you have a chance because time is of the essence. In fact, bible apps are free on your phone therefore you have no excuse. Some of the greatest genocides in history have been on Christians by religion and that includes catholicism, so we have definitely misinterpreted much of what we think we know outside of historical and biblical truth. If religion was the pathway to God then Jesus would have followed and conformed himself to the teaching of the religions that surrounded him at the time, but he didn't. He was an independent revolutionary. He witnessed they're convoluted hypocrisy firsthand and flipped the money changers tables over himself because of the perception the world attributed to God, and would in the future. He even says in John 2, "The zeal of your house has consumed me." Faith in him is independent of religion and he's given us this release from it because of the hypocrisy in the carnal entitlement of man. I'm not saying it's not important to meet together with a community of believers as the bible insists we do, but it doesn't take four walls for us to have a relationship with God.

A relationship with God becomes even stronger at times in contemplation with him alone through prayer and the study of his Word. Even getting together with a half a dozen people interactively can be more beneficial than being in a big congregation, where your voice and opinions are never heard. I feel there's a balance and maturity somewhere in-between and beneath it all that is a productive and cohesive way of growth and faith that pleases him. If we feel pressured from the control or entitlement of man and we back away, God's love is greater because man doesn't dictate or determine God's interaction inclusively to any individual. I've left churches and it actually taught me more about God and myself through the process. There's obviously men and women more mature and experienced in the faith that we can all learn from but I've also seen a lot of immaturity, complacency and abuse from an entitled position that I was wise and stubborn enough to not let myself be subject to. I've got an old Christian friend that's been a missionary for years and he once said to me, "It's a dangerous thing when we think we've arrived." It wasn't even what he said, it was how he said it. We're all fallen sinful creatures and sometimes the deception is in the ranks or positions we think we've gained. As soon as the door closes we're on the same level as everyone in the general population regardless of what we think of ourselves otherwise. I'm glad God's made it this way because I wouldn't attend church or be interested in learning about God otherwise. 1 John 2:26 says, "These things I have written to you concerning those who try to deceive you. The anointing which you have received from him abides in you, and you do not need that anyone teach you, but as the same anointing teaches you concerning all things, and is true, and is no lie, and even as it has taught you, you shall abide in him." Ultimately, what control does anyone have over you if God's spirit abides in you. It's a gift of wisdom and of independence. You're actually more spiritually inclined than them because of the position they feel they have over you. You're in a relationship with him regardless and he's invited us all into this inclusive relationship with him. God doesn't need the pope, a priest, a new profit, denomination or any premonition or inclination of man to communicate anything. This is where so much of our confusion and contention comes from. In some respects they served their purpose for a time but now it's for us to learn from. Hebrews1 says, "God, who at various times and in various ways spoke in time past to the father's by the prophets, has in these last days spoken to us by his Son." The more we draw attention to ourselves, the more we corrupt the gospel. It's a complete absurd mockery of God on so many levels that deceives millions and has prostituted his glorious name in the process. There's one spiritual conduit and mediator between God and man and that is Jesus Christ and unless a man is directing us to that conduit, things will always go astray because of our self-entitled narcissism and greed. 1 Timothy 2:3-5 says, "God our savior, who desires all men to be saved and to come to the knowledge of the truth. For there is one God and mediator between God and men, the man Jesus Christ, who gave himself a ransom for all." I don't need man to dictate or regulate a timeline to where I can understand that. It speaks to me anytime of the day, all week long. As soon as man speaks from a position of entitlement, he's lost his humility and my attention almost instantaneously. Entitlement triggers so much of our childhood trauma and the trauma generated by the conformity of the world, therefore God would not leave us subject to it. Obviously there's cases of discipline and obedience within the four walls that need to be handled maturely, but again, God is not a religious entity of conformity. He's about structure and common sense. He's not there with a butcher knife waiting to cut off our hands and feet when we make mistakes, nor does he give us the power to do so. There were severe cases in the bible when Paul was setting the foundation and grounds for the church and needed to establish his leadership and authority, but they were also performing lewd sexual acts and things that wouldn't even be mentioned in church nowadays. It was the reformation of the conscious mind of the world and the stakes were far more severe and intentional. I think my point is that anyone in leadership or in a position to teach has to live by example and that takes a mature level of humility to do so. Who we are before knowing Christ is who we are without him, therefore entitlement is completely contradictory to the truth of Christ in a believer, as is self-righteousness. Leadership is a gift given of God and some of us just don't have that capacity to productively endure it. For me personally, I'm too new of a Christian first of all and I just don't care enough. Nor do I possess the patience, maturity, experience or humility to do it. James 3:1 says, "Let not many of you become teachers, knowing that we shall receive a stricter judgement. For we all stumble in many things." An even stricter scripture to those in positions of authority is in Romans 2. It says, "Therefore you are inexcusable, O man, whoever you are who judge, for in whatever you judge another you condemn yourself, for you who judge practice the same things. But we know that the judgement of God is according to truth against those who practice such things. And do you know this, O man, you who judge those practicing such things, and doing the same, that you will escape the judgement of God?"

Apart from the obvious physical definition of conduit piping, it's also defined as a natural channel through which something is conveyed or a way of connecting two people or organizations. With

God the conduit is pure and undefiled because our filter isn't clean or transparent enough to transmit the frequency sincerely, nor has it ever been and that's why Jesus came. Our sin and hypocrisy gets in the way and always has, so God has made the way himself in Christ and unless man humbles itself to this truth, we'll continue to fail delivering the message of the cross. Anyone else is an imposter who substitutes or compromises this direct conduit. They create the gap so they can stand in it for money and control and again, there was a time in history when the supposed Christian church who we all know as catholicism sent anyone to death reading or proclaiming true doctrine for fear the masses would come to know the truth of their apostasy and they'd have to relinquish their control. William Tyndale was one of the leaders of the protestant reformation and initially translated the bible into English. He was then subsequently charged with heresy by the catholic church, strangled to death and burned at the stake. They hated people finding true liberty, empowerment and independence outside of their control methods and four walls. The catholic church is one of the worst representations of Jesus Christ the world has ever seen and unfortunately the majority of people I've conversed with see Jesus and the bible through their convoluted misrepresentation. It's frustrating and you even see it now through this pandemic when the news addresses the effects on church services and how the media and news outlets subconsciously attribute Christianity to Roman Catholicism as though that's its representation to the world. It couldn't be further from the truth and I just shake my head in disgust because people won't actually open the bible and inquire themselves, nor have they studied the protestant movement to understand their level of abuse and apostasy. It's atrocious and no wonder people are leery and turn away from Christianity with this religious heretical garbage as their imprint and guide, especially being ingrained in children growing up. I could write a book on the topic itself and probably should one day but you're better off reading the book that opposes it all the most, the bible.

There are many churches that do it right and don't compromise and it just takes some simple research, prayerful diligence and discernment for it to be revealed to us. There's definitely depth to the scriptures and theology that take time to study but again, much of it is just common moral sense. I understand it's very difficult these days from an ecumenical standpoint, appeasing everyone's feelings and opinions and there's definitely a dividing imbalance within the word church these days, but the way to salvation doesn't change whether the door is open or shut. The bible is confrontational and offensive to our will and isn't supposed to appease everybody's feelings. There's a new ecumenical movement going on right now trying to bring all of these denominations and centuries of division together in supposed unity but all they are are band-aids to clean up the scars from the heretical typhoon that's unfolded. For me it just enables the heresy even more in the tolerance and justification we carnally live for and presume is of importance. Regardless of our introspection, this has been satan's plan all along. The church has been his number one target and adversary because of the effect on his objectives. Of course he's going to disrupt our unity and clarity especially if it's providing a place for refuge, support, healing and salvation. He hates when people turn from their sin and come to the Lord but it's our responsibility to dig a little deeper into the word faith and into the Word of God to diffuse all of the heresy the enemy has conjured up in our minds. It's just for lack of knowledge, humility and in our selfishness that the church becomes divided and gives the enemy a foothold. When I read the bible I don't find any of their religious jargon or ritualistic nonsense between the covers at all. When our opinions are held together in humility by sound doctrine and hermeneutics and when we're not living for the benefit of ourselves, we stand as a united front of service for the greater cause. There's got to be some sort of moral order and delegation in this world especially in regards to family and children, and God's Word definitely harmonizes that together proficiently. That's the sustaining power of faith and the church and where all of these apostates and new age prophets fall short in their immaturity and selfish ambition. This worldwide pandemic is a perfect example of how far off course we can get with religion, our carnal premonitions and our supposed prophetic knowledge from God. You'd think the pope who is the supposed representation of God on earth would have known all this and warned the world let alone these new age prophets. What's even crazier is he probably did know it and was partially the cause of it and didn't tell anybody. They're all a bunch of power hungry, attention-seeking money hounds who live in the financial overhead of their hypocrisy and those who have believed in them have to repent themselves of the covetousness they yearned for themselves.

Now that I've come to this knowledge and place in my faith, there's no going back for me, in fact the spirit within me won't allow it. So much of the contention and deception in the world has been clarified in my mind by God's Word, as has the contention within the church. It's all right there for us to study and evaluate and the gravity of its significance to me is infallible. 2 Timothy 3:12-17 says, "All who desire to live godly in Christ Jesus will suffer persecution. But evil men and impostors will grow worse and worse, deceiving and being deceived…….. All scripture is given by instruction of God, and is profitable for doctrine, for reproof, for correction, for instruction in righteousness, that the man of God may be complete, thoroughly equipped for every good work." I don't see the entitlement or control of man in those words whatsoever. There's a transparent and redeeming clarity in the heart of God through his Word that only a born-again believer can experience. He's become that reassuring relationship that I always yearned for and needed to sustain me. Again, It's convicting at times but it bears the truth that frees the conscience to live unabated, justified, accepted and rejuvenated. I think back at some of the things I used to do and it scares me to think where I'd be without him and where I'd end up on judgement day. It also scares me to think where I'd be amidst this pandemic and where others are in their heads right now. Once enlightened to that truth and the power of his forgiveness, we all need to stand in reverence of God and live in compliance.

Reverence

How awful and disobedient would I be to go back to my old ways and willfully disobey the commandments and truth God has instilled in my heart and the past he's forgiven me from. As the world does every day, it's like slapping him in the face while he's on that cross crucifying him all over again and I think he takes it personally. In fact the Word says so. Hebrews 6 says, "It's impossible for those who were once enlightened, and have tasted the heavenly gift, and have become partakes of the Holy Spirit, and have tasted the good Word of God and the powers of the world to come, if they fall away, to renew them again to repentance, since they crucify again for themselves the Son of God, and put Him to an open shame."

I have an old pastor friend who has a crazy testimony. He was addicted to cocaine and in the gang life selling drugs and guns since he was a teenager. He finally hit rock bottom fearing for his life and decided to turn his life over to Jesus. Ironically, after his conversion he was asked to build a large cross for the church and to beat on it with a hammer to make it look old and rustic. He said he was beating away at the pristine edges of the new wood when God spoke to him in the process and said, "You're doing this to me Dave, you're doing this to me," as he swung the hammer. He then fell on his face and broke down in tears as he lay on the cross being convicted of sin and has never looked back. It just crushed him at the reality of his sin on the cross. He's definitely had his ups and downs as we all have but has dedicated his life to sharing the gospel to those marginalized and addicted on the streets ever since. This is a severe reminder of how the world perceives the sacrifice of Jesus Christ especially when we'll be judged by him. Romans 14:10-12 says, "We shall all stand before the judgment seat of Christ. For it is written, as I live, says the Lord, every knee shall bow to me, and every tongue shall confess to God… Every one of us shall give account of himself to God."

When I was fourteen I was sent up north to a ranch for delinquent kids. We were building a huge house and my job was to throw precut pieces of 2x10 down into the excavation for the foundation. I started acting like an idiot and was launching them all over the place to impress another guy on site, not paying attention. Next thing you know this huge foreman guy walked up the steep hill with blood pouring down from his forehead. I was a strong kid with a wicked arm and literally split his head wide open, but it's incredible what happened next. I was so scared standing there petrified, thinking that was the end for me. He was going to either kill me or I'd be fired and sent to a foster home which would have been disastrous for me at the time. Amazingly he didn't do either, he walked up to me and said, "I forgive you, be more careful next time." I couldn't believe it, he took that pain upon himself to free me from the punishment I rightfully deserved. His words were stern but in that short walk up that hill he had the heart to forgive me and it changed the course of my life, even with that pain going through him. He was such a tough, strong man not just physically but mentally and I had such respect, appreciation and reverence for him and what he did for me that I still tell the story 30 years later. The point is, how awful would it be if I saw him from the top of that same hill and deliberately threw another piece of wood at his head? For me it's an illustration of what God has done for us through Jesus Christ and the reverence we should live in.

He is the saviour of the world and the historical transition in accountability, dignity and a million other synonyms the world didn't generate on its own. The question is where would have the world gone without him if he didn't intervene? That's a scary revelation in itself. He's taken upon himself the sins of man so that the world's relationship with him can be reconciled and restored. 1 John 2:2 says,

"He himself is the propitiation for our sins, and not for ours only but also for the whole world." It gives God joy when people come to him through what Christ has done. Hebrews 12:2-3 says, "Looking unto Jesus the author and finisher of our faith; who for the joy that was set before him endured the cross, despising the shame and is set down at the right hand of the Throne of God. For consider him that endured such contradiction of sinners against himself, less you be wearied and faint in your hearts." I love how the King James Bible says contradiction there, especially considering the title of my book. I also love how it says, "despising the shame" as though God lived and died to release us from our shame and regrets. It goes so much deeper into the heart than the word religion could ever define. In Luke it says that there is joy in the presence of the angels of God over one sinner that repents. This is the entire spiritual battle taking place around us and is what salvation in Christ is based upon. God was in Christ feeling the emotional toil and humiliation of humanity and feeling the nails being driven into his body. It says in Luke 22:44 that before going to the cross Jesus was in agony and his sweat was like drops of blood falling down to the ground. Sin is the cause of this world's discourse so he offered himself up and died for the cause. God has taken sin personally on the cross by interceding on our behalf and we need to take that seriously.

Encouragement

Somehow I want this truth to register more clearly to those struggling in their own identity, feeling trapped, inadequate and internally imploding. There's no better time than now through this pandemic to surrender your heart to Jesus Christ, especially with what's on the horizon and with people in isolation feeling more and more confused and introverted. I've been there myself and can relate on so many levels, especially now due to my accident. The world has made us feel like we're the only ones dealing with these issues and sometimes the ones with the biggest hearts are the ones most affected by the world's discourse. We're the most vulnerable and sensitive to it, but God came to strengthen us and use us and our giftings for inspiration and encouragement to others. I've been so confused and lonely in my life, weakened by the pressures of the world and the pressures I put on myself. I've felt the insecurity and fear of being judged and scrutinized. I've suffered deeply with social anxiety and spiritual torment in my life. I've had severe times of anger and depression. Times of poverty and lack of support. I've battled through serious health issues, bankruptcy, car accidents, drug and alcohol abuse, overdoses by friends, adultery, murder, divorce and just distrust and unloyalty from friends and family.

Life hasn't pulled many punches my way but I see a lot of it was relative to the choices I was making and the choices people were making around me. An old saying is that you are the company you keep and it's definitely hard to expect anything else with so much drugs and alcohol abuse around. Other afflictions in my journey have just been the life and circumstances that surround us in this fallen world into which many of us suffer. Some people have dealt with far worse circumstances than me, but again, whoever we are and whatever we've been through, we can't feel sorry for ourselves and play the victim role expecting the world to be empathetic. We've got to push through in faith because God doesn't change and will continue to strengthen our hearts and walk alongside us regardless of our shortcomings or circumstances. He's that good if we are transparent and seek him through the process and only out of sheer mercy does he seek us in our ignorance, much like Paul in the New Testament. 1 Timothy 13-16 says, "I was formerly a blasphemer, a persecutor, and an insolent man; but I obtained mercy because I did it ignorantly in unbelief. And the grace of our Lord was exceedingly abundant, with faith and love which are in Christ Jesus. This is a faithful saying and worthy of all acceptance that Christ came into the world to save sinners, of who I am chief. However, for this reason I obtained mercy, that in me first Jesus Christ might show all long-suffering, as a pattern to those who are going to believe on him for everlasting life." Paul is an incredible example to follow especially to those who feel unworthy of forgiveness. God called him not only worthy but inspired him to write a good portion of the New Testament. 2 Timothy 2 says that if we deny him he will deny us, but if we struggle in believing or are faithless, he remains faithful because he cannot deny himself. Sometimes this single revelation alone is miraculous enough for me to believe and to persevere through in faith. It generates an overwhelming appreciation for him and shows us the true unselfish and merciful nature of God. He's got many characteristics but thank God patience and mercy are on the list. Why doesn't he turn away in bitterness like we all do with an offense against us? Why doesn't he whine and complain and make up excuses? Why doesn't he judge like we judge each other? The question not only is why doesn't he but why didn't he in Jesus Christ? That's where the revelation of God is unprecedented. James 2:13 says, "Judgment is without mercy to the one who has shown no mercy. Mercy triumphs over judgement."

Ultimately, there was nothing in me when I needed him the most but he saw something in me and drew me to himself, persevering for my cause along the way. He's become a saviour to so many that have been lost and confused and unfortunately the world disregards such irrefutable transformations. He sees potential in the most dire and disastrous of circumstances. Somehow new flowers sprout and blossom after forest fires and we don't plant the seeds but unless we allow God's seed to grow within us, we're merely living spiritually dead in the ashes. 1 John 5:12 says, "He that has the Son has life, and he that does not have the Son of God does not have life." This is a bold scripture and kind of rules out the purpose and philosophy of man entirely. It's offensive to anyone that's become wise in their own eyes. The carnal world doesn't see that God's hand of mercy will slowly rise and more and more the world will fall victim to its own subjective reasoning, bound in its own self-deceived determination, bringing the scriptures more and more alive and relevant. The greatest hypocrisy is many will wonder why and even blame the God they were irreverent to all along.

The End is Near

I feel the end of the age is here, especially considering this pandemic and seeing the global deception and domino's beginning to fall. The weeds of evil have interwoven themselves so deeply and seductively within our world that it's carnally irreversible and inevitable. What's being promoted, and what we think is pulling us forward into a promising future is actually pulling us to the end that much quicker. There's a new Sprint commercial that states that they were the first to bring 5G technology nationwide. The commercial says, "We're turning up the speed, upgrading over a thousand towers a month with ultra-capacity 5G that will bring speeds as fast as Wi-Fi to cities and towns across America and we're adding more every week." It ends the commercial by saying, "Who says you can't have it all," meanwhile the Queen song "I want it all, I want it now" is playing in the background throughout the whole commercial. You can see how they manipulate our subconscious in how they define what having it all and wanting it all is for us socially and impulsively. To the complacent mind of innovative comfort and convenience it all seems beneficial and desirable but unfortunately each button we press makes us more vulnerable to conformity and to their accessibility to us. The comfort we seek and feel we're entitled to, I feel, has become the greatest deception. I just can't express it enough and that's why it's so imperative to acknowledge the bible for its truth and severity moving forward. It's a comprehensive look at life we just can't disregard anymore.

Our desire needs to be turned from the world to an eternal desire because as the world and its accessibility to resources diminishes, so will our hopes in them. It's going to get ugly as our desperation increases along with our selfishness and entitlement to it all. Without eternity as our refuge and hope, the world will turn into a frantic, confused hysteria, lost in its own lack of discipline and impulsive dependencies. It's happening right now where I live. We've had some heavy rains that have caused some severe flooding in the area. It's thrown people into a panic and they've raided all the grocery stores. They're even rationing off gas as of last night. This is just a precursor to what's on the horizon. Whether it's a month or ten years, we will soon be completely under siege by their New World Order, New International Economic Order or whatever they're calling it these days. They've taken bits and pieces of socialist philosophy, Imperialism, Zionism and technocracy stemming from the 1930s, along with many other conforming methods and have developed a system to which they will completely control and monopolize the world into their desired goal of totalitarianism. Economically, it's much like the board game monopoly itself. A brief definition of technocracy from Google is an ideological system of governance in which a decision-maker or makers are elected by the population or appointed on the basis of their expertise in a given area of responsibility, particularly with regard to scientific or technical knowledge. That is kind of vague to which I hope to discuss more after my testimony but it just gives you an idea of how calculated and sophisticated these global elite lunatics are. It's basically the pinnacle of innovation in the hands of the wrong people, to put it mildly. Technology is so advanced nowadays that the world will not only become a slave to the lender but be conformed into the control of a database monitoring system which they own and operate. This pandemic is simply to set that all in motion just as the bible indicates. My definition of them is a bunch of demon-possessed psychopaths with nothing better to do than to cowardly amalgamate together in secret to destroy and control the world. What a pathetic and meaningless existence they live. The more I've researched, the more evident it is of how their decisions impact our lives. They have an infinite financial overhead and simply buy out the resources, dictating the world's economy through the stock market like I was saying before. They own the majority of the entertainment industry and media for brainwashing and push their psychological algorithms and narratives forward. They even have the power to manipulate the election polling systems. They also buy out the patent companies along with all the technological, scientific and biological development and use it for their benefit. They manipulate and bankrupt governments and collapse the whole system so we all live beyond our means and become enslaved and dependent upon them to survive. They've created this system right before our eyes with impulse and convenience as the illusion and now they'll dictate its rise and fall. People love capitalism because of the opportunity generated but unfortunately they've used it to capitalize on us all. They generate a reward system in our minds to reward themselves. Welcome to the world of evil and the pessimism of the Bible that people don't think is an imminent reality. God not only reveals himself to us, he reveals the spirit of evil and its intentions and helps us become more consciously aware of our spiritual surroundings. In this book I hope to broaden the spectrum of understanding to those struggling for answers and reluctant to open this book we call the bible. I don't see a need to over analyze it all in regards to conspiracy, it's actually quite simple. It doesn't matter what "ology" or "ism" you call it, these are evil people doing extremely evil things and they are willfully conscious of it. We just don't perceive that level of omnipotence financially but it definitely exists on our planet. It's the spiritual magnitude of it all that is so blinding without God. Again, people say pessimism is negative but every dramatic movie has a climactic ending with the credits on the screen, this unfortunately isn't a fictional story, this is the truth of the world at large and we better have our names written in God's Book of Life.

I'm a common, simple man that I feel a lot of people can relate to. I have no college degree and barely graduated high school as you can probably tell by my writing style. If it were up to me outside of faith, my dream would be to be up in a cabin somewhere with a nice down-to-earth gal, rebuilding an old Datsun, fishing and golfing every day without any of this in my mind, but I don't feel that's my inevitable destiny or calling. Part of me feels like Jonah in the Bible as I can see it all unfolding around me and I know what I should do but I don't know if I have the courage or strength to carry it out. I also know without God I don't care enough to voice a concern. It's crazy the truth God puts before you when you become a believer. I said before that I hate that it's the truth and that's because it's about dying to yourself. I naturally want to live for myself, not die to myself but that's what faith compels us to do. There's something God has called me to as there is in each of us, and I've yet to fully grasp what that is but maybe this book is the beginning of that destination. I feel like many Christians are in this state of mind and are reluctant to push forward for their fear of losing their identity in the world whether it be socially or financially but now is a crucial and pivotal time in history for us to let go and bear this objective. We need to test our faith and help the cause before the world is consumed and another soul is lost.

I feel I have to somehow express to others what's happened in me and by sharing my testimony in writing, hopefully it will encourage others to surrender their lives over to Jesus and do the same. I've tried public speaking but I don't think I'm quite ready to take on that level of pressure and scrutiny. It's obviously not my gift because I get overcome with anxiety and whatever intellect is in my mind does not come through my lips. I'm quite sensitive as we all are to a barrage of opinions focussed upon us and I admire speakers, especially pastors who handle it without biblical compromise and with such eloquence and dignity. They take on far more than anyone realizes. I thought about music as a way to share my faith but I'm lackluster on the guitar at best and my voice kind of sounds like an ogre yodeling down a hallway. I tried playing five songs for a street ministry downtown awhile ago and it was extremely nerve racking for me. I forgot the words and chords and totally froze up on stage. It triggers my rejection trauma which can be extremely painful for me. Regardless, I'm going to start with this book and see where God takes me from there, even if it inspires one person. It's been a struggle writing this book to be completely honest. First of all I gave it to a friend's son who's an apparent computer wiz to transcribe and edit for me but his computer crashed and he lost about 80,000 words. That was a bit of a setback because I have a horrible short-term memory since this accident and had to start all over again from scratch. I also struggle with ADD and bouts of depression and anxiety so reliving and referencing everything has brought out a lot of emotions in me that I like to put in the past. Regardless, I've persevered and I think it's all happened for a reason to make me that much more genuine and transparent. I'll be honest, I've learned a lot about myself writing this book. So much goes on in the journey of life that none of us actually document and even though it can be painful reliving some of it, it's healthy to see how much we've persevered through. Many of us should be far more proud of ourselves than we are at what we've endured and persevered through.

At first I didn't focus on adding the scriptures in relation to my own circumstances and I'm so glad that I've done that now. It's like the scriptures come alive when you're trying to convey the spirit's work within you. Galatians 1:15-16 Paul says, "It pleased God, who separated me from my mother's womb, and called me by his grace, to reveal his son in me." Paul's transformation has revolutionised the gentile world and that same spirit is what transformed me and is still alive and at work around the globe. God has revealed to me things so severe and detrimental to the destiny of our souls, that aren't for the timid or faint of heart. There's a darkness that looms over this earth that is about to swallow us whole and unless we surrender to

God and accept the salvation he offers, we will be consumed by it. The truth is God is not trying to save this world and however good we perceive ourselves to be, it still doesn't force a gift from the hand of the giver. It's all mercy at the end of each day and we'll all come to realize that very shortly. If you're reading this, you're a sinner, admit it, ask for forgiveness from God and accept his sacrifice for it on his cross. Let it be from the heart and let it be sincere and out of that acknowledgment. That confession is what God asks for from within the heart of man. Don't be stubborn, it's free and God wanted it to be free so our mind isn't contrived and can process grace unabated without man-centered regulations impeding our conscience, spiritual development and peace of mind. Romans 10:9-10 says, "If you confess with your mouth the Lord Jesus and believe in your heart that God has raised him from the dead, you will be saved. For with the heart one believes unto righteousness, and with the mouth confession is made unto salvation."

Spiritual Veil

I see life now as a spiritual veil. A veil that can be lifted or one that remains over our eyes and our heart like a closed curtain, continually blinding us from the truth. Whether we're believers or not, most of us will admit there's two heartstrings pulling us in opposite directions over our choices whether they be good or bad, productive or counterproductive. It's like the old analogy of the angel and demon on either shoulder voicing their persistence. These voices are like a persisting commentary at times that seem to oppose each other, but again, in Christ we see their directives and can clearly identify with them. It's amazing that the more you identify with true biblical spirituality, the more you come into your own identity. Without this spiritual consciousness man's consciousness is held to its own inconclusive theories and philosophies which bear so much more weight on the human vessel and allow the mind to be deceived and battered in torment with the spiritual warfare that surrounds us. The most prominent scientists, philosophers, and intellectual mind's in history, along with all the atheists, and agnostics around the world are lost in secular humanism, sitting around conversing with pens full of ink and blank sheets of paper in front of them unable to explain any means to the supernatural phenomenon that's taking place in them and all around them. They're lost in faithless disassociation as is the entire unbelieving world. Many live justified in their theories and affirmations yet each one will fall asleep and be awakened to another realm in their dreams. Their body of matter is unconscious on their bed but their mind is awakened to a whole nother world with seemingly predetermined storylines with feeling, emotion and physical properties and substance sometimes greater than that if they were awake. It's a third of our daily life and a completely unexplainable and mysterious phenomenon, full of intuition, premonitions and meaning that are seemingly from another realm and world beyond our own. We are asleep in the natural realm, but our conscious will is in operation in a dream realm as though we're simultaneously two separate beings at the same time. How can something we can't even fathom or comprehend in the natural realm be comprehended, formulated and predetermined inside of us? It's one thing to imagine something but how can we be conscious of something unimaginable and how can we remember it when we awaken? If it's only in our imagination as science claims it to be, how can we remember what we've imagined when we are not conscious of it when we're asleep? The scientific study of dreams is called oneirology but it's all based on theories and through all of its extensive research and diagnosis has simply defined dreams as a product of random brain activation. Their word random is a pretty inconclusive determination that's occurring within billions of people every night. Wikipedia says one of the central questions of sleep research is what part of the brain is driving dreams video-auditory experience. We have a video auditory experience taking place in the natural realm while we're awake through our eye's lens of perception and through our other senses but we also have the same while we're asleep and our eyes are closed. My point is, how do we know we won't be in that state when we die? How do we know it won't be a permanent nightmare? What conclusive proof does science have to say otherwise?

I had an intensely vivid dream a few years ago where I was on a concrete roof top with concrete dividers on it. I remember I could feel this premonition of an approaching paradigm shift in the world. I sensed it coming and all of a sudden, simultaneously, time seemed to end in the natural world and this bright blue, green and yellow piercing light shined so bright I couldn't bear to look at it the colours were so magnificent. I remember cowering in the corner of the concrete divider pleading for mercy over my life and all that I'd done, hoping my faith would save me. It was so terrifying that I was in the fetal position paralyzed with fear. I then remember the back of my mouth and tongue tasting like cold steel and I could feel and taste the presence of death in me and all around me. I had this tiny glimmer of life left in me but there were empty, zombie-like souls walking by in agony, destitute of life and suffering in torment. The point again is, how can my mind formulate or even imagine or articulate something that's not even perceivable in the natural realm? The sensory motor cortex is functioning to produce our perspective in the natural but how does it transition into the supernatural in our dreams, with emotions and senses that exceed that in the natural? It's impossible unless it actually exists somewhere or is somehow foreordained otherwise it wouldn't precede itself in our intuition. Our imagination wouldn't have the capacity to generate it.

I was dating a gal recently for a couple months. We had a strong attraction and a lot in common but she had an extremely domineering and controlling spirit about her that was at times abusive and overbearing. The attraction was so strong that I justified dating her but was still leery and confused if she was a good fit for me. I then had this crazy dream about her one night that seemed to reveal who she truly was. It was like a warning to me to let it go and end it as soon as possible. I remember trying to calm her down in the dream and be understanding about something but she was fearsome and brutally contentious about it. It's almost as if I could see into her genealogy and that controlling spirit that I was leery of. After the dream I could see it so clearly in her mannerisms of how true the dream was about her character. The only explanation to this outside of an impartation of some sort is that my intuition is actually more conscious of my life while I'm unconscious. The only other alternative is there's a spirit world interceding on my behalf. Again, these are unexplainable phenomena taking place in each of us on a nightly basis.

The truth is we're all extremely intricate in our design and there's far more than merely operating matter taking place outside and within our vessel. We have a soul with spiritual dimensions existing every present moment of our lives whether we believe it or not. The actual word soul again, has no matter attached to it and is actually defined by Google as the spiritual or immaterial part of a human being regarded as immortal. It says the soul is the principle of life, feeling, thought, and actions in humans, regarded as a distinct entity separate from the body, and commonly held to be separable in existence from the body. The question is how did Google define that, let alone science? The principle of life, feeling, thought, and actions seems like a rather essential component to me from something science can't establish as real.

Incarnate God

Again we can try to disregard it all as irrelevant but we are only lying to ourselves and with it the opposing forces of evil enhance further into the influence of our mind. We can't physically see God so that justifies science's unbelief, therefore for him to reveal himself to us in a relative way, he took on humanity, incarnating himself in the person of Jesus Christ, subjecting himself to our limitations with the objective of becoming our overriding influence unto salvation. Colossians 1 says, "We have redemption through his blood, even the forgiveness of sins: Who is the image of the invisible God, the firstborn of every creature, for by him were all things created, that are in heaven, and that are in earth, visible and invisible, whether they be thrones, or dominions, or principalities, or powers: all things were created by him and for him." And again Hebrews 1 says, "In these last days God has spoken to us by his son, whom he has appointed heir of all things, through whom also He made the worlds, who being the brightness of His glory and the express image of His person, and upholding all things by the Word of his power, when He had by Himself purged our sins." There's many more scriptures concerning the incarnation of God through Jesus Christ which becomes the fascination and mystery within the Bible, but one more is 1 Timothy 3:16, it says, "Without controversy great is the mystery of godliness; God was manifest in the flesh, justified in the spirit, seen by angels, preached unto the gentiles, believed on in the world, received up into glory."

I realize it's a mystery and it takes faith to believe but if what God's saying to us through his Word is true, then eternity lies in the balance. No one truly comprehends the fullness of God's incarnation in Jesus Christ nor has he allowed us the ability to do so. If we could he wouldn't subject humanity to faith, nor would he make us accountable to it. He's left it a mystery and he declares it a mystery. Colossians 2:2 says, "The mystery of God, and of the Father, and of Christ; in whom are hid all the treasures of wisdom and knowledge." He's left us subject to our limitations but in Hebrews 2 says that God has put all things in subjection under his feet. It says, "He put all in subjection under him, he left nothing that is not put under him. But now we do not yet see all things put under him. But we see Jesus, who was made a little lower than the angels, for the suffering of death crowned with glory and honour, that he, by the grace of God, might taste death for everyone. For it was fitting for him, for whom are all things and by whom are all things, in bringing many sons to glory, to make the captain of their salvation perfect through suffering."

If I were to try to convey how I perceive it in simpleton terms it would be like taking an old Dodge Aries or station wagon, stripping it of all its driving components and running gear and just leaving the shell. You take the engine and transmission out along with all the brakes, steering column and suspension and replace them with the components of a Formula 1 racing car. From the outside it would seem the same but on the inside is a hidden driveline full of pristine power, breaking and control, but if you were to crash it, all the components would feel the impact together as one unified vessel. It's much like how God felt the impact of life in the vessel of Jesus Christ through his sacrifice on the cross. The soul of God was in the person of Jesus Christ. For those who don't believe that Jesus Christ is the incarnation of God, even those who claim to be Christians like the Jehovah Witnesses? Zechariah 12:10 God says, "They will look upon me whom they have pierced, and they shall mourn for him as one mourns for his only son, and shall be in bitterness for him as one is in bitterness for his firstborn." It's amazing how God speaks in the second and third person throughout the Word and this scripture is no different. He speaks of his own preordained incarnation. Again, it's a mystery but a glorious one at that. In Ephesians 3 Paul repeatedly says that Christ is a mystery. He says, "I was made a minister, according to the gift of the grace of God given to me by the effectual working of his power. To me, who am less than the least of all saints, is this grace given, that I should preach among the gentiles the unsearchable riches of Christ. And to make all men see what is the fellowship of the mystery, which from the beginning of the world has been hid in God, who created all things by Jesus Christ. To the intent that now the principalities and powers in heavenly places might be known by the church the manifold wisdom of God. According to the eternal purpose which he purposed in Christ Jesus our Lord. In whom we have boldness and access with confidence by the faith of him."

See how it says that we have access with confidence by the faith of him? Hebrews 12 says that Jesus is the author and finisher of our faith and it's extremely important to understand what he's accomplished for us. The mystery is in his will and he's left that a mystery for us to abide in so we're not bound in entitlement, defining and determining faith ourselves. Again, we do not generate this regeneration within ourselves, it's a supernatural transformation within the soul that only a born again believer can comprehend.

Christianity in its purest form isn't necessarily about religion as so many perceive it to be. It's not defined by traditions, oppressive regulations or ritualistic symbolism. There weren't suits and ties two thousand years ago, nor were there organs or synthesizers. They met in small groups in homes and in caves, hiding from persecution most of the time. His disciples were mostly fishermen and John the Baptist walked around wearing camel's hair as his garment with a leather girdle wrapped around his loins. He never cut his hair and the bible says he ate locusts and wild honey scooped out of the hollow part of trees. He had absolutely no ties to religion other than to plead to the world to repent and make the way for the coming savior until eventually he was beheaded. Christianity is not a man-made organization or system, nor does it define itself by showing up to church on Sundays. These things can help draw us to the truth (sometimes by them even exposing the truth) but they don't define the intention. They'll all fail and continue to do so to some degree because we all fall short of the glory of God. Christianity is the incarnation of God to mankind. How we as coherent, competent individuals entertain and perceive this revelation in our minds will determine eternity for us. Sin separates us from God and that's what he came to expose and reconcile. He came to open our eyes to true spiritual awareness and expose the carnal mind in all its depravity, something we could not and still don't provingly do on our own. He encapsulated the highest level of personal conduct under the uttermost and burdensome set of circumstances to save us from ourselves and to regenerate the heart of the world. With all the power and reason to turn away from the objective set before him, he walked through it with courage and selfless love in every one of his footsteps. Where we have always failed, he becomes our champion and saviour and those who love him glorify and worship him for this service and sacrifice. It's such a riveting and profound proclamation of God on so many levels. We just don't have the wisdom, imagination or intellect to create a story like this in our minds. It's either fiction or nonfiction and it's our choice to decide which one. If the story is really fictional as many supposed it to be, it's still been more influential than any other devised in history. It's actually the cornerstone of documented time in history. All of documented time descends on him and now descends from him. The terms Anno Domini and BC, being before Christ, are used to label or number years in the Julian and Gregorian calendars which is the most widely used calendar around the world. It says this calendar era is based on the traditionally reckoned year of the conception or birth of Jesus of Nazareth, with AD counting years from the start of this epoch and BC denoting years before the start of the era. That is fascinating in of itself and if it doesn't give reason for reference or reverence, I don't know what can. An epoch is defined as a period of time in history or a person's life, typically one marked by notable events or particular characteristics. It says the beginning of a distinctive period in the history of someone or something or a division of time that is a subdivision of a period and is itself subdivided into ages corresponding to a series in chronostratigraphy.

The Bible's Relevance

However we perceive it to be, the Bible is the number one produced book of all time and subsequently the number one read book of all time and is to this very day. When I type in any combining words from the bible, google instantly brings up the scripture or a variation of those similar. It's fascinating to me how powerful that is because no other book does that. Over six billion bibles have been circulated throughout history. The number of bibles that are sold, given away or otherwise distributed in America are 168000 per day not to mention China which is now the fastest growing Christian country in the world. It's in hotel room drawers in over 190 countries. That in itself is an incredible statement to its levity and relevance. It's built hundreds of thousands of churches throughout history, not to mention thousands of colleges and universities. It's actually the first book people learned to read and write modern English as we know it, which is the most predominant language being spoken around the world today. These are the words that have formed the very language we speak and have developed our conscience morally and spiritually. Ironic that every word spoken in unbelief is from a book where the language originated. There's been missions, charities and philanthropy that have circulated the world through faith in Christ that have delivered millions of resources globally to sustain our world in compassion and empathy. It's the governing conscience of our judicial system and constitution as I was stating before and the foundation to regulate our principles and ethics. The president's of the United States of America put their hand on a bible to swear into office. It's incredible the impact Christ has made on the world. One of the biggest contradictions concerning unbelievers is that they use churches for weddings and funerals. Why then if it's so irrelevant? They'll even put a cross in the grass or on a tree of their loved ones who've died in a car accident. There's dozens of them around where I live. It's like it's a symbol of life and death and when we cross to the other side. Vertically it's a symbol of heaven and hell and horizontally it's a symbol of life here on earth. We disregard the severity of its relevance yet we depend on its relevance in so many aspects of life, especially for its governing law to constitute our justice system and the freedoms we all yearn for. I feel the printing and distribution of the King James Bible is the second most pivotal and revolutionary time in the history of the world, second only to the cross of cavalry. It was written chronologically throughout centuries by over 40 different authors which didn't receive a dime for their efforts, not to mention being recorded genealogically. It goes even deeper than that for me in its symbolism and typology. To be honest, it's too profound for me to articulate or compartmentalize the depth of it all. It just doesn't make plausible sense without an omnipresent being and spiritual author being conscious of its prophetic progression from generation to generation. 2 Peter 1:20-21 says, "No prophecy of scripture is of any private interpretation, for prophecy never came by the will of man, but holy men of God spoke as they were moved by the Holy Spirit." The more you study it, the more relevant, believable and undeniable it becomes. It's impossible otherwise and the truth is it's real and a persisting prophecy that is reaching its climactic conclusion. Our disregard of its relevance is a testament to its relevance because of the consequences we are living in and again, it will only progressively get worse in the near future as we put our faith and trust in the world.

Failures of Man

The world has ultimately failed in its own philosophy and in its own definition of accountability and responsibility. We fail on so many levels in regards to influence and morality as humans, but especially in positions of leadership. When we hold a position or seat of power, judgment or authority at any level, we so easily fail in hypocrisy and greed. It's also the access to money that becomes too insatiable to deny. I just watched an American Greed episode where the mayor of New Orleans got charged with twenty counts of conspiracy around the time of hurricane Katrina. It was appalling how vindictive he became in the seat of power. Every single decision he made was to fill his wallet. That show is incredible in witnessing the lengths people will go for money and the fulfillment of the American dream. We ignore and hide behind the truth for the preservation and benefit of ourselves. We grow entitled and narcissistic, feeding our egos instead of implementing constructive directives for the benefit of others and the community that surrounds us. The power of control, admiration, wealth and impunity become too appealing and it blinds us in our ordinances and directives. It's happened throughout history wherever man holds a position of empowerment whether it be in capitalism, communism, socialism or systems of democracy. They're just tiers in a conforming monopoly and none of them follow suit with their original philosophy because their leaders have never had the population's best interest in mind outside of their own. They get enthralled with the power of social and financial impunity, living uninhibited from the overhead of taxpayers money, meanwhile imposing regulations and laws while somehow exonerating themselves in the process.

Apart from idolatry, I think impunity is my favorite word in writing this book. It's synonyms are words like exemption, immunity, nonliability, amnesty, and pardon and is defined as an exemption from punishment or freedom from the injurious consequences of an action. Welcome to leadership in our world. America is an obvious disaster but our prime minister here in Canada is a devil in disguise as well, caught up in so many allegations and scandals of embezzlement, fraud and treason but somehow continues on untouchable, living beyond the law. We'd be appalled at what really goes on behind the scenes and what they hide from the public.

Another American Greed episode was about a congressman in California who ran for four terms between 2009 to 2018. Without going into too many details, he was finally indicted on 60 counts of conspiracy with charges of bank fraud, wire fraud, falsifying records and campaign fund violations, to name a few. He and his wife would actually steal the donor funds from the public to finance their own lifestyle. They stole hundreds of thousands of dollars for lavish vacations and shopping excursions all around the world. They even gambled the donor money on horse races! He was eventually found to have several mistresses along the way and when confronted on national TV, he lied about it all and blamed his wife for everything. Finally, the day before his trial he confessed to some of the allegations as his wife was planning to testify against him. He pleaded guilty and was sentenced to 11 months in prison but what's crazy is that he didn't serve one day behind bars. Donald Trump granted him a full pardon along with 19 other convicted felons. He was not only pardoned, he still received his salary. A statement on the show says that not one single member of Congress has ever been stripped of their federal pension. He can start receiving his pension as early as age 55 and if he lives to life expectancy to 81, he'll collect over 1.2 million dollars funded by the American taxpayer. This is one story in a thousand that takes place behind closed doors every day. Their selfish greed draws them into the snare of living beyond their means and the means of the country and they become entrapped by extortion themselves in the contract, having to uphold and feed the lie, further bankrupting their countries and communities in the process. It's not just in government, it's in any philosophy where man is exalted or glorified, including religion. It's the whole philosophy behind church and state and the Roman Catholic Church. They live beyond the laws they impose and regulate because in their own irreverent, godless minds they've become the overriding authority to impose the law. What's even scarier is when they hold the power to print money. In a sense they've become God in their own minds. The majority are hypocrites and history continues to repeat itself along this path of destruction whether be in government, in religion or simply being a parent or teacher on a smaller scale. When man becomes entitled or in a position of control, we fail in integrity, also, when man puts his dependence and faith in man the inevitable immoral fall transpires due to the selfish, immature and prideful intentions of man. This is why Solomon at the end of ecclesiastes says, "Let us hear the conclusion of the whole matter, fear God, and keep his commandments, for this is the whole duty of man. God shall bring every work into judgment, with every secret thing, whether it be good, or whether it be evil."

When it comes to hypocrisy and entitlement, they're extremely destructive. I've witnessed and been a victim of it all myself, as we all have. It's a shame it happens within the church and in government but it happens within family as well. My adopted dad was a selfish, entitled narcissist who verbally abused my mom their entire marriage. From within his own fears and trauma he manipulated, demoralized and suppressed her freedom socially and financially to use her and gain control. He belittled her and destroyed her confidence while somehow gaining a pathetic superiority complex and confidence of his own. I wasn't a part of their lives much after the age of 14 but in my early thirties my mom became extremely ill and needed a double lung transplant. She had about a month to live awaiting a lung donor. I remember sitting across the table from my dad and her and he still belittled and demeaned her with every word out of his mouth. I was trying to talk to her and he kept interrupting as though we were both worthless idiots. I finally stood up to him and said, "How would you like it if I told you to shut up every time you said a word? At first I don't think he took me seriously but I was dead serious and asked him again, "How would you like it if I told you to shut up every time you said a word? I remember him muttering a word and I told him to shut up and there was dead silence. The look on his face was of total shock. He then said another word and I told him to shut up again just to show him how it felt. He had gained such an abusive control over her that it became normal but when confronted with the same abuse he was paralyzed with fear and speechless.

Again, it's not only within our families, it's in everyday life that we see so much of an interactive contradiction taking place around us in the fallen state of man. There's obviously a need for moral structure into which God has so graciously rendered to us, but we've screwed it up royally ourselves and that's why there's such distrust and fear in the world. Entitlement and surrender do not coincide yet we battle for the power of entitlement and then wonder why we can't peacefully coexist. Some people have been subject to that power of entitlement and oppression their whole lives and it destroys them. Even in a democracy our freedom is oppressed psychologically wherever individual entitlement holds a sense of control. Unfortunately that's become our entire ideology and identity. We live and fight for the pride and entitlement that tears us apart and no one sees it.

Through my own experiences I would say that kind of discernment has become my greatest gift as a Christian in regards to intention and the objectives of man. I would say not only the intentions but also the inclinations and the premonitions of men and women. I can detect not only the morals and authenticity in regards to scripture, but I can hear it in people's voices and in how they socially interact. I can detect it so easily because of my own trauma. Sometimes the pain we've endured makes us wise to the pain around us and the pain we give. It's a gift of God but it's also him and his Holy Spirit that intercedes alongside the world's carnal intentions.

I have a friend or should I say acquaintance, that corrects you every time you speak a word. We all know somebody like that but he can't listen long enough to your opinion without interrupting with an opinion of his own. It's so condescending and it's like he's simultaneously contemplating how to discredit and manipulate you as you're speaking to further exalt himself and demoralize you. He'll even make up lies to further his narcissistic and domineering control over the conversation or situation. He thinks he's doing you and everyone else a favour by the conversation and time he's spending with you. He's like talking to the end of a vacuum hose and you regret uttering a word when you're around him. Much like my dad, when I finally confronted him about it, he had no idea because of how entitled he'd become and how manipulated he was by his own fears. People can not only be physically abusive and controlling but they can be spiritually and psychologically abusive and controlling as well. I just hate how people attribute this abuse to Christianity and hopefully in reading this people can look past that perception. A lot of the control we so adamantly desire is for fear of relinquishing it and it all comes from our own insecurities. I know because I've not only been the victim of it but been guilty of it at times, as we all have.

For 40 years my dad justified his life and based his entire security on oppressing and conforming one person into his control and it was all from his own insecurity and fear of being alone. He treated my mom as though she was worthless but he was nothing without her. He even planned his entire future with a woman up the street as my mom was dying and awaiting a miracle lung transplant. Fortunately she did, which I share a bit about in my testimony, but my point is in his power of entitlement and how he lived with no regard or consideration for her whatsoever. He just lived year after year using her for his own selfish benefit and she lives with the trauma of it to this day. Again, this is where entitlement and narcissism don't coincide with servitude and surrender and where faithlessness bears it's disparaging fangs. This type of psychology is hard to detect in this generation with our narcissistic self preservation and impulsive desire so emphatically emphasized and driven to satisfy every moment. We suffer from the effects of it but very few of us see it within ourselves. We want to gain autonomy and control over our lives and we're driven to use any means necessary to do so, whoever that hurts in the process. It's amazing that the first teaching and words out of Jesus's mouth in Matthew we're about humility, entitlement and hypocrisy and the world disregards it all as irrelevant.

Glory of Christ

For those who are struggling to take this initial leap of faith, I'll admit I struggled at first with it all as well. It's such an imposing conviction to our own will and carnal desires but I'm glad my stubborn spirit has pushed through into the truth and I feel blessed that instead of turning away from the faith, the Word of God has come that much more alive within me at the revelation of Jesus Christ. He encapsulates all of these failures in one person. The more we come to realize the failures of man the more the carnal nature gets exposed and the more we're drawn to the spirit of Christ in our faith. The more man claims to uphold its own righteous fortitude, especially in religious entitlement, the more it fails in hypocrisy. In Paul's letter to the Romans he states this very thing in chapter 10. He says, "Brethren, my heart's desire and prayer to God for Israel is that they may be saved. For I bear them witness that they have a zeal for God, but not according to knowledge. For they, being ignorant of God's righteousness, and seeking to establish their own righteousness, have not submitted to the righteousness of God. For Christ is the end of the law for righteousness to everyone who believes." The Christian faith does not endorse or exalt the carnal vindication or entitlement within man, it convicts and exposes that complacent and entitled vindication for its intended means and it's for this purpose Jesus came. Romans 3 says, "There is none righteous, no, not one, there is none who understands, there is none who seeks after God. They have all turned aside, they have together become unprofitable, there is none who does good, no, not one. Their throat is an open tomb; With their tongues they have practiced deceit, the poison of asps is under their lips, whose mouth is full of cursing and bitterness. Their feet are swift to shed blood; Destruction and misery are in their ways, and the way of peace they have not known. There is no fear of God before their eyes." He came to give us independence and to crush the esteem and entitlement of man to release us from it's slavery. 1 Corinthians 3:18-19 says, "Let no man deceive himself. If any man among you seems to be wise in this world, let him become a fool, that he may be wise. For the wisdom of this world is foolishness with God. For it is written, he takes the wise in their own craftiness. And again, the Lord knows the thoughts of the wise, that they are vain. Therefore let no man glory in men." It becomes such a relevant and overwhelming truth that he reveals and his eternal hope carries us through our lives in a far deeper sense of security and hope than anything this world has offered or will moving forward. It brings strength, wisdom and refuge to the common and humble at heart.

I love the red-letter Bibles that pronounce the words of Jesus. His first words spoken in Matthew are totally contrary to our carnal and philosophical way of thinking and even how these new age teachers perceive faith to be. He says, "Blessed are the poor in spirit: for theirs is the Kingdom of Heaven. Blessed are they that mourn: for they shall be comforted. Blessed are the meek: for they shall inherit the earth. Blessed are they that hunger and thirst for righteousness sake: for theirs is the Kingdom of Heaven. Blessed are the merciful: for they shall obtain mercy. Blessed are the pure in heart: for they shall see God. Blessed are the peacemakers: for they shall be called the children of God. Blessed are they which are persecuted for righteousness sake: for theirs is the Kingdom of Heaven. Blessed are you, when men shall revile you, and persecute you, and shall say all manner of evil against you falsely, for my sake. Rejoice, and be exceedingly glad: for great is your reward in heaven: they also persecuted the prophets that were before you."

Jesus has declared such a prophetic moral decree that is unheard of in the voices of men. He's created such a paradigm shift in ethics and faith that is unfathomable in our limited philosophy and perspective. Colossians 2:8 says, "Beware lest anyone cheat you through philosophy and empty deceit, according to the tradition of men, according to the basic principles of the world, and not according to Christ." It's only intrinsically inclusive to him and is a weight far too heavy to bear in our feeble minds and hands. It's a wisdom too deep and an influence and burden too overwhelming to exemplify. In writing this I'm trying to look up more synonyms for the words exemplify and intrinsic but Jesus is an unexplainable phenomenon that words just can't do justice. Synonyms for exemplify are to epitomize, personify, embody and represent but they still can't define the attributes of Christ and his impact on the world. It's like an eternal ball of fire in a pair of dollar store oven mitts. We can't hold it long enough to instill its purpose or directive without God interceding and taking the reins himself. In simpleton terms, he bit off far more than we can chew, to say the least. We couldn't do it then without him and we certainly can't productively do it now without him, so when he came, he gave his spirit to the world through faith. Those without faith just can't see it and will remain carnally blind in the deception and affliction that surrounds them. Hence the title again, "Blind in Affliction."

Decision to Make

The problem on the horizon is now he'll come for the final time and those who deny him will suffer for their choices. Daniel 12:2-3 says, "Many of them that sleep in the dust of the earth shall awake, some to everlasting life, and some to shame and everlasting contempt. And they that are wise shall shine as the brightness of the firmament, and they that turn many to righteousness as the stars forever and ever." What grieves my heart and soul more than anything and is one of my primary incentives for this book, is the world's preconceived notions and misconceptions concerning Christianity, due to the actions and hypocrisies of man. Nothing angers and sickens my stomach more than these heretical monsters who use the bible or Jesus's name as a personal credit card for money and control. They've used faith as an opportunity and not a responsibility. It's so frustrating and again, I hope this book is a way people can see through it all and seek the truth for themselves. God has mercifully given this world that hates him an abundance of resources to share and be content with, imagine what he'll give to those who love him and persevere in faith through the clouds of misconception for the world to come. Hebrews 10:22-23 says, "Let us draw near with a true heart in full assurance of faith, having our hearts sprinkled from an evil conscience....let us hold fast the profession of our faith without wavering; for he is faithful that promised." Hebrews 12:1 says, "Since we are surrounded by so great a cloud of witnesses, let us lay aside every weight, and the sin which so easily ensnares us, and let us run with endurance the race that is set before us, looking unto Jesus, the author and finisher of our faith." James 1:12 says, "Blessed is the man that endures temptation; for when he is tried, he shall receive the crown of life, which the Lord has promised to them that love him."

I had a dream soon after my conversion that was incredible. I remember being awakened to incomparable beauty on the horizon. It's as if all time and reason was interconnected but I was set free from it all. I could see what looked to be an eternal sunset but it was also an eternal resolution in its simplicity as if it had no restriction to time or suppression attached to it. There was a complete resolve and detachment from any condemnation in me and around me. I could feel this euphoric bliss and clarity all around me and remember looking down at my hands and sifting through this pure gold-like sand and as if I'd arrived at a place I was internally longing for. I then looked to my right and my friend that initially brought me to church was jumping around with a childlike grin on his face and kept saying, "We did it, we did it!" Everything was pure and I felt this adolescent bliss and elation that far exceeded the capability of our natural senses. I'll never forget that dream and I feel it was God cementing the promise of faith into my newly converted mind to help keep my eyes and heart on what is above and not what's down below. Colossians 3:2-4 says, "Set your affection on things above, not on things on the earth. For you are dead, and your life is hid with Christ in God. When Christ, who is our life, shall appear, then shall you also appear with him in glory." 1 John 2:15-17 says, "Do not love the world or the things in the world. If anyone loves the world, the love of the Father is not in him. For all that is in the world, the lust of the flesh, the lust of the eyes, and the pride of life, is not of the Father but is of the world. And the world is passing away, and the lust of it; but he who does the will of God abides forever."

When these heretical teachers and imposters read these scriptures, I'm not sure how they can follow along with their apostasy but they do, further condemning themselves in the process, whether it be through religious oppression, prosperity teaching or the miraculous. It's unfortunately destroying so many people in their overriding perception of the Christian faith. There's a core issue of sin that is and will be seen as the overriding objective of God and premise to our faith when all is revealed. When we die in faith we'll look down on all these false teachers and apostates with all their irrelevant claims and clusters of pride and entitlement and shake our heads at how petty, selfish and insignificant they'll look in the light of eternal salvation. Matthew 10 says, "Do not fear those who kill the body but cannot kill the soul. But rather fear Him who is able to destroy both soul and body in hell......Do not fear them; for there is nothing covered that will not be revealed, and hidden that will not be known."

A friend of mine's dad unfortunately passed away from cancer recently. He was a devout Christian and family man who honoured his wife and his faith until he passed on. There wasn't a fear or concern in his family through his battle with the disease or since he's been gone. There was obviously some grieving and tears along the way from his friends and family, especially at his funeral, but they accepted his fate as eternal optimists and were otherwise calm and resilient. Sure there's a loss of life but there's also so much hope and gain in salvation that brings peace and resolve knowing he's with Christ for eternity. The funeral was a celebration of his life and people rejoiced at his service to God and his family. I guarantee he's in a place where prosperity on earth bears no significance. I realize it sucks having to face the inevitability of death and the fears that arise, but that's part of life and billions have had to face the same inevitable and inescapable formality throughout history. There's an incredible passage in Hebrews 2 that says, "Inasmuch then as the children have partaken of flesh-and-blood, he himself likewise shared in the same, that through death he might destroy him who had the power of death, that is, the devil, and release those who through fear of death were all their lifetime subject to bondage." The definition of bondage means the state of being a slave or of being severely constricted or restrained by obligations or circumstances. I see how bondage can be a physical constriction but I also see it as being a spiritual or psychological constriction, especially in this day and age in the constriction and conformity of our minds.

I'm pleading with people to take the word salvation and God's definition of it more seriously and I hope through this book people will dig a little deeper into history and into the written Word of God and come to their own conclusion, ignoring their misconceptions and the hypocrisies of man. God is sovereign and independent over it all and yearns for a personal relationship with each of us no matter our ethnicity, cultural background, IQ, accolades, or what sins we've committed. His shoulders are wide and his spirit is powerful, and it just takes a leap of faith to begin the journey. For me it took me to see death for a change to occur and I pray people don't have to go that far and have to experience what I have to come to receive salvation in Christ. I realize there are some circumstances in life that are horrible and hard to fully comprehend and understand the reasons why. We try to reason with them but it just seems unfair. I've endured much affliction throughout my life and was nearly killed by a drunk driver but it still hasn't turned me from the truth of faith. It actually compelled me to write this book. I'm trying to be sensitive to people's trauma and emotions but at the same time be unwaveringly persistent. I realize people have suffered far more traumatic circumstances than me and for them the justification of faith is a hard pill to swallow. I can't relate to some of the physical and sexual abuse people have endured nor other tragedies, especially children, but God allows our free will to progress unabated without physically restraining us and that bears it's unfortunate consequences. There was a Christian carpenter on my jobsite recently who's daughter was randomly stabbed to death along with another child in they're high school. It grieved my heart when I heard that and left me speechless. You could tell it left him torn in his faith and he had every right to feel that way. Some things I'll admit are unexplainable and beyond reason but others are simple common sense into which we are certainly responsible. My mother and her sister have suffered from severe lung complications since they were born. My Mom finally needed a double lung transplant as I mentioned before. She's bitter and again, completely detests the thought of God because of the circumstances of her life. She's had a horrible time of suffering throughout her life but my grandpa chain-smoked raw unfiltered tobacco throughout the majority of his life as did many in his generation, which unfortunately bear its hereditary consequences. It's the same with alcohol and drug addiction or even having a bad diet. People don't consider these truths and the fact that for decades we breathed in asbestos and lead particles that were in our insulation, drywall and paint throughout our homes. Ultimately, the seed has been poisoned, not only by original sin but it also gets poisoned by us not being health conscious and further altering and compromising life's natural course. Some of the poisoning has been heinously deliberate and outside of our control in too which God allows, but that's just part of the fallen world we live in. When we come to recognize the depth of conspiracy and how sinful the world truly is, we don't necessarily understand why God allows it, but we revert the blame onto ourselves much easier.

The remainder of my book is my testimony of coming to Christ and some closing remarks to ponder for how I see some of the things taking place around us. I'll share a little more of my opinions because I feel we're all entitled to do so and ultimately, contemplation should generate an opinion however confrontational some issues may seem. My testimony won't be long but it's basically the story of my childhood through to eventually becoming a child of God. I won't go into detail about every waking moment of my life but I'll share some pivotal moments that have shaped my journey and brought me to where I am today. It's a testimony to the transformation of the human heart, from someone extremely angry, confused and weighed down by the afflictions of childhood and everyday life, to someone that's been shown mercy, enlightened and given new meaning, purpose and hope. I hope it encourages people to keep pressing forward and persevering in faith and not to give in to all the deception and external pressures that surround us and mislead us. I want people's eyes to be opened to a deeper awareness from the eternal hope God has freely given us through his Word and in his son Jesus Christ. A hope and promise that we will forever be released into his loving arms for eternity.

Chapter 13

Testimony

I was born in St Paul's hospital in Vancouver British Columbia Canada. My mother had three kids in total that were all taken from her at birth and given over to the foster care system due to her mental illness and instability. My father's identity is in question as she was extremely promiscuous during my conception and had even resorted to prostitution to survive. I would only come to know a lot of this as I went on a search for her in my early twenties and ended up tracking her down at a mental institution. I'll talk about her a little more in a few pages but to describe her would be a hard core 1970's street hippie with a severe case of paranoid schizophrenia. She was raw and unfiltered and lived as though the world was out to get her.

I was in a foster home separate from my other siblings when my older sister was eventually adopted and her parents ended up bringing me along for the ride adopting us both as we were within two years of each other. Apparently there's another older brother roaming the earth somewhere but I'm not sure where he ended up.

I remember very little of my early childhood but for the most part it wasn't that bad. If you're born under my conditions, Canada would probably be one of the best in the world considering the social services and resources available. As pertaining to faith, I would consider my parents and their family agnostic or bordering on atheists as God or faith were never questioned or even mentioned growing up in any conversation. My mom's side, who I was closer to, was British and my grandma grew up with some sort of Catholicism or Anglican in her background, but nothing was practiced. My adopted dad had two adopted kids from his previous marriage but his wife had passed away so there were four of us all together for the first few years of me and my sister's childhood. They eventually separated when I was around 6 or 7 and me and my sister went with my mom and my older sister and brother went with my dad. It's all very vague because of how young I was but for the most part we were doing okay with my mom from what I've heard and remember. Her sister had two adopted kids our age that lived close by and me and my cousin were nearly inseparable. My parents seem to go their separate ways and even started dating other people until somehow they got back together and everything went downhill from there. My mom still admits that it was the worst decision of her life. I think it was to do with my mom's financial situation but my dad also needed someone to mother his children as he was incapable of doing so on his own. My dad wasn't a physically abusive man but was verbally abusive and constantly degraded and demoralized my mom their entire relationship. He was very charming and manipulative but was also a selfish narcissist who used demoralization to control my mom, based on his own insecurities and fears. It suppressed her to where she turned emotionless, bitter and cold towards us kids with me being the brunt of her hostility as my sister lived with a disability. I think deep down my mom truly cared but my dad's abuse wore her down and how she communicated was horribly insensitive. They were both very strict and unaffectionate people and I was an extremely sensitive kid which merely compounded the friction between us all. There were no hugs or "I love you's" in our household growing up nor has there ever been since. All my dad cared about was money and we seemed to be the burden in the way of what he was trying to achieve or acquire. I think my older brother suffered the most because he was even more sensitive than me. I started acting up in elementary school and as my parents moved around I became more and more lonely, insecure and problematic. I think with my sister being partially handicapped it added to my frustration with their attention and responsibility more focussed towards her. Again, my parents weren't these horribly abusive people, nor did they abuse drugs or alcohol, but were focussed on their own business and career and were unattentive and despondent towards me. It's like they were there but they weren't. They owned a travel agency that took up all their time and energy and were in a tax bracket that forced them to pay over 50% of their income which made it nearly impossible to get ahead. I think being adopted as it probably is in many cases, there's not as tight of a bond as there would be with maternal or paternal birth parents. Again, I was an extremely emotional and sensitive kid and that bond and security would have probably helped me deal with my childhood and gave me a sense of support and belonging. Unfortunately these are the consequences of mindless fornication and that was an impossible scenario considering my conception and my mom's mental health condition. To my parents' defense, they saved me, but either way, I always felt alone with a sense of rejection and abandonment growing up with very few friends it seemed. I remember having a birthday party in grade 4 or 5 where only one kid showed up along with my cousin. It was at a wave pool and I misjudged jumping from the pool deck into the wave and cracked my head open on the pool floor. I remember the PA announcing my birthday party was over and me being completely dejected and humiliated.

I was a good little soccer player growing up and a few years later I remember going to a soccer tournament in California when I was around 12 and my parents were the only ones that didn't come on the trip. I was the goalie and we won the whole tournament with tickets to Disneyland for 3 days but there was no one there to congratulate me in support and it felt that way in everything. My brother would usually drive me to my soccer outings in his little Audi Quattro as they were always busy. Again, it was like my parents were there but they weren't committed as though they were just going through the parental motions to justify their own selfishness. My mom's words were harsh and the sound of her voice was cruel and demoralizing as it still is to this day. She judges and makes you feel like a worthless failure which is, ironically, the same way my dad treated her her whole life. It was not only in her actions and words, it was in the tone of her voice that triggered such bitter hatred and anger within me. I grew to hate my mother growing up because she'd tear me down instead of lifting me up and treat me as if I was to blame for her misfortune or as if I was inconveniencing her on her path. I ended Elementary School pretty dysfunctional and agitated. I started becoming a very aggressive and problematic child to say the least. My French immersion class had planned a trip in grade 7 across Canada to Quebec but I was held back due to my behaviour. I feel there was a lot of potential within me but I was becoming more and more introverted and unpredictable, evolving into a ticking time bomb. Ironic how kids grow more and more insecure when there's no security and support at home.

Next thing was High School and within only a few months I completely fell apart. My best friend I'd met in elementary school left for another school 50 kms away to live with his dad so I felt all alone in a school of over 1800 kids. I started growing extremely insecure and more introverted with each day that passed by. I hated going to school and I hated going home and my mind grew extremely dark and hostile. It was too much for me to handle and it was around this time I felt there was something else wrong with me genetically. There seemed to be a narrative voice condemning me in my thoughts and tormenting me along my path. It was relentless and wouldn't leave me alone. It turned into an obsessive compulsive disorder where I'd question every thought or action. I'd also come home to my room and my sister in the room next to me would be having these conversations with herself out loud for hours and hours which further made me feel like I was going crazy and that there was something wrong with us genetically.

The first friend I met in grade 8 was a drug dealer and everything spiralled downhill from there. He mainly dealt marijuana and acid but the acid is what derailed me completely. I don't even think I enjoyed it as much as I'd do anything to escape my reality and not feel alone anymore. I feared and hated rejection and wasn't scared to prove how brazen I was to try drugs or guzzle alcohol to gain acceptance or attention. Again, I guess this is what can happen when there's no acceptance, support or attention at home. We'd even do acid at school and trip out in class which posed enough problems on their own but the worst is when I got home and tried navigating around my parents, high as a kite. Acid is an extremely strong hallucinogenic drug for anybody of any age but especially an aggressive 14 year old with OCD and schizophrenia in my bloodline. The acid would hit my system and my whole mind would go psychotically dark and volatile. I remember lying in the fetal position for hours shaking in torment thinking maggots were eating me from the inside out. Somehow I would justify the suffering with the reality I faced at home and within who I felt I was. I hated the perception I had of myself and I grew to hate my mother even worse. I remember writing a letter to myself as a reminder to never forgive her for how awful and insensitive she was to me. I was finally taken to a psychiatrist who diagnosed me as an anti-social psychopath. Things at home were reaching a boiling point until finally one day I was arguing with my sister and punched her in the leg for tattle tailing on me about something. My mom intervened and slapped me across the face and I launched her into the kitchen railing. That was the final straw for me and my parents. My dad took me to his work where I had to stay in his car overnight and then I was apparently going to a foster home. I don't think they knew what to do with me but my mom luckily stumbled upon a ranch for juvenile delinquent kids about 2000 kilometres away up north here in British Columbia.

Whiplash Ranch

We flew up there and they dropped me off for about two years. Looking back now it probably saved my life but it was an extremely difficult transition for me at first. I knew no one and knew I had no support from home so I felt completely rejected and abandoned. I already had severe issues with loneliness, depression and separation anxiety and this merely compounded the problem. It was a lot to overcome and I remember when I initially got to the ranch, they put me in a room and I didn't come out for two days. I could hear the voices outside but was so scared, broken and confused that I just wouldn't come out. It took me a few months to get acquainted and come out of my shell but then I seem to adapt quite well. I didn't have my mom's demeaning voice coming down on me, nor did I have the peer pressure of high school bearing down on me either. There were no drugs or alcohol up there and there were kids close to my age that were always up for doing something fun and adventurous. The ranch was an hour or so into the bush off the main highway and was completely self-contained with their own farm with cows, chickens, pigs and horses. They had even built their own mechanic shop for all the equipment and a lumber mill to cut their own lumber. The story behind the ranch that I remember was two draft dodgers bought a massive piece of property and brought a few of their friends along with them to build the ranch. They had a bunch of kids along with their friends which amalgamated together and formed a community of about a hundred or so people. They hired a few tradesmen to live there and help sustain the property along the way and it seemed to work quite well. All in all it was pretty neat especially for an introverted city kid. There were two other boys my age that were sent there from the city and we grew pretty close over the months, adventuring all over the hectares of land. There was a school there but I quit right away and started working alongside the men and my two friends building log homes, fixing fences and whatever else was needed to sustain the property. I even spent a few months bucking up logs with a chainsaw in the bush which was a really neat and challenging experience for a 14 year old city kid. The men were really rugged and tough but also very down-to-earth and transparent. There was no external influence from television or the media at all. The only time I ever saw the television on was to watch the NHL playoff hockey games. They just lived off the land and in the simple pleasures of life and of hard work. It was below freezing for 8 months of the year so the kids spent their time riding horses, playing hockey on the outdoor rink and tobogganing all over the property. When it comes to faith, they weren't religious at all from what I remember but I was oblivious to faith at that time so I wouldn't have recognized otherwise. I do recall them having these adult meetings called "floors" where everyone would share their concerns and feelings, but I was never invited. As far as I knew, they were just old-fashioned, hardworking folks, united for the common goal. It was a lot for a city kid to endure at first but again, it seems as soon as I was away from the pressures at school and away from my parents, my true character came out and I wasn't that bad of a kid at all. I did lose my temper with a few of the kids but seemed to get along with everybody as time went on. The whole place was a story in itself but we'd go on horse rides and ATV adventures all over the place. The river flooded every year as the snow melted and we'd ride tractor tire tubes down the river for hours. Whenever you needed to get somewhere you'd just start walking down the road until a truck drove by and then hop in the back of the pickup box. It was the off-the-grid way of life. There's so many stories to share but for the sake of the book's general directive I won't go on and on. It's just a part of my testimony and I'm trying to share the overall perspective.

Me and my one friend Liam we're living in this old trailer down by the garbage dump. We heard something outside scraping along the trailer wall early one morning at about 4 AM. We woke up and started walking down the trailer hallway to the front door. We both kind of looked at each other in fear and just as we opened the door we heard two gunshots and a black bear drop dead outside the door. The ranch mechanic named "Mitro" must have seen it from atop the hill in his cabin and blew it away from over a hundred yards. I'd never seen anything like that before but before we even had a chance to process it, he came down in his truck and had us lift it into the back of the pickup box. I'll never forget that drive in the back of his truck and feeling the arms of that bear and feeling its teeth. We then drove it up past the mechanic shop where Mitro slit its throat and hung it upside down from the front end loader to bleed it out. This is what real men do in the country and I was just a little smart-ass city kid who had a lot to learn about being a man and I knew it right then and there.

Back Home

The two years elapsed and I decided to come home and try to catch up in a work and learn program and finish High School. My two friends stayed up at the ranch which now looking back might have been a better decision for me but it's also important to finish High School in the city. I do remember coming back in those two years on a bus to go to a Guns & Roses concert with my brother but my parents didn't want me around their house so my only alternative was to go back to the ranch. My brother got me hammered at a strip joint before the concert and I ended up puking everywhere and passing out in the bathroom stall for the whole concert until he came and found me. That was a long 22 hour bus ride there and back for that memory and the rejection I got from my parents. Nevertheless they allowed me back into the house just before I turned 16 to finish High School. It was a big decision on their part but much of my behaviour had been rehabilitated and verified by the elders at the ranch to which they were surprised and relieved about. I lived at home until I graduated but my rehabilitation started dissolving again into the same recurring theme. Nothing really changed at home with my parents and the atmosphere and peer pressure at school was the same. I wasn't into the heavy drugs like acid anymore but everyone I knew smoked marijuana and drank and I followed along to fit in and to make friends. My parents finally decided to sell their house and move up off the mainland about 2 and 1/2 hours away. My sister went to live with my grandma and I was out on my own after I graduated. My other two siblings were long gone as they were 10 years older and that was how our family was left pretty much to this day 25 years later. We'd see each other at Christmas and maybe once or twice a year but otherwise us kids were left to fend for ourselves emotionally and financially. It actually started petering out to where we wouldn't see each other at all. I saw my older sister for the first time in 15 years last year and hadn't even heard my dad's voice in over 12 years until I called him at Christmas this year. There weren't phone calls or family dinners as there is in normal families. There weren't birthday parties or get-togethers. We were cut loose and we all fell apart because of it. To put it into better perspective, I didn't hear from either of my parents after my recent accident for 2 years. Neither of them called to ask if I was okay or offer any sort of support or empathy. They just didn't care and that's who they were and who they still are. Luckily my birth sister lived with my grandma and was part of a church community where she found security and support but my older sister fell apart with severe depression and anxiety until she came to Christ in her early thirties. My brother became addicted to drugs and alcohol into which he still struggles to this day.

Of course I'd like to have had more loving and supportive parents growing up but I don't fully blame them for the decisions I made along the way. I was a lot to handle and I scared them both, especially my dad. I think everyone's intentions are somewhat genuine going through the adoption process and when they see a little baby lying there in a waiting room, but you're kind of rolling the dice in genetics on who's coming out of it. So much of our problematic society these days that's lost in the blame is based on the physical and mental health of the individuals upon conception and also the conditions that surround it. Unfortunately mine wasn't conducive to a productive environment or outcome. My mother was an extremely promiscuous, drug and alcohol induced street hippie which holds its unfortunate hereditary consequences. I sometimes wonder about the mercy of God upon conception and how and why he brings us out of these horrible circumstances. It's a complete mystery to us what will transpire when a sperm fertilizes an egg in a uterus that only God has the power to understand or determine but we are definitely accountable to initiating the process. Unfortunately for some the circumstances upon conception not only become difficult hereditarily or biologically but geographically as well into which God is most certainly not to blame especially considering his warnings concerning fornication. I don't see what we should expect otherwise and is why I don't hold as much resentment towards my adopted parents as I did growing up. In a sense, I feel the whole world is living in a fallen state of its own unaccountability and irresponsibility. Regardless, I was left to raise and fend for myself which definitely posed its challenges. I just turned into survival mode without any guidance to help me.

Strange Days

When I turned 19 I was legal to buy alcohol and rented a house next to the beer store on the main street of my hometown. My best friend from elementary school ended up moving in with me for the next year or so and every night seemed to be a gong show of loud music, partying and buffoonery. The whole town started taking note of us without us truly being aware of it. It was a busy and bustling town and we were naked to everyone's eyes but too young and naive to recognize it all. Somehow the circumstances changed to where I needed another roommate and this Mark guy answered my ad in the paper and ended up moving in with his dog Kyuss. All was fine for a month or so but he was heavy into cocaine and things started to get really awkward and weird. I hated the stuff personally but my other friends joined in the debauchery and that's when the weirdness and paranoia seemed to set in. If there was ever proof to the entrance into the demonic realm, cocaine takes you there with no mercy. You feel this euphoric high like you're the centre of the world for a few minutes, then your feet get pulled out from under you and you feel like you're the laughingstock of that same world. Mark was a strange guy sober but cocaine made him even more erratic and unpredictable. He had a massive temper and one day I came home to him beating the crap out of his dog in the backyard. He was going way overboard and I told him if he did that again he was gone and I would keep the dog. A week or so later I heard the dog squealing in his room across the hallway in the middle of the night. I broke into the room and found him beating on the dog again. I kicked him out and kept the dog with his family condoning both decisions on my part. Unfortunately, word got out on the street that he had sex with his dog and I somehow became the brunt of the town's scrutiny especially from those who I grew up with in high school. I tried to handle it and be tough about it but it was overwhelming and it seemed everywhere I went people would snicker at me and gossip about the whole ordeal.

People definitely love to kick you when you're down in this world and now I was trapped in this house to bear the scrutiny. I was already a pretty troubled and insecure kid but whatever reputation I had or held within myself in the eyes of others was lost by my roommate's story. I had a few confrontations and run-ins with people after I moved out but no one ever messed with me even though the talk of the town was of me getting beat up. They might have thought about it but knew I'd hold my own with anyone one on one, plus there's always the risk when someone gets older into which I don't think they were willing to risk. This is what stemmed from the guy I pushed over in the bar and his friend blowing his head off while he talked to his mom on the phone. I also remember punching a bartender in the face for laughing and mocking me and punching through a car window chasing a guy around in a parking lot for doing the same. I started getting really paranoid and remembered a phone call I got that said on the answering machine "You sir are the real geek." I was pretty sure I knew who it was and it just continued to compound my fears and insecurities. There was a spoiled jock in school who bullied everyone and would laugh and mock me when he'd see me around. (Just for reference, this was the time I saw that tape on the ground and smashed it into pieces that said "let go, let God.") Nevertheless, I'll admit the scrutiny wore me down and hurt me deeply. I went from being sent away to a ranch then becoming the derision of a whole town a few years later. It wasn't just the humiliation that bothered me, this was around the time I had mentioned earlier in the book of how I felt called for something. People around thought I was succumbing to the scrutiny which I was to some degree but I was under far more of an attack than any of them realized. I felt chosen or selected for some unforeseen reason that only God knew the answer to. It's like I could see the spiritual world moving in parallel alongside my own at times as though something about me was preordained or predestined.

I had an older friend that was affiliated with the Hells Angels living in a trailer in the back of the house that saw it too and thought I was some chosen prodigy which added to the confirmation. It's hard to explain in words but it was a severity and pressure I couldn't bear on my own. It felt like I was walking in concrete everywhere I went. It's like the air around you is some sort of spiritual sphere with you being the centre of its intended focus or purpose. I think we all have these spiritual spheres encompassing us but some of them are more critical and crucially preordained than others. This is not to say that I thought I was anything special but something other than me thought otherwise. The Bible even says that many are called and few are chosen but I had no idea what I was chosen for or called to do, let alone by whom. Regardless of how I see it now spiritually, at the time I was a broken and sensitive kid, oblivious to anything spiritual and grew even more insecure and jaded from it all. I didn't understand why this was all happening to me and whatever false front I put out to the world around me and with the friends I had, I took it personally and it deeply affected me. I didn't know where to release all these emotions and I needed some sort of outlet.

My Outlet

I ended up getting into boxing right around this time and fought competitively for the next four or five years. When word on the street got out that I was a boxer, the gossip stopped and people seemed to leave me alone. I think people thought I was tough and a bit crazy but now I was training and learning how to fight professionally and that was a dangerous combo. To be completely honest, I wasn't the best boxer in the world. I wasn't mentally or emotionally strong enough in the ring as it becomes quite a chess match of discipline and wit in there, but I was physically strong and got fairly good over the years. I could hold my own with pretty much anyone they threw in the ring with me. I remember an offensive lineman for the CFL came into the gym with a huge ego saying he could take on anyone my coach put in the ring. I was a few years into training at this point and my coach put me in to spar with him. I was around 170lb and he was around 300lb and full of aggression and confidence. He was a powerful man and came at me with everything he had but I held my ground, bobbing and weaving and blocking punches as I moved around the ring. I could see he was getting frustrated and tired and I kind of snickered at him and said, "It's my turn now big fella," and just started pummelling him to where he left the gym and never came back. I had a couple dozen amateur fights but again, I just didn't have the mind for it and wasn't a violent person by nature. It was a great outlet for me but my personal life outside the ring was unstable and problematic and I just couldn't balance the two. I also framed houses during the day for work which was too much for my body to handle. I finally got hurt pretty bad in the ring that made me want to quit and hang up the gloves. I fought my sparring partner who was an absolute beast that ended up fighting in the UFC later on. He hit me so hard in the chin, I dropped to a knee and knew it just wasn't for me anymore. I held my own with him fairly well sparring but as soon as I was in the ring competitively and people were watching, I fell apart and lost focus. It was like that with many of my fights. I just had no self confidence.

Origin

Around this time I went on a search for my original birth mom. I was lost and was searching for answers to my origin and to what was going on in my head. I felt tormented like there was something after me everywhere I went. My girlfriend at the time, who was ironically my friend's daughter that was living in the backyard, helped me try to find her. She was an amazing person and their family took me in as one of their own. Without her and her family at that time I don't know where I'd be right now, even though her dad was a bit of an alcoholic lunatic at times. British Columbia was the only place in Canada you could get your original birth registration outside of hiring a private investigator. For fifty bucks you could mail away and they'd send a photocopy of it with your parents signature upon childbirth in the hospital. There was no name of my father but we searched and searched, phoning dozens of numbers with her name in the Yellow Pages, until one person almost hung up, but said, "Oh Angela?" It was a distant cousin of hers from what I remember but it was the right Angela and we ended up tracking her down in a government-funded care facility and arranged to meet at a local white spot nearby. Hearing her voice for the first time on the telephone was surreal enough but meeting her in person was like being in a movie. The instant I sat down across the table from her everything seemed to make more sense and resolve itself within me. I didn't know what to say for the first few minutes and just started crying. She was an extremely ill woman with schizophrenia and the intensity and ora she carried with her was severe. I wasn't delusional or paranoid to the degree she was but I definitely struggled with things in my mind that were uncommon to the people around me. I think the resolve for me came in seeing where some of these internal struggles originated genetically and that I wasn't to blame. Schizophrenia is a mysterious and varying illness in its degree of severity from patient to patient but my mom's was definitely in the higher degree of severity. She had over 35 admissions to the psych ward in Riverview Hospital here in BC throughout her lifetime. She actually described my conception as the "Thrill on Riverview Hill," although she admitted my birth father could have been three different men. Although there was some resolve meeting her it was also very hard and discouraging to see someone in that much anguish and pain. She triggered a trauma in me that was indescribable. She even said to me one day what a horrible thing it would be to be one of her offspring. Again, I had some suffering mentally and emotionally but it was nothing to this level. It's like she was coherent for moments at a time but extremely sensitive and emotionally unstable to people's words that would make her very abrasive and volatile. She's hard to describe without meeting her in person but it's as though the world was after her and she lived completely off the grid in her mind. She was like a child with an IQ of a genius and just couldn't navigate rationally through situations and circumstances in society. She would even resort to intentionally getting arrested because she felt safer in the psych ward then she did out in the public. It's like she had a severe obsessive-compulsive disorder assuming everyone's perception of her was constantly fixated upon her and it became a detriment to her well being and peace of mind. There was no filter in her mind and everything affected her emotions and responsive evaluation to the extreme degree. Much of mental illness is defined scientifically as a chemical imbalance which is true because serotonin is produced in the body to balance our levels of stress and anxiety. Serotonin is defined as the key hormone that stabilizes our mood, feelings of well-being and happiness. It says it impacts our entire body and enables brain cells and other nervous system cells to communicate with each other. It also affects our motor skills along with our sleeping, eating and digestion but my mother was definitely being tormented by the spiritual realm outside of any philosophy or scientific diagnosis that I could relate to now being her biological son. Google defines schizophrenia as a serious mental disorder in which people interpret reality abnormally. It says it may result in some combination of hallucinations, delusions, and extremely disordered thinking and behaviour that impairs daily functioning, that can be disabling. Interestingly, it actually says that the causes of schizophrenia are unknown to which even more confirms a spiritual impartation. Many believe it can be brought on genetically, by trauma or can be triggered with cases of severe paranoia from drugs like marijuana and cocaine. Regardless, my mother was certainly suffering from this mysterious illness and in seeing the anguish within her soul, I don't wish it upon my worst enemy. She was adopted herself so it's hard to trace anything genetically concerning the disease but she suffered much trauma in her life along with much drug use, so it's hard to truly know. She said her favourite boyfriend had been killed by an 18-wheeler right in front of her and many others close to her had died, even committing suicide. My heart says it was brought on or most certainly enhanced by the trauma of living an extremely promiscuous lifestyle. That type of lifestyle is extremely draining emotionally and damaging to your self worth and dignity. I feel that's where much of her shame and anger came from. You most certainly didn't cross her and she told me a story of it taking five officers to restrain her one time in the psych ward. I felt compelled to visit her for a few years after our initial meeting, but she was extremely ill and it wasn't healthy for me anymore. She had a boyfriend that she'd bring along in our visits that was suffering from the illness even worse than her. He was a man so internally bound and burdened in his illness that it completely debilitated him. This to me was the definition of a mental health issue as opposed to the common systems of emotional depression and social inadequacy. It's like the disease holds you captive into such a paranoid state of fear from the perception and opinions of others that you're held mentally paralyzed, with no way out. Every circumstance is overemphasized and every thought is overanalyzed without any reprieve and all they can do to manage the interactive imbalance is to heavily medicate you to avoid your reactive state of mind. It's an extremely complicated and concerning disease but regardless, I would get so angry after seeing her, I once pulled over by the front lawn of Riverview hospital hyperventilating at how agitated she made me feel. She was a manipulative and possessed demoniac and I most certainly did not need that in my life and ended up cutting her out of it completely. That was about 18 years ago now and I've thought about tracking her down again merely concerning her salvation but haven't been compelled to do so. I'm scared for what emotions will arise and a part of me isn't willing to risk it. Her stories were so vile and disturbing of her life that I just don't want to subject myself to that anymore. How I came out of that mess is a miracle in itself. Interestingly, the definition of reprieve is a cancellation of a painful or otherwise lousy situation. It says, ironically, that if you're being tortured, a reprieve is a break from whatever's tormenting you but that is unfortunately what's taking place in the mind of some of these poor people with mental illness without it.

Danny Dayton

I was around 25 at this time and I'd quit boxing and my relationship with my girlfriend had come to an end. She was an incredible person and had helped me through such a difficult and heavy time in my life but we both needed to move on. The old saying is "If you love someone, let them go," and she did it gracefully. She saw that I needed time alone to figure out my life and was strong and independent enough to allow that to happen. Even though I loved her, I just couldn't give her what she deserved in a relationship. There was no love loss and we stayed mutual friends as I was close to the family. Unfortunately after we broke up and quit boxing the void and release they filled turned me back to drugs and alcohol. My friends outside of boxing drank heavily, smoked marijuana, dabbled with cocaine and I intermingled within it all. I framed houses everyday which kept me afloat but I was emotionally drowning outside of work. I felt empty and alone and the marijuana and alcohol were merely my medicine to cope with it all. I just didn't know any other way. Things were getting pretty crazy until finally when I was 27 my best friend Dan was murdered outside of his house in the middle of the street. I was with him that whole weekend and knew he was up to no good but had no idea to what level. I remember even saying to him that weekend that if he keeps scrapping people and doing what he's doing somebody's going to shoot him. Ironically, that's exactly what happened. I would have been there if it wasn't for our dogs constantly fighting the night before in his house. I remember calling his work the next morning after he didn't answer my calls and they told me he was gone. I raced over there and it was like a movie with all the yellow tape circling his house and street. It was all so surreal but I remember having to go in and get his two psychotic dogs as the cops were scared to go into his house. There was a lot of speculation to what happened but years went by and the case eventually went cold. There was rolled up money and cocaine on the kitchen counter and there was also a grow up in the house which probably stereotyped him from the cops priority. There was a suspect that apparently shot himself in the face playing Russian roulette but otherwise that's all we heard for years. I was devastated as we were very close friends and my heart turned cold to the world. The pain and lack of closure was also killing his parents emotionally and in regards to their health, when finally years later something strange happened. I was working with this guy Al for several months and he always complained about his long commute to work. I finally asked him one day where he lived and he said, "96th and 126th." It rang a bell to me and then I recognized the address as being by my friend's house where he was killed. I said, "Pretty violent neighbourhood eh? He then went on telling me in detail the whole story of my friend's murder without me even mentioning it. He lived a couple houses down and said my friend chased away the prostitutes from the street corner outside his house and one day he had an altercation with the pimp that all the neighbours could hear. They were arguing back and forth and the pimp said the next day he was going to kill him and sure enough, he must have followed through with his threat. I won't go into any more of the details but chills came over me as he was telling the story and what's even crazier, is the day I showed up on the crime scene, he was the guy I was talking to behind the yellow tape eight years earlier and I didn't even realize it. This was a traumatic time for me to say the least. My alcoholic brother had just moved in with me at the time as I'd rescued him from a disastrous situation and my friends' dogs were two 190-pound vicious Great Danes that I grabbed from the crime scene.

Kona and Kita

Normally Great Danes are passive aggressive and docile but these things were savage beasts as he taught them to be aggressive and protect his property. There was so much surrounding the incident and I turned cold and into complete survival mode especially with these two dogs to tend to. I was also living in a grow up and had two big dogs of my own which further enhanced the stress of the situation. I lived in a townhouse complex where the limit was 45lbs for pets and I was harbering over 600! I had to separate them in rooms and walk them in intervals as they didn't get along.

As soon as I'd open the door to take them for a walk the neighbours would run back inside and you'd see cats running for their lives. The male named "Kona" got out the front door one day and when I went out to get him he was on top of a MPV minivan chasing after a cat. I had an old Delta 88 4 door car where the back window only rolled down halfway. Kona put his head through while I was driving and then shattered the window trying to come back inside. It was chaotic and hard to manage the situation especially with my brother who was a lot more vulnerable and sensitive than myself. They destroyed everything and even turned on me a few times but I somehow felt obligated to figure it out for my friend. His parents and girlfriend told me to just put them down but I was persistent and wanted to persevere. There was also a good side to them behind all the confusion and chaos as there is in most rescue dogs. Regardless, they were beasts and I'd have to make sure no one was around when I walked them or they'd team up and attack them.

I took them to the park close by and this one time I could see a man walking the opposite way with a baby carriage and a golden lab. They were about a hundred yards away so I figured the coast was clear but for whatever reason they changed directions and were headed right for us. The two dogs overpowered me, broke free and started tearing the lab apart. I caught up and had to pull a Mike Tyson on both of them. I can't even imagine what was going on in that poor guy's mind, whether he should be scared of me or the dogs. I finally got one dog tied to a tree but the male had the lab's head stuck in his mouth and wasn't letting go. I finally pried his jaws open enough to where the dog could get his head out but it was a pretty traumatic situation for the guy. There's so many chaotic stories with those crazy dogs but another one that I remember is, I'd take them to the high school close by and let them run in the upper field to do their business. I was under so much stress that I'll admit I could care less about cleaning up after them. They took massive craps the size of mountains that I was ignorant of to my default. I remember getting home early from work and taking them to the upper field around the time high school was out. I was walking down the chain link fence pathway towards the school and could hear voices saying, "That's him, that must be him." I didn't really catch on but I guess that's where the rugby team practiced their scrimmages and obviously weren't too happy sliding around in immense piles of dogshit. I then turned the corner to go up to the field and their big crazy rugby coach was walking towards me and the dogs. He walked straight for me without any fear of the dogs and Kita the female lunged at him and bit his arm really badly, drawing blood as he threatened to fight me. He was really ignorant and kept baiting me into a fight as I made my way into the upper field. When I got in there I realized I was trapped and the only way out was the entry gate he was standing in. He phoned the cops and kept screaming at me that the dogs were finished and I was going to get arrested. He was such an abrasive and ignorant jerk and held the phone up mocking me as I could hear the sirens in the background approaching. He kept saying, "What are you going to do now, you're trapped!? The fence was over 6 feet high but I went into beast mode myself and somehow heaved the dogs over the fence with all my adrenaline pumping before the cops got there. I was ignorant for not cleaning up after the dogs but that guy was an obnoxious jerk and it felt so good waving him goodbye on the other side of the fence. The dogs were a lot to handle but I persevered and finally found good homes for them both. Their behaviour had a lot to do with my friends training but they were also scared and traumatized by the entire situation. They've got a pack dog mentality in them but as soon as I separated them they were actually real sweethearts.

Dozens of people phoned and came to look but thought they were too vicious until finally the big male ironically went to a running back on a football team. I knew he needed to go to someone strong and this guy was perfect. I remember telling him to roll up his windows when he left or Kona would bite someone and sure enough when he pulled into the gas station on his way home Kona bit the gas station attendant filling up his truck. Kita the female went to a lady who tragically lost her husband in a car accident and was left in a large home all alone in a dangerous neighborhood. Kita was far more aggressive than the male but as soon as that lady got out of her car, Kita ran up and curled up under legs as if she knew her and her traumatic situation already. Somehow the dog sensed her pain and I just gave her the dog for free.

Life Goes On

27 passed away along with my friend and the years following were troubled and empty. I filled my void with all I knew which was marijuana and alcohol. I started learning to play the guitar and played in some garage bands over the years with my friends but I was still empty inside. It was a way to vent but I needed healing

from my childhood and some of the trauma I'd endured over the years. I got pretty heavy into the music the next few years and even made demo tapes in the studio. There were a lot of good times along the way but also falling outs because it always involved a lot of egos, drugs and alcohol. Everything seemed so desperate and temporary. You smoke some dope and drink some beer sensualizing everything for a few hours, then you wake up and do it all over again. It's definitely a creative outlet but it also creates such an emotional imbalance and separation from true reality, chasing the high night after night. Nothing productive outside of the music ever seemed to get accomplished, as I was saying earlier.

Finally when I was about 30 I met my future wife. She was about nine years younger but we hit it off right away. I grew really close to her and her family and we seemed to get along quite well. We had our ups and downs as any relationship does but we became best friends over the next few years. The one thing that divided us was my commitment to the band and the heavy drinking with my friends. The music was getting serious and we were heavily committed to the songs. We started recording and practiced almost everyday. Our upbringings were very different so I don't think she understood my passion for the music and what generated so much hostility towards life. She also was jealous of the time and dedication I put into something other than herself. Around this time I started getting severe chest pains. I'd be singing with the band or even just doing my everyday routine at work and these horrible chest pains would be unbearable. I'd even collapse at times from the pain. I went to the emergency room and visited my doctor several times at the walk-in clinic but no one could figure out what was wrong with me. The chest pains would progressively get worse and worse but I kept playing our music and tried to work through the pain. I could hardly sing or play guitar anymore the pain was so bad and my drummer was getting frustrated. I'd try here and there in intervals but something was definitely wrong inside my chest that the doctors were unable to diagnose. I didn't know if it was anxiety or some sort of overexertion but I felt like I was going to have a heart attack and die. We were determined to make an album at this time but it was like God intervened in his mercy, protecting me from my own distorted ambition and blind determination. The music was good but I wasn't some professional musician or rock and roll star. I could hardly handle the emotions of my own life let alone the pressure of being a lead singer in a band and drawing more attention to myself. Although I loved the music with all my heart, it wasn't in my character to be the centre of attention. I was leading myself into a false reality that I just couldn't handle. There was just too much of an imbalance going on in my head and ironically one of our songs was called "Little demons." The lyrics were,

These little demons inside,
that are messing with your mind
You got to let them out
You gotta let them out
Let them out loud,
so you stand out in the crowd
Grab a pick and a set of sticks,
start to rock and roll,
it'll soothe your soul
Let that feeling hit the ceiling,
when you hear that band a playin
Who gives a fuck what people are sayin,
just grab a guitar and start wailin,
and let them out
Turn the volume up high
We can't let this spirit die
You got to let them out,
before we all go crazy....

Another song I wrote lyrics went,

Cry me a river, cry me a storm
Look to the future, but I've been warned
Always that trailer who passes by,
as a reminder, that bird don't fly..
Get down to that river,
float downstream,
Worst drowning you've ever seen,
Forget them sorrows, no one cares,
look to the future,
What are we going to do about our future,
What are we going to do as our future fades away
Learn to keep the rhythm, before I die
Can't let this talent pass me by
Learn to keep the rhythm, learn to fly,
Ain't going to find the answers, unless I try...

I share them just because it's interesting to me how I perceived life before faith and what came through me in my lyrics.

We put a lot of time and effort into the songs and we had a lot of fun but we were way over our heads in dealing with any kind of music industry or record label. We were just crazy, broken and insecure buffoons trying to find an outlet to vent all of our pain and frustration. My bassist and drummer had a horrible childhoods growing up as well and wanted to push forward but I'd come to a place where my body couldn't do it anymore and that's where my testimony comes to where I came to know Jesus.

Calling Out God

My chest pains were getting so severe I had to take time off work and unfortunately had to break up with my girlfriend. I was at my wits end trying to balance it all and was smoking dope and drinking heavily every night, completely at a loss with what to do. One night after playing a few songs me and my drummer went out on the deck to have a drink. It was a torrential downpour and we were under the overhang, hiding out from the rain. We were kind of joking around facetiously about the meaning of life and then I went out in the pelting rain, looked up to the sky and said, "God if you're out there, show yourself!" As soon as those words left my ignorant mouth, a bolt of lightning hit the tree in the neighbor's yard not 30 yards from the deck. Even in my drunken stupor and ignorance I recognized that as being more than just coincidence. I ran for cover and from that moment on everything seemed to change around the house we were living in. I felt this weird presence in the house as if it was haunted or something. It seemed to grow progressively worse and my friends could feel it too. For whatever reason it was inclusively targeting me and I'd wake up to this presence of death all around me in the middle of the night. I'd felt it before a few times but this was a deplorable feeling that was not from this world. It's like a momentary detachment from the presence of physical reality and you can see the demonic realm as it moves alongside but you have no protection from it. It's as though the stillness of the air is magnified upon you. It's completely fixated upon you and you know it but can't escape from it. I went to a guy's house years before that was a striker for the Hell's Angels whose house and ora were very similar. Him and his friend had shot and killed two people in their driveway in supposed self-defense and you could feel that same severity around him and that same presence of death as you walked through the front door of their house. The difference with them is they seemed to embrace it, but I was completely petrified.

It was an eerie feeling and I finally pulled my mattress out on the deck to sleep outside, but the presence didn't go away. I remember my dog ferociously barking at the air as if something was there that I couldn't see. The presence started getting so severe I couldn't bear it anymore. This was far more severe than even those Hell's Angels could handle and if they could they were embracing an evil that I was not interested in. It's like I had nowhere to hide from it. I'd wake up at 2 in the morning for about four or five nights in a row with the presence of death all around me until one night I was completely terrified. It was an unexplainable spiritual phenomena especially to me with no spiritual knowledge or experience concerning this kind of thing. I got up, phoned my friend in the middle of the night and went to his house to try to sleep. I fell asleep on his couch for about 15 minutes and woke up to the presence of hell in me and all around me ten times more severe than before. Whatever spirit was after me or closing in on me followed me from my house and manifested itself right there in my friends living room. It was like that detachment and other realm completely opening up and for a few moments I felt the feeling of eternal hell and condemnation. I can try to describe it but it was far worse than any words could ever justify or articulate. It was like the whole room closed in on me and I was permanently sandwiched in between two 400-ton chunks of concrete with only an inch to spare and there was no way out and no one to cry to. It was like I was forever encased in my own head. Again, words can't do it justice but I wish that upon no one, not even my worst enemy. It's as if God lifted his hand of mercy off me to show me the demonic realm and the truth of where humanity was headed in it's sin. I've had dreams similar to it, much like my rooftop dream but this was manifest to me in the natural realm and I was dead sober. There was a time years ago where I experienced something similar in real life but it was drug-induced. I was at my friend's house who got murdered and we all smoked this drug called Salvia. It's surprisingly legal here in Canada but when refined and increased in potency much as hash is with marijuana, it packs a serious punch. Google says Salvia divinorum is a plant species with transient psychoactive properties when its leaves are consumed by chewing, smoking, or as a tea. The leaves contain opioid-like compounds that induce hallucinations. I would describe the hallucinations much like acid but far more severe and most people only ever try it once. I remember taking this huge toke on his deck and was instantly opened into another realm. The drug only lasts for about 5 minutes but those 5 minutes feel like hours and are the most terrifying moments any mind or physical body can handle. It's like the whole spiritual world comes alive and encloses itself upon you as though there's some sort of a protective chasm between you otherwise outside the influence of the drug. It's hard to explain the severity of it but it's like you open some sort of portal or gateway into another realm. I remember a spirit launching me into the corner of the wall and me cowering in fear, wanting it all to end. What's interesting is my friends that smoked it with me saw that same spiritual impartation fixated upon me and wanted it to be about them. I remember emphatically saying, "No you don't, you don't want this!!" My point in the story is that the experience in my friend's living room was much similar but ten times worse as though I was in a permanent state of confined claustrophobia. I'm minimizing the severity of it, but if this is a precursor to hell, I suggest to anyone who reads this, to ask God for forgiveness and the salvation he offers in Jesus Christ. I'd say the experience only lasted about 30 seconds or so but I felt a paralyzed state of fear and my left side collapsed as if I had a stroke. I somehow drove to the emergency thinking I was going to die. They did a bunch of tests on me but eventually deemed me to be fine and sent me back home. I survived the night and remember walking through a grocery store the next morning and wondering what on earth was going on with me. It was like some spiritual force was out to kill me.

Christ Intervenes

I had one Christian friend who we all hung out with in our early twenties who had given over his life to Jesus back then. I phoned him in the grocery store and told him what was going on with me. I found it strange how he reacted to what I told him, as though he knew the answer already. He just calmly said, "I've heard of this kind of stuff before and said to come to church the next Sunday." I'd only ever been to church once before and had no idea what to think. I do remember crying the one time I went years before and feeling a sense of peace and unity but for whatever reason I never went back. I sat down at my friend's church and actually fell asleep right away. It's as though whatever demonic spirit was hunting me down and tormenting me wasn't allowed in that room. I then remember the pastor saying, "If no one knows Jesus, raise your hand and come up to the front." I had reached such a low in my life and was living in such fear that I raised my hand and went to the front. The pastor then put his hand on my chest and prayed for me. At that moment a spirit completely enveloped me. I remember looking up at the crowd of people and just breaking down in tears. This spirit of peace and grace overtook me and it's like all the fear, pain and turmoil of my life came out right there in my tears. All the walls I'd built up, all the trauma and rejection and all the anger and loneliness of life since I was a child just poured out in front of everyone in that church. I was overcome with gratitude because all my vulnerability and insecurities were actually being accepted and not scrutinized and that is what I feared my whole life. It was a support and encouragement that was completely foreign to me. I remember looking up at the crowd through my tears and seeing an angelic haze and what looked like a sheet of glass over top and covering the congregation. I was in awe and couldn't contain my tears. That was the breakthrough my pride was holding me back from seeing that only God could reveal to me. It was a supernatural phenomenon that took place that day that science or philosophical reasoning just can't explain. God was drawing me to himself in his love and mercy but I was so blinded by my pride and afflictions, I couldn't see it until then. I was extremely stubborn and physically strong and he knew that taking my physical strength and revealing the demonic realm was the only way for me to see how I was destroying myself. I needed the fear of God to see and comprehend the saving grace of God.

Everything changed and looked different to me from that day forward. Something entered in when I let go on that stage and surrendered my life to God. The days and months following were difficult and challenging but my chest pains were gone and that horrible presence of death never returned. I started attending that same church regularly and was compelled to learn more about Jesus. The more I learned, the more all my preconceived notions and skepticism were peeling away. I remember saying to myself over and over, "How could I not see this before?" 2 Corinthians 5:17 says, "Therefore, if anyone is in Christ, he is a new creation, old things have passed away, behold, all things have become new." This was so true with what was going on inside of me. It also reminds me of 2 Corinthians 3 when Paul says that when one turns to the Lord, the veil is taken away because where the spirit of the Lord is, there is liberty. There's a lot you wrestle with when you initially become a believer but I kept persevering through the social changes around me and the character changes going on within me. It's like as soon as my purpose and initiatives changed and got resolved, so did the expectation and pressures I was putting on myself. I got back together with my girlfriend who at first seemed to support the change, especially in regards to sobriety, which would turn out to be a bad decision on my part, unfortunately. Regardless, I moved from that rental house and later found out from the neighbours that it was a social housing psych ward for schizophrenic's and those with severe mental illness. I always wondered why the rooms had dividing curtains in them but otherwise didn't give it much attention. They told us of hearing constant screaming and erratic behaviour for years prior to us being there, but regardless of what went on there with the patients and concerning myself, it was all in the past and I felt renewed and given new hope in life. There was some sort of demonic portal that was opened in that house and I'm so glad that it got closed. I eventually got baptized and was learning more and more about God through the Word and fellowship with other believers. I felt like a bull in a china shop walking into church and still do at times to be honest, but it all fascinated me, especially the person of Jesus Christ and the community and purpose that his teaching generated. So much was getting revealed to me about the truth of life and faith and the spiritual world that surrounds us. It wasn't just that, it was the emotions and hostility inside me that never had a safe place to vent or find resolve that were all coming out in the open. People supported my transparency and didn't judge me for my past or the insecurities within me. It's like whatever was being released in me had already been released and reconciled in them and we could communicate humbly and on level terms. I was also learning to forgive myself which is the greatest struggle many of us have in life and where much of our healing begins. I'd never exposed that side of me with others and I'd never exposed that within myself. Again, it was all foreign to me and what I always considered a weakness in my prideful determination, I now saw as a strength. The more I learned about the true character of God, the more I came to realize that it is this emotional insecurity and transparency that God lives to resolve within us through a relationship with him and where so much of our confusion and despair lie in this world. Pride is a blinding weakness and stronghold that isolates us to its dependency. It also conforms us and holds us back from communitive and relative interaction. When I'd close my eyes in prayer, especially with other people around, I realized the vulnerability and weakness within me and where it lies in all men and women. It's this threshold in our pride where the veil gets lifted in prayer. I was emotionally immature and only God could expose and resolve that insecurity within me. It's amazing to me that the more you reveal your insecurities to God, the more secure you become. It's like you're oppressing yourself by your own fears otherwise. We think we are weak by expressing how we feel and being vulnerable but the weakness is actually in the unwillingness and fear to do so. It takes courage and it's the first time I learned what a real man was. If we can't even face ourselves when our eyes are closed then how do we expect to face the perceptions of the world when our eyes are open being lost in the perception of ourselves? I'd also never experienced someone praying for me, especially right beside me and never even thought to pray for anyone else. It was a selfless act of courage and maturity that I'd never seen before or even considered. Life to me was a battle for self-preservation and a life driven to be the beneficiary of my own actions and this was all new to me. Prayer was extremely uncomfortable for me at first but I saw it as an endearing quality that Jesus brought out in people and again, I saw the insecurities within myself as a lack of emotional and spiritual development that faith compels us all to grow and mature in. To me it was a noble and commendable discipline and direction to life. The world loves to judge and analyze what everyone else is doing wrong but is scared to confront what's going on within themselves and this is where prayer and faith in Christ brings us to a humility the world cannot generate.

Being Sanctified

I kept growing and learning in the months and years that followed but I remember something significant that happened to me just before my conversion that would later tie in to my faith and understanding. A Jehovah Witness would frequently come to that rental house and bring along a different sidekick with him each time. He was a charming young fellow and we got to be friends over the months I lived there. I actually ended up chasing him down with a tire iron thinking he was robbing my house but that's another story. He would talk about God but it seemed like a contrived sales pitch to me and would go in one ear and out the other. Nothing he said struck me as revolutionary or awe inspiring and although he was kind and knowledgeable, he didn't seem sure of himself. It's as if he was under an oppressive tutelage and following what someone told him was true and not necessarily independent of himself. After I got saved and had moved he somehow tracked me down at my new place and came around the back patio with one of his new minions, unannounced. We sat down and started talking about God but we seemed to have conflicting opinions about the deity of Christ and many other critical fundamentals concerning the Christian faith and the Bible. He started getting really upset because he couldn't convince me and even started shaking as he was holding his Bible. Everything he denied was the spirit that was transforming and revolutionizing me. He lived to be justified by the law and in his religious works and hated the fact that I had a sense of liberty and freedom otherwise. He seemed so oppressed and enslaved to me and what I saw as redemption, reconciliation and regeneration, he saw as heresy. I was coming to the revelation through the word that Jesus Christ was the incarnation of God and their whole religion emphatically denied that. Their religion has actually taken the Bible and removed and manipulated scriptures where Christ's deity is solidified and exemplified. Again, he became so agitated as I refuted his claims that he was shaking as he held his Bible in front of me. What's significant about it all is that it took me on a path of research and truth I would have never imagined and was the turning point of how I saw the element of evil through the gospel lens. The greatest evil especially from a spiritual perspective aims to tear down the greatest truth and that truth is in the deity of Jesus Christ. I started researching their religion along with other cults and secret societies as I'd mentioned before. Again, it's a dark road to go down but it's alive and real and affecting us all to a degree most don't realize. I started stripping away the hidden truths of the world's progressive evil and affiliated corruption and it all drew me closer and closer to Christ as the Word came alive at what it exposed. It's like the words knew more of what's going on now in our generation than we do and no one could foretell that unless it was prophetically revealed to them by God. The truth is hard to bear but it's still the truth and becomes such an irrefutable revelation in defining the elements of evil and how they are bearing down and monopolizing our world. The only thing that can truly expose and define the magnitude of evil at work is defining righteousness and holiness and what is in opposition to them and that is only defined biblically and exemplified in Jesus Christ.

The Word also started exposing and convicting me of my own sin and that's when the heavy drinking, marijuana and fornication came to an end along with my foul mouth and bitterness towards the world. God's spirit was within me confirming the Word's truth and was persistent in killing these desires and peeling away other bad habits, dependencies and character flaws I wasn't even aware of before. The fear and truth of God is revolutionising and it's like a new purpose, humility and appreciation for life was birthed within me that was in complete contrast to my way of life and perspective before. It's amazing how our accountability changes when we have something or someone to respect and be reverent and accountable to. God was transforming me and the process was a continuously regenerating confirmation as though his spirit worked alongside and cared about me more than I cared about myself, much like a good father would be to his wayward son. God was forgiving, loving, and patient with me and this sanctification process is only something a born again Christian can experience. It's a relationship that inclusively grows as the world continues on around you as it would otherwise.

Around this time is when I smoked some marijuana in our jam room and knew it was over with me and the band. Again, the music was fun but something in me was changing and the lifestyle was problematic and detrimental to my health. Shortly after my drummer overdosed on painkillers and my bassist's psychotic girlfriend flipped her car over in the ditch outside my house, absolutely hammered, screaming she was going to kill me and him. There was definitely a lot of transitioning going on within me and in the lives and spirit world around me but I was holding on in faith as Christ became that much more real to me. I started feeling a sense of belonging regardless of my surroundings and how people felt about my new faith. Christ changes the atmosphere and you can see the repercussions of our actions so much more clearly when you become a believer. Your faith starts shaking the spirit world and all the complacencies and strongholds it thought it had in you and around you. This was also the time my girlfriend got baptized and I saw the demon over top of the bed in our room. This level of spirituality was all new to me and to my girlfriend and was a lot for her to take in. I felt torn between faith and the world and also the social pressures and expectations from the people and friends around me. I speak for myself but I know it was happening within her as well. I think a part of her believed but it was all very confusing and she wasn't willing to compromise her status and identity in the world. She felt like she had to give up so much of what she was living for. I know how this can be such a difficult time for new believers to persevere through, especially considering the social pressures of our world today. We were both battling through all of this and it reminds me of Jesus's parable of the seeds being sown in Matthew 13 and in 1 Peter 4:4 where it says, "In regards to these, they think it strange that you do not run with them in the same flood of dissipation, speaking evil of you." Regardless, I eventually asked her to marry me and we would a year or so later. She seemed happy and went along with the faith for a while after we got married but deep down she wasn't fully committed. In my wedding speech I thanked Jesus for saving me and saving our relationship but looking back now I realize hardly anyone in the audience were Christians and I think it embarrassed her. She tried following along in support of me but it was such a drastic change and wasn't something that interested her anymore. Her whole life was reality television, facebook and partying with her softball friends and she wasn't willing to surrender. I was fascinated by Jesus and the bible but it all made her uncomfortable and a part of her grew jealous and bitter at the attention I gave my faith. She was still attached to the world and showed no signs of wanting to change. I got involved in street ministry pretty intensely and something in her just didn't see a future in the church or in a life together with me. It was partially my fault because I think at first when we become Christians we want to change and take on the world and get way ahead of ourselves, putting everything else secondary. We also can become religiously entitled and abusive which can push people away trying to expose the sin within them. Regardless, we were unequally yoked and it was only a matter of time until our relationship would end. I think at first she thought it would be a good way for me to get sober and start a family but I was fully committed to the whole transformation and lifestyle. I remember her dad years later saying it was my faith that she just couldn't contend with. About a year into our marriage I found out she was sleeping with some guy on her softball team.

It was devastating for me and we ended up getting divorced soon after. We were just two different people going in two different directions and looking back now it's almost better that it happened sooner than later. She was chasing after the world and I was dying to it and unfortunately that's a place where many people become divided in marriages and between family and friends in regards to faith. He was a popular party guy on her softball team that gave her the attention she desired and I was done with that lifestyle completely. She ended up having a couple kids with the guy and has apparently been with him ever since. The divorce was about seven years ago and I've pressed on in faith and been single ever since. It was an extremely painful experience but I finally called her one day and told her I forgave her and wished her the best moving forward. Deep down I loved her and wished her no harm and the phone call was a release we both needed. I've learned that forgiveness is the most powerful word in the english language but have also learned that apart from murder, adultery is one of the greatest evils because it knows its victim personally and uses and exploits them for all their worth, while willfully embracing the lie. That's why God is so attement about the consequences of fornication and adultery. Proverbs 6:32 says, "Who commits adultery with a woman lacks understanding; He who does so destroys his own soul." I find it interesting that it wasn't the sex that hurt me as much as it was her ability to blatantly lie to my face. There was a night we got together to try to figure things out and I asked her straight up if there was another guy into which she adamantly denied and went on with the evening as if everything was normal and she just needed time to sort things out. She left that night but had dropped her phone in the kitchen while we were talking. It must have broken and she had to reconnect her old phone into which all of her emails and text messages were coming through her iPad which I still had. I remember hearing the iPad notification going off in the morning and seeing all these messages coming through from the night before. My heart just died inside as I read them because they were at the exact time she had left that evening. She had walked out the door from seeing me, phoned him and went straight to his house and had sex with him without any care or consideration for me whatsoever and it was all there in the messages along with all the steamy details in the morning. It's a horrible and empty feeling to go through and I sympathize with anyone that's had to endure something like this. Your whole life is flipped upside down within seconds and I had every right to be angry and hate them both for what they did. All the love and trust we'd build up and all the memories we shared over the years meant nothing to her and were wiped away forever. She was dead to me and it took me years to let go and to make that phone call to forgive her but what ultimately compelled me to do it was thinking of Jesus and what compelled him to go to the cross. This one offense caused so much insecurity, trauma and bitterness in my life. I felt dejected, hopeless and demoralized but Jesus came into a world that hates him and willfully and voluntarily paid the penalty for the offense. It would be like me laying my life down for my wife and her new man after finding out of their adultery, but Jesus has done this for the sin of the whole world. I had to forgive her because of the forgiveness that's been shown to me. This is the forgiving love of God in Jesus Christ and is the only way we can truly know him and have a relationship with him. Every other carnal perspective or perception of God does not personify him or revolutionize us to where his spirit can work within us. Romans 5 says, "Therefore, have been justified by faith, we have peace with God through our Lord Jesus Christ, through whom also we have excess by faith into his grace to which we stand, and rejoice in hope of the glory of God. And not only that, but we also glory in tribulations, knowing that tribulation produces patience and patience, experience; and experience, hope. Now hope does not make us ashamed, because the love of God is being poured out into our hearts by the Holy Spirit who was given to us. For when we were still without strength, in due time Christ died for the ungodly. For scarcely for a righteous man will one die; yet perhaps for a good man someone would even dare to die. But God demonstrates his own love towards us, in that while we were still sinners, Christ died for us. Much more than, having now been justified by his blood, we shall be saved from wrath through him. For if when we were enemies we were reconciled to God through the death of his son, much more, having been reconciled, we shall be saved by his life. And not only that, but we also rejoice in God through our Lord Jesus Christ, through whom we have now received the atonement."

The years have gone by with ups and downs along the way that finally led me to my accident and the book that you're reading. That's kind of my life and testimony in a nutshell. I was a hard shell to crack but once God got in there, I started to see the light. I'm not saying the Christian life is easy by any means but when we believe, he continuously reveals to you the power of forgiveness and the liberty, truth and grace that comes from the cross. Again, the truth is hard to bear and many of us are reluctant to face it, but however painful it is, that nut in the shell is in complete darkness until its shell is opened up and exposed to the light and I hope that whoever reads this has enough courage to allow God to do so.

Chapter 14

Conclusion

In closing, I want to say thank you for taking the time to read my book. There's definitely more to this life than meets the eye and I hope I've given more insight into that and into the deception that surrounds us all. I tried to just be myself and write as though I'm speaking to a friend in everyday life. I don't profess to be an overly philosophical or intellectual person, especially after the concussion from my accident. I've had a hard time putting a sentence together at times so it's been challenging trying to articulate my thoughts into words. Even before the accident I wasn't much into intellectual conversation nor were my friends and family. It's just not in my character. I can see what's going on in the world now but I don't see being overly philosophical as being a good way to communicate it. It just seems to just incite more contention in people. Paul says he was all things to all people for the gospels sake that he might save some. Even to the weak he became weak to form a relationship and get his message across clearly. There's just no need to be overanalitical and complicate things. You can go into depths with some people but the majority of us are simpleminded. I remember reading a book years ago and it's like the author had a thesaurus beside her trying to find the biggest words to prove how intelligent and intellectual she was. I guess being intellectual is being intelligent but anyways, it was so irritating I couldn't even finish the first chapter. I don't even see how she could relate to her own book. The end of Ecclesiastes says, "And moreover, because the preacher was wise, he still taught the people knowledge, yes, he pondered and sought out and set in order many proverbs. The preacher sought to find acceptable words; and what was written was upright, words of truth. The words of the wise are like goads, and the words of scholars are like well driven nails, given by one Shepherd. And further, my son, be admonished by these. Of making many books there is no end, and much study is wearisome to the flesh." I hope this book isn't wearisome, I hope it's a book people can relate with and find some clarity through the turmoil of life. It can definitely be a vigorous emotional and spiritual battle finding truth amidst the madness of this deceiving, volatile, contentious and self-entitled world. It's not only the contentious world outside we're battling, it's the contentious battle within us all, but again, there's such a release when we can let it go. I succumbed to much of it myself but now I see that so much of my anxiety and incentives in life were driven by deception and vanity. It's like they were ingrained into my subconscious since I was a child. The world trains us to live for the pride that destroys us and it was most certainly destroying me. Honestly, I don't blame people for being consumed and succumbing to the anxiety the world generates for itself. It's maddening. Everything seems to be conspiring against us. When I process the world these days, many other C words come to mind, like contrived, contention, conflicting, contradicting and confusing, to name a few. The entire world has become a collateral implosion with these words and within our perception of truth and reality, but ultimately, it's due to our own irreverence and denial of God and his Word. This is the real global pandemic going on and unfortunately with that denial and dissociation the lion's fangs sink deeper and deeper under our faithless and impressionable skin. It can be exhausting analyzing all of the opinions, perspectives, theories and controversy circulating every outlet and within our personal interaction with others these days, especially in regards to covid-19 and vaccinations. People have become extremely divisive, contentious and opinionated and with that we've all become even more introverted, self conscious and insecure. I guess we're all entitled to our opinion but we're sure not finding common ground. For me, if you're secure in your opinion then you shouldn't take such offence to the opinions around you. They shouldn't have such an effect on your disposition but it seems the opposite and has more proved the ever increasing instability within us all. It seems everyone has an answer but nothing is getting resolved. It just keeps getting worse and noyone truly understands why. Proverbs 26:12 says, "Do you see a man wise in his own eyes? There is more hope for a fool than him." Romans 1 says, "They became futile in their thoughts, and their foolish hearts were darkened. Professing to be wise, they became fools."

People take offence to anything these days and I see so much of that as being manipulated, disillusioned and built up into a false sense of democratically promoted security by satan and his pathetic minions. Instead of standing affirmed or assured in what we believe, we're lossed in our own prideful entitlement and in our search for control and self-affirmation. Freedom in democracy has become a deceiving ideology and philosophy and with it we've become lost in how we've perceived independence physically and psychologically. It opens doors of opportunity that we can't see in the natural realm. Again, the basis of the word capitalism is to capitalize and we don't quite see the level into which that extends itself or impacts our lives financially or psychologically. We are definitely being manipulated and impulsively coerced into complacency but with accessibility to information and as advanced as technology is these days, if you dig deeper, you can break down much of the world's discourse throughout history with a little research and discernment, even carnally speaking. I watched a show on Fox called "Unfiltered" with Dan Bongino the other day that was incredible. He's on every Saturday at 10pm and is extremely informative on the truth of corruption taking place politically and economically. Again, it's a dark road to go down and unearth that will make your stomach turn and will eventually lead you to much of what's manifesting itself before our eyes but unfortunately there's still a void and unseen spiritual veil that's disguised and continues to persist alongside, just outside of our carnal rationality and perception that's two steps ahead no matter how much information we take in or research. The money trail can definitely reveal a lot and will get you close to the crest of the pyramid but even more truth reveals itself in the progressive intentions the finances hold from the demonic impunity of the global elite. 2 Corinthians 10:3-4 says, "Though we walk in the flesh, we do not war after the flesh. For the weapons of our warfare are not carnal but mighty through God in the pulling down of strongholds, casting down imaginations, and every high thing that exalts itself against the knowledge of God." There is a deep evil in this world and our carnal wisdom is nonsensical to the prevailing imminence of the relentless and persisting spiritual realm whether we think so or not. Satan is too sophisticated of an adversary to contend with or comprehend carnally and God is too strong in wavering in his convictions and in the fulfillment of his prophetic Word for the salvation of our souls. There's an undisclosed barrier of illumination in procession in the spiritual realm that is impossible to decode, detect or ascertain outside of the biblical revelation of Jesus Christ and our personal confession and testimony to and of God. He's the only exposition of that which imposes itself upon us all. Until we die to ourselves, we are completely blind to it otherwise. The world's most intellectual minds and philosophers cannot process the compounding implications of sin because outside of Christ and his spiritual admonishment, there isn't a bar of correction to be reverent or accountable to. They're merely lost as we all are in unbelief and in our own pursuit, entitlement, and optimism as the consequences of sin persistently prevail and compile alongside. It's impossible to see outside of ourselves when we're consumed by living for ourselves.

Much of the biblical worldview is actually a simple overview in common sense and self exaltation. 2 Corinthians 11:3 says, "But I fear, lest somehow, as the serpent deceived Eve by his craftiness, so your minds may be corrupted from the simplicity that is in Christ." Paul goes on in chapter 1:12 and says, "For our boasting is this: the testimony of our conscience that we conducted ourselves in the world in simplicity and godly sincerity, not with fleshly wisdom but by the grace of God." Mankind just can't rationalise intellectually outside of the purpose, service and benefit to and of ourselves and the impulses we desire. Much is mere selfishness and gluttony but we've also been blinded by the fear of losing in this life what we'll gain in the life to come by surrendering in repentance and faith. In this our wisdom has been restricted and restrained by its own pursuit, socially and financially. Ultimately, satan relishes in it all and is why he incessantly promotes the incentive. He loves human philosophy, especially gnosticism and has ever since the first century that succeeded Christ. Gnosticism is defined as the emphasis of personal spiritual knowledge above the orthodox teachings, traditions, and authority of the church. This is the demise of the world in its philosophy and it is all rooted in entitlement, greed and pride. I just watched a two hour documentary about Bernie Madoff who was a stock market guru in the 90's. He built one of the biggest ponzi schemes in history amassing over 65 billion dollars that was all built on a lie. He lured tens of thousands of investors in and built an empire but it all came crashing down as soon as that lie was exposed. He was deceived by his own greed and it eventually destroyed everything in his life. He got a 150 year prison sentence. His one son committed suicide while the other died of stress related cancer. His largest investor comitted suicide by slitting his wrist and all his partner's ended up in jail having to relinquish their assets. The collateral damage of his lie lives on to this day with people investing billions into his lie. To me, it shows how far our own pursuit can take us and what damage it causes.

Proverbs 16:25 says, "There is a way that seems right to a man but its end is the way of death." Proverbs 28:11 says, "The rich man is wise in his own eyes but the poor who has understanding searches him out." In Ecclesiastes 16:18 Solomon says, "I communed with my heart saying, look, I have attained greatness and have gained more wisdom than all who were before me in Jerusalem, my heart has understood great wisdom and knowledge and I set my heart to know wisdom and to know madness and folly, I perceived that this also is grasping for the wind, in much wisdom is much grief and he who increases knowledge increases sorrow." Isaiah 29:14-16 says, "For the wisdom of their wise man shall perish and the understanding of their prudent men shall be hidden, woe to those who seek deep to hide their counsel far from the Lord and their works are in the dark. They say, who sees us? And who knows us? Surely you have things turned around! Shall the potter be esteemed as the clay? Shall the thing made say of him who made it, he did not make me? Or shall the thing formed say of him who formed it, he has no understanding?" Isaiah 47:10-14 says, "Your wisdom and your knowledge have warped you and you have said in your heart I am and there is no one else besides me therefore evil shall come upon you, you shall not know from where it arises and trouble shall fall upon you, you will not be able to put it off and desolation shall come upon you suddenly which you shall not know. Stand now with your enchantments and the multitude of your sorceries in which you have laboured from your youth, perhaps you will be able to profit. Perhaps you will prevail. You are wearied in the multitude of your counsels; Let now the astrologers, the stargazers and the monthly prognosticators stand up and save you, from what shall come upon you. Behold, they shall be as stubble, the fire shall burn them; they shall not deliver themselves from the power of the flame...."

Wisdom of God

I love how the Bible speaks for itself so I don't have to. It's incredible the depth and power it holds between the covers. In regards to wisdom, Proverbs 11:30 simply says, "The fruit of the righteous is a tree of life, and he who wins souls is wise." There's many other scriptures concerning human wisdom and man-centered philosophy and again, this is where Solomon met vanity in writing Ecclesiastes. He initially asked God for wisdom which God granted him but he inevitably failed in not adhering to and retaining that wisdom for Israel's benefit. He sought after the wisdom and pleasures of the world for the benefit of himself. He became egocentric and narcissistic and as he gained favour, opulence and fame, he attributed that to the wisdom of God. With all his impulses and pleasures being met, he eventually saw it all as vanity and a chasing after the wind and only in that did he finally become truly wise in writing Ecclesiastes. He asked for wisdom but he only truly got it when he died to himself. He fell as all humanity has at the seat of judgement, prosperity or influence. He fell to the wisdom he claimed was being generated from within himself. It's easy to be confident and become wise in your own eyes as you stand behind equity, pleasure and achievement but try being confident and revolutionizing the world standing behind no equity at all. Solomon's life was recorded and written for us to learn from and not for us to aspire to be yet we continue to prove ourselves to be gullible gluttons of punishment. We attribute wisdom solely to the acquisition of wealth and prestige but God's wisdom in Christ strikes a far deeper and more productive cord than that of our own.

It's baffling to me how everything we've witnessed in history and everything were witnessing now whether it be in the news, media outlets, TV shows, movies, books, or just within our interactive and apparently perceptive world, isn't enough proof of the depravity within us all and reason for us to change and turn to God. We are so proovingly stubborn and prideful and everything is an undeniable illumination of the consequences of faithlessness and sin as it has been throughout history, yet we still pursue what's destroying us and somehow trust in the process we're generating as though a productive outcome awaits the world. Jeremiah 17:5-10 says, "Cursed is the man who trusts in man and makes flesh his strength, whose heart departs from the Lord, for he shall be like a shrub in the desert and shall not see when good comes, but shall inhabit the parched places in the wilderness in a salt land which is not inhabited, blessed is the man who trusts in the Lord and whose hope is in the Lord, for he shall be like a tree planted by the waters which spreads out its roots by the river and will not fear when heat comes, but its leaf will be green and will not be anxious in the year of drought nor will cease from yielding fruit. The heart is deceitful above all things and desperately wicked, who can know it? I the Lord search the heart, I test the mind, even to give every man according to his ways, according to the fruit of his doings."

Outside of God and the salvation he offers, we're putting our faith, hope, and dependence on man and on a world run by pathological liars, political tyrants and luciferian psychopaths as though they have our best interests in mind, but it couldn't be further from the truth as proven in the empowerment of communism and the tens of millions of people slaughtered in a supposed common and united goal. It's not only in communism, it's in all systems generated by men with autonomous impunity and access to the financial overhead. For this reason I am pleading for people to get right with God and accept the salvation he offers through Jesus Christ, no matter where you are in the world or what system you're under.

Warning

I love defining words because collusion comes to mind when defining these cowardly and insubordinate leeches of our world.

Collusion means a secret or illegal cooperation or conspiracy especially in order to cheat or deceive others. I'll read Isaiah 10:1-4 just for a warning to anyone who this complies. It says, "Woe to those who decree unrighteous decrees, who write misfortune, which they have prescribed to rob the needy of justice, and to take what is right from the poor of my people, that widows may be their prey, and that they may rob the fatherless. What will you do in the day of punishment, to whom will you seek for help? In where will you leave your glory? Without me they shall bow down among the prisoners and they shall fall among the slain, for all this his anger is not turned away."

The common man or proletarian as some call the masses, have the greatest insight into the imbalances of power and injustice from a carnal perspective but fail to identify with the eternal destiny of the soul. It also isn't identifying with the spiritual realm, its own conscience or in the expectation it desires morally from those they entrust in. God has our best interests in mind by voluntarily paying the price for our sins on the cross of calvary. No politician would ever do that for us nor any idol we're aspiring to become. God was in Christ reconciling the world to himself, it's just so hard to articulate the severity of it all in words. It frustrates me to no end. What more can I say to persuade you? It's like everything is coming to light but we are so blinded and deceived in our own pursuit, further succumbing to that darkened mirage and abyss. It's crazy how the Bible specifically identifies with all of this especially from an oppressive state of mind but we continue to deny its relevance. So much of the Bible is a severe warning to those in the power and liberty and salvation to those under its yoke, but unfortunately satan is who the world pursues in its disassociation to Christ from system to system and from generation to generation, whether it be in power or in the common man.

Only in Jesus Christ is there a testimonial witness to the divine and destined purpose of a reverent and obstinate will. He is the justifier to moral compliance and of salvation. He is the initial ambassador and initiator to the construct of community and family structure and ultimately, he is the formulation and institution of our moral law, historically. He is also the fulfilment of it in Christ and to deny him is to deny life entirely, especially based on morality, integrity and eternal justice. If conviction is the restrainer to consequence then we only have that to be reverent and appreciative of. His impact goes beyond what any genius could even formulate in their mind. In John 1 it says, "In him was life and the life was the light of men and the light shines in the darkness and the darkness did not comprehend it." It says, "He was in the world and the world was made by him, and the world did not know him, He came to his own and his own did not receive him, but those that did receive him, to them he gave the right to become children of God, to those who believe in his name, who were born not of blood, nor of the will of flesh, nor of the will of man, but of God." 1 John 5-12 again says, "He who has the Son has life, he who does not have the Son of God does not have life." These words are definitely offensive to the will and pride in man and the disdain under the tongue toward God because it takes the power, ego and control from our hands and gives accountability and eternal consequence to the conscience in everything we do. In Christ, our conscience finds the identity of its refinement. It's literally insane to think where we'd be as a world without that accountability, conviction and eternal fear to ponder. His life is a mercy offering to the entire world and his standard is the saving grace of the world, even in it's denial of him.

In John 3 it says, "This is the condemnation, that the light has come into the world, and men loved darkness rather than light, because their deeds were evil. For everyone practicing evil hates the light and does not come to the light lest his deeds be exposed, but he who does truth comes to the light that his deeds may be clearly seen." The truth is Jesus Christ is this light and until we humble ourselves and confess our sin, a cloud of darkness blinds us in our own wills intention and we further ensnare ourselves and collectively implode in the objective and entrapment of satan. There's a show on TV called "catch a contractor" where a team goes out to help victims of fraudulent construction contractors who have taken their money. A private investigator tracks them down and then they confront them with all their lies with the victims in the same room. Many find excuses and lie their way through till the end but some break down in tears at the devastation they've caused the families. It becomes not only a transformation for the victims but a transformation within themselves in confessing their sin. It brings you to tears watching when the victims actually forgive the contractors. This power of reconciliation is the regeneration within God's Word.

Without it, all the hidden sin and tolerance we neglect to abstain from and identify with prosper in satan's hand and continue to have their progressive and cumulative effects on the world and within ourselves, further separating ourselves from the source of life which is Jesus Christ. Even the most unassuming sins like gossip, criticism or embellishment take root on the wings and backs of demons in this sensitive, volatile and emotionally reactive world, without us even knowing it. This is also the consequence in a world with no influence to bear especially from an eternal perspective. It's only the Holy Spirit within us that convicts, exposes and withholds our natural propensity to react, pursue and selfishly commit sin when we come to faith and believe. Ultimately denying him is denying the solution. Again, the truth is impossible to decode without this regeneration from God. We just live to justify ourselves in our own ethical standard of morality and stand affirmed in our progression as though we have and hold the solution within us. To be frank, it doesn't seem to be working individually or collectively. We're only lying to ourselves trying to solve it within ourselves.

Exposing the Darkness

From a carnal sense, I'll admit, there are many courageous whistleblowers coming out exposing conspiracies, secret societies, government cover ups and corruption like Dan Bonafino and much gets exposed through investigative reporting, journalism, documentaries and literature, but it's so hard to know who or what to believe anymore. People don't realize that part of conspiracy is to flood the world with conspiracy as a diversion. I had an old drummer in my band who was consumed by conspiracy theories. He believed everything he read on the internet as though the sky would fall at any second. He thought everyone was out to get him and everyone was an idiot for not believing what he was saying. He might have been right about some of it but that was over 10 years ago and last time I checked, the sky was still up there. He didn't realize that much of the conspiracy he thought he was exposing was actually designed to generate the fear that was disabling him from living a productive and proactive life. For me it's good to be aware of but not if we let it affect our lives in a detrimental way. He wasn't a Christian so he couldn't see it from a spiritual or biblical perspective and it all consumed him with anxiety and depression. I've gone to those places in my head but have worked hard to stay close to God and be balanced and discerning. Like I've said before, there's definitely psychological manipulation, subversion and bribery cohersing us all into a false narrative but it's imperative how we process it. I don't see how anyone can watch these new pharmaceutical commercials and not see how morbidly psychotic they truly are. They've even stooped so low as to come after our pets! It's like a constant bombardment of more fear and more drugs day in and day out. Regardless, the inflation in our economy is enough proof of conspiracy on it's own. It's the highest it's been in over 30 years. Six months ago it was 37$ for a sheet of plywood. We just bought one for 162$ for a work project and we have the most trees in the world here in Canada. If you don't believe in conspiracy and want to live indifferent to it all, that's your choice but it's not going to change what evil is conspiring to do. Our own government grows marijuana with people still in jail for marijuana related offenses. If that isn't a contradiction, I don't know what is. It's naive to think there's no conspiracy when they've generated a digital currency equivalent to our regular currency that goes even beyond the government's control. How is that justifiable? There's that "they" word again. The question is who are "they" and how can they hold so much power and influence over our world? If you listen closely, even Joe Biden will say "they" in regards to who wrote his speeches as though he's merely a little puppet to another narrative. Many people despise Donald Trump but I found him quite bold in how he'd constantly profess to there being "fake news." Here you have the leader of the supposed free world with the largest military ever constructed in history, completely powerless to the media. Why can't he just shut it down? Much like my old drummer, I can see how people get consumed by it all because a lot of it is true. We don't hold the answers to a lot of what dictates our democracy and that can make you feel helpless and vulnerable. It's very allusive in pinpointing the actual perpetrators to conspiracy but it's still real. You've got to be pretty ignorant to think otherwise. In defining a false narrative it says. "To convey a story that isn't real but to characterise it as if it is by creating a false story behind the situation in order to make it factual when the history itself never happened." So much is owned and been infiltrated by a discretionary power of impunity and censorship that's filtered and undisclosed to the public for its own sadistic agenda. It's amazing how one little rutter can steer a massive cruise ship and that's much like how they influence our culture. The lens can be a powerful tool in exposition but as we are all learning, can also be a powerful tool in control and in the conformity over our impressionable minds to which we are all guilty of and victims of to some degree. So much of it bases its objective in fear and within the psychology of the envious and impulsive mind. James 2 says, "If you have bitter envy and self-seeking in your hearts, do not boast and lie against the truth. This wisdom does not descend from above, but is earthly, sensual and demonic. Where envy and self-seeking exist, confusion and every evil thing are there."

I lived in anxiety and a state of fear and insecurity my whole life until I came to faith but again, I can see now how so much of that was built on a fabricated lie and what I was subjecting myself to and what was subjecting itself upon me. Is it a conspiracy? Yes, but it's what I chose to believe about myself and what I was being told the requirements should be to be accepted. I was in an identity crisis into which many of us are but now I can identify with that in Christ and am not ashamed to admit it. When we are wise to it and can admit it, conformity has no control over our identity and in our minds disposition or self worth. We can let go of our pride and our grip on the world especially from a social perspective and learn what true freedom really is. I say let them conspire against us but let us not conspire against ourselves. The regenerated mind of faith can take a step back, prioritise, and see the psychological and spiritual deception of evil unfolding around us within our carnal aspirations and pride. No matter how prestigious, honourable or wise we perceive ourselves to be, our initial propensity and responsive evaluation is wayward intellectually in the worship, contrived opportunism and entitled philosophy on life. We will justify any philosophy that gives us attention or puts money in our hands and that's how we conspire against ourselves without even knowing it. What we claim to know won't selflessly die to the benefit, position or affirmation we receive in our claim and that's where the revelation of Jesus Christ transcends our own limited philosophy and maturity level. 1 Corinthians 1:18-25 says, "For the message of the cross is foolishness to those who are perishing, but to us who are being saved it is the power of God. For it is written: I will destroy the wisdom of the wise, and bring to nothing the understanding of the prudent. Where is the wise? Where is the scribe? Where is the disputer of this age? Has not God-made foolish the wisdom of this world? For since, in the wisdom of God the world through wisdom did not know God, it pleased God through the foolishness of the message preached to save those who believe. For Jews request a sign, and Greeks seek after wisdom; but we preach Christ crucified, to the Jews a stumbling block and to the Greeks foolishness, but to those who are called both Jews and Greeks, Christ the power of God and the wisdom of God. Because the foolishness of God is wiser than men, and the weakness of God is stronger than men."

If you had all the greatest philosophers and intellectual minds of our generation and in centuries past at a table, along with all scientists and whistleblowers exposing conspiracy, I guarantee the world still couldn't get to the bottom of its progressive and descending calamity outside of the revelation of Jesus Christ. We analyze it to death but still nothing changes. We innovate to the extreme but still nothing changes. We claim to be adapting and evolving but we're just giving God's word more relevance by our ignorance of it. The truth of it all is that it's been written and the spirit behind the prophetic word is the exposition the world lives to deny and disregard and this is why we stumble and suffer like we do. We don't take heed to the warning and we don't see God's discipline as a benefit to ourselves. Hundreds of years before Christ came to earth, Isaiah wrote, "I lay in Zion a stone for a foundation, a tried stone, a precious cornerstone, a sure foundation, whoever believes will not act hastily." Then after Christ comes to earth, Peter reiterates those words and writes, "Behold, I lay in Zion, a chief cornerstone, elect, precious, and he who believes on him will by no means be put to shame. Therefore to you who believe he is precious, but to those who are disobedient, the stone which the builders rejected has become the chief cornerstone, and a stone of stumbling and a rock of offense. They stumble being disobedient to the word, to which they were also appointed." These are powerful and prophetic words the world is neglecting to adhere to and the more the world consciously exposes its own failings, the more it brings to light the man into which there was no sin or failure and our undeniable need for him. It also brings to light the revelation God destined in himself to exemplify through Christ and to save the world from the pursuit of itself.

I learned a lot myself during the process of writing this book that I wouldn't have otherwise unless I took the time to research some of the questions and doubts I've had along my journey, especially in regards to faith, history and theology. So much of man's philosophy bases itself in circular reasoning to which, again, it lives to justify itself outside of faith for its own benefit. That's where my word contrived comes from in defining our priorities in life. Contrived is defined as being deliberately created rather than arising naturally and interestingly a synonym for it is to be artificial. We sometimes don't ask questions to find an answer or reason, we ask the questions merely to reason with or justify ourselves in, apart from accountability. We will usually reason with faith's morality for a time but then as circumstances arise especially from an unfulfilling or negative standpoint, we don't see a reason for its dependence. For many it becomes an inconvenience because we just don't want to relinquish our control. The word faith in itself can be complicated and is certainly a stumbling block to the world and to myself, I'm not going to lie, but that's why it's called faith. It's not actually faith that's complicated, it's me who complicates it in my lack of faith. Much of our fight in faith as Christians is for the faith and at times that doesn't always generate a result or an immediate outcome our desires are looking for. At times in faith we're living for and serving a purpose greater than that of our own and that puts our will in a compromising position because we want it to be circumstantial. Our world has become about the "now" and we want immediate results in everything we do. It's just so hard for people to see past themselves into the bigger picture that faith illuminates. I have a stubborn and skeptical mind as many of us do but so much truth gets exposed and resolved in humility and reverence to God when we close our eyes in prayer into which the world provides no answers outside of faith. All we've become is an evolving manifestation of our own wisdom and capacity. We're neglecting to discover who we're created to be when we hold on to life in our pride. It's become a detriment to our soul. 1 Corinthians 3:18 says, "Let no man deceive himself. If any man seems to be wise in this world, let him become a fool, that he may be wise."

Faith is a powerful word in light of scripture and I wouldn't have learned as much myself unless I persevered in faith through the situation with my accident and the excuses and procrastination that naturally followed. No matter what situation or circumstance we find ourselves in, the spiritual realm seems unrelenting in its pursuit of us but sincere faith definitely gives us perspective and compelling reason and strength to persevere forward. I love the word sincere because it's the most productive adjective in regards to ethical principles, conduct and humility. The definition of sincere is being genuine, true and honest and it says an example of sincerity is a friend who helps you without an expectation of you doing something for them in return. In other words, uncontrived. Sincerity comes from the heart and a wilful conscious choice to do so and what the world is failing to recognize is to what extent God will go to extract that sincerity from within us all. He will sanctify and break you down to teach and build you up and as the world adamantly seeks its own recognition don't be surprised to see God breaking it down in mercy for its own good. It happened to me and it was painful, but it's what I needed. God's not in the business of supporting what's destroying us. This is the unrelenting love of God that's too holy and unperceivable for the carnal mind to fathom intellectually. 2 Peter 3:14-15 says, "Be diligent to be found by Him in peace, without spot and blameless, and consider that the long suffering of our Lord is salvation."

I think very few, including myself, consider or acknowledge the selflessness and patience of God on a daily basis." It's ridiculous how he suffers for our cause. Think of the pain we feel when someone we love brings harm upon themselves. It's a horrible and helpless feeling but that's why God came into the world and how he proved his love for us.

Victim Mentality

This being said, life at times can be a fierce battle and this love seems elusive especially for people faced with afflictions like mine and my injury. I'll admit at times after my accident I became bitter and insecure and played the victim role even as a Christian. I started searching for sympathy, into which in many respects, I was completely justified. The drunken idiot totally altered my life and future, mentally, physically, emotionally and financially. I've had every right to harbour resentment for what he did and let it dictate my emotions. I'd also have every right to turn from my faith if I based it on my circumstances.

It's not just the accident though. I'll admit, looking back, my whole life I've played the victim role to some degree but I used that as an excuse to excuse my own responsibility, accountability and vigilance. It became my identity but unfortunately all that did was further victimize myself. In truth, it somehow gave me a justified excuse to sin, but sin still held its consequence in the excuse no matter how justified I was or felt I was. It somehow became my overriding dependence in my life. It was like I could escape because I had an excuse to but this is where we all stand in a hypocritical contradiction of ourselves because so much of our frustration, trauma and calamity stems from sin imposed upon us yet we still continue to do it ourselves. I am a victim of sin yet I further victimized myself and the world around me by playing the victim role and living in that victim mentality and I feel many of us do the same thing. The deeper psychological aspect of the victim role is that we are actually simultaneously in agreement to the innate structure of moral confiance. The sympathy and victimization actually reveals our hearts true desire especially in relation to family. We yearn for what we don't want to give. If we didn't yearn for them then what are we a victim of in our minds? The problem with playing the victim role is we harbour resentment and bitterness and again, it gives us the self justified vindication we feel we deserve to not be proactive in perseverance or integrity. Unfortunately with that, we merely enable each other and no one sees or has a relatable influence to follow and be encouraged to persevere. Noyone sees a reason to move forward for the greater good and for a greater hope. We just play on each other's emotions to justify ourselves. Jesus wasn't lying when he said the harvest is plentiful but the workers are few.

Thankfully, our strength in faith is wise to that and independent of it all, especially within our emotions. The psychology of it also reveals how we've been manipulated and conformed by the narcissistic promotion of the world. We've come to believe each of us is the center of the universe and weigh ourselves and the world down by that disillusion. Also, in playing the victim role our resentment is a form of faith that bases its dependence on the integrity, compassion and empathy of others to which we are all falling victim to in its capacity and expectation. Some are obviously true victims but others definitely and exhaustingly draw attention to themselves for merely that, attention. This is much of the blindness I speak of within our afflictions into which Jesus was transcendently victorious. He wasn't dependent on anyone to be proactive in accomplishing his objective. Sometimes in life we must bear the sufferings to recognize what it means to bear the influence and this is where Jesus is most worthy of worship and praise. He transcended it all and became the center of the universe for us to realize we're not. It's a level of maturity that takes courage and selflessness to exemplify. He initiated it and now we must learn to implement it. As victims our resentment is like a united front against injustice but the cycle never comes to an end because satan is the spiritual instigator in our unforgiveness. It's not only him, it's the obvious fruit of unforgiveness and forgiveness within us that bear such significance. Some people harbour unforgiveness their entire life. It's literally life-and-death spiritually, psychology and even neurologically. Ephesians 4:32 says, "Be kind and compassionate to one another, forgiving each other, just as in Christ, God forgave you." 2 Timothy 2:24-26 says, "A servant of the Lord must not quarrel but be gentle to all, able to teach, patient, in humility correcting those who are in opposition, if God will perhaps grant them repentance so that they may know the truth, and that they may come to their senses and escape the snare of the devil, having been taken captive by him to do his will."

What transformed me and ultimately revolutionized the world is the disposition and forbearance of Jesus Christ in his affliction. Jesus had every justifiable right to play the victim role and cower with the burden laid before him but he pressed on in faith and defined it's cause as we all should now in service and in reverence to him.

Hebrews 12:3 says, "Consider him who endured such hostility from sinners against himself, lest you become weary and discouraged in your souls." The unrivalled weight of glory and admiration I have for and see in Jesus is the wisdom and influence he instituted amidst the affliction and contention that surrounded him. The anxiety and fears that debilitate us did not intimidate him. He didn't succumb to the fear physically nor from a social, spiritual or psychological perspective, he was independent of it all because as his Word indicates in 1 John, "There is no fear in love, but perfect love casts out fear; because fear has torment." There is a profound distinction and maturity level within him that is something only God himself could personify.

We're all victims to some degree in this world whether it be from a broken family, poverty, health issues, abusive relationships, racial discrimination, social injustice, or merely the taxes we pay the government but if we are seeking sympathy or empathy from others and using that victim mentality as an excuse to sin and not be proactive, were contradicting ourselves and denying the truth we're confessing to in our heart. If it wasn't true, noyone would be a victim of anything and life would just be a meaningless course of natural selection. We are subconsciously and subsequently declaring a standard and precedence of ethics but expecting that compassion and integrity from others that we're denying within ourselves. We're also succumbing to the emotional entrapment the enemy has devised for us to react in our faithless instability. He's drawn the whole world into that volatile and reactive state of hostility and watches it unfold as we all point fingers in blame at injustice and oppression, but again, all we are doing collectively by reacting is further oppressing ourselves, especially in a democracy like America. This is why I can't stress enough the danger within social media and Hollywood and the influence they generate within our naive and impressional culture. People that refute conspiracy should turn on their TV more often. These scripts in Hollywood and the agendas behind social media are ruthlessly and morbidly induced evils. It's literally diabolical how sophisticated they've become and how they've affected our perception of reality. There's the old saying, "perception is reality" but our perception has been completely altered. There was just a trial that came out on the news about a supposed white supremacist cop who gunned down 3 blacks for no reason. The whole country was up in arms with mobs and riots everywhere, even outside the courthouse. When the actual facts got to the judge and the jury laid down their verdict, he was innocent of all charges. Nothing the media said was true. They weren't even black! There was a drone that filmed the whole thing that contradicted everything the media put out to the public. It's not just the media, movies have paralleled society's oppressive psyche psychologically and have had us relate and sympathise to these characters in their affliction but always vindicate the reaction in their revenge, much like the new movie, "The Joker" which is the pinnacle of that influential and psychological deception in our generation. One scene has him act revenge on a coworker for berating and belittling him. He viciously stabs him in the neck over and over with no remorse or emotion, as though he was justified to do so. It's hard to watch, it's so horrific but it's been seen by millions of people across the globe, enhancing that resentment and victim mentality within us all. What's even worse is how young the minds are that watch this garbage nowadays. We are all victims of an enemy far bigger, wiser and more sinister than the carnal eye can see that's unbiased and unrelenting no matter how justified we feel we are. It's also why he bases his initiative not only on the incentives of life but the acceptance and expectation we have of ourselves in the supposed requirement. Everything becomes about envy and comparison and we all become resentful and divided. He's the ultimate conspirator no matter what country, ethnicity or culture we're from. I realize some people are victims of unbearable afflictions, oppression and circumstances far worse than I can relate to or have experienced myself into which I've got to be sensitive of, but that injustice will be judged by God eternally and we need to leave those emotions for him however hard that seems. If we are all desperately yearning and complaining for our world to uphold a perfect standard of judgement and justice then again, we can't be angry at God or blame him for wanting that judgment to be upheld within ourselves, nor can we be angry at him for executing that judgement and justice eternally. Ultimately, the gospel message is that the justice we all deserve, God executed on himself in Christ.

To Skeptics

It's kind of a reverberating theme in my book, but again, this is where our contradiction lies and where our conscience is inexcusably exposed. We know what is right and wrong whether we admit it or not and to those who don't feel that way, God says otherwise. Romans 2:14-16 says, "When gentiles, who do not have the law, by nature do the things in the law, these, although not having the law are a law to themselves, who show the work of the law written in their hearts, their conscience also bearing witness, and between themselves their thoughts accusing or else excusing them.... In the day when God will judge the secrets of men by Jesus Christ." It's called the Word of truth for a reason and goes on in Romans 12 and says, "Recompense no evil for evil. Provide things honest in the sight of all men, if it's possible, as much as lies in you, live peaceably with all men, don't avenge yourselves, but rather give place unto wrath; for it is written, "Vengeance is mine, I will repay," says the Lord. Don't be overcome by evil, but overcome evil with good."

The only way to win this war and to come to true knowledge, wisdom and understanding is to repent of our own sin, humble ourselves and not react to the deception and hostility that surrounds us. Even more importantly, we must forgive each other as we've been forgiven in Christ and stand united in the spiritual battle that ensues and that lies ahead. There's a bigger picture going on around us and so much of our divisiveness is petty and selfish. We think the people around us are a hindrance to our path in life but it's the path we're pursuing that's destroying us and where so much of our volatility is rooted. It's all such vanity and as Solomon says, "A chasing after the wind". Galatians 3:26-28 says, "You are all sons of God through Jesus Christ. For as many of you as were baptised into Christ have put on Christ. There is neither Jew nor Greek, there is neither slave nor free, there is neither male or female, for you are all one in Christ Jesus." No matter what ethnicity or culture you're from, these words are for you. We need to let our entitlement and contention go and treat others as we wish to be treated. The people asked Jesus in Matthew 22:36 saying, "Master, which is the great commandment in the law? He answered saying, "You shall love the Lord your God with all your heart, with all your soul, and with all your mind. This is the first and great commandment. And the second is like it, you shall love your neighbour as yourself. On these two commandments hang all the law and the prophets." Ephesians 2:14 says, "He is our peace, who has made both one, and has broken down the middle wall of partition between us." It's impossible to defuse all of this hostility and divisiveness without a united cause and that's what we're surrendering to in Christ. All of the hostility and contention we see around us is merely the effects of the unregenerate, faithless and entitled mind therefore we can't harbour that same resentment because again, it's as though we are looking at a reflection of our old selves in the mirror before coming to Christ. We can't take offence to it as many of us do because we're subjecting ourselves to its capacity and subjecting our faith to its hope as though there's optimism for the world outside of Jesus Christ. The more we expose the world's carnal depravity the more we agree with God to its need of it's regeneration. This goes for unbelievers as well and is the evolving contradiction I speak of in my subtitle. What excuse do we have if we hate what we've become? We actually don't hate people as much as we hate the carnality within them. People hate billionaire entrepreneurs like Donald Trump but he's the outcome of what many of them are living for. I'm not saying faith is easy but it's a reasonable and justifiable compliance to adhere to and the more technology exposes sin and injustice through the lens, the more it gives prevalence to God's word and its irrefutability. Again, we are fighting an enemy far more encompassing than we realize outside of faith. Where fighting the enemy of our soul. It says in 2 Timothy 2:3-4, "Endure hardness, as a good soldier of Jesus Christ, no man that wars entangles himself with the affairs of this life, that he may please him who has chosen him to be a soldier." Solving the affairs of this life outside of Christ are futile because of the free will of man and the friction generated in its carnal pursuit. The desire has been too deeply ingrained in our subconscious for us to stand down or see otherwise. We can't ascertain this spiritual and progressive development carnally and in that limitation satan wraps us around our own perception of justice and tolerance and collapses us in our perceived consciousness.

These new age teachers speak of consciousness and spiritual enlightenment but if we are not conscious of God through the revelation of Jesus Christ we are spiritually dead and conscious of nothing. Ephesians 2 says, "And you he made alive, who were dead in trespasses and sins, in which you once walked according to the course of this world, according to the prince of the power of the air, the spirit who now works in the sons of disobedience, among whom also we all once conducted ourselves in the lusts of our flesh, fulfilling the desires of the flesh and of the mind, and were by nature children of wrath, just as the others. But God who is rich in mercy, because of his great love with which he loved us, even when we were dead in trespasses, made us alive together with Christ. For by grace you have been saved through faith, and that not of yourselves, it is the gift of God, not of works, lest anyone should boast."

The world yearns for a standard to be met but outside of Christ the example hasn't been set and if it hasn't supposedly been historically set by Christ then we need to ask ourselves what we are supposing or expecting the moral standard should be. We continually conclude truth is recognized in our conscience by our accusations and in our admonishment of the world, yet we deny its origin in Christ. The conviction from God is the saving standard of justice our conscience is at war with in its own self-justification and autonomy. The definition of autonomy is to be self-governed or to have independence in one's thoughts or actions. We just won't willingly surrender to what is designed to save us from ourselves and that's why we are in need of a saviour that was obedient to the conscience's objective. This is where atheists, agnostics, evolutionists or anyone else who denies the significance of God, hit a wall in their beliefs and theories and why it is so dangerous how they fail to identify with the historical implementation and institution of the law. It's not only the historical basis for the law, it's the historical record of Jesus Christ and how each of their licenses and birth certificates signify the yearly ascension from Christ's life on earth, along with billions of others around the world. The question to those in unbelief is where did the judicial law come from if it didn't come from the God of the Bible and its written account, and what is so significant about this time in history that we're all ascending from? Why is BC-AD the centerpiece of how we've established time and how does one man change the entire course of how time is documented? It's far more significant than people realize. They're ignorantly leapfrogging the world's sustaining historical pillars of moral influence, justice and conviction. Where would civilization be without these ordinances set in place? The only other alternative apart from God is that the law somehow formed itself through an evolving conscience to which contradicts itself in its paralleled judicial implementation to the Bible and its influence constitutionally. We've put our hand on and swore oaths to the Bible for decades here in the Western world and around the globe because it's the only pillar of historical morality that justifiably overrides and convicts our own conscience whether we're hypocrites of it or not. Even the judge is subject, reverent and accountable to its ethical principles and guilty to its charge. The law itself and our consciousness to it is like a refining fire of unfulfillment that God purified within himself for us to be released from its condemnation through faith. Everyone has heard of John 3:16 but if you follow on in John 3:17-18 it says, "God did not send his Son into the world to condemn the world, but that the world through him might be saved. He that believes on him is not condemned, but he that doesn't believe is condemned already, because he has not believed in the only begotten Son of God." In John 3:36 it says, "He that believes on the Son has everlasting life and he that doesn't believe on the son shall not see life, but the wrath of God abides on him." In Acts 13:38-39 it says concerning Jesus, "Through this man is preached to you the forgiveness of sins, and by him everyone who believes is justified from all things from which you could not be justified by the law of Moses." In speaking of the law 2 Corinthians says, "The letter kills but the spirit gives life"... "Even to this day when Moses is read, a veil

432

lies on their heart. Nevertheless when one turns to the Lord, the veil is taken away. Now the Lord is the spirit, and where the spirit of the Lord is, there is liberty."

This is not only for the Israelites, it's for all humanity. The law bears down on a man till his death to which we all stand guilty to its charge, but God fulfilled its task in Christ. God sees our penalty justified through our belief in what he endured through Christ. Isaiah 53 prophesied concerning Jesus saying, "He is despised and rejected by men, a man of sorrows and acquainted with grief. And we hid, as it were, our faces from him, he was despised, and we did not esteem him. Surely he has borne our griefs and carried our sorrows; Yet we esteemed him stricken, smitten by God, and afflicted. But he was wounded for our transgressions, he was bruised for our iniquities; the chastisement for our peace was upon him, and by his stripes we are healed. All we like sheep have gone astray; We have turned, every one, to his own way and the Lord has laid on him the iniquity of us all. He was oppressed and he was afflicted, yet he opened not his mouth; He was led as a lamb to the slaughter."

I was so stubborn and skeptical when I first started learning of Christ myself but this passage and so many others were foretold hundreds of years before his coming to earth and definitely started making a believer out of me along with these truths concerning the law, regardless of my personal circumstances. Again, to some people God's Word seems rash or too black-and-white but as we all see the world imploding in on itself, the imminent severity of them become more and more relevant and irrefutable. I've heard many people say Christians are narrow minded and that there's so much more to life and to spirituality. In Mathew 7 Jesus says, "Enter by the narrow gate, for wide is the gate and broad is the way that leads to destruction, and there are many who go in by it. Because narrow is the gate and difficult is the way which leads to life, and there are few who find it." If you are reading this, and you are an unbeliever or still skeptical, lay aside your preconceived notions concerning religion in regards to christianity and start taking heed. Pick the book up and begin the journey of faith. You're only lying to yourself otherwise and tomorrow isn't promised. Romans 11:22 says, "Therefore consider the goodness and severity of God; on those who fell, severity, but toward you, goodness if you continue in his goodness." Hebrews 11:6 says, "Without faith it is impossible to please Him, for he who comes to God must believe that he is, and that he is a rewarder of those who diligently seek Him."

I have a Christian friend who's sister is in severe trouble. She's been using heavy drugs with some shady characters and now fears for her life. She keeps coming to him asking for help in what to do as long as he doesn't mention Jesus or faith. He's stuck between a rock and a hard place because there's no other way for her and he knows it. She's exhausted every option but just won't surrender her sin and pride. It's like she'd rather die than relinquish her identity in the world and admit she needs help. My brother and many of my friends growing up are the same way. They're at the end of their rope but just won't let go. They're holding on to what's pulling them down and won't admit they're doing it to themselves. It's literally psychotic how far people take their pride. It's become more important than life itself. Only the spirit of God can deliver us from this pride and instill a sustainable and applicable compass of morality for us to live a productive life. He gives us direction and purpose that isn't religious at all. Swallowing our pride is not that deep of a philosophy but it's the most critical and revolutionary in transforming our mind, especially when we give that pride to God. Human philosophy has led us on a wild goose chase of self analysis but is a detriment to our maturity and growth. Literally within a few seconds of giving our pride and sin to God, we're transformed. It's that simple. You can throw all the self help books out the window. They're just masking the problem. Corinthians 2 says, "God has revealed them to us through his spirit, for the spirit searches all things, yes, the deep things of God. For what man knows the things of a man except the spirit of the man which is in him? Even so, no one knows the things of God except the spirit of God, now we have not received the spirit of the world but the spirit who is from God, that we might know the things that have been freely given to us by God. These things we also speak, not in words men's wisdom teaches, but which the Holy Spirit teaches, comparing spiritual things with spiritual. But the carnal man does not receive the things of the spirit of God, for they are foolish to him, nor can he know them because they are spiritually discerned. But he who is spiritual judges all things, yet he himself is rightly judged by no one. For who has known the mind of the Lord that he may instruct him? But we have the mind of Christ."

This passage speaks of a gift freely given to us, but unless we are willing to receive it, it remains unopened. The greatest challenge I find in faith is not only persevering through personal circumstances but it's how to convey and articulate what's been revealed to me verbally to others, and for them not to take offence. Satan has built the pride and validation up in man to such a level that we're offended by any sort of conviction, but the conviction of the Lord is meant to save us from the entitlement that pride produces. Much of the gospel is offensive to the path we're on and to the entitlement or position we've established. I struggle with sharing the gospel without allowing my emotions to get involved and I know many are the same because it is convicting and confrontational. Even though we know it's the truth it's hard to convey that truth with the world around us that is so bound and determined for validation and acceptance. The only way I've ever articulated my emotions verbally in the past is through anger, resentment and bitterness and usually under the influence of drugs or alcohol. The world turned me cold, stubborn and abrasive but God is patient and merciful in our afflictions and sanctifies us who believe until we're humble and wise. It's definitely a maturing process handling contention peacefully. I'm kinda laughing inside because that most certainly isn't the strong suit in my personality otherwise. I'm a work in progress in verbal communication but I've found writing to be a healthy outlet for my thoughts and emotions to register and to find release whether other people read them or not. I've procrastinated writing this book but salvation is at stake and I know others can relate to my story. I found much of my procrastination wasn't only a result of my accident but the insecurities I've built up in my mind for years from what I've been trained to perceive about myself through the deceptive lenses that surround us in the world. The world crushes you in your identity and never relents. The pressure can be overwhelming but when I changed my priority to faith in God, he shifted my priorities into the benefit of others and I now see that purpose far greater to live for than that of my own. I started to see the cohesive manipulation that surrounds us into which I was previously enslaved. It's an elusive spirit blinding this world but when we can step back from the priority of ourselves we can see far more clearly how the spiritual world operates. I needed to see my own disillusion and weaknesses to relate to the weakness and blindness within us all. It's a healthy place to be when we can look inside the internal mirror of observation and not be ashamed of what we see anymore. Philippians 3:13-15 says, "I press on, that I may lay hold of that which Christ Jesus has also laid hold of me. Brethren, I do not count myself to have apprehended but one thing I do, forgetting those things which are behind and reaching forward to those things which are ahead, I press towards the goal for the prize of the upward call of God in Christ Jesus. Therefore let us, as many as are mature, have this mind, and if in anything you think otherwise, God will reveal even this to you."

Satan's greatest adversary is forgiveness but especially when we can forgive ourselves and become proactive in our pursuit of truth. When we get to that place, especially with God's unconditional love, salvation and acceptance as our refuge and strength, Satan's accusations become futile allegations that we become wise to in our faith. 2 Timothy 1:7 says, "God has not given us the spirit of fear, but of power and of love and of a sound mind." The pride of man sees us weak who dropped to our knees in prayer but that same pride becomes wise in its own eyes and is weakened by what he stands affirmed in and in what it assumes to be of importance. The greatest weakness and disillusion within man is the praise he gives himself for the attention or benefit he receives and satan knows how to entice and enhance that all within our ego. On our knees is where truth is found and where the true war is won and lossed in this world. Without that place of refuge, accountability and sanctification the affairs of this world become an endless and futile battle of recirculating injustices without resolution. People don't change until God's justice has been resolved within them and that justice in God's eyes is only resolved through the cross. I'll admit the truth of God is painful and can be grievous to endure but becomes more and more proof of the righteous standard he upholds in sanctifying the world, especially to us called for his purpose.

What I found fascinating about writing the book was finding synonyms and defining certain words in the English language. It's as though the conscious mind becomes a revealing thesaurus of truth in of itself. I find the innate and intuitive response in our language to be a fascinating tale to the undeniability of our conscience to God's moral law and his design within us, whether we believe it or not. The word sanctification is defined as "the state of proper functioning" it says, "to sanctify someone or something is to set that person or thing apart for the use intended by its designer." Again, the world sees the conviction from God as a suppression to our freedom but it's actually the proof of his unwavering love in the sanctification, to free us. If the world would only define the words mercy and grace it would open itself up to a whole new paradigm shift consciously and spiritually. In defining mercy it says, "Compassion or forgiveness shown toward someone whom it is within one's power to punish or harm." In defining grace it says, "Grace is unmerited divine assistance given to humans for their regeneration or sanctification." Jesus's parables surely come alive in defining many of these words especially relating to mercy and moral conduct. Science or should I say the science we are led to believe seems to emphatically deny God and his Word as relevant, yet it consciously lives and depends on the moral law and standard it's generated. It yearns and depends on the justice it ignorantly denies for its own opportunity to be liberated and unabated to prove its denial, and to me that's conclusive proof of God in its contradiction. We as a world can't say we don't believe in God when we live for his standard of justice to be upheld in the world around us. The more frustrated and angry we get at injustice the more we're subconsciously admitting to our knowledge of it. My point is science gives no explanation to the conscious mind or to justice, nor does it set a precedent to uphold it. It actually vindicates and justifies the world's unaccountability to justice and that's an extremely dangerous and contradictory theory to base our lives on. I'm finishing this book amidst the coronavirus and the black lives matter movement that's sweeping across the globe. You see thousands of people standing up for these causes and emphatically marching and protesting for justice wether it be political, social, economical or racial discrimination. The whole world seems to have their finger pointing at an offence or injustice, especially in America, but they don't realize the evolving contradiction of it all. They are simultaneously proving the truth of God and his standard of morality and justice within their own heart. The world yearns for what it denies and is suffering in what it defines. Times like these are when the Old Testament comes alive in the rise and fall of the nation of Israel. If people would see God's heart for a nation and his anger towards its leaders and their oppressive tyranny they would come to understand the implosion we're seeing around us and rejoice in the salvation he offers in Christ. Jeremiah 44 says, "Why do you commit this great evil against yourselves?" It says, "They have not been humbled, to this day, nor have they feared, they have not walked in my law or in my statutes that I set before you and your fathers. Therefore thus says the lord of hosts, the God of Israel, behold, I will set my face against you for catastrophe." Jeremiah 22 says, "Woe to him who builds his house by unrighteousness and his chambers by injustice, who uses his neighbours service without wages and gives him nothing for his work…..You're eyes and your heart are for nothing but your covetousness, for shedding innocent blood, and practicing oppression and violence…..I spoke to you in your prosperity, but you said, I will not hear, this has been your manner from your youth, that you did not obey my voice, the wind shall eat up all your rulers, and your lover's shall go into captivity, surely then you will be ashamed and humiliated for all your wickedness." Isaiah spoke of the same oppression and injustice we see today. In chapter 10 it says, "Woe to those who decree unrighteous decrees, who write misfortune, which they have prescribed to rob the needy of justice, and to take what is right from the poor of my people, that widows may be their prey, and that they may rob the fatherless. What will you do in the day of punishment, and in the desolation which will come from a far? To whom will you flee for help and where will you leave your glory? There are hundreds of scriptures concerning these issues but one that hits the heart is Isaiah 29:13, it says, "These people draw near with their mouths and honor Me with their lips, but have removed their hearts far from Me, and their fear towards Me is taught by the commandments of men." Also in Jeremiah 9:23-24 it says, "Let not the mighty man boast in his might, let not the rich man boast his riches, but let him who boasts boast in this, that he understands and knows me, that I am the Lord who practices steadfast love, justice and righteousness in the earth. For in these things I delight, declares the Lord," In Hosea 4 it says, "Hear the Word of the Lord, you children of Israel, the Lord has a controversy with the inhabitants of the land because there is no truth, nor mercy, nor knowledge of God in the land. By swearing and lying and killing and stealing and committing adultery they break out and blood touches blood. Therefore the land shall mourn and everyone that dwells there shall languish, my people are destroyed for lack of knowledge, because they have rejected knowledge, I will also reject them, as they saw increase, they sinned against me therefore I will turn their glory into shame."

Bigger Picture

I wish America and many other nations that are on the verge of collapse would have read these words for their own self examination and reproof but these are the ramifications of a godless world living to define and substantiate its own form of governing justice and freedom without God. Unfortunately America has become a gullible pawn of satan as the illuminated model to exemplify the extent of these implications for the world to witness its own contradictions in freedom, justice and tolerance. He's got the carnal mind so consumed in its own individual pursuit and philosophies on life that it doesn't know why, who to blame or where to turn anymore. Without God all we've come to rely on and draw from is ourselves. He's masterminded the democratic American dream and ideology as a product to which man is fully liberated to pursue all his or her carnal aspirations and has used Hollywood and the media to sell it around the world through sensationalism and idolatry. It's become the full expression and exaltation in self desire and in the allure of sensuality and overstimulation. I'm trying to define democracy as I'm writing this and in my research I'm finding no one has truly defined these governing systems or theories, whether it be democracy, socialism, capitalism or communism. They've all become ambiguous counterproductive smoke screens to imperialism as far as I'm concerned and to the far greater looming power and monopolizing threat of zionism. I researched the founder of zionism, Theodore Hertzle and it blew my mind at how his philosophy has impacted our world today psychologically and economically. He initialized the domino effect of the world and is definitely one of satan's greatest ambassadors in history. Revelation 2:9 says, "I know the blasphemy of them which say they are Jews, and are not, but are of the synagogue of satan." This all relates itself to Israel becoming a Jewish nation in 1948 in which the Zionists initiated and established. The problem is they weren't Jewish and it's much of that initial lie that has superseded and become our world's calamity.

In regards to governing systems, it's not my area of expertise but they all seem to guide themselves by their initial philosophy or theory but never achieve their intended goal. (Or at least the goal initially advertised). Unfortunately imperialism is the Zionists philosophy in achieving their desired goal but it's now reaching its global directive. For reference, Imperialism is defined as a state policy, practice or advocacy of extending power and dominion, especially by direct territorial acquisition or by gaining political and economic control of other territories and people's. This one word is the best definition to what my book is trying to expose because if we've defined the word imperialism then who is behind its conspiring deliberation? In defining American imperialism it says it consists of policies aimed at extending the political, economic, and cultural influence of the United States over areas beyond its boundaries. Interesting how it says "cultural influence." Point being is the initial theory of a democracy sounds good and optimistic as does capitalism from a carnal sense, especially to those feeling oppressed because of the opportunity generated but we are now seeing the implications in America's collapse and the promotionary implications around the world. The definition of implication says," The conclusion that can be drawn from something although it's not explicitly stated, which in a sense leaves it to be determined." It says, "Implications are effects and consequences that may happen in the future." Again, I see a democracy actually working initially to a degree in sectors, but as it and the world is sold into its apparent personal and individual liberty, it's also sold into it for the purpose and benefit of itself because of its diplomatic view on self-expression and religious entitlement. It's hard to be wrong in a generic ideology that says everyone is right and in a country that's pride is built on fighting for that human right of diplomacy. In a general sense it's fighting for the freedom and entitlement that's destroying it. There's been 131 mass shootings in America this year and it's only the middle of April. Everyone is wondering why there's such a struggle for unity but it's impossible to be united with such contrasting views and diversity immigrating into a country, especially with the goal promoted being the entitled benefit to and of yourself. How can people live for the same purpose if the purpose to live for is yourself and your own entitled opinions, feelings and philosophy? Entitlement means having a right to something or the belief that one is inherently deserving of privileges or special treatment. This is the deception that has inherently come to divide us all. There has to be a moral line drawn by the law but with human rights as the buffeter, prejudice and discrimination actually allow the tolerance to escalate. It's reverse psychology within the pride of ideology, similar to how sports or even the Olympics are seen as positive unifying outlets but actually increase our pride and division internally and globally between teams and countries. It's as though satan has pushed the barriers of supposed democracy with tolerance and drawn the world into an epicenter of its own diversity to further increase man's level of entitlement and narcissism. We see what is obtainable and it generates an insatiable sense of opportunity. Again, a democracy supposedly gives power to the people to which we are entitled to our human rights, beliefs and opinions but as these grow within our cultural and ethnical diversity so does the pride and entitlement to our claim. We come to feel a sense of empowerment but satan knows outside of faith in Christ, the carnal mind lives to stand affirmed in its own feelings, opinions and perceptions on life therefore he's designed at ego centred culture to drive this narcissism in man to its climax and with that draws the whole world into support of its ideology. That's why America is seen as the centerpiece of the world when all it was all along was a buffer. While the supposed individual freedom in it grows so does satan's enhancement of the patriotism within it and then uses that pride for his own agenda. People may feel a form of unity and worth patriotically but individually their self worth is devalued due to the level of idolatry that's generated. Within the borders we actually end up hating what we love and loving what we hate. Satan even further divides the culture within by enhancing the stereotypes he forms through the entertainment industry and social media. Whether it be expressive freedom, sexual freedom, or religious freedom, without a common goal especially from a moral sense, these views on freedom and tolerance are bound to clash as they cross paths and coexist together. Again, a democracy seems to be good theoretically as many experience a sense of individual independence and personal liberty but it also allows the darkness of this world to be justified in its freedom of expression and unfortunately in that freedom, satan, his demons and imperialistic earthly minions have impressed the American influence upon the whole world. This is why Hollywood and the entertainment industry are the most dangerous influences in the world spiritually and psychologically. With the freedom of expression in art as the justifiable vindicator and without prejudice, it's become an open forum and demons run rampant seducing the world into its illusionary lens and sinful demise. Almost every script has an intended purpose and an intended target audience for an undisclosed agenda unbenounced to the viewer to further increase the conflict within us all. Ultimately, this is the outcome of democracy because the word itself can be defined however you wish it to be defined psychologically or economically. Politicians have to promote the ideology to increase their votes but then it becomes an economic power struggle with the concept of capitalism that's generated within the power of the people and free enterprise. We've basically reached the climax of both concepts in the western world and become victims to the promotion.

While researching democracy, I read an interesting article that was simply titled, "The criticism of democracy." It read, "Criticism of democracy is grounded in democracy's purpose, process and outcomes. Since classical antiquity and through the modern era, democracy has been associated with the rule of the people, rule of the majority and free selection or election either through direct participation or elect representation respectively, but has not been linked to a "particular outcome." Political thinkers approach their critique of democracy from different perspectives. Many do not necessarily oppose democracy's "rule of the people" but rather seek to expand or question its popular definition. In their work, they distinguish between democratic principles that are effectively implemented through undemocratic procedures; Undemocratic procedures that are implemented through democratic procedures and variations of the same kind. For instance, some critics of democracy would agree with Winston Churchill famous remark, "No one pretends that democracy is perfect or all wise, indeed, It been said that democracy is the worst form of government except all those other forms that have been tried from time to time"...While others, may be more prepared to describe existing democratic regimes as anything but "rule of the people" critics of democracy have tried to highlight democracies inconsistencies, paradoxes and limits by contrasting it with other forms of government."

Quite an interesting article to say the least. Google defines democracy as a system of government in which power is vested in the people and exercised by them directly or through freely elected representatives. Another definition says a democracy is a system with institutions that allows citizens to express their political preferences, has constraints on the power of the executive, and provides a guarantee of civil liberties. I've just scratched my head at all because I don't see much power in the people's hands to elect anything nor a guarantee of civil liberties, all I see is the lesser of two evils and the system bordering on socialism. The system is at a loss within itself. There's sure a lot of taxpayers money feeding the overhead without much disclosure to those paying for its services. The governing body invests billions of undisclosed amounts of taxpayers money and somehow justifies it all as legal. I've heard of these 2025 pandemic bonds the government has invested in and all sorts of other fraudulent activity and conspiracy going on but I'm gonna stop right there trying to figure it all out whether it be democracy, capitalism, communism, socialism or whatever other "ism" or system of government has ruled or dictated the world's societies. Again, they all seem to amalgamate together with no productive result other than to further oppress and enslave the common man psychologically and economically. John Adams was quoted saying, "Remember, democracy never lasts long. It soon wastes, exhausts, and murders itself. There was never a democracy yet that did not commit suicide. It is in vain to say that democracy is less vain, less proud, less selfish, less ambitious, or less avaricious than aristocracy or monarchy. It is not true in fact, and nowhere appears in history. Those passions are the same in all men, under all forms of simple government. And when unchecked, produce the same effects of fraud, violence, and cruelty. When clear prospects are opened before vanity, pride, avarice, or ambition, for their easy gratification, it is hard for the most considerate philosophers and the most conscientious moralists to resist the temptation. Individuals have conquered themselves."

It's amazing that all the intellectual and philosophical minds throughout history and even now in the 20th century with all our resources and technology can't generate a sustainable solution. It's because again, without God we're restricted by our own moral diligence and capacity. We're only reverent to ourselves and like John Adams states, we succumb to the temptation and indulgences of our world. It reminds me of 1 Samuel in the Old Testament when he started to get old and appointed his son's judges over Israel. Unfortunately his sons did not walk in God's ways and the scriptures say they turned aside after dishonest gain, took bribes and perverted justice. Finally the elders of Israel pleaded to Samuel to appoint them a king like the rest of the nations, similar to a system of democracy as we see today. This upset Samuel because he knew God's way was their only hope of peace and sustainability. Samuel then prayed to God and God answered him by saying, "Heed the voice of the people in all that they say to you; for they have not rejected you, but they have rejected me that I should not reign over them... They have forsaken me and served other gods --so they are doing to you also....you shall solemnly forewarn them, and show them the behavior of the king who will reign over them." Samuel then told them all that the king would do to oppress and enslave them but they refused to obey the voice of Samuel and further oppressed and enslaved themselves to their dependence upon man. All of man's systems are blind to the spiritual pursuit of our souls and with that satan continues his siege dismantling every system and theory that's been devised by man for his own sadistic cause, just as the Bible indicates. We're driven by our superiority complexes and have become gods in our own mind without God. The Bible says satan deceives all the nations and you can see much of how he's done that through the influence of the American ideology. Satan has fooled America into believing they are the centre and saviour of the world but all along used them and their ideology as a gullible pawn and prostitute for an alternative agenda. Revelation 17 and 18 describe an allegory of a harlot. Just for reference, as a literary device, an allegory is defined as a narrative in which a character, place or event is used to deliver a broader message about real world issues and occurrences. John has prophetic visions of the future that are far from fictional. It says, "An angel showed John a great whore that sits on many waters, with whom the kings of the earth have committed fornication, and the inhabitants of the earth have been made drunk with the wine of her fornication....The waters where the whore sits are peoples, and multitudes and nations and tongues....She has seven heads and ten horns having a golden cup in her hand full of abominations and filthiness of her fornication.

Ironically, the statue of liberty has seven points from her crown and she's standing on a massive concrete pillar with ten points surrounded by water. It says, "The woman is that great city which reigns over the kings of the earth." These visions that John saw were of the end days into which we are now in where the whole world will fall victim to the deception of the devil and of its own carnal propensity and aspirations. In John's visions he saw a powerful angel who cried out saying, "Babylon the great is fallen and has become the habitation of devils, and the hold of every foul spirit, all nations have drunk of the wine of wrath of her fornication, and the kings of the earth have committed fornication with her and the merchants of the earth have become rich through the abundance of her delicacies." Revelation is a lot to process but what God is trying to reveal to the world is that without him we buy into the lie, whether it be the homeless guy on the street, a rich entrepreneur or prestigious leaders of nations. We've become consumed and overcome by impulse, pride and envy and satan has enhanced it all through the root of oppression outside of sincere faith. He knows that as the benchmark and bar of acceptance increases through idolatry so does the feeling of rejection, which generates a sense of personal restitution within us all. To some it becomes an insatiable vengeance. Benchmark is defined as a standard or point of reference in which things may be compared or assessed and that has definitely become the driving compulsion within us all. We're not battling a war on social injustice as much as we're battling a war internally within our social security. This is what generates our insecurities. Even if we're not being oppressed physically, we feel a sense of oppression psychologically in what we desire to be or attain. Social oppression is when a single group in society unjustly takes advantage of, and exercises power over another group using dominance or subordination. This results in the exploitation of a group of individuals by those in power. Finally in defining social oppression wikipedia says that it derives from power dynamics and imbalances. It's so true in how these imbalances filter down and affect our priorities in everyday life. People have come to disregard the Bible but this is what it exposes and helps us to live independent of.

The world outside of Christ wants both sides of the word accountable. It wants to be autonomously free in unaccountability to God but is pleading for accountability to be met in the world around it. It's much the same with the word responsibility. It's lossed in its own hypocrisy, yearning for justice for all these offences yet lives for the freedom to be justified in its sin and irreverence to God. Our own Prime Minister here in Canada said, "Evangelical Christianity is the worst thing for Canadian society," yet he can't regulate our society without God's justice and standard. We are all hypocrites and contradict ourselves in so many facets of our lives. Every presumption of ours, every perception and every habitual tendency is exploited fuel for satan to further implode our world collectively in our blindness and faithlessness. He promotes the American dream of fame and fortune so we're all consumed by its desire whether it be in government, Hollywood, sports or in the music industry. There's always two chairs with an offer on the table beside a cheque or a wad of cash. Unfortunately there's hidden clauses and mandates in those contracts we don't see. It's a hidden network and coalition of coercion where the most sinister evil has been personified and orchestrated. It hides in the conscious lie for its own gain and has for centuries. Unbenounced to the public, there's an unassuming and anonymous luciferian society in deliberation that exists outside of the perceivable mind that has an infinite supply of money that invests in the bribe in all facets of life. There's also a conscious decision and element of evil at the table that only the Bible testifies to and where science or philosophy provide no answers. Psalm 15 says, "Who may dwell on your holy hill? He who walks uprightly, and works righteousness, and speaks truth in his heart; He who does not backbite with his tongue, Nor does evil with his neighbour....He who does not put out his money at interest, Nor does he take a bribe against the innocent." How is this not relevant when the entire world is run by men who lend money with interest and invest in the bribe? Ephesians 2 says satan is the prince of the power of the air and in the air between those two chairs is where satan most inclusively operates. Psalm 26:9-10 says, "I do not gather my soul with sinners, Nor my life with bloodthirsty men, in whose hands is a sinister scheme, and whose right hand is full of bribes." The Bible says the love of money is the root of all evil and many have surrendered their souls to the desires of the flesh, but unfortunately with that have allowed satan to further his ruthless agenda. Mathew 6:24 says, "No one can serve two masters, either he will hate the one and love the other, or else he will be loyal to the one and despise the other. You cannot serve both God and money." So much of the world's implosion and hidden truths have been carried along by the truth people won't expose do to the bribe that bought them. Not only does he invest in the bribe he invests in the enticement for the bribe to be too alluring for the impulses to deny. He's manipulated the human mind to live for achievement, validation and acceptance which further separates us from the unconditional and unselfish love of God. Unfortunately the love from the world is always provisional and conditional. Whether it be a smile and wave from a president, an acting role, a new patent, a scientific discovery, a vaccine or a pole dance at the Super Bowl by Jennifer Lopez, they're all linked to a residual agenda with extortion, bribery and a contract attached to them and everyone under its power is used progressively to collapse the mirage it generates. Evil is proactive in its deliberation and overrides the conscience for the effects that transpire. Again, collusion is defined as a secret or illegal cooperation or conspiracy especially in order to cheat or deceive others and this is the collusion that transpires and is utilized by the effects of the American dream. It sells the world out to its own greed and blind optimism. This is why the conviction of the Holy Spirit and the eternal judgement of God are the only convictions strong enough to restrict us from the allure of the bribe because the vast majority of men and women can be bought with a price. Not only can we be bought with a price, we get deceived and sell ourselves out to the lie the bribe generates. Revelation 22:14-15 says, "Blessed are those who do his commandments, that they may have the right to the tree of life, and may enter in through the gates into the city. But outside are dogs and sorcerers and sexually immoral and murderers and idolaters and whoever loves and practices a lie."

The truth encroaching upon us is that if our hope is solely in the world then we become subject to its coercive manipulation into which we grow naive and blind in our optimism, but if our hope is in the promise of God's salvation, then we can release our grip on this life's deception, whether it be financially or the social pressure it generates and live for the life to come. This is the trial in life and in faith into which we're all torn, much like Paul's journey in the Bible. In 2 timothy 4:3-7 he says, "For the time will come when they will not endure sound doctrine, but according to their own desires, they shall heap up for themselves teachers, having itching ears, and they shall turn away their ears from the truth, and shall be turned to fables. But you be watchful in all things, endure afflictions, do the work of an evangelist, fulfill your ministry.... The time of my departure is at hand. I have fought the good fight, I have finished the race, I have kept the faith."

I realize there's so much good to life that people yearn for and work hard to attain, establish and protect, especially in regards to family and books like mine seem cynical and pessimistic, but the evil of this world has progressed alongside in a far greater capacity than the general masses are aware of and we can't blame God for telling us the truth of it however unfair that seems. Ultimately, God is not trying to save the world, he's trying to save us from the world.

I've said it before but I see a fierce battle ahead between biblical imminence and carnal optimism that will shear the heart of man to the core, even to those in faith. Biblical faith is a daunting revelation and at a critical point in history. I'm in a severe battle with it myself that at times leaves me in a conflicting state of depression. I've worked so hard and persevered through so much to get to where I am in my life, but it all seems redundant at times especially in this pandemic and with what will transpire in the near future. It's like you're trapped in truth. Again, I don't want to die to myself, I want to live for myself. Regardless, the more optimistic I am for the future, the more I deceive myself because of what I know is a lie. It's difficult wrestling with an impending inevitability and leaves you feeling torn and helpless at times. It's like every human desire and accomplishment seems so vain with the impending truth that is unfolding.

The Olympics are going on in Tokyo as I'm finishing this book and although I like watching some of the events, it all seems so contradictory, not only to salvation and the vanity of life but in regards to the apparent pandemic going on around the world. There's just so many variables that prove how selfish and unempathetic the world truly is. It's not only that, it's how driven and determined we are in pursuing vanity and how we justify ourselves in doing so. What are we really accomplishing while millions are supposedly perishing around the world? It's sociopathic negligence on every level. Every telecast and interview is about chasing history and leaving a legacy behind but what does it even matter in light of eternity? It's just so difficult to put it in words. The question will soon become who we are when these opportunities are inaccessible and unattainable? That's when the true vanity of it all will set in and completely derail us. Of course people are going to cast a blind eye and oppose pessimistic books like mine with all they've got invested in the world. People have not only invested their time and emotions in athletics, idols and sports organizations, they've invested billions in the future financially through mortgages, student loans, real estate, and the stock market. That's what their faith and dependence are upon but that's the whole grand illusion. They've also invested so much of their emotions in their social identity which I feel is the most blinding. We all struggle with these truths and priorities in life. A part of me hates the fact that the truth is just that, the truth. I ask myself, how can I live and pray for a future that I know doesn't exist? Yet a part of me still does. How can I desire a family when the future of the world looks so ominous? Ultimately, biblical faith does not define itself on a philosophy or methodology on tomorrow's life. This is life and death and critical elements to our souls' immortality. I'll admit, I've been demoralized by it all and become extremely fatalistic into which I feel our emotions are completely justified at times. I've hit ruts so low, only the Word of God could pull me through. I feel this is the crossroads where many people will fall away in how they've defined faith in their minds. We're at that time where this is critical.

The Burden of The Word of the Lord

Matthew 24:24 says, "False Christs and false prophets will rise and show great signs and wonders to deceive, if possible, even the elect." Again, the truth is hard to bear even for believers, but however hard it is to bear, it is still the truth. It's called the burden of the Word of the Lord for a reason. Faith is an enduring responsibility into which many will choose to deny and refuse to accept until it's imminence consumes them. It's happened to millions throughout history in regards to circumstance.

I watched a movie called Dante's peak with Pierce Brosnan where he was a volcano analyst. He tried to warn this town with all the evidence he'd accumulated but they didn't take his warnings seriously enough and complacently and optimistically went along with their lives. Eventually the volcano erupted and consumed the whole town. It won't seem fair to many people but a positive attitude doesn't change the course of volcanic lava. Not only do we have apocalyptic scientific evidence encroaching upon us from a carnal perspective, we have biblical imminence that we should strongly consider in regards to the destiny of our soul. Optimism sounds positive and encouraging but isn't relative to the truth that surrounds us, not only biblically but from a scientific perspective as well. The world is not regenerating itself fast enough for any sort of productive outcome to unfold in the future and deep down, we all know that. Conservation efforts are minimal in balancing the scale. It's like we know it but the impulse and optimistic promotion of life lures us to be indifferent and complacent to it all. We also just don't want to process that level of severity in our minds. Fortunately God has offered an escape and refuge through Jesus Christ that far outweighs it all. Again, if we saw what awaits us who believe we'd rejoice in elation and be patient and blameless but it's not easy sometimes in this relentless and psychotic world. Bondage is the perfect word in describing our state of mind without the hope of God. It's defined as the state of being bound by or subjected to some external power or control. This external power is not only in the physical realm but in the spiritual as well in how it's affected us psychologically. Hebrews 6:17-19 says, "Thus God, determining to show more abundantly to the heirs of promise the immutability of his counsel, confirmed it by an oath, that we might have strong consolation, who have fled for refuge to lay hold of the hope set before us. This hope we have as an anchor for the soul, both sure and steadfast, and which enters the presence behind the veil, where the forerunner has entered for us, even Jesus." I'll end this book with a warning, be careful what you think you know because I guarantee there's a spiritual world that knows you better than you know yourself and it's after your opportunity of salvation. There's a relentless evil encroaching upon the world that has severed its own opportunity and is consciously bound to implode and destroy our world and no amount of good deeds, human intelligence, charity, philosophy or scientific discovery will stop it. Revelation 12:10-12 says, "Now salvation, and strength, and the Kingdom of our God, and the power of his Christ have come, for the accuser of the brethren, who accused them before our God day-and-night has been cast down. And they overcame him by the blood of the Lamb and by the word of their testimony, and they did not love their lives to the death. Therefore rejoice, oh heavens, and you who dwell in them! Woe to the inhabitants of the Earth and the sea! For the devil has come down to you, having great wrath because he knows that his time is short." 2 Peter 3:15 says, "Scoffers will come in the last days, walking according to their own lusts and saying where is the promise of his coming? For since the fathers fell asleep all things continue as they were from the beginning of creation. For this they are willfully ignorant of; that by the Word of God the heavens were of old, and the earth standing out of water and in the water, by which the world that then existed perished being flooded with water. But the heavens and earth which are now preserved by the same Word, are reserved for fire until the day of judgement and perdition of ungodly men. But, beloved, do not forget this one thing, that with the Lord one day is as a thousand years, and a thousand years one day. The Lord is not slack concerning his promise, as some count slackness, but is longsuffering toward us, not willing that any should perish but that all should come to repentance. But the day of the Lord will come as a thief in the night, in which the heavens will pass away with a great noise, and the elements will melt with fervent heat; Both the earth and the works that are in it will be burned up. Therefore, since all these things will be dissolved, what manner of persons ought you to be in holy conduct and godliness, looking for and hastening the coming of the day of God, because of which the heavens will be dissolved, being on fire, and the elements will melt with fervent heat? Nevertheless we, according to His promise, look for new heavens and new earth in which righteousness dwells. Therefore, beloved, look forward to these things, be diligent to be found by him in peace, without spot and blameless and consider that the long suffering of our Lord is salvation."

The end....

CPSIA information can be obtained
at www.ICGtesting.com
Printed in the USA
LVHW111311030922
727549LV00019B/329